FOOTBALL

NORTHERN IRELAND

– a statistical record

1881 to 2021

Michael Robinson

British Library Cataloguing in Publication Data

A catalogue record for this book is available from the British Library

ISBN 978-1-86223-453-6

Copyright © 2021, SOCCER BOOKS LIMITED (01472 696226) www.soccer-books.co.uk
72 St. Peter's Avenue, Cleethorpes, N.E. Lincolnshire, DN35 8HU, United Kingdom

All rights are reserved. No part of this publication may be reproduced, stored in a retrieval system or transmitted, in any form or by any means, electronic, mechanical, photocopying, recording, or otherwise, without the prior written permission of Soccer Books Limited.

Printed in the UK by 4edge Ltd

INTRODUCTION

This book features a statistical history of football in Ireland from 1881 to 1920 and of Northern Ireland from 1920 to 2021. More precisely, this follows the clubs who were members of the Irish Football Association and Irish League formed initially to cover the whole of Ireland but which continued to oversee football in Northern Ireland after the partition of the country in 1921.

The Irish Football Association was founded on the 18th November, 1880 at a meeting in the Queen's Hotel in Belfast presided over by Mr John Sinclair. The original idea had come from Mr John McAlery (founder of Cliftonville FC, Ireland's first football club in 1879), who was intrigued after seeing football being played while on his honeymoon in Edinburgh in 1878. Mr McAlery arranged for a challenge match between local players from Belfast and a selection of players from the Scottish clubs Queen's Park FC and Caledonian FC. This match was played on 24th October, 1878 at Ulster Cricket Ground, Ballynafeigh and was won 3-1 by the Scots.

The meeting of 18th November, 1880 was attended by representatives of Belfast clubs Avoniel FC, Cliftonville FC, Distillery FC, Knock FC, Oldpark FC and also Alexander FC (Limavady) and Moyola Park FC (Castledawson). Major Spencer Chichester was appointed as the first president of the Association and Mr McAlery as the first secretary. Having formed an official association the next step was to introduce an official tournament and the draw for the inaugural Irish F.A. Cup was made on 10th January, 1881 with the above named clubs as entrants. The entrance fee for the IFA Cup was 1/- (one shilling = 5 pence in today's currency) which was the same as the annual fee for membership of the IFA.

Following the success of the Irish Cup, the Irish League was formed in 1890 with Mr W. McNeice as the first president. The founding members of this league were: Clarence FC, Cliftonville FC, Distillery FC, Glentoran FC, Linfield FC, Milford FC (Armagh), Oldpark FC, Ulster FC. All the clubs were based in the city of Belfast except for Milford FC whose home town was Armagh. Football in Ireland remained strictly an amateur affair until 1894 when a vote in favour of professionalism was passed with a 64-30 majority at the IFA annual meeting, a similar motion having been previously defeated since first proposed in 1882.

In 1920 all clubs from the south of Ireland resigned from the Irish League and the Irish FA to join the newly formed Irish Free State FA and Irish Free State League, today's Football Association of Ireland (Republic of Ireland). As the majority of the members of the Irish League were located in Northern Ireland, this did not prove to be a problem and the League continued much the same as before with the number of members increasing in subsequent years. The first major change to the League structure occurred in 1995 when the League was split into two divisions – the "Premier Division" and the "First Division" – both are covered in this book. In 1999, a "Second Division" was also added to the League structure after the Intermediate level "B Divison – Section 1" was renamed, but the next major change came in 2003 when the Irish FA took charge of the top flight of Northern Irish football. The Premier Division became the new "Irish Premier League" and was the only senior league in Northern Irish football as the First Division dropped down to Intermediate level alongside the Second Division. The following season, the Irish Football League was effectively wound up altogether as the Irish FA took over the running of the two IFL divisions and renamed them as the IFA Intermediate League First Division and Second Division, both operating below the Premier League. In 2008, the Premier League was renamed to the "IFA Premiership" and at the same time, the IFA Intermediate League was closed down, with Division One becoming the new "IFA Championship". For the 2008-09 season only, there was also an "IFA Interim Intermediate League" comprising the former members of the IFA Intermediate League who did not meet the criteria for membership of the new IFA Championship. Members of this interim league had one season to make the necessary changes to qualify for membership of the IFA Championship and 10 out of 12 clubs were successful, joining a new "IFA Championship 2" the following season. A new body, the "Northern Irish Football League" took over the running of league football for the 2013-14 season. No change was made to the structure of the league, but the divisions were all renamed to "NIFL" from the "IFA". At the end of the 2015-16 season, the NIFL Championship 1 gained senior status and was renamed the NIFL Championship. The NIFL Championship 2 remained at Intermediate level and was renamed the NIFL Premier Intermediate League.

In addition to the results of various League matches, Final League tables and Irish Cup results, this book also lists the top goalscorers for each season, where known. The full names of clubs are used whenever possible and are listed in the following format: Club Name (Home Town/City/Village).

In an attempt to ensure accuracy, the information has been checked and collated. However, if any errors are found, readers are invited to notify Soccer Books using the contact information at the front of the book.

1881

IRISH CUP FINAL (Cliftonville Ground, Belfast – 09/04/1881 – 1,500)
MOYOLA PARK FC (CASTLEDAWSON)   1-0   Cliftonville FC (Belfast)
Morrow   *(H.T. 0-0)*

Moyola: Mackrell, Hewison, Dowd, McLernon, McSwiggan, R.Redmond, McKenna, W.J. Houston, T. Houston, M. Redmond, Morrow.
Cliftonville: Kennedy, Howell, McAlery, Martin, Baird, R.M.C. Potts, Davidson, Beyer, Williams, McKeague, Hannay.

Semi-finals

Knock FC (Belfast)	2-2, 1-2	Cliftonville FC (Belfast)
Moyola Park FC (Castledawson)	3-0	Alexander FC (Limavady)

Round 1

Knock FC (Belfast)	11-0	Distillery FC (Belfast)
Moyola Park FC (Castledawson)	2-0	Avoniel FC (Belfast)
Oldpark FC (Belfast)	0-2	Cliftonville FC (Belfast)

Alexander FC (Limavady) received a bye

1881-82

IRISH CUP FINAL (Ulster Ground, Ballynafeigh, Belfast – 13/05/1882 – 2,000)
QUEEN'S ISLAND FC (BELFAST)   1-0   Cliftonville FC (Belfast)
Bell

Queen's Island: W. Gilmour, Gouk, Cunningham, Orr, J. Gilmour, Kerr, Stewart, Bell, Drummond, McMillan, Monroe.
Cliftonville: Parlane, Hull, McAlery, Martin, Baird, Hannay, R.M.C. Potts, Davidson, Jackson, Spiller, Waring.

Semi-finals

Cliftonville FC (Belfast)	1-1, 0-0, 2-0	Avoniel FC (Belfast)
Queen's Island FC (Belfast)	w/o	Castlederg FC (Castlederg)

Round 1

Avoniel FC (Belfast)	1-1, 3-1, 1-0	Distillery FC (Belfast)
(A replay was ordered after a protest that the 2nd match was ended 4 minutes early)		
Castlederg FC (Castlederg)	2-1	Banbridge FC (Banbridge)
Knock FC (Belfast)	0-2	Cliftonville FC (Belfast)
Moyola Park FC (Castledawson)	1-1, 1-2	Queen's Island FC (Belfast)

1882-83

IRISH CUP FINAL   (Bloomfield Ground, Belfast – 05/05/1883 – 2,000)
CLIFTONVILLE FC (BELFAST)   5-0   Ulster FC (Belfast)
J. Potts 1, McWha 2, Davison   *(H.T. 3-0)*
Cliftonville: Houston, McAlery, Browne, Hannay, Martin, Davidson, McWha, R.M.C. Potts, J.T. Potts, Dill, Spiller.
Ulster: McCracken, Watson, Hamilton, Hastings, Elliott, Williams, J. Reid, J. Johnston, Jackson, Waring, Andrews.

Semi-finals

Cliftonville FC (Belfast)	7-0	Alexander FC (Limavady)
Ulster FC (Belfast)	4-1	Queen's Island FC (Belfast)

Quarter-finals

Alexander FC (Limavady)   1-0, 1-0   Strabane FC (Strabane)
(The result of the 1st match was changed to 0-0 after a protest)
Distillery FC (Belfast)   1-2, 0-1   Queen's Island FC (Belfast)
(The result of the 1st match changed to 1-1 after a protest)
Moyola Park FC (Castledawson)   0-1 (aet)   Cliftonville FC (Belfast)
Ulster FC (Belfast) received a bye

1883-84

IRISH CUP FINAL   (Ulster Ground, Ballynafeigh, Belfast – 19/04/1884 – 2,000)
DISTILLERY FC (BELFAST)   5-0   Wellington Park FC (Belfast)
Hogg 2, Stewart 2, S. Johnston   *(H.T. 3-0)*
Distillery: Millar, M. Wilson, R. Wilson, Baxter, W. Crone, McClatchey, Hogg, S. Johnston, J. Johnston, Condy, Stewart.
Wellington: McCarroll, Gibb, King, Elliott, Hazlett, Herd, Totton, Dodds, Gibb, McCoull, McCashin.

Semi-finals

Distillery FC (Belfast)	3-0	Ulster FC (Belfast)
Wellington Park FC (Belfast)	4-2	Moyola Park FC (Castledawson)

Quarter-finals

Distillery FC (Belfast)	1-0	Cliftonville FC (Belfast)
Moyola Park FC (Castledawson)	2-0	Alexander FC (Limavady)
Wellington Park FC (Belfast)	w/o	Dublin Association (Dublin)

Ulster FC (Belfast) received a bye

1884-85

IRISH CUP FINAL (Ulster Ground, Ballynafeigh, Belfast – 21/03/1885 – 2,000)

DISTILLERY FC (BELFAST) 3-0 Limavady FC (Limavady)
(Johnston 2, Rankine) *(H.T. 2-0)*

Distillery: Millar, Cunningham, Wilson, W. Crone, Baxter, McClatchey, Hogg, S. Johnston, Beattie, Sinclair, Stewart.

Limerick: Rankin, Jack Sherrard, Devine, Douglas, Allen, Ferguson, Joe Sherrard, McLean, Magennis, Connell, Doyle.

Semi-finals

Limavady FC (Limavady) 2-1 Cliftonville FC (Belfast)
Distillery FC (Belfast) received a bye

Quarter-finals

Distillery FC (Belfast) 1-0 Oldpark FC (Belfast)
Hertford FC (Lisburn) 0-1 Limavady FC (Limavady)
Cliftonville FC (Belfast) received a bye

1885-86

IRISH CUP FINAL (Ulster Ground, Ballynafeigh, Belfast – 27/03/1886 – 1,000)

DISTILLERY FC (BELFAST) 1-0 Limavady FC (Limavady)
J. Johnston *(H.T. 0-0)*

Distillery: Page, M. Wilson, R. Wilson, Baxter, W. Crone, McClatchey, McArthur, S. Johnston, J. Johnston, Bell, Condy.

Limerick: Fleming, Jack Sherrard, Devine, M. Douglas, Allen, Phillips, Joe Sherrard, Fleming, R. Douglas, Ferguson, McLean.

Semi-finals

Distillery FC (Belfast) 4-0 Dublin University AFC (Dublin)
Limavady FC (Limavady) 1-0 Belfast Y.M.C.A. (Belfast)

Quarter-finals

Dublin University FC (Dublin) 6-0 Banbridge FC (Banbridge)
Limavady FC (Limavady) 6-0 Moyola Park FC (Castledawson)
Belfast Y.M.C.A. (Belfast) and Distillery FC (Belfast) both received byes

1886-87

IRISH CUP FINAL (Distillery Ground, Broadway, Belfast – 12/02/1887 – 4,000)

ULSTER FC (BELFAST) 3-1 Cliftonville FC (Belfast)
Mears, Jack Reid, Watson *(H.T. 3-1)* *Turner*

Ulster: Barclay, Fox, Watson, Moore, Hastings, Campbell, Miller, E. Reid, Jack Reid, John Reid, Mears.
Cliftonville: Phillips, Browne, Stewart, Molyneux, Rosbotham, Baxter, Turner, Dobbin, Barry, Ferguson, Elleman.

Semi-finals

Cliftonville FC (Belfast)	2-0	Limavady FC (Limavady)
Ulster FC (Belfast)	2-1	Glentoran FC (Belfast)

Quarter-finals

Cliftonville FC (Belfast)	10-1	St. Malachy's College FC (Belfast)
Glentoran FC (Belfast)	2-1	Distillery FC (Belfast)
Millmount FC (Banbridge)	0-5	Limavady FC (Limavady)
Ulster FC (Belfast)	2-2, 3-2	Belfast Y.M.C.A. (Belfast)

1887-88

IRISH CUP FINAL (Ulster Ground, Ballynafeigh, Belfast – 17/03/1888 – 3,000)

CLIFTONVILLE FC (BELFAST) 2-1 Distillery FC (Belfast)
Barry, Gibb *(H.T. 1-1)* *Stanfield*

Cliftonville: Clugston, Browne, Wilson, Williamson, Rosbotham, Molyneux, Elleman, Gibb, Barry, McPherson, Turner.
Distillery: Irwin, R. Crone, Ritchie, W. Crone, Spencer, Crawford, McClatchey, Stanfield, McManus, Stewart, Johnston.

Semi-finals

Cliftonville FC (Belfast)	5-0	Linfield Athletic FC (Belfast)
Distillery FC (Belfast)	3-1	Oldpark FC (Belfast)

Quarter-finals

Limavady FC (Limavady	3-3, 5-3	Cliftonville FC (Belfast)
Oldpark FC (Belfast)	1-1, 3-2	Mount Collyer FC (Belfast)
Ulster FC (Belfast)	0-2	Distillery FC (Belfast)

Linfield Athletic FC (Belfast) received a bye

1888-89

IRISH CUP FINAL   (Ulster Ground, Ballynafeigh, Belfast – 16/03/1889 – 3,500)

DISTILLERY FC (BELFAST)   5-4   Belfast Y.M.C.A. (Belfast)
R.Stewart 2, McClatchey 2, Stanfield   *Lemon 2, Millar, Small*

Distillery: Galbraith, R. Crone, Ritchie, W. Crone, Spencer, Crawford, McClatchey, Stanfield, R. Stewart, W. Stewart, McIlvenny.

Belfast: Pinkerton, Ervine, Watson, E. Reid, Leslie, Cooke, Dalton, Small, Miller, Lemon, Percy.

Semi-finals

Belfast Y.M.C.A. (Belfast)	3-1	Glentoran FC (Belfast)
Distillery FC (Belfast)	13-0	Hilden FC (Lisburn)

Quarter-finals

Distillery FC (Belfast)	10-0	Oldpark FC (Belfast)
Glentoran FC (Belfast)	8-0	Limavady FC (Limavady)
St. Columb's Court FC (Londonderry)	1-3	Belfast Y.M.C.A. (Belfast)

Hilden FC (Lisburn) received a bye

1889-90

IRISH CUP FINAL   (Ulster Ground, Ballynafeigh, Belfast – 08/03/1890 – 4,500)

GORDON HIGHLANDERS REGIMENT   2-2   Cliftonville FC (Belfast)
Swan, Archibald   *Wilton, Small*

Gordon Highlanders: Grant, Thompson, Buchanan, Maguire, Milne, Johnston, Swan, Hall, Archibald, McCormack, Beveridge.

Cliftonville: Clugston, Nelson, Ervine, Willianson, Crawford, Cooke, Elleman, Small, Barry, Lemon, Wilton.

IRISH CUP FINAL REPLAY   (Ulsterville, Belfast – 12/03/1890 – 3,500)

GORDON HIGHLANDERS REGIMENT   3-0   Cliftonville FC (Belfast)
Swan 2, Beveridge

Cliftonville: Clugston, Nelson, Gibb, Williamson, Crawford, Cooke, Stewart, Small, Barry, Wilton, Turner.

Gordon Highlanders: Grant, Thompson, Buchanan, Maguire, Milne, Johnston, Swan, Reid, Hall, McCormack, Beveridge,

Semi-finals

Cliftonville FC (Belfast)	3-2, 4-2	Dublin Association (Dublin)
	(The replay was ordered after a protest)	
Gordon Highlanders Regiment	2-1	Linfield FC (Belfast)

Quarter-finals

Dublin Association (Dublin)	6-2	Limavady FC (Limavady)

Cliftonville FC (Belfast), Gordon Highlanders Regiment and Linfield FC (Belfast) all received byes

1890-91

Irish League 1890-91	Clarence	Cliftonville	Distillery	Glentoran	Linfield	Milford	Oldpark	Ulster
Clarence FC		2-5	0-4	5-4	1-3	+:-	1-3	2-6
Cliftonville FC	2-2		7-3	0-0	0-8	3-2	2-2	4-1
Distillery FC	4-3	1-6		5-2	2-1	+:-	2-0	3-5
Glentoran FC	9-1	4-3	0-3		0-7	4-2	3-2	-:+
Linfield FC	5-2	10-2	6-2	6-0		9-1	14-0	9-5
Milford FC	-:+	-:+	1-9	0-8	1-6		-:+	2-5
Oldpark FC	+:-	2-3	2-4	0-2	0-3	5-0		2-10
Ulster FC	4-2	9-0	4-4	5-3	2-2	10-1	4-4	

	Irish League	**Pd**	**Wn**	**Dw**	**Ls**	**GF**	**GA**	**Pts**	
1.	LINFIELD FC (BELFAST)	14	12	1	1	89	18	25	
2.	Ulster FC (Belfast)	14	9	3	2	70	38	21	
3.	Distillery FC (Belfast)	14	9	1	4	46	37	19	
4.	Cliftonville FC (Belfast)	14	7	3	4	37	46	17	
5.	Glentoran FC (Belfast)	14	6	1	7	39	39	13	
6.	Oldpark FC (Belfast)	14	4	2	8	22	48	10	
7.	Clarence FC (Belfast)	14	3	1	10	21	49	7	#
8.	Milford FC (Armagh)	14	-	-	14	10	59	-	#
		112	50	12	50	334	334	112	

Top goalscorers 1890-91

1) Robert HILL   (Linfield FC)   20
2) John PEDEN   (Linfield FC)   19
3) Sam TORRANS   (Linfield FC)   18

\# Milford FC (Armagh) resigned from the league on 20/01/1891 with 5 games still to play. These remaining games were awarded to their opponents (-:+) and a 0-0 scoreline was registered.

Other matches shown as +:- or -:+ were awarded to (+) with a 0-0 score-line being recorded.

Clarence FC (Belfast) withdrew from the league on 01/09/1891 and disbanded later in the same year. Their place was given to the Lancashire Fusiliers Regiment (Belfast) who were unable to play their opening game due to the short notice being given.

Elected: Belfast Y.M.C.A. (Belfast), Ligoniel FC (Belfast), Milltown FC (Belfast)

The league was extended to 10 clubs for the next season

IRISH CUP FINAL   (Solitude, Belfast – 14/03/1891 – 5,000)

LINFIELD FC (BELFAST)   4-2   Ulster FC (Belfast)
Hill, Torrans, Gaffiken, Flanelly o.g.   *(H.T. 4-2)*   *Tierney, McIlvenny*

Linfield: T. Gordon, W. Gordon, Morrison, McKeown, Milne, Moore, Dalton, Gaffiken, Hill, S. Torrans, Peden.
Ulster: Johnstone, Purvis, Campbell, Flanelly, Reynolds, Cunningham, McIlvenny, Tierney, McCabe, McAuley, Haig.

Semi-finals

Linfield FC (Belfast)	9-0	St. Columb's Court FC (Londonderry)
Ulster FC (Belfast)	6-2	Clarence FC (Belfast)

Quarter-finals

Omagh Wanderers FC (Omagh)	0-6	St. Columb's Court FC (Londonderry)
St. Columb's Hall FC (Londonderry)	0-7	Ulster FC (Belfast)

Clarence FC (Belfast) and Linfield FC (Belfast) both received byes

1891-92

Irish League 1891-92	Cliftonville	Distillery	Glentoran	Lancs. Fus.	Ligoniel	Linfield	Milltown	Oldpark	Ulster	Y.M.C.A.
Cliftonville FC	■	---	1-1	2-3	4-1	0-5	8-0	7-1	0-3	3-3
Distillery FC	3-1	■	-:+	5-0	2-1	---	7-0	5-3		---
Glentoran FC	4-4	4-3	■	2-3	3-1	1-7	11-0	15-1	6-5	---
Lancashire Fusiliers Regiment	1-0	(a)	1-1	■	13-2	0-0	4-0	+:-	2-5	---
Ligoniel FC	(b)	---	0-9	1-5	■	3-8	4-0	+:-	2-4	---
Linfield FC	8-0	6-1	8-0	6-2	7-1	■	14-0	9-0	8-1	---
Milltown FC	-:+	0-4	0-9	0-8	7-3	1-3	■	+:-	0-4	3-2
Oldpark FC	-:+	1-5	0-7	3-10	3-0	1-7	-:+	■	0-2	+:-
Ulster FC	4-0	---	7-1	5-0	+:-	1-5	3-1	9-2	■	5-2
Y.M.C.A. Belfast	---	2-10	0-7	3-4	2-4	0-4	---	---	---	■

	Irish League	Pd	Wn	Dw	Ls	GF	GA	Pts	
1.	LINFIELD FC (BELFAST)	17	15	1	1	106	14	31	
2.	Lancashire Fusiliers Regiment (Belfast)	17	11	3	3	56	30	25	#
3.	Ulster FC (Belfast)	16	12	-	4	61	34	24	
4.	Glentoran FC (Belfast)	16	9	3	4	80	41	21	
5.	Distillery FC (Belfast)	12	8	1	3	45	18	15	-2
6.	Cliftonville FC (Belfast)	16	5	4	7	30	37	14	
7.	Milltown FC (Belfast)	16	4	-	12	12	77	8	#
8.	Ligoniel FC (Belfast)	16	3	1	12	22	70	7	#
9.	Oldpark FC (Belfast)	17	2	-	15	12	78	4	#
10.	Belfast Y.M.C.A. (Belfast)	9	-	1	8	14	40	1	
		152	69	14	69	439	439	150	

On 02/02/1892 Distillery FC were fined £10.00 and had 2 points deducted for fielding an ineligible player versus Linfield FC but the result 2-1 was allowed to stand. They were later expelled from the league on 10/02/1892 for failing to pay the fine but were reinstated on 24/02/1892 after paying a reduced amount. However, some teams refused to accept this decision.

On 12/04/1892 Glentoran FC were fined £15.00 for refusing to play against Distillery FC

(a) On 18/04/1892, the Lancashire Fusiliers were awarded 2 points for the opening match of the season which they had been unable to play due to late acceptance to league status. They were also awarded 1 point for their unplayed match against Distillery FC, but they then resigned from the league prior to the start of the 1892-93 season. (All matches had been played on their opponents grounds).

Unplayed Distillery matches against Glentoran, Milltown, Ulster, Cliftonville and Ligoniel were declared void (---).

The Cliftonville FC vs Glentoran FC match was not played but was registered as a 1-1 draw by the Irish League.

(b) The Ligoniel FC vs Cliftonville FC match was not played but both teams were awarded 1 point by the Irish League.

Belfast Y.M.C.A. (Belfast) resigned from the league on 19/12/1891, their remaining fixtures were declared void (---).

Oldpark FC (Belfast) resigned from the league on 20/04/1892 after hostility had been shown towards them for playing against Distillery FC. Their remaining fixtures were awarded to their opponents (+:- or -:+)

Top goalscorers 1891-92

1)	Tom MORRISON	(Glentoran FC)	21
2)	Robert HILL	(Linfield FC)	15
3)	Robert McILVENNY	(Ulster FC)	14

(not fully recorded)

Ligoniel FC (Belfast) and Milltown FC (Belfast) were excluded from the league from the next season.

Elected: Derry Olympic FC (Londonderry)

IRISH CUP FINAL   (Solitude, Belfast – 12/03/1892)

LINFIELD FC (BELFAST)	7-0	Black Watch Regiment (Limerick)
Hill 4, S. Torrans, R. Torrans, Dalton	*(H.T. 4-0)*	

Linfield: T. Gordon, W. Gordon, Arnott, McKeown, Milne, S. Johnston, Dalton, Gaffiken, Hill, S. Torrans, R. Torrans.
Black Watch: Mann, Cassels, Barr, McGee, Porter, Clarke, McAuley, Connor, Reynolds, Malcolm, Thom.

Semi-finals

Black Watch Regiment (Limerick)	4-1	St. Columb's Court FC (Londonderry)
Linfield FC (Belfast)	3-0	Ulster FC (Belfast)

Quarter-finals

Black Watch Regiment (Limerick)	8-2	Lancashire Fusiliers Regiment (Belfast)
Linfield FC (Belfast)	6-0	Glentoran FC (Belfast)
Ulster FC (Belfast)	4-2	Cliftonville FC (Belfast)

St. Columb's Court FC (Londonderry) received a bye

1892-93

Irish League 1892-93	Cliftonville	Derry Olympic	Distillery	Glentoran	Linfield	Ulster
Cliftonville FC	■	8-1	3-2	2-1	0-3	3-1
Derry Olympic FC	1-2	■	0-9	1-2	-:+	2-3
Distillery FC	5-3	2-2	■	0-4	1-1	7-0
Glentoran FC	1-3	+:-	3-3	■	1-2	3-0
Linfield FC	3-3	+:-	3-0	5-0	■	3-1
Ulster FC	0-1	+:-	2-3	0-1	1-7	■

	Irish League	Pd	Wn	Dw	Ls	GF	GA	Pts	
1.	LINFIELD FC (BELFAST)	10	8	2	-	27	7	18	
2.	Cliftonville FC (Belfast)	10	7	1	2	28	18	15	
3.	Distillery FC (Belfast)	10	4	3	3	32	21	11	
4.	Glentoran FC (Belfast)	10	5	1	4	16	16	11	
5.	Ulster FC (Belfast)	10	2	-	8	8	30	4	
6.	Derry Olympic FC (Londonderry)	10	-	1	9	7	26	1	#
		60	26	8	26	118	118	60	

Top goalscorers 1892-93

1)	Robert HILL	(Linfield FC)	9
	James PERCY	(Cliftonville FC)	9

Derry Olympic FC (Londonderry) resigned from the league after only 6 games. The remaining games were awarded to their opponents with a 0-0 scoreline being registered.

Elected: Ligoniel FC (Belfast)

IRISH CUP FINAL   (Ulsterville, Belfast – 11/03/1893)

LINFIELD FC (BELFAST)	5-1	Cliftonville FC (Belfast)
T. Torrans, Milne 2, McKeown, Turley	*(H.T. 5-0)*	*J. Williamson*

Linfield: T. Gordon, W. Gordon, S. Torrans, McKeown, S. Johnston, R. Torrans, T. Torrans, Peden, Gaffiken, Milne, Turley.

Cliftonville: Clugston, R. Stewart, Thompson, Crawford, McKee, Anderson, Small, G. Williamson, J. Williamson, Turner, Blayney.

Semi-finals

Cliftonville FC (Belfast)	10-1	Ulster FC (Belfast)
Linfield FC (Belfast)	4-1, 4-0	Distillery FC (Belfast)
	(The replay was ordered after a protest)	

Quarter-finals

Distillery FC (Belfast)	6-0	Leinster Nomads FC (Dublin)
Ivy FC (Londonderry)	0-8	Linfield FC (Belfast)

Cliftonville FC (Belfast) and Ulster FC (Belfast) both received byes

1893-94

Irish League 1893-94	Cliftonville	Distillery	Glentoran	Ligoniel	Linfield	Ulster
Cliftonville FC	■	3-2	0-1	2-2	3-1	1-3
Distillery FC	2-1	■	1-0	1-2	4-4	2-0
Glentoran FC	8-0	4-2	■	5-1	1-3	5-1
Ligoniel FC	1-5	0-6	0-2	■	0-5	3-4
Linfield FC	3-3	6-0	0-1	4-0	■	5-2
Ulster FC	2-4	4-3	2-4	5-1	1-5	■

	Irish League	Pd	Wn	Dw	Ls	GF	GA	Pts	
1.	GLENTORAN FC (BELFAST)	10	8	-	2	31	10	16	
2.	Linfield FC (Belfast)	10	6	2	2	36	15	14	
3.	Cliftonville FC (Belfast)	10	4	2	4	22	25	10	
4.	Distillery FC (Belfast)	10	4	1	5	23	24	9	
5.	Ulster FC (Belfast)	10	4	-	6	24	33	8	#
6.	Ligoniel FC (Belfast)	10	1	1	8	10	39	3	#
		60	27	6	27	146	146	60	

Top goalscorer 1893-94

1) Michael McERLEAN   (Linfield FC)   9

Ligoniel FC (Belfast) and Ulster FC (Belfast) were not in the league for next season. As no new teams were elected the league was reduced to 4 clubs.

IRISH CUP FINAL   (Solitude, Belfast – 17/03/1894 – 5,500)

DISTILLERY FC (BELFAST)   2-2   Linfield FC (Belfast)
Stanfield 2   *Milne, McAllen*

Distillery: Thompson, Brown, Ponsonby, Myles, J. Stilges, Burnett, Stanfield, Shannon, Emerson, W. Stilges, McClatchey.

Linfield: T. Gordon, H. Gordon, W. Gordon, McKeown, S. Johnston, J. Jordan, Dalton, Gaffiken, Milne. T. Jordan, McAllen.

IRISH CUP FINAL REPLAY   (Solitude, Belfast – 18/04/1894)

DISTILLERY FC (BELFAST)   3-2   Linfield FC (Belfast)
Emerson 2, Stanfield   *Jordan, McErlean*

Linfield: T. Gordon, S. Torrans, W. Gordon, McKeown, Milne, H. Gordon, Dalton, Gaffiken, McErlean, T. Jordan, McAllen.

Distillery: Thompson, J. Stilges, Mawhinney, Ponsonby, McClatchey, Myles, Thompson, Stanfield, Burnett, W. Stilges, Emerson.

Semi-finals

Distillery FC (Belfast)	8-3	St. Columb's Court FC (Londonderry)
Linfield FC (Belfast)	3-2	Cliftonville FC (Belfast)

Quarter-finals

Ligoniel FC (Belfast)	2-4	Cliftonville FC (Belfast)
St. Columb's Court FC (Londonderry)	3-4, w/o	Bohemian FC (Dublin)

(A replay was ordered after a protest but Bohemian refused to play)
Distillery FC (Belfast) and Linfield FC (Belfast) both received byes.

1894-95

Irish League 1894-95	Cliftonville	Distillery	Glentoran	Linfield
Cliftonville FC	■	1-2	2-2	0-5
Distillery FC	4-3	■	3-1	2-2
Glentoran FC	1-3	3-1	■	2-2
Linfield FC	3-1	3-1	3-0	■

	Irish League	Pd	Wn	Dw	Ls	GF	GA	Pts
1.	LINFIELD FC (BELFAST)	6	4	2	-	18	6	10
2.	Distillery FC (Belfast)	6	3	1	2	13	13	7
3.	Glentoran FC (Belfast)	6	1	2	3	9	14	4
4.	Cliftonville FC (Belfast)	6	1	1	4	10	17	3
		24	9	6	9	50	50	24

No clubs were promoted or relegated

Top goalscorers 1894-95

1)	George GAUKRODGER	(Linfield FC)	4
	Joe McALLEN	(Linfield FC)	4
	William SHERRARD	(Glentoran FC)	4
	Oliver STANFIELD	(Glentoran FC)	4
	J.H. TORRANS	(Cliftonville FC)	4

IRISH CUP FINAL (Solitude, Belfast – 23/03/1895 – 2,000)

LINFIELD FC (BELFAST)	10-1 (H.T. 3-1)	Bohemian FC (Dublin)

Milne 3, McAllen 3, H. Gordon, Williamson, Gaffiken, Gaukrodger *Blayney*

Linfield: T. Gordon, H. Gordon, S. Torrans, S. Johnston, Milne, R. Torrans, G. Williamson, Gaffiken, Gaukrodger, T. Jordan, McAllen.

Bohemian: Morrogh, Murray, Whelan, McCaughey, Fitzpatrick, O'Sullivan, Farrell, Wilson, Sheehan, Murray, Blayney.

Semi-finals

Bohemian FC (Dublin)	4-1	St. Columb's Hall Celtic FC (Londonderry)
Linfield FC (Belfast)	6-1	Belfast Celtic FC (Belfast)

Quarter-finals

Bohemian FC (Dublin)	6-4	Glentoran FC (Belfast)
Dublin University FC (Dublin)	1-3	Belfast Celtic FC (Belfast)
Linfield FC (Belfast)	0-0, 4-1	Distillery FC (Belfast)
St. Columb's Hall Celtic FC (Londonderry)	3-1	St. Columb's Court FC (Londonderry)

1895-96

Irish League 1895-96	Cliftonville	Distillery	Glentoran	Linfield
Cliftonville FC	■	2-2	2-1	2-3
Distillery FC	2-2	■	6-1	2-1
Glentoran FC	1-3	6-2	■	2-3
Linfield FC	1-3	0-3	2-2	■

Play-off (Solitude, Belfast – 11/01/1896)

DISTILLERY FC (BELFAST)　　　　　2-1　　　　　Cliftonville FC (Belfast)

	Irish League	Pd	Wn	Dw	Ls	GF	GA	Pts
1.	Distillery FC (Belfast)	6	3	2	1	17	12	8
1.	Cliftonville FC (Belfast)	6	3	2	1	14	10	8
3.	Linfield FC (Belfast)	6	2	1	3	10	14	5
4.	Glentoran FC (Belfast)	6	1	1	4	13	18	3
		24	9	6	9	54	54	24

Elected: Belfast Celtic FC (Belfast), North Staffordshire Regiment (Belfast)

The league was extended to 6 clubs for next season

IRISH CUP FINAL (Solitude, Belfast – 14/03/1896 – 6,000)

DISTILLERY FC (BELFAST)　　　　　3-1　　　　　Glentoran FC (Belfast)
Riley, Baird, Campbell　　　　　　　　　　　　　　　　　　　　　　　*Carmichael*

Distillery: Thompson, Brown, Ponsonby, McCoy, Farrell, McClatchey, Baird, Rylie, Stanfield, Campbell, Peden.
Glentoran: E. Johnston, Purvis, McFall, Hatty, Shannon, Burnett, Carmichael, Hall, P. Johnston, Kelly, Somerset.

Semi-finals

Distillery FC (Belfast)	4-1	Cliftonville FC (Belfast)
Glentoran FC (Belfast)	8-2	Derry North End FC (Londonderry)

Quarter-finals

Cliftonville FC (Belfast)	1-0	Linfield FC (Belfast)
Derry North End FC (Londonderry)	0-0, 1-1, 4-1	St. Columb's Court FC (Londonderry)
Distillery FC (Belfast)	3-1	Bohemian FC (Dublin)
2nd Battalion Scots Guard Regiment (Dublin)	2-2, 0-3	Glentoran FC (Belfast)

1896-97

Irish League 1896-97	Belfast Celtic	Cliftonville	Distillery	Glentoran	Linfield	North Staffs.
Belfast Celtic FC		1-3	2-1	1-3	3-3	1-1
Cliftonville FC	3-1		2-3	1-3	1-1	2-2
Distillery FC	2-0	2-2		2-0	0-6	1-1
Glentoran FC	2-0	3-2	2-1		1-0	6-0
Linfield FC	4-2	3-4	7-4	2-2		7-1
North Staffordshire Regiment	3-0	1-2	1-1	1-2	6-1	

	Irish League	Pd	Wn	Dw	Ls	GF	GA	Pts
1.	GLENTORAN FC (BELFAST)	10	8	1	1	24	10	17
2.	Cliftonville FC (Belfast)	10	4	3	3	22	20	11
3.	Linfield FC (Belfast)	10	4	3	3	34	24	11
4.	Distillery FC (Belfast)	10	3	3	4	17	23	9
5.	North Staffordshire Regiment (Belfast)	10	2	4	4	17	23	8
6.	Belfast Celtic FC (Belfast)	10	1	2	7	11	25	4
		60	22	16	22	125	125	60

2nd/3rd Place Play-Off   (Solitude, Belfast)

Cliftonville FC (Belfast)   3-2   Linfield FC (Belfast)

No clubs were promoted or relegated

Top goalscorers 1896-97

1)	John DARLING	(Linfield FC)	6
	Richard PEDEN	(Linfield FC)	6
3)	George HALL	(Distillery FC)	5
	HIGERTY	(North Staffordshire Regiment)	5
	Tom JORDAN	(Linfield FC)	5
	Sam MARTIN	(Cliftonville FC)	5
	James PYPER	(Cliftonville FC)	5

IRISH CUP FINAL   (Grosvenor Park, Belfast – 20/03/1897 – 5,000)

CLIFTONVILLE FC (BELFAST)   3-1   Sherwood Foresters FC (Curragh)
Jas. Campbell, Martin, Pyper   *Bedford*

Cliftonville: Scott, Gibson, Foreman, Jack Campbell, Polland, Jack Pyper, James Campbell, McCashin, Barron, James Pyper, Martin.
Shelbourne: Lewis, Pykett, Vernon, Locker, Cleland, Murphy, Thorpe, Porter, Roberts, Hoare, Bedford.

Semi-finals

Cliftonville FC (Belfast)   2-1   Distillery FC (Belfast)
Sherwood Foresters FC (Curragh)   3-2   St. Columb's Hall Celtic FC (Londonderry)

Quarter-finals

Bohemian FC (Dublin)	0-1	Sherwood Foresters FC (Curragh)
Cliftonville FC (Belfast)	2-1	Linfield FC (Belfast)
Derry North End FC (Londonderry)	2-2, 3-4	St. Columb's Hall Celtic FC (Londonderry)
Distillery FC (Belfast) received a bye		

1897-98

Irish League 1897-98	Belfast Celtic	Cliftonville	Distillery	Glentoran	Linfield	North Staffs.
Belfast Celtic FC	■	1-2	5-1	1-5	0-3	2-1
Cliftonville FC	1-0	■	4-3	1-1	0-1	3-1
Distillery FC	0-2	5-0	■	0-6	1-1	2-0
Glentoran FC	1-0	3-0	6-0	■	2-4	1-2
Linfield FC	2-1	2-4	1-0	2-1	■	3-0
North Staffordshire Regiment	3-3	0-8	3-1	2-5	1-3	■

	Irish League	Pd	Wn	Dw	Ls	GF	GA	Pts
1.	LINFIELD FC (BELFAST)	10	8	1	1	22	10	17
2.	Cliftonville FC (Belfast)	10	6	1	3	23	17	13
3.	Glentoran FC (Belfast)	10	6	1	3	31	12	13
4.	Belfast Celtic FC (Belfast)	10	3	1	6	15	19	7
5.	Distillery FC (Belfast)	10	2	1	7	13	28	5
6.	North Staffordshire Regiment (Belfast)	10	2	1	7	13	31	5
		60	27	6	27	117	117	60

No clubs promoted or relegated

IRISH CUP FINAL   (The Oval, Belfast – 19/03/1898 – 3,000)

LINFIELD FC (BELFAST)   2-0   St. Columb's Hall Celtic FC (Londonderry)
Darling, Jordan

Linfield: White, Howard, S. Torrans, Anderson, Milne, Maginnis, Stevenson, Darling, T. Jordan, R. Rea, S. Rea.
St. Columb's: P. Boyle, Hassan, Gallagher, McComb, McNulty, Phillips, Gallagher, Maginnis, McIntyre, Lynch, G. Boyle.

Semi-finals

Linfield FC (Belfast)	1-1, 2-1	Belfast Celtic FC (Belfast)
St. Columb's Hall Celtic FC (Londonderry)	1-0	Bohemian FC (Dublin)

Quarter-finals

Bohemian FC (Dublin)	0-0, 1-2, w/o	Yorkshire Regiment

Belfast Celtic FC (Belfast), Linfield FC (Belfast) and St. Columb's Hall Celtic FC (Londonderry) all received byes

1898-99

Irish League 1898-99	Belfast Celtic	Cliftonville	Distillery	Glentoran	Linfield	North Staffs.
Belfast Celtic FC		1-2	1-2	2-3	1-6	2-0
Cliftonville FC	4-0		1-3	3-0	1-2	3-0
Distillery FC	0-2	2-1		0-2	2-1	5-2
Glentoran FC	2-1	1-2	1-2		1-2	3-0
Linfield FC	0-0	2-0	2-0	0-1		2-0
North Staffordshire Regiment	3-4	1-2	3-4	0-3	2-4	

Play-off

DISTILLERY FC (BELFAST)   2-0   Linfield FC (Belfast)

	Irish League	Pd	Wn	Dw	Ls	GF	GA	Pts	
1.	Distillery FC (Belfast)	10	7	1	2	23	17	15	
1.	Linfield FC (Belfast)	10	7	1	2	21	8	15	
3.	Cliftonville FC (Belfast)	10	6	-	4	19	12	12	
4.	Glentoran FC (Belfast)	10	6	-	4	17	12	12	
5.	Belfast Celtic FC (Belfast)	10	2	2	6	15	25	6	
6.	North Staffordshire Regiment (Belfast)	10	-	-	10	11	32	-	#
		60	28	4	28	106	106	60	

\# The North Staffordshire Regiment (Belfast) resigned from the league due to the regiment being posted to serve in South Africa.

Elected: Royal Scots Regiment (Belfast)

IRISH CUP FINAL   (Solitude, Belfast – 18/03/1899 – 7,000)

LINFIELD FC (BELFAST)   1-0   Glentoran FC (Belfast)
Peden
(The match ended early after Glentoran players refused to continue claiming that a Linfield player had punched a shot clear from the goal-line and no penalty had been awarded).
Linfield: Murray, Swan. S. Torrans, Maginnis, Milne, Wilson, John Peden, Darling, T. Jordan, Doherty, McAllen.
Glentoran: J. Lewis, Purvis, Kerr, Lyttle, McCann, McMaster, Gill, Smith, P. Johnston, Seaton, Duncan.

Semi-finals

Glentoran FC (Belfast)   2-2, 2-1, 2-0   Belfast Celtic FC (Belfast)
(The 2nd replay was ordered after a protest)
Linfield FC (Belfast)   4-2   Bohemian FC (Dublin)

Quarter-finals

Glentoran FC (Belfast)   8-0   King's Own Rifles Regiment (Cork)
Belfast Celtic FC (Belfast), Bohemian FC (Dublin) and Linfield FC (Belfast) all received byes

1899-1900

Irish League 1899-1900	Belfast Celtic	Cliftonville	Distillery	Glentoran	Linfield	Royal Scots
Belfast Celtic FC	■	5-1	3-1	2-1	2-0	1-0
Cliftonville FC	0-0	■	3-1	4-1	0-4	2-2
Distillery FC	4-3	3-3	■	0-0	1-1	4-0
Glentoran FC	0-1	1-4	0-1	■	4-4	2-4
Linfield FC	4-2	1-1	0-0	2-0	■	5-0
Royal Scots Regiment	---	4-1	0-2	---	---	■

	Irish League	Pd	Wn	Dw	Ls	GF	GA	Pts	
1.	BELFAST CELTIC FC (BELFAST)	9	6	1	2	19	11	13	
2.	Linfield FC (Belfast)	9	4	4	1	21	10	12	
3.	Distillery FC (Belfast)	10	4	4	2	17	13	12	
4.	Cliftonville FC (Belfast)	10	3	4	3	19	22	10	
5.	Royal Scots Regiment (Belfast)	7	2	1	4	10	17	5	#
6.	Glentoran FC (Belfast)	9	-	2	7	9	22	2	
		54	19	16	19	95	95	54	

\# The Royal Scots Regiment (Belfast) resigned from the league after only 7 games due to the regiment being posted to serve in South Africa because of the "Boer War".

Elected: Derry Celtic FC (Londonderry)

Note: Some publications show the following final table which excludes the record of the Royal Scots Regiment:

	Irish League	Pd	Wn	Dw	Ls	GF	GA	Pts
1.	Belfast Celtic FC (Belfast)	8	5	1	2	18	11	11
2.	Linfield FC (Belfast)	8	3	4	1	16	10	10
3.	Cliftonville FC (Belfast)	8	3	3	2	16	16	9
4.	Distillery FC (Belfast)	8	2	4	2	11	13	8
5.	Glentoran FC (Belfast)	8	-	2	6	7	18	2
		40	13	14	13	68	68	40

IRISH CUP FINAL   (Grosvenor Park, Belfast – 24/03/1900 – 5,500)

CLIFTONVILLE FC (BELFAST)　　　　　2-1　　　　　　　　　Bohemian FC (Dublin)
Campbell, Martin　　　　　　　　　　　　　　　　　　　　　　　*Sheehan*

Cliftonville: McAlpine, John Pyper, Jack Sheppard, Cochrane, McCoull, McShane, James Campbell, Wheeler, James Pyper, Martin, Thompson.
Bohemian: Farrell, McCausland, Whelan, Fulton, H. Barry, Crozier, Sheehan, Hooper, Pratt, Curtis, A. Barry.

Semi-finals

Bohemian FC (Dublin)	2-1	Belfast Celtic FC (Belfast)
Cliftonville FC (Belfast)	w/o	King's Own Scottish Borderers Regiment

Quarter-finals

Belfast Celtic FC (Belfast)	3-1	St. Columb's Court FC (Londonderry)
Cliftonville FC (Belfast)	5-1	Derry Celtic FC (Londonderry)
Distillery FC (Belfast)	1-5	Bohemian FC (Dublin)
King's Own Scottish Borderers Regiment	1-1, 5-2	Richmond Rovers FC (Dublin)

1900-01

Irish League 1900-01	Belfast Celtic	Cliftonville	Derry Celtic	Distillery	Glentoran	Linfield
Belfast Celtic FC	■	1-1	6-2	1-1	1-0	1-0
Cliftonville FC	1-0	■	3-3	3-4	2-4	0-0
Derry Celtic FC	0-1	2-3	■	0-6	2-4	1-4
Distillery FC	4-1	1-1	9-0	■	3-1	3-0
Glentoran FC	3-1	3-1	3-1	3-1	■	0-0
Linfield FC	1-0	0-2	4-1	0-1	1-3	■

	Irish League	Pd	Wn	Dw	Ls	GF	GA	Pts
1.	DISTILLERY FC (BELFAST)	10	7	2	1	33	10	16
2.	Glentoran FC (Belfast)	10	7	1	2	24	13	15
3.	Belfast Celtic FC (Belfast)	10	4	2	4	13	13	10
4.	Cliftonville FC (Belfast)	10	3	4	3	17	18	10
5.	Linfield FC (Belfast)	10	3	2	5	10	12	8
6.	Derry Celtic FC (Londonderry)	10	-	1	9	12	43	1
		60	24	12	24	109	109	60

Elected: St. Columb's Court FC (Londonderry) and Ulster FC (Belfast)

The league was extended to 8 clubs for the next season

IRISH CUP FINAL   (Grosvenor Park, Belfast – 13/04/1901)

CLIFTONVILLE FC (BELFAST)	1-0	Freebooters FC (Dublin)

Scott

Cliftonville: McAlpine, Gibson, Sheppard, Cochrane, McKee, Anderson, Scott, Wheeler, James Pyper, Kirkwood, James Campbell.

Freebooters: Nolan-Whelan, Finney, Ryan, Fottrell, Crozier, H. Thomas, McCann, T. Thomas, B. O'Reilly, H. O'Reilly, J. O'Reilly.

Semi-finals

Cliftonville FC (Belfast)	3-1	Derry Celtic FC (Londonderry)
Freebooters FC (Dublin)	2-1	Linfield FC (Belfast)

Quarter-finals

Cliftonville FC (Belfast)	2-0, 4-2	Belfast Celtic FC (Belfast)

Derry Celtic FC (Londonderry), Freebooters FC (Dublin) and Linfield FC (Belfast) all received byes

1901-02

Irish League 1901-02	Belfast Celtic	Cliftonville	Derry Celtic	Distillery	Glentoran	Linfield	St. Columb's	Ulster
Belfast Celtic FC	■	0-0	2-1	0-0	1-3	0-3	4-0	6-1
Cliftonville FC	2-0	■	1-0	1-2	1-2	3-0	3-0	1-0
Derry Celtic FC	3-2	2-0	■	1-1	2-1	0-1	2-0	1-2
Distillery FC	1-1	2-1	5-1	■	1-2	2-1	4-1	5-1
Glentoran FC	4-0	3-3	4-1	3-1	■	0-2	7-1	5-2
Linfield FC	4-0	2-0	4-0	2-0	5-1	■	3-0	4-2
St. Columb's Court FC	2-5	1-5	1-7	2-10	0-4	1-3	■	3-4
Ulster FC	1-1	0-3	2-2	3-4	2-4	1-4	1-1	■

	Irish League	Pd	Wn	Dw	Ls	GF	GA	Pts
1.	LINFIELD FC (BELFAST)	14	12	-	2	38	10	24
2.	Glentoran FC (Belfast)	14	10	1	3	43	22	21
3.	Distillery FC (Belfast)	14	8	3	3	38	20	19
4.	Cliftonville FC (Belfast)	14	7	2	5	24	14	16
5.	Belfast Celtic FC (Belfast)	14	4	4	6	22	25	12
6.	Derry Celtic FC (Londonderry)	14	5	2	7	23	26	12
7.	Ulster FC (Belfast)	14	2	3	9	22	44	7
8.	St. Columb's Court FC (Londonderry)	14	-	1	13	13	62	1 #
		112	48	16	48	223	223	112

St. Columb's Court FC (Londonderry) did not compete in the Irish League for the next season.

Elected: Bohemian FC (Dublin)

IRISH CUP FINAL   (Solitude, Belfast – 15/03/1902)

LINFIELD FC (BELFAST)	5-1	Distillery FC (Belfast)
Mercer 2, Milne, Peden 2		*Cairns*

Linfield: W. Scott, Darling, S. Torrans, Crothers, Milne, Maginnis, Mercer, Maxwell, Carnegie, John Peden, McAllen.

Distillery: Andrews, Ponsonby, McCracken, Cochrane, Parsons, McFarlane, Kearns, McArthur, Jones, Cairns, Kirkwood.

Semi-finals

Distillery FC (Belfast)	5-3	Richmond Rovers FC (Dublin)
Linfield FC (Belfast)	2-0	Bohemian FC (Dublin)

Quarter-finals

Derry Celtic FC (Londonderry)	1-4	Bohemian FC (Dublin)
Distillery FC (Belfast)	2-1, 2-0	Cliftonville FC (Belfast)
Freebooters FC (Dublin)	0-5	Linfield FC (Belfast)
Richmond Rovers FC (Dublin)	1-0	Shelbourne FC (Dublin)

1902-03

Irish League 1902-03	Belfast Celtic	Bohemian	Cliftonville	Derry Celtic	Distillery	Glentoran	Linfield	Ulster
Belfast Celtic FC	■	2-1	1-1	2-0	1-2	3-1	4-2	4-0
Bohemian FC	1-4	■	1-1	3-3	2-1	1-3	0-3	5-1
Cliftonville FC	2-1	2-3	■	2-0	1-3	1-0	0-2	1-0
Derry Celtic FC	3-3	2-1	2-2	■	3-1	4-1	1-1	6-0
Distillery FC	2-1	5-0	1-3	3-1	■	1-1	2-1	2-1
Glentoran FC	2-1	4-0	2-1	6-0	2-2	■	0-1	4-1
Linfield FC	6-1	2-2	4-0	3-0	2-4	1-1	■	5-1
Ulster FC	0-7	3-2	1-0	3-2	1-5	1-3	0-5	■

	Irish League	Pd	Wn	Dw	Ls	GF	GA	Pts	
1.	DISTILLERY FC (BELFAST)	14	9	2	3	34	20	20	
2.	Linfield FC (Belfast)	14	8	3	3	38	16	19	
3.	Glentoran FC (Belfast)	14	7	3	4	30	18	17	
4.	Belfast Celtic FC (Belfast)	14	7	2	5	35	23	16	
5.	Derry Celtic FC (Londonderry)	14	4	4	6	27	31	12	
6.	Cliftonville FC (Belfast)	14	5	3	6	17	21	11	-2
7.	Bohemian FC (Dublin)	14	3	3	8	22	36	9	
8.	Ulster FC (Belfast)	14	3	-	11	13	51	6	#
		112	46	20	46	216	216	110	

Note: Cliftonville FC (Belfast) had 2 points deducted for fielding an ineligible player.

Ulster FC (Belfast) did not compete in the league for the next season.

Elected: K.O.S.B. Regiment (Belfast) (K.O.S.B. = King's Own Scottish Borderers)

IRISH CUP FINAL   (Dalymount Park, Dublin – 14/03/1903)

DISTILLERY FC (BELFAST)	3-1	Bohemian FC (Dublin)
Kearns, Hunter, Hamilton		*Pratt*

Distillery: J. Andrews, W. McCracken, G. McMillan, J. Hunter, W. Morton, Jos. Burnison, J.T. Mercer, Aitken, A. Kearns, David McDougall, W.J. Hamilton.

Bohemian: Monson, Meadows, Crane, Caldwell, D.B. Fulton, Bastow, H.A. Sloan, H. Pratt, W.F. Hooper, Callinan, Greene.

Semi-finals

Bohemian FC (Dublin)	6-1	Derry Celtic FC (Londonderry)
Distillery FC (Belfast)	2-1	Linfield FC (Belfast)

Quarter-finals

Bohemian FC (Dublin)	4-1	Shelbourne FC (Dublin)
Glentoran FC (Belfast)	1-2	Linfield FC (Belfast)

Derry Celtic FC (Londonderry) and Distillery FC (Belfast) both received byes

1903-04

Irish League 1903-04	Belfast Celtic	Bohemian	Cliftonville	Derry Celtic	Distillery	Glentoran	K.O.S.B.	Linfield
Belfast Celtic FC		6-0	3-0	1-0	1-2	1-0	5-1	0-2
Bohemian FC	2-2		3-1	2-1	0-2	0-0	8-0	2-4
Cliftonville FC	2-1	1-2		1-0	3-3	1-1	5-1	1-8
Derry Celtic FC	0-0	4-1	0-2		1-1	2-3	2-0	2-3
Distillery FC	2-1	5-1	3-1	2-1		1-1	7-0	0-1
Glentoran FC	2-1	2-0	4-2	1-0	0-0		3-0	1-1
K.O.S.B. Regiment	3-2	2-2	1-2	2-3	0-6	1-2		0-7
Linfield FC	1-0	3-1	1-0	7-1	2-1	0-0	7-0	

	Irish League	Pd	Wn	Dw	Ls	GF	GA	Pts	
1.	LINFIELD FC (BELFAST)	14	12	2	-	47	9	26	
2.	Distillery FC (Belfast)	14	8	4	2	35	13	20	
3.	Glentoran FC (Belfast)	14	7	6	1	20	10	20	
4.	Belfast Celtic FC (Belfast)	14	5	2	7	24	17	12	
5.	Cliftonville FC (Belfast)	14	5	2	7	22	31	12	
6.	Bohemian FC (Dublin)	14	4	3	7	24	33	11	
7.	Derry Celtic FC (Londonderry)	14	3	2	9	17	26	8	
8.	K.O.S.B. Regiment (Belfast)	14	1	1	12	11	61	3	#
		112	45	22	45	200	200	112	

\# K.O.S.B. Regiment (Belfast) did not compete in the league the for the next season.

Elected: Shelbourne FC (Dublin)

IRISH CUP FINAL   (Grosvenor Park, Belfast – 17/03/1904)

LINFIELD FC (BELFAST)	5-0	Derry Celtic FC (Londonderry)

Hagan 3, Milne, Darling

Linfield: Scott, McCartney, Sheppard, Anderson, Milne, Maginnis, Darling, Hagan, Carnegie, Stewart, Whaites.
Derry: McGonagle, Sheeran, McCourt, N. Blayney, Gallaher, Taylor, McGinnis, E. Blayney, Ward, Lynch, McClure.

Semi-finals

Derry Celtic FC (Londonderry)	9-3	Derry Hibernians FC (Londonderry)
Linfield FC (Belfast)	1-0	Cliftonville FC (Belfast)

Quarter-finals

Bohemian FC (Dublin)	0-2	Derry Celtic FC (Londonderry)
Cliftonville FC (Belfast)	1-0, +:-	Belfast Celtic FC (Belfast)
Linfield FC (Belfast)	3-3, 2-0	Freebooters FC (Dublin)

Derry Hibernians FC (Londonderry) received a bye

1904-05

Irish League 1904-05	Belfast Celtic	Bohemian	Cliftonville	Derry Celtic	Distillery	Glentoran	Linfield	Shelbourne
Belfast Celtic FC	■	3-1	2-0	3-0	0-3	1-1	0-0	2-1
Bohemian FC	0-1	■	3-1	4-0	0-1	1-2	1-1	0-2
Cliftonville FC	0-1	5-0	■	2-1	2-1	1-2	3-0	0-2
Derry Celtic FC	2-4	3-3	0-0	■	0-3	0-2	0-0	3-1
Distillery FC	0-2	2-0	0-1	0-0	■	2-0	0-2	0-0
Glentoran FC	1-0	1-0	3-0	3-1	1-1	■	1-0	2-0
Linfield FC	0-1	3-2	2-0	4-0	1-2	2-2	■	2-0
Shelbourne FC	1-1	1-0	0-2	2-2	2-1	3-1	0-1	■

Play-off
GLENTORAN FC (BELFAST)   3-1   Belfast Celtic FC (Belfast)

	Irish League	Pd	Wn	Dw	Ls	GF	GA	Pts
1.	Glentoran FC (Belfast)	14	9	3	2	22	12	21
1.	Belfast Celtic FC (Belfast)	14	9	3	2	21	10	21
3.	Linfield FC (Belfast)	14	6	4	4	18	12	16
4.	Distillery FC (Belfast)	14	6	3	5	16	11	15
5.	Cliftonville FC (Belfast)	14	6	1	7	17	17	13
6.	Shelbourne FC (Dublin)	14	5	3	6	15	17	13
7.	Derry Celtic FC (Londonderry)	14	1	5	8	12	31	7
8.	Bohemian FC (Dublin)	14	2	2	10	15	26	6
		112	44	24	44	136	136	112

No clubs promoted or relegated

IRISH CUP FINAL   (Solitude, Belfast – 11/03/1905)
DISTILLERY FC (BELFAST)   3-0   Shelbourne FC (Dublin)
Magill 2, Soye

Distillery: Sloan, Watson, McMillan, Grieve, Johnston, Ferguson, Hunter, Andrews, Soye, Murray, Magill.
Shelbourne: Rowe, Heslin, Connor, Abbey, Doherty, Lawless, Owens, John, Byrne, Harris, Clery.

Semi-finals
Distillery FC (Belfast)	1-0	Derry Celtic FC (Londonderry)
Shelbourne FC (Dublin)	4-1	Glentoran FC (Belfast)

Quarter-finals
Derry Celtic FC (Londonderry)	3-1	Linfield FC (Belfast)
Distillery FC (Belfast)	1-0	Cameron Highlanders Regiment
Shelbourne FC (Dublin)	2-1	Bohemian FC (Dublin)

Glentoran FC (Belfast) received a bye

1905-06

Irish League 1905-06	Belfast Celtic	Bohemian	Cliftonville	Derry Celtic	Distillery	Glentoran	Linfield	Shelbourne
Belfast Celtic FC	■	2-1	1-1	3-1	2-2	3-0	1-3	2-3
Bohemian FC	1-2	■	2-0	1-1	1-2	3-2	1-0	2-0
Cliftonville FC	1-0	3-0	■	2-0	0-1	5-1	2-2	1-0
Derry Celtic FC	0-1	0-4	0-0	■	1-0	3-1	3-1	3-0
Distillery FC	1-0	3-1	0-0	5-1	■	1-0	2-2	1-0
Glentoran FC	1-2	0-0	1-1	1-0	1-2	■	1-2	3-2
Linfield FC	0-0	3-0	0-1	3-0	2-0	1-0	■	1-0
Shelbourne FC	3-1	2-0	0-2	0-0	2-0	1-1	3-1	■

Play-off

CLIFTONVILLE FC (BELFAST)   0-0, 3-3   DISTILLERY FC (BELFAST)

(After 2 drawn matches it was decided that the clubs should share the championship)

	Irish League	Pd	Wn	Dw	Ls	GF	GA	Pts
1.	Cliftonville FC (Belfast)	14	7	5	2	19	8	19
1.	Distillery FC (Belfast)	14	8	3	3	20	13	19
3.	Linfield FC (Belfast)	14	7	3	4	21	14	17
4.	Belfast Celtic FC (Belfast)	14	6	3	5	20	18	15
5.	Bohemian FC (Dublin)	14	5	2	7	17	20	12
6.	Shelbourne FC (Dublin)	14	5	2	7	16	18	12
7.	Derry Celtic FC (Londonderry)	14	4	3	7	13	22	11
8.	Glentoran FC (Belfast)	14	2	3	9	13	26	7
		112	44	24	44	139	139	112

No clubs promoted or relegated

IRISH CUP FINAL   (Dalymount Park, Dublin – 28/04/1906)

SHELBOURNE FC (DUBLIN)   2-0   Belfast Celtic FC (Belfast)

James Owens 2 (1 pen.)

Shelbourne: Rowe, Heslin, Kelly, Abbey, Doherty, Ledwidge, John Owens, Byrne, James Owens, Harris, Clery.
Belfast: Haddock, McClelland, Pinkerton, McColl, Connor, Nicholl, Gall, Mulholland, Runnigan, Maguire, Maxwell.

Semi-finals

Belfast Celtic FC (Belfast)	2-0	Bohemian FC (Dublin)
Shelbourne FC (Dublin)	3-0	Derry Celtic FC (Londonderry)

Quarter-finals

Belfast Celtic FC (Belfast)	3-1	Cameron Highlanders Regiment
Cliftonville FC (Belfast)	0-1	Derry Celtic FC (Londonderry)
Glentoran FC (Belfast)	0-2	Shelbourne FC (Dublin)

Bohemian FC (Dublin) received a bye

1906-07

Irish League 1906-07	Belfast Celtic	Bohemian	Cliftonville	Derry Celtic	Distillery	Glentoran	Linfield	Shelbourne
Belfast Celtic FC		0-2	0-1	1-0	3-1	4-2	0-1	1-2
Bohemian FC	2-3		1-0	1-1	1-1	1-1	2-4	1-3
Cliftonville FC	0-0	2-2		5-1	2-1	2-1	0-1	1-1
Derry Celtic FC	1-1	0-4	1-1		1-2	3-1	2-3	1-0
Distillery FC	6-3	0-0	3-1	2-0		3-2	2-1	2-2
Glentoran FC	3-0	1-2	1-1	2-0	1-1		0-2	2-2
Linfield FC	1-1	3-0	1-1	3-0	1-0	1-1		7-0
Shelbourne FC	3-1	3-0	2-1	2-0	4-3	3-0	0-1	

	Irish League	Pd	Wn	Dw	Ls	GF	GA	Pts
1.	LINFIELD FC (BELFAST)	14	10	3	1	30	9	23
2.	Shelbourne FC (Dublin)	14	8	3	3	27	21	19
3.	Distillery FC (Belfast)	14	6	4	4	27	22	16
4.	Cliftonville FC (Belfast)	14	4	6	4	18	16	14
5.	Bohemian FC (Dublin)	14	4	5	5	19	22	13
6.	Belfast Celtic FC (Belfast)	14	4	3	7	18	25	11
7.	Glentoran FC (Belfast)	14	2	5	7	18	25	9
8.	Derry Celtic FC (Londonderry)	14	2	3	9	11	28	7
		112	40	32	40	168	168	112

No clubs promoted or relegated

IRISH CUP FINAL   (Celtic Park, Belfast – 23/03/1907)

CLIFTONVILLE FC (BELFAST)   0-0   Shelbourne FC (Dublin)

Cliftonville: McKee, Seymour, McIlroy, Wright, Martin, McClure, Blair, Robertson, Beattie, Hull, Shanks.
Shelbourne: Rowe, Heslin, Kelly, Abbey, Doherty, Moran, Harris, Murphy, James Owens, John Owens, Clery.

IRISH CUP FINAL REPLAY   (Dalymount Park, Dublin – 20/04/1907)

CLIFTONVILLE FC (BELFAST)   1-0   Shelbourne FC (Dublin)

Beattie

Shelbourne: Rowe, Heslin, Moran, Abbey, Doherty, Ledwidge, Harris, Murphy, John Owens, James Owens, Clery.
Cliftonville: McKee, Seymour, McIlroy, Spence, Martin, McClure, Blair, Robertson, Campbell, Beattie, Shanks.

Semi-finals

Cliftonville FC (Belfast)	2-2, 3-2	Linfield FC (Belfast)
Shelbourne FC (Dublin)	1-0	Belfast Celtic FC (Belfast)

Quarter-finals

Belfast Celtic FC (Belfast)	1-0	Derry Celtic FC (Londonderry)
Cliftonville FC (Belfast)	6-1	Reginald FC (Dublin)

Linfield FC (Belfast) and Shelbourne FC (Dublin) both received byes

1907-08

Irish League 1907-08	Belfast Celtic	Bohemian	Cliftonville	Derry Celtic	Distillery	Glentoran	Linfield	Shelbourne
Belfast Celtic FC		7-0	0-0	1-2	5-2	2-1	1-2	0-3
Bohemian FC	0-1		0-3	3-0	3-1	1-3	2-4	1-2
Cliftonville FC	3-1	3-0		2-0	1-1	1-1	1-1	0-2
Derry Celtic FC	1-0	1-1	2-3		1-2	2-1	2-4	1-0
Distillery FC	0-1	1-0	1-2	2-1		3-1	0-1	4-1
Glentoran FC	0-2	3-1	2-0	4-3	1-1		2-2	3-2
Linfield FC	3-0	1-0	3-1	4-0	3-1	2-3		1-0
Shelbourne FC	3-0	1-1	2-2	3-0	0-2	1-2	2-0	

	Irish League	Pd	Wn	Dw	Ls	GF	GA	Pts	
1.	LINFIELD FC (BELFAST)	14	10	2	2	31	15	22	
2.	Cliftonville FC (Belfast)	14	6	5	3	22	16	17	PO
3.	Glentoran FC (Belfast)	14	7	3	4	27	23	17	PO
4.	Distillery FC (Belfast)	14	6	2	6	21	21	14	
5.	Shelbourne FC (Dublin)	14	6	2	6	22	17	14	
6.	Belfast Celtic FC (Belfast)	14	6	1	7	21	20	14	
7.	Derry Celtic FC (Londonderry)	14	4	1	9	16	30	9	
8.	Bohemian FC (Dublin)	14	2	2	10	13	31	6	
		112	47	18	47	173	173	112	

2nd/3rd Place Play-off

Cliftonville FC (Belfast)   3-2   Glentoran FC (Belfast)

No clubs promoted or relegated

IRISH CUP FINAL   (Dalymount Park, Dublin – 21/03/1908)

BOHEMIAN FC (DUBLIN)   1-1   Shelbourne FC (Dublin)
Sloane   *Lacey*

Bohemian: O'Hehir, Balfe, Thunder, Bastow, Healy, Curtis, R.M. Hooper, Hannon, W. Hooper, Sloan, Slemin.
Shelbourne: Reilly, Heslin, Kelly, Harris, Doherty, Moran, John Owens, Murphy, Merrigan, James Owens, Lacey.

IRISH CUP FINAL REPLAY   (Dalymount Park, Dublin – 28/03/1908)

BOHEMIAN FC (DUBLIN)   3-1   Shelbourne FC (Dublin)
R.M. Hooper 2, W. Hooper   *James Owens*

Shelbourne: Reilly, Heslin, Kelly, Abbey, Harris, Ledwidge, John Owens, Murphy, Merrigan, James Owens, Lacey.
Bohemian: O'Hehir, Balfe, Thunder, Bastow, Healy, McElhinny, W. Hooper, Hannon, R. Hooper, Sloan, Slemin.

Semi-finals

| Bohemian FC (Dublin) | 2-2, 2-0 | Belfast Celtic FC (Belfast) |
| Shelbourne FC (Dublin) | 0-0, 2-0 | Distillery FC (Belfast) |

Quarter-finals

Belfast Celtic FC (Belfast)	w/o	Reginald FC (Dublin)
Bohemian FC (Dublin)	2-2, 2-1	Linfield FC (Belfast)
Distillery FC (Belfast)	2-0	Derry Celtic FC (Londonderry)
Shelbourne FC (Dublin)	1-1, 2-0	Cliftonville FC (Belfast)

1908-09

Irish League 1908-09	Belfast Celtic	Bohemian	Cliftonville	Derry Celtic	Distillery	Glentoran	Linfield	Shelbourne
Belfast Celtic FC	■	---	2-1	2-1	2-3	1-1	2-3	3-2
Bohemian FC	0-1	■	2-2	2-1	1-0	6-1	0-4	3-1
Cliftonville FC	0-2	---	■	5-0	0-1	1-1	2-1	1-3
Derry Celtic FC	2-1	2-1	1-0	■	3-2	0-1	0-2	0-1
Distillery FC	2-2	3-0	1-3	3-1	■	0-1	0-1	1-2
Glentoran FC	6-0	4-2	4-1	3-1	2-1	■	2-2	2-1
Linfield FC	3-2	2-1	0-1	2-0	0-2	4-1	■	1-0
Shelbourne FC	3-0	2-4	1-0	1-0	1-3	2-0	0-2	■

	Irish League	Pd	Wn	Dw	Ls	GF	GA	Pts
1.	LINFIELD FC (BELFAST)	14	10	1	3	27	13	21
2.	Glentoran FC (Belfast)	14	8	3	3	29	22	19
3.	Shelbourne FC (Dublin)	14	7	-	7	20	20	14
4.	Distillery FC (Belfast)	14	6	1	7	22	19	13
5.	Bohemian FC (Dublin)	12	6	1	5	27	24	13
6.	Cliftonville FC (Belfast)	13	4	2	7	17	19	10
7.	Belfast Celtic FC (Belfast)	13	4	2	7	21	32	10
8.	Derry Celtic FC (Londonderry)	14	4	-	10	12	26	8
		108	49	10	49	175	175	108

Note: Bohemian FC (Dublin) away matches versus Belfast Celtic FC (Belfast) and Cliftonville FC (Belfast) were not played.

IRISH CUP FINAL   (Windsor Park, Belfast – 03/04/1909)

CLIFTONVILLE FC (BELFAST)   0-0   Bohemian FC (Dublin)

Bohemian: O'Hehir, Curtis, Thunder, Doyle, Healy, Sloan, D. Hooper, Hannon, McDonnell, W. Hooper, Slemin.
Cliftonville: McKee, Seymour, Neilly, Wright, Martin, Palmer, McComb, Robertson, Houghton, McAuley, Thompson.

IRISH CUP FINAL REPLAY   (Dalymount Park, Dublin – 10/04/1909)

CLIFTONVILLE FC (BELFAST)   2-1   Bohemian FC (Dublin)
McAuley, McComb   *W. Hooper*

Bohemian: O'Hehir, Curtis, Thunder, Doyle, Healy, Sloan, W. Hooper, McDonnell, R.M. Hooper, Slemin.
Cliftonville: McKee, Neely, Seymour, Martin, Wright, Palmer, McComb, Robertson, Houghton, McAuley, Thompson.

Semi-finals

Bohemian FC (Dublin)	2-1	Glentoran FC (Belfast)
Cliftonville FC (Belfast)	2-0, 2-3, 3-2	Distillery FC (Belfast)

Quarter-finals

Bohemian FC (Dublin)	10-2	St. James's Gate AFC (Dublin)
Cliftonville FC (Belfast)	+:-	Dublin University AFC (Dublin)
Glentoran FC (Belfast)	1-1, 2-0	Belfast Celtic FC (Belfast)
Linfield FC (Belfast)	0-4	Distillery FC (Belfast)

1909-10

Irish League 1909-10	Belfast Celtic	Bohemian	Cliftonville	Derry Celtic	Distillery	Glentoran	Linfield	Shelbourne
Belfast Celtic FC	■	1-0	2-0	2-1	0-1	2-0	1-2	5-0
Bohemian FC	1-3	■	4-3	1-2	1-0	2-1	1-1	2-2
Cliftonville FC	2-1	4-1	■	1-0	1-0	1-0	2-1	4-2
Derry Celtic FC	2-0	3-1	1-1	■	2-2	5-4	2-2	0-0
Distillery FC	0-1	0-1	1-1	2-0	■	0-1	1-0	3-0
Glentoran FC	1-4	6-1	1-4	1-0	1-2	■	4-0	2-0
Linfield FC	3-2	3-2	0-0	0-0	3-1	2-1	■	1-1
Shelbourne FC	0-1	2-2	1-1	4-1	1-1	0-0	2-1	■

	Irish League	**Pd**	**Wn**	**Dw**	**Ls**	**GF**	**GA**	**Pts**
1.	CLIFTONVILLE FC (BELFAST)	14	8	4	2	25	15	20
2.	Belfast Celtic FC (Belfast)	14	9	-	5	25	13	18
3.	Linfield FC (Belfast)	14	5	5	4	19	20	15
4.	Distillery FC (Belfast)	14	5	3	6	14	13	13
5.	Derry Celtic FC (Londonderry)	14	4	5	5	19	21	13
6.	Bohemian FC (Dublin)	14	4	3	7	20	31	11
7.	Glentoran FC (Belfast)	14	5	1	8	23	23	11
8.	Shelbourne FC (Dublin)	14	2	7	5	15	24	11
		112	42	28	42	160	160	112

No clubs promoted or relegated

IRISH CUP FINAL   (The Oval, Belfast – 26/03/1910)

DISTILLERY FC (BELFAST)	1-0	Cliftonville FC (Belfast)

Johnston

Distillery: Sloan, Burnison, Creighton, Flannagan, Donnelly, Scott, Wright, Hamilton, Johnston, Uprichard, Heggarty.

Cliftonville: McKee, Sterling, Seymour, Wright, Martin, Palmer, McComb, Robertson, Neville, McAuley, Thompson.

Semi-finals

Cliftonville FC (Belfast)	3-0	Bohemian FC (Dublin)
Distillery FC (Belfast)	4-0	Glentoran FC (Belfast)

Quarter-finals

Belfast Celtic FC (Belfast)	0-2	Bohemian FC (Dublin)
Cliftonville FC (Belfast)	2-0, +:-	Shelbourne FC (Dublin)

Distillery FC (Belfast) and Glentoran FC (Belfast) both received byes

1910-11

Irish League 1910-11	Belfast Celtic	Bohemian	Cliftonville	Derry Celtic	Distillery	Glentoran	Linfield	Shelbourne
Belfast Celtic FC	■	3-3	3-0	2-1	0-0	1-3	0-1	3-2
Bohemian FC	1-3	■	1-1	4-0	0-2	0-1	0-2	2-2
Cliftonville FC	1-1	1-0	■	1-0	2-0	1-4	0-1	4-1
Derry Celtic FC	2-1	2-1	3-3	■	1-0	3-1	2-2	5-2
Distillery FC	1-1	5-2	1-1	0-0	■	1-2	0-1	0-1
Glentoran FC	1-2	2-0	4-0	9-0	2-1	■	3-0	4-0
Linfield FC	1-1	1-0	3-0	2-2	4-0	2-2	■	6-1
Shelbourne FC	2-0	0-0	0-1	1-0	2-2	1-1	0-3	■

Play-off

LINFIELD FC (BELFAST)	3-2	Glentoran FC (Belfast)

	Irish League	Pd	Wn	Dw	Ls	GF	GA	Pts	
1.	Linfield FC (Belfast)	14	9	4	1	29	11	22	
1.	Glentoran FC (Belfast)	14	10	2	2	39	12	22	
3.	Belfast Celtic FC (Belfast)	14	5	5	4	21	19	15	
4.	Cliftonville FC (Belfast)	14	5	4	5	16	22	14	
5.	Derry Celtic FC (Londonderry)	14	5	4	5	21	29	14	
6.	Shelbourne FC (Dublin)	14	3	4	7	15	31	10	
7.	Distillery FC (Belfast)	14	2	5	7	13	19	9	
8.	Bohemian FC (Dublin)	14	1	4	9	14	25	6	#
		112	40	32	40	168	168	112	

\# Bohemian FC (Dublin) did not compete in the league for next season.

Elected: Glenavon FC (Lurgan)

IRISH CUP FINAL   (Dalymount Park, Dublin – 25/03/1911)

SHELBOURNE FC (DUBLIN)	0-0	Bohemian FC (Dublin)

Shelbourne: Rowe, Dunne, Bennett, Watson, Doherty, Moran, Clarkin, Murphy, Merrigan, Halpin, Devlin.

Bohemian: O'Hehir, Bill McConnell, Thunder, Hannon, Brennan, Magwood, Johnston, W.Hooper, McDonnell, West, Willett.

IRISH CUP FINAL REPLAY (Dalymount Park, Dublin – 15/04/1911)

SHELBOURNE FC (DUBLIN)　　　　　　　2-1　　　　　　　　Bohemian FC (Dublin)

Moran pen., Devlin　　　　　　　　　　　　　　　　　　　　　　　　　*R.H. Hooper*

Bohemian: O'Hehir, McConnell, Thunder, Hannon, Brennan, Hagwood, Ryder, R.H. Hooper, McDonnell, West, Willets.

Shelbourne: Rowe, Dunne, Bennett, Watson, Doherty, Moran, Clarkin, Murphy, Merrigan, Halpin, Devlin.

Semi-finals

Bohemian FC (Dublin)	2-2, 2-2, 2-1	Cliftonville FC (Belfast)
Shelbourne FC (Dublin)	3-0	Derry Celtic FC (Londonderry)

Quarter-finals

Derry Celtic FC (Londonderry)	2-3, +:-	Linfield FC (Belfast)
Shelbourne FC (Dublin)	+:-	St. James's Gate AFC (Dublin)

Bohemian FC (Dublin) and Cliftonville FC (Belfast) both received byes

1911-12

Irish League 1911-12	Belfast Celtic	Cliftonville	Derry Celtic	Distillery	Glenavon	Glentoran	Linfield	Shelbourne
Belfast Celtic FC		0-0	4-1	1-1	1-0	1-3	2-1	1-1
Cliftonville FC	0-2		0-1	4-5	2-1	0-1	1-2	1-0
Derry Celtic FC	0-2	4-2		1-3	4-3	1-1	1-0	1-0
Distillery FC	1-1	5-0	3-1		3-0	2-3	0-0	4-1
Glenavon FC	0-2	0-1	2-0	0-1		1-5	1-3	3-1
Glentoran FC	1-1	10-0	2-0	2-1	3-2		1-0	7-0
Linfield FC	2-2	3-2	2-2	0-1	2-2	2-1		5-1
Shelbourne FC	0-1	2-1	2-0	0-2	2-2	2-5	0-0	

	Irish League	Pd	Wn	Dw	Ls	GF	GA	Pts
1.	GLENTORAN FC (BELFAST)	14	11	2	1	45	13	24
2.	Distillery FC (Belfast)	14	9	3	2	32	14	21
3.	Belfast Celtic FC (Belfast)	14	7	6	1	21	11	20
4.	Linfield FC (Belfast)	14	6	4	4	25	16	16
5.	Derry Celtic FC (Londonderry)	14	5	1	8	16	29	11
6.	Shelbourne FC (Dublin)	14	2	3	9	12	33	7
7.	Cliftonville FC (Belfast)	14	3	1	10	14	36	7
8.	Glenavon FC (Lurgan)	14	2	2	10	17	30	6
		112	45	22	45	182	182	112

Elected: Bohemian FC (Dublin), Tritonville FC (Dublin)

The league was extended to 10 clubs for next season

After a dispute between the Irish FA and the County Antrim FA, a new but unofficial Association was formed on 22/12/1912 with the following clubs as members: Belfast Celtic FC (Belfast), Cliftonville FC (Belfast), Derry Celtic FC (Londonderry), Distillery FC (Belfast), Glenavon FC (Lurgan), Glentoran FC (Belfast) and Shelbourne FC.

However, after a series of meetings and proposals, agreement was reached and the "rebel" clubs were re-admitted to the Irish FA and competed in the league/cup for the next season.

IRISH CUP
LINFIELD FC (BELFAST)

The competition was completed to the quarter-final stage on 17th February 1912. However, on 21st February 1912, Cliftonville, Glentoran and Shelbourne resigned from the Irish Football Association, leaving Linfield as the only remaining competitor. These three clubs were among the 7 who resigned from the IFA after a dispute between the Irish FA and the County Antrim FA over ground levies for international matches. These 7 clubs formed an "unofficial" association on 22/12/1912. Another team of mainly Linfield Swifts FC players (Linfield's reserve team) also joined the "new" IFA as Belfast Blues FC. The dispute was however settled in time for the start of the 1912-13 season.

On the 7th May 1912 Linfield were declared holders of the Irish Football Association Challenge Cup for season 1911/12. Winners medals were presented to the Linfield Team which had defeated Bohemians 3-2 in Dublin on 3rd February 1912.

1912-13

Irish League 1912-13	Belfast Celtic	Bohemian	Cliftonville	Derry Celtic	Distillery	Glenavon	Glentoran	Linfield	Shelbourne	Tritonville
Belfast Celtic FC		1-0	3-1	3-0	1-1	0-0	2-3	0-0	2-0	5-3
Bohemian FC	4-0		1-1	3-0	1-4	1-0	4-1	1-2	3-0	4-2
Cliftonville FC	1-2	3-0		1-0	1-0	3-2	0-1	1-1	0-0	2-1
Derry Celtic FC	3-2	0-1	1-2		0-1	0-0	0-0	4-2	3-1	2-2
Distillery FC	0-2	5-1	1-0	3-0		3-0	1-0	1-2	1-1	4-1
Glenavon FC	1-0	3-0	2-0	3-0	2-1		2-3	0-1	3-1	2-0
Glentoran FC	2-0	2-1	0-2	5-0	0-1	2-0		0-0	2-0	8-0
Linfield FC	4-0	1-1	3-0	2-1	0-1	1-4	2-4		1-0	4-3
Shelbourne FC	1-1	2-0	3-0	4-2	2-1	1-0	0-2	1-1		1-0
Tritonville FC	2-0	1-5	2-5	4-1	3-5	0-1	1-2	1-2	1-2	

	Irish League	Pd	Wn	Dw	Ls	GF	GA	Pts	
1.	GLENTORAN FC (BELFAST)	18	12	2	4	37	16	26	
2.	Distillery FC (Belfast)	18	11	2	5	34	17	24	
3.	Linfield FC (Belfast)	18	9	5	4	29	23	23	
4.	Glenavon FC (Lurgan)	18	9	2	7	25	17	20	
5.	Cliftonville FC (Belfast)	18	8	3	7	23	23	19	
6.	Bohemian FC (Dublin)	18	8	2	8	31	28	18	
7.	Belfast Celtic FC (Belfast)	18	7	4	7	24	26	18	
8.	Shelbourne FC (Dublin)	18	7	4	7	20	23	18	
9.	Derry Celtic FC (Londonderry)	18	3	3	12	17	39	9	#
10.	Tritonville FC (Dublin)	18	2	1	15	27	55	5	#
		180	76	28	76	267	267	180	

\# Derry Celtic FC (Londonderry) and Tritonville FC (Dublin) did not compete in the league which was reduced to 8 clubs for next season.

IRISH CUP FINAL (Celtic Park, Belfast – 29/03/1913)
LINFIELD FC (BELFAST)　　　　　　　2-0　　　　　　　　　　Glentoran FC (Belfast)
McNeill, McEwan
Linfield: Kelly, Darling, Sterling, Rollo, Clifford, Bartlett, Brown, Nixon, Smith, McNeill, McEwan.
Glentoran: Murphy, McAlpine, Waters, Ferrett, Ritchie, Reid, Lyner, J. Lunday, Napier, McKnight, Monroe.

Semi-finals

Glentoran FC (Belfast)	5-1	Belfast Celtic FC (Belfast)
Linfield FC (Belfast)	4-1	Tritonville FC (Dublin)

Quarter-finals

Linfield FC (Belfast)	4-0	Derry Guilds FC (Londonderry)
Shelbourne FC (Dublin)	0-0, 0-1	Glentoran FC (Belfast)
Tritonville FC (Dublin)	5-1	St. James's Gate AFC (Dublin)

Belfast Celtic FC (Belfast) received a bye

1913-14

Irish League 1913-14	Belfast Celtic	Bohemian	Cliftonville	Distillery	Glenavon	Glentoran	Linfield	Shelbourne
Belfast Celtic FC	■	4-1	1-0	2-1	2-0	1-0	1-2	1-0
Bohemian FC	4-5	■	2-3	0-0	2-1	2-5	3-1	0-1
Cliftonville FC	0-1	4-2	■	0-1	6-2	0-3	0-3	0-3
Distillery FC	1-0	3-1	3-1	■	1-0	0-0	1-3	1-0
Glenavon FC	0-0	1-0	1-0	2-1	■	2-3	1-1	1-0
Glentoran FC	4-0	5-1	3-1	0-0	1-0	■	2-2	3-2
Linfield FC	2-1	3-1	2-0	2-0	5-1	4-2	■	1-0
Shelbourne FC	3-0	0-0	2-0	1-1	1-0	3-1	0-1	■

	Irish League	**Pd**	**Wn**	**Dw**	**Ls**	**GF**	**GA**	**Pts**
1.	LINFIELD FC (BELFAST)	14	11	2	1	32	13	24
2.	Glentoran FC (Belfast)	14	8	3	3	32	18	19
3.	Belfast Celtic FC (Belfast)	14	8	1	5	19	18	17
4.	Distillery FC (Belfast)	14	6	4	4	14	12	16
5.	Shelbourne FC (Dublin)	14	6	2	6	16	10	14
6.	Glenavon FC (Lurgan)	14	4	2	8	12	23	10
7.	Bohemian FC (Dublin)	14	2	2	10	19	36	6
8.	Cliftonville FC (Belfast)	14	3	-	11	15	29	6
		112	48	16	48	159	159	112

No clubs promoted or relegated

IRISH CUP FINAL (Grosvenor Park, Belfast – 28/03/1914)

GLENTORAN FC (BELFAST)	3-1	Linfield FC (Belfast)
W. Lindsay 2, Lyner		*McEwan*

Glentoran: Murphy, McCann, Annesley, Ferrett, Scraggs, Emerson, Lyner, J. Lindsay, Napier, Boyd, W. Lindsay.
Linfield: Kelly, Rollo, Foye, McConnell, Clifford, Wallace, Lyner, Nixon, Young, McNeill, McEwan.

Semi-finals

Glentoran FC (Belfast)	1-1, 1-1, 0-0, 3-1	Shelbourne FC (Dublin)
Linfield FC (Belfast)	4-2	Glenavon FC (Lurgan)

Quarter-finals

Shelbourne FC (Dublin)	1-1, +:–	Belfast Celtic FC (Belfast)

Glenavon FC (Lurgan), Glentoran FC (Belfast) and Linfield FC (Belfast) all received byes

1914-15

Irish League 1914-15	Belfast Celtic	Bohemian	Cliftonville	Distillery	Glenavon	Glentoran	Linfield	Shelbourne
Belfast Celtic FC	■	1-1	5-0	1-0	3-0	1-0	2-1	1-0
Bohemian FC	0-3	■	1-2	2-3	2-4	0-3	2-5	0-3
Cliftonville FC	1-3	2-0	■	0-1	3-1	0-3	1-2	1-3
Distillery FC	0-1	3-0	4-0	■	4-2	1-2	0-0	0-1
Glenavon FC	2-2	6-0	1-1	0-3	■	0-0	5-1	0-0
Glentoran FC	2-0	3-0	2-0	4-3	5-0	■	1-1	1-0
Linfield FC	0-0	5-2	3-0	3-0	1-1	3-0	■	2-2
Shelbourne FC	0-1	2-0	0-2	0-1	3-2	1-1	2-0	■

	Irish League	Pd	Wn	Dw	Ls	GF	GA	Pts
1.	BELFAST CELTIC FC (BELFAST)	14	10	3	1	24	7	23
2.	Glentoran FC (Belfast)	14	9	3	2	27	10	21
3.	Linfield FC (Belfast)	14	6	5	3	27	18	17
4.	Distillery FC (Belfast)	14	7	1	6	23	16	15
5.	Shelbourne FC (Dublin)	14	6	3	5	17	12	15
6.	Glenavon FC (Lurgan)	14	3	5	6	24	28	11
7.	Cliftonville FC (Belfast)	14	4	1	9	13	29	9
8.	Bohemian FC (Dublin)	14	-	1	13	10	45	1
		112	45	22	45	165	165	112

The league was suspended due to World War 1 but the Irish Cup and some "unofficial" league competitions continued to be contested until the resumption of the "official" Irish League for the 1919-20 season.

IRISH CUP FINAL (Solitude, Belfast – 27/03/1915)

LINFIELD FC (BELFAST)	1-0	Belfast Celtic FC (Belfast)
Bovill		

Linfield: McKee, Rollo, Foye, Wallace, Clifford, Bartlett, Young, Nixon, Hamilton, Bovill, McEwan.
Belfast: MeHaffey, Nelson, Barrett, Leatham, Hamill, Norwood, Kerr, McKnight, Williams, Cowell, Hegan.

Semi-finals

Belfast Celtic FC (Belfast)	0-0, 1-0	Shelbourne FC (Dublin)
Linfield FC (Belfast)	2-0	Distillery FC (Belfast)

Quarter-finals

Bohemian FC (Dublin)	0-4	Belfast Celtic FC (Belfast)
Distillery FC (Belfast)	4-1	Glenavon FC (Lurgan)
Glentoran FC (Belfast)	1-2	Shelbourne FC (Dublin)
Linfield FC (Belfast)	3-2	Cliftonville FC (Belfast)

1915-16

Belfast & District League 1915-16	Belfast United	Cliftonville	Distillery	Glenavon	Glentoran	Linfield
Belfast United FC		0-0	0-2	3-1	2-2	1-0
Cliftonville FC	2-1		0-2	0-0	1-1	0-2
Distillery FC	1-1	1-1		7-0	1-0	0-1
Glenavon FC	0-4	2-3	0-1		1-2	1-6
Glentoran FC	2-1	4-0	4-2	5-2		0-0
Linfield FC	3-1	1-0	2-1	2-0	0-0	

	Belfast & District League	Pd	Wn	Dw	Ls	GF	GA	Pts
1.	LINFIELD FC (BELFAST)	10	7	2	1	17	4	16
2.	Glentoran FC (Belfast)	10	5	4	1	20	10	14
3.	Distillery FC (Belfast)	10	5	2	3	18	9	12
4.	Belfast United FC (Belfast)	10	3	3	4	14	13	9
5.	Cliftonville FC (Belfast)	10	2	4	4	7	14	8
6.	Glenavon FC (Lurgan)	10	-	1	9	7	33	1
		60	22	16	22	83	83	60

No clubs promoted or relegated

IRISH CUP FINAL   (Celtic Park, Belfast – 25/03/1916)

LINFIELD FC (BELFAST)	1-1	Glentoran FC (Belfast)
Nixon		*Ferrett pen.*

Linfield: McKee, Rollo, Foye, McCandless, Clifford, Bartlett, Houston, Nixon, Bovill, Campbell, McEwan.
Glentoran: Steele, Stafford, Grainger, Ferrett, Scraggs, Emerson, Lyner, Seymour, Boyd, West, Bookman.

IRISH CUP FINAL REPLAY   (Grosvenor Park, Belfast – 01/04/1916)

LINFIELD FC (BELFAST)	1-0	Glentoran FC (Belfast)
Nixon		

Glentoran: Steele, Stafford, Frainger, Ferrett, Scraggs, Emerson, Lyner, Seymour, Boyd, West, Bookman.
Linfield: McKee, Rollo, Foye, McCandless, Clifford, Bartlett, Houston, Nixon, Bovill, Campbell, McEwan.

Semi-finals

Belfast Celtic FC (Belfast)	0-1	Linfield FC (Belfast)
Glentoran FC (Belfast)	4-2	Bohemian FC (Dublin)

Quarter-finals

Bohemian FC (Dublin)	0-0, 3-0, 1-0	Shelbourne FC (Dublin)
	(The 2nd match was abandoned)	
Distillery FC (Belfast)	0-3	Glentoran FC (Belfast)

Belfast Celtic FC (Belfast) and Linfield FC (Belfast) both received byes

1916-17

Belfast & District League 1916-17	Belfast United	Cliftonville	Distillery	Glenavon	Glentoran	Linfield
Belfast United FC	■	0-1	1-1	1-1	1-3	0-3
Cliftonville FC	3-0	■	0-1	3-2	0-2	1-1
Distillery FC	1-1	1-0	■	5-3	3-3	1-1
Glenavon FC	1-0	0-0	1-5	■	2-3	0-5
Glentoran FC	2-1	1-1	4-3	4-3	■	4-0
Linfield FC	3-2	2-0	0-2	2-0	2-2	■

	Belfast & District League	Pd	Wn	Dw	Ls	GF	GA	Pts
1.	GLENTORAN FC (BELFAST)	10	7	3	-	28	16	17
2.	Distillery FC (Belfast)	10	5	4	1	23	14	14
3.	Linfield FC (Belfast)	10	5	3	2	19	12	13
4.	Cliftonville FC (Belfast)	10	3	3	4	9	10	9
5.	Glenavon FC (Lurgan)	10	1	2	7	13	28	4
6.	Belfast United FC (Belfast)	10	-	3	7	7	19	3
		60	21	18	21	99	99	60

No clubs promoted or relegated

IRISH CUP FINAL   (Windsor Park, Belfast – 31/03/1917)

GLENTORAN FC (BELFAST)	2-0	Belfast Celtic FC (London)

Seymour 2

Glentoran: Steele, G.Moore, Grainger, Bennett, Scraggs, Ferrett, Lyner, Seymour, Boyd, Emerson, W.Moore.
Belfast: Scott, Kennedy, McIlroy, Norwood, Hamill, Stewart, McKinney, Kelly, Heaney, Johnston, Frazer.

Semi-finals

Belfast Celtic FC (Belfast)	4-0	Bohemian FC (Dublin)
Glentoran FC (Belfast)	1-1, 3-1	Distillery FC (Belfast)

Quarter-finals

Belfast Celtic FC (Belfast)	1-1, 2-0	Linfield FC (Belfast)
Bohemian FC (Dublin)	3-1	Strandville FC (Dublin)

Distillery FC (Belfast) and Glentoran FC (Belfast) both received byes

1917-18

Belfast & District League 1917-18	Belfast United	Cliftonville	Distillery	Glenavon	Glentoran	Linfield
Belfast United FC	■	1-1	1-0	4-1	1-3	0-1
Cliftonville FC	1-1	■	0-0	3-0	0-4	1-3
Distillery FC	3-2	3-2	■	5-0	0-2	2-2
Glenavon FC	1-0	1-0	0-1	■	1-4	1-5
Glentoran FC	2-1	0-0	2-0	1-0	■	0-0
Linfield FC	4-0	3-1	3-0	7-0	2-0	■

	Belfast & District League	**Pd**	**Wn**	**Dw**	**Ls**	**GF**	**GA**	**Pts**	
1.	LINFIELD FC (BELFAST)	10	8	2	-	30	5	18	
2.	Glentoran FC (Belfast)	10	7	2	1	18	5	16	
3.	Distillery FC (Belfast)	10	4	2	4	14	14	10	
4.	Cliftonville FC (Belfast)	10	1	4	5	9	16	6	
5.	Belfast United FC (Belfast)	10	2	2	6	11	17	6	
6.	Glenavon FC (Lurgan)	10	2	-	8	5	30	4	#
		60	24	12	24	87	87	60	

\# Glenavon FC (Lurgan) did not compete in this league for the next season.

Elected: Belfast Celtic FC (Belfast)

IRISH CUP FINAL   (The Oval, Belfast – 30/03/1918)

BELFAST CELTIC FC (BELFAST)   0-0   Linfield FC (Belfast)

Belfast: Scott, McStay, Barrett, Mulligan, Hamill, Stewart, McKinney, McIlroy, Ferris, Johnstone, Norwood.
Linfield: McKee, Rollo, Foye, Dunlop, Lacey, McCandless, Cochrane, Nixon, West, Rea, McEwan.

IRISH CUP FINAL REPLAY   (Solitude, Belfast – 13/04/1918)

BELFAST CELTIC FC (BELFAST)   0-0   Linfield FC (Belfast)

Belfast: Scott, McStay, Barrett, Mulligan, Hamill, Stewart, McKinney, McIlroy, Ferris, Johnstone, Frazer.
Linfield: McKee, Rollo, Foye, Dunlop, Lacey, McCandless, Campbell, Nixon, Cochrane, West, McEwan.

IRISH CUP FINAL 2ND REPLAY   (Grosvenor Park, Belfast – 24/04/1918)

BELFAST CELTIC FC (BELFAST)   2-0   Linfield FC (Belfast)

Foye o.g., Stewart
Belfast: Scott, McStay, Barrett, Mulligan, Hamill, Stewart, McKinney, McIlroy, Ferris, Johnston, Frazer.
Linfield: McKee, Rollo, Foye, Dunlop, Fulton, McCandless, Rea, Stitt, McLaughlin, Lacey, McEwan.

Semi-finals

Belfast Celtic FC (Belfast)	2-1	Belfast United FC (Belfast)
Linfield FC (Belfast)	2-1	Distillery FC (Belfast)

Quarter-finals

Belfast Celtic FC (Belfast)	0-0, 4-0	Glentoran FC (Belfast) 2nd XI
Belfast United FC (Belfast)	3-0	Shelbourne FC (Dublin)

Distillery FC (Belfast) and Linfield FC (Belfast) both received byes

1918-19

Belfast & District League 1918-19	Belfast Celtic	Belfast United	Cliftonville	Distillery	Glentoran	Linfield
Belfast Celtic FC		2-1	2-0	1-0	2-1	0-1
Belfast United FC	2-2		2-2	2-4	2-1	1-2
Cliftonville FC	0-3	0-1		1-1	1-0	2-3
Distillery FC	0-1	2-0	1-1		0-0	0-2
Glentoran FC	0-2	1-0	2-0	3-2		1-0
Linfield FC	2-0	3-1	1-0	1-1	0-2	

Play-off
BELFAST CELTIC FC (BELFAST)   1-0   Linfield FC (Belfast)

	Belfast & District League	**Pd**	**Wn**	**Dw**	**Ls**	**GF**	**GA**	**Pts**	
1.	Belfast Celtic FC (Belfast)	10	7	1	2	15	7	15	
1.	Linfield FC (Belfast)	10	7	1	2	15	8	15	
3.	Glentoran FC (Belfast)	10	5	1	4	11	9	11	
4.	Distillery FC (Belfast)	10	2	4	4	11	12	8	
5.	Belfast United FC (Belfast)	10	2	2	6	12	19	6	#
6.	Cliftonville FC (Belfast)	10	1	3	6	7	16	5	
		60	24	12	24	71	71	60	

Belfast United FC (Belfast) were not included in the "official" Irish League which started next season, 1919-20. Bohemian FC (Dublin), Glenavon FC (Lurgan) and Shelbourne FC (Dublin) were elected in addition to the other 5 clubs in the above Belfast & District League.

IRISH CUP FINAL   (Celtic Park, Belfast – 29/03/1919)
LINFIELD FC (BELFAST)   1-1   Glentoran FC (Belfast)
Featherstone   *Lyner*

Linfield: McKee, Rollo, B. McCandless, Seymour, Lacey, Pollins, J.McCandless, Lindsay, Featherstone, McDonald, McEwan.

Glentoran: Liddell, Spencer, Grainger, Bennett, Scraggs, Emerson, Lyner, Ferrett, Chambers, Mathieson, Moore.

IRISH CUP FINAL REPLAY   (Grosvenor Park, Belfast – 05/04/1919)
LINFIELD FC (BELFAST)   0-0   Glentoran FC (Belfast)

Linfield: McKee, Rollo, B.McCandless, Houston, Lacey, Pollins, Campbell, Lindsay, Featherstone, McDonald, McEwan.

Glentoran: Liddell; Spencer, Christie Grainger, Bennett, Scraggs, Emerson, Lyner, Chambers, Boyd, Mathieson, Moore.

IRISH CUP FINAL 2ND REPLAY   (Solitude, Belfast – 07/04/1919)

LINFIELD FC (BELFAST)	2-1	Glentoran FC (Belfast)
McEwan 2		*Scraggs*

Linfield: McKee, Rollo, McCandless, Houston, Lacey, Pollins, Campbell, Lindsay, Featherstone, McDonald, McEwan.

Glentoran: Liddell, Spencer, Grainger, Bennett, Scraggs, Emerson, Lyner, Chambers, Boyd, Mathieson, Moore.

Semi-finals

Glentoran FC (Belfast)	2-0	Belfast Celtic FC (Belfast)
Linfield FC (Belfast)	2-0	Shelbourne FC (Dublin)

Quarter-finals

Linfield FC (Belfast)	4-0, 1-0	Distillery FC (Belfast)

Belfast Celtic FC (Belfast), Glentoran FC (Belfast) and Shelbourne FC (Dublin) all received byes

1919-20

Irish League 1919-20	Belfast Celtic	Bohemian	Cliftonville	Distillery	Glenavon	Glentoran	Linfield	Shelbourne
Belfast Celtic FC		5-0	4-0	0-0	3-0	1-0	1-0	1-0
Bohemian FC	0-4		1-0	0-2	0-4	2-2	0-1	1-3
Cliftonville FC	1-2	2-0		0-1	0-4	0-0	0-0	2-2
Distillery FC	0-0	4-1	0-0		0-0	2-2	1-0	7-3
Glenavon FC	1-2	5-1	2-3	1-7		1-3	0-0	0-0
Glentoran FC	2-0	6-0	3-1	1-0	4-0		2-0	4-0
Linfield FC	1-3	0-1	1-1	1-2	2-0	1-0		1-0
Shelbourne FC	1-1	0-0	2-1	0-0	3-3	2-0	0-0	

	Irish League	Pd	Wn	Dw	Ls	GF	GA	Pts	
1.	BELFAST CELTIC FC (BELFAST)	14	10	3	1	27	6	23	#
2.	Distillery FC (Belfast)	14	7	6	1	26	9	20	
3.	Glentoran FC (Belfast)	14	8	3	3	29	10	19	
4.	Shelbourne FC (Dublin)	14	3	7	4	16	21	13	#
5.	Linfield FC (Belfast)	14	4	4	6	8	11	12	
6.	Glenavon FC (Lurgan)	14	3	4	7	21	28	10	
7.	Cliftonville FC (Belfast)	14	2	5	7	11	22	9	
8.	Bohemian FC (Dublin)	14	2	2	10	7	38	6	#
		112	39	34	39	145	145	112	

\# Belfast Celtic FC (Belfast) resigned from the league after being expelled from the Irish Cup and did not compete in the league for the next season. Bohemian FC (Dublin) and Shelbourne FC (Dublin) resigned from the Irish League to join the newly-formed League of Ireland in the newly constituted Irish Free State (later to become the Republic of Ireland).

The Irish League was reduced to 5 clubs for next season

IRISH CUP

SHELBOURNE FC (DUBLIN)

Shelbourne were awarded the cup after both Belfast Celtic and Glentoran were expelled from the competition

Semi-finals

Glentoran FC (Belfast)   1-1, 0-0   Belfast Celtic FC (Belfast)

During the replay on 17th March 1920, Celtic left-back Fred Barrett was ordered off the field of play. This resulted in a spectator running on to the field firing a revolver at the Glentoran fans. This caused panic and rioting in the crowd and the match was abandoned after 70 minutes. A number of spectators were injured, Celtic were found guilty of "lack of control of fans" and were expelled from the cup on 20th March 1920. Belfast Celtic then protested that Glentoran had fielded H. McIlveen who was ineligible as his name was not included on the list submitted to the referee. Glentoran were duly expelled from the competition also. As a result of this double expulsion Shelbourne, the only remaining competitors, were awarded the cup.

Shelbourne FC (Dublin)   3-0   Glenavon FC (Lurgan)

Quarter-finals

Bohemian FC (Dublin)   0-2   Belfast Celtic FC (Belfast)
Glentoran FC (Belfast)   0-0, 2-0   Cliftonville FC (Belfast)
Glenavon FC (Lurgan) and Shelbourne FC (Dublin) both received byes

1920-21

Irish League 1920-21	Cliftonville	Distillery	Glenavon	Glentoran	Linfield
Cliftonville FC	■	4-1	0-0	0-2	0-0
Distillery FC	2-0	■	0-1	0-3	0-1
Glenavon FC	3-0	4-3	■	3-1	0-0
Glentoran FC	2-0	5-1	3-0	■	1-0
Linfield FC	3-1	1-0	1-1	2-3	■

	Irish League	Pd	Wn	Dw	Ls	GF	GA	Pts
1.	GLENTORAN FC (BELFAST)	8	7	-	1	20	6	14
2.	Glenavon FC (Lurgan)	8	5	2	1	14	8	12
3.	Linfield FC (Belfast)	8	3	3	2	8	6	9
4.	Cliftonville FC (Belfast)	8	1	1	6	5	15	3
5.	Distillery FC (Belfast)	8	1	-	7	7	19	2
		40	17	6	17	54	54	40

Elected: Queen's Island FC (Belfast)

The league was extended to 6 clubs for the next season

Note: All "southern" clubs resigned from the Irish FA to join the newly formed Irish Free State FA.

IRISH CUP FINAL   (Windsor Park, Belfast – 26/03/1921)

GLENTORAN FC (BELFAST) 2-0 Glenavon FC (Lurgan)

Crooks, Snape

Glentoran: McHaffey, McSeveney, Ferguson, Ferrett, Scraggs, Emerson, McGregor, Crooks, Davey, Meek, Snape.
Glenavon: Mehaffey, Curran, Burnison, Campbell, Barbour, Rollins, McMullan, W. Brown, J. Brown, Steele, Clarke.

Semi-finals

Glenavon FC (Lurgan)	0-0, w/o	Shelbourne FC (Dublin)

(Glenavon were awarded a walk over after Shelbourne refused to replay in Belfast on St. Patrick's Day, claiming that the replay should be held in Dublin on a different day).

Glentoran FC (Belfast)	4-3	Brantwood FC (Belfast)

Quarter-finals

Glenavon FC (Lurgan)	1-0	Linfield FC (Belfast)
Glentoran FC (Belfast)	2-1	Forth River FC
St. James's Gate AFC (Dublin)	0-0, 1-2	Shelbourne FC (Dublin)

Brantwood FC (Belfast) received a bye

1921-22

Irish League 1921-22	Cliftonville	Distillery	Glenavon	Glentoran	Linfield	Queen's Island
Cliftonville FC		0-2	2-1	0-2	0-1	0-1
Distillery FC	1-0		2-1	2-2	2-3	3-0
Glenavon FC	1-0	2-1		1-1	1-3	2-1
Glentoran FC	3-1	3-1	1-0		0-0	0-1
Linfield FC	1-0	4-0	1-1	1-0		1-1
Queen's Island FC	0-0	2-4	2-1	0-2	1-3	

	Irish League	**Pd**	**Wn**	**Dw**	**Ls**	**GF**	**GA**	**Pts**
1.	LINFIELD FC (BELFAST)	10	7	3	-	18	6	17
2.	Glentoran FC (Belfast)	10	5	3	2	14	7	13
3.	Distillery FC (Belfast)	10	5	1	4	18	17	11
4.	Glenavon FC (Lurgan)	10	3	2	5	11	14	8
5.	Queen's Island FC (Belfast)	10	3	2	5	9	16	8
6.	Cliftonville FC (Belfast)	10	1	1	8	3	13	3
		60	24	12	24	73	73	60

No clubs promoted or relegated

IRISH CUP FINAL   (Solitude, Belfast – 25/03/1922)

LINFIELD FC (BELFAST) 2-1 Glenavon FC (Lurgan)

Savage, McCracken *Boyd*

Linfield: Harland, Gaw, Frame, Wallace, Morgan, McIlveen, Cowan, McCracken, Savage, McIlreavey, Scott.
Glenavon: Morrow, Brown, Curran, Barbour, Short, Killen, McMullan, Thompson, Rushe, Boyd, McMahon.

Semi-finals

Glenavon FC (Lurgan)	2-1	Linfield Rangers FC (Belfast)
Queen's Island FC (Belfast)	0-1	Linfield FC (Belfast)

Quarter-finals

Distillery FC (Belfast)	1-5	Linfield FC (Belfast)
Glenavon FC (Lurgan)	1-0	Glentoran FC (Belfast)
Linfield Rangers FC (Belfast)	3-1	Forth River FC
Queen's Island FC (Belfast)	1-1, 1-1, 2-0	Cliftonville FC (Belfast)

1922-23

Irish League 1922-23	Cliftonville	Distillery	Glenavon	Glentoran	Linfield	Queen's Island
Cliftonville FC	■	2-2	1-0	1-1	1-2	1-2
Distillery FC	0-2	■	1-0	1-0	1-0	2-3
Glenavon FC	4-1	2-3	■	2-1	0-0	0-1
Glentoran FC	3-0	1-0	3-1	■	1-2	2-0
Linfield FC	1-0	1-0	4-1	1-1	■	3-0
Queen's Island FC	4-2	2-2	4-2	1-1	0-6	■

	Irish League	Pd	Wn	Dw	Ls	GF	GA	Pts
1.	LINFIELD FC (BELFAST)	10	7	2	1	20	5	16
2.	Queen's Island FC (Belfast)	10	5	2	3	17	21	12
3.	Glentoran FC (Belfast)	10	4	3	3	14	9	11
4.	Distillery FC (Belfast)	10	4	2	4	12	13	10
5.	Cliftonville FC (Belfast)	10	2	2	6	11	19	6
6.	Glenavon FC (Lurgan)	10	2	1	7	12	19	5
		60	24	12	24	86	86	60

Elected: Ards FC (Newtownards), Barn FC (Carrickfergus), Larne FC (Larne), Newry Town FC (Newry)

The league was extended to 10 clubs for next season

IRISH CUP FINAL   (Solitude, Belfast – 31/03/1923)

LINFIELD FC (BELFAST)	2-0	Glentoran FC (Belfast)

McCracken, Savage

Linfield: Diffin, Maulstaid, Frame, Wallace, Moorhead, Robinson, Cowan, McCracken, Savage, McIlreavy, McGrillen.

Glentoran: McCormick, Peden, Ferrett, Reid, Burns, Evans, Swindell, Elwood, Keenan, McAnally, Topping.

Semi-finals

Glentoran FC (Belfast)	2-1	Glenavon FC (Lurgan)
Linfield FC (Belfast)	1-0	Distillery FC (Belfast)

Quarter-finals

Dunmurry Recreation FC (Dunmurry)	3-2	Distillery FC (Belfast)
(Distillery were awarded the match after a protest)		
Glenavon FC (Lurgan)	1-1, 3-2	Queen's Island FC (Belfast)
Glentoran FC (Belfast)	0-0, 2-2, 2-2, 4-1	Brantwood FC (Belfast)
Linfield FC (Belfast)	2-0	Cliftonville FC (Belfast)

1923-24

Irish League 1923-24	Ards	Barn	Cliftonville	Distillery	Glenavon	Glentoran	Larne	Linfield	Newry Town	Queen's Island
Ards FC		0-0	0-2	1-0	1-1	1-2	2-0	4-3	1-0	1-2
Barn FC	1-2		0-1	2-2	2-0	2-1	3-1	0-0	3-2	4-2
Cliftonville FC	1-1	4-1		1-2	3-3	0-1	3-2	1-0	0-0	1-1
Distillery FC	4-0	0-0	2-1		4-4	0-3	3-1	1-2	3-2	1-1
Glenavon FC	2-1	1-0	3-2	1-1		2-1	0-0	1-1	0-0	0-2
Glentoran FC	2-0	4-1	0-1	1-2	4-0		5-1	2-1	2-2	0-3
Larne FC	5-2	1-0	1-1	4-3	3-3	2-1		3-3	4-1	0-5
Linfield FC	2-0	2-1	2-0	1-1	1-2	1-2	4-1		3-1	3-2
Newry Town FC	1-1	2-3	5-2	1-2	2-2	1-0	1-3	1-2		3-4
Queen's Island FC	2-0	4-0	0-0	4-1	2-2	3-1	3-1	4-0	4-0	

	Irish League	Pd	Wn	Dw	Ls	GF	GA	Pts	
1.	QUEEN'S ISLAND FC (BELFAST)	18	12	4	2	48	18	26	-2
2.	Distillery FC (Belfast)	18	7	6	5	32	30	20	PO
3.	Linfield FC (Belfast)	18	8	4	6	31	27	20	PO
4.	Glenavon FC (Lurgan)	18	5	10	3	27	30	20	PO
5.	Glentoran FC (Belfast)	18	9	1	8	32	23	19	
6.	Cliftonville FC (Belfast)	18	6	6	6	24	24	18	
7.	Barn FC (Carrickfergus)	18	6	4	8	23	29	16	
8.	Larne FC (Larne)	18	6	4	8	33	43	16	
9.	Ards FC (Newtownards)	18	5	4	9	18	30	14	
10.	Newry Town FC (Newry)	18	2	5	11	25	39	9	
		180	66	48	66	293	293	178	

2nd Place 2nd Play-off

Distillery FC (Belfast)	2-1	Linfield FC (Belfast)

2nd Place Play-off	Linfield	Distillery	Glenavon
Linfield FC		---	4-0
Distillery FC	2-2		---
Glenavon FC	---	1-3	

Play-off (2nd Place)	Pd	Wn	Dw	Ls	GF	GA	Pts
1. Linfield FC (Belfast)	2	1	1	-	6	2	3
1. Distillery FC (Belfast)	2	1	1	-	5	3	3
3. Glenavon FC (Lurgan)	2	-	-	2	1	7	-
	6	2	2	2	12	12	6

Note: Queen's Island FC (Belfast) had 2 points deducted by the Irish League committee.

Elected: Belfast Celtic FC (Belfast), Portadown FC (Portadown)

The league was extended to 12 clubs for the next season

IRISH CUP FINAL   (Windsor Park, Belfast – 29/03/1924)

QUEEN'S ISLAND FC (BELFAST)	1-0	Willowfield FC (Belfast)

Burns

Queen's Island: Gough, McKeown, Fergie, Kennedy, Gowdy, Murdough, Cowan, Croft, Burns, McCleery, Morton.
Willowfield: Jackson, Savage, Fulton, Ingram, Kirkwood, McClure, Bothwell, Clarke, Hewitt, Johnston, Snape.

Semi-finals

Queen's Island FC (Belfast)	1-1, 1-0	Crusaders FC (Belfast)
Willowfield FC (Belfast)	1-0	Larne FC (Larne)

Quarter-finals

Crusaders FC (Belfast)	5-4	Distillery FC (Belfast)
Willowfield FC (Belfast)	2-2, 1-1, 3-0	Newry Town FC (Newry)

Larne FC (Larne) and Queen's Island FC (Belfast) both received byes

1924-25

Irish League 1924-25	Ards	Barn	Belfast Celtic	Cliftonville	Distillery	Glenavon	Glentoran	Larne	Linfield	Newry Town	Portadown	Queen's Island
Ards FC		4-0	7-0	2-1	3-2	2-0	0-3	0-3	0-2	4-0	1-0	1-4
Barn FC	1-0		2-1	1-2	1-1	0-2	1-1	2-0	2-3	5-1	3-2	0-0
Belfast Celtic FC	2-2	0-0		2-1	4-1	0-1	0-1	2-0	2-1	4-1	2-1	1-1
Cliftonville FC	3-0	4-0	2-2		1-0	3-1	0-1	1-0	0-3	1-1	0-0	0-3
Distillery FC	1-1	1-0	1-5	2-0		3-0	1-3	1-1	1-2	4-2	0-1	2-3
Glenavon FC	5-2	2-1	1-3	2-0	2-1		2-1	4-1	1-2	10-2	1-2	1-2
Glentoran FC	2-1	2-1	4-0	1-0	2-2	1-0		7-2	4-0	6-2	5-1	1-0
Larne FC	5-4	2-1	0-2	0-0	1-0	2-5	0-2		2-1	2-0	2-2	1-4
Linfield FC	0-1	1-2	0-0	4-1	1-2	0-2	2-1	0-0		3-0	2-1	2-3
Newry Town FC	4-3	4-2	1-2	3-0	3-2	2-2	1-2	1-3	1-0		1-2	1-1
Portadown FC	1-0	4-2	1-2	3-1	3-1	1-1	1-2	6-2	4-3	3-1		2-2
Queen's Island FC	2-1	3-2	2-0	1-0	1-2	5-0	1-1	2-1	1-2	6-1	1-1	

	Irish League	Pd	Wn	Dw	Ls	GF	GA	Pts
1.	GLENTORAN FC (BELFAST)	22	17	3	2	53	18	37
2.	Queen's Island FC (Belfast)	22	13	6	3	48	23	32
3.	Belfast Celtic FC (Belfast)	22	11	5	6	36	31	27
4.	Portadown FC (Portadown)	22	10	5	7	42	35	25
5.	Glenavon FC (Lurgan)	22	11	2	9	45	36	24
6.	Linfield FC (Belfast)	22	10	2	10	34	31	22
7.	Ards FC (Newtownards)	22	8	2	12	39	41	18
8.	Larne FC (Larne)	22	7	4	11	30	47	18
9.	Barn FC Carrickfergus)	22	6	4	12	29	40	16
10.	Cliftonville FC (Belfast)	22	6	4	12	21	32	16
11.	Distillery FC (Belfast)	22	6	4	12	31	40	16
12.	Newry Town FC (Newry)	22	5	3	14	33	67	13
		264	110	44	110	441	441	264

No clubs were promoted or relegated

IRISH CUP FINAL (Solitude, Belfast – 21/03/1925)

DISTILLERY FC (BELFAST)　　　　　2-1　　　　　　　　　　Glentoran FC (Belfast)

McKenzie, Burnison pen.　　　　　　　　　　　　　　　　　　　　　　　*Burns*

Distillery: Fitzroy, Thompson, Burnison, Garrett, Sloan, Anderson, McKenzie, Dalrymple, Rushe, Blair, McMullan.

Glentoran: Bowden, McSeveney, Reid, Inch, Burns, Emerson, McKeague, Rainey, Keenan, Meek, Allen.

Semi-finals

Distillery FC (Belfast)	2-0	Glenavon FC (Lurgan)
Glentoran FC (Belfast)	2-0	Crusaders FC (Belfast)

Quarter-finals

Crusaders FC (Belfast)	2-0	Belfast Celtic FC (Belfast)
Distillery FC (Belfast)	0-0, 1-0	Barn FC (Carrickfergus)
Glentoran FC (Belfast)	5-3	Newry Town FC (Newry)
Glenavon FC (Lurgan) received a bye		

1925-26

Irish League 1925-26	Ards	Barn	Belfast Celtic	Cliftonville	Distillery	Glenavon	Glentoran	Larne	Linfield	Newry Town	Portadown	Queen's Island
Ards FC		3-1	1-2	1-1	1-2	3-1	2-1	1-3	6-1	5-1	3-3	4-2
Barn FC	3-4		0-2	1-2	2-1	0-2	0-6	2-1	1-3	4-4	1-1	0-2
Belfast Celtic FC	2-0	5-1		3-2	2-1	0-1	2-1	5-2	5-3	4-3	1-3	2-1
Cliftonville FC	0-2	3-2	3-0		1-3	0-1	2-3	2-2	2-2	1-2	0-2	2-2
Distillery FC	2-5	2-1	0-0	1-1		1-1	2-1	1-0	4-1	3-2	3-2	2-0
Glenavon FC	0-2	3-1	0-2	1-4	2-1		2-1	2-2	2-3	1-2	4-1	3-1
Glentoran FC	4-2	4-1	2-3	2-1	2-1	4-1		2-1	3-2	5-1	2-2	2-2
Larne FC	4-1	2-0	3-1	3-0	4-1	3-3	1-1		3-0	1-0	4-1	2-0
Linfield FC	1-0	6-1	2-4	2-1	3-1	4-1	0-1	2-2		5-0	0-1	1-2
Newry Town FC	3-3	3-1	1-2	1-0	0-0	0-2	2-3	1-2	1-1		3-2	2-2
Portadown FC	2-2	4-2	2-3	0-0	2-2	1-3	0-2	4-0	3-3	4-1		1-2
Queen's Island FC	3-5	3-0	6-2	3-1	2-3	1-0	1-1	3-0	2-2	2-0	0-2	

	Irish League	Pd	Wn	Dw	Ls	GF	GA	Pts
1.	BELFAST CELTIC FC (BELFAST)	22	16	1	5	52	38	33
2.	Glentoran FC (Belfast)	22	13	4	5	53	31	30
3.	Larne FC (Larne)	22	11	5	6	45	33	27
4.	Ards FC (Newtownards)	22	11	4	7	56	42	26
5.	Distillery FC (Belfast)	22	10	5	7	37	35	25
6.	Queen's Island FC (Belfast)	22	9	5	8	42	37	23
7.	Glenavon FC (Lurgan)	22	10	3	9	36	37	23
8.	Linfield FC (Belfast)	22	8	5	9	47	46	21
9.	Portadown FC (Portadown)	22	7	7	8	43	41	21
10.	Newry Town FC (Newry)	22	5	5	12	33	53	15
11.	Cliftonville FC (Belfast)	22	4	6	12	29	39	14
12.	Barn FC (Carrickfergus)	22	2	2	18	25	66	6
		264	106	52	106	498	498	264

IRISH CUP FINAL   (Solitude, Belfast – 27/03/1926)

BELFAST CELTIC FC (BELFAST)	3-2	Linfield FC (Belfast)
Curran 3		*Andrews, Cooke*

Belfast: Fitzmaurice, Scott, Ferguson, Pollock, Moore, Perry, McGrillen, Ferris, Curran, S. Mahood, J. Mahood.
Linfield: McMeekin, Holmes, Frame, Stewart, Moorehead, Grant, Coates, Cooke, Andrews, McIlreavy, Morton.

Semi-finals

Belfast Celtic FC (Belfast)	3-0	Newry Town FC (Newry)
Linfield FC (Belfast)	2-2, 2-2, 3-2	Glentoran FC (Belfast)

Quarter-finals

Belfast Celtic FC (Belfast)	2-1	Glenavon FC (Lurgan)
Glentoran FC (Belfast)	2-1	Belfast United FC (Belfast)
Newry Town FC (Newry)	1-1, 3-1	Portadown FC (Portadown)
Linfield FC (Belfast) received a bye		

1926-27

Irish League 1926-27	Ards	Barn	Belfast Celtic	Cliftonville	Distillery	Glenavon	Glentoran	Larne	Linfield	Newry Town	Portadown	Queen's Island
Ards FC	■	4-1	1-6	0-1	3-0	0-1	3-2	2-1	2-1	4-2	3-3	1-1
Barn FC	1-3	■	2-6	0-4	3-7	3-2	2-6	2-1	2-2	3-3	3-8	2-3
Belfast Celtic FC	1-1	4-1	■	1-0	3-0	3-1	4-1	3-1	4-2	7-2	0-0	1-0
Cliftonville FC	4-1	3-1	1-1	■	0-1	4-1	0-2	0-2	1-3	0-1	2-6	2-1
Distillery FC	2-2	4-0	1-2	5-3	■	5-1	3-2	4-0	1-0	2-1	5-1	1-2
Glenavon FC	2-2	5-0	2-4	3-2	1-4	■	2-3	3-1	0-1	1-4	0-4	1-1
Glentoran FC	2-2	3-2	3-3	3-2	1-1	3-1	■	2-4	3-1	3-2	3-2	1-3
Larne FC	5-1	4-1	3-3	1-1	6-6	3-0	2-6	■	3-1	2-1	4-2	3-3
Linfield FC	4-1	3-0	2-2	4-0	1-1	3-3	0-1	3-0	■	2-1	3-1	1-3
Newry Town FC	0-0	2-2	0-4	2-0	1-1	3-2	1-1	2-4	4-2	■	2-0	3-4
Portadown FC	0-3	5-1	1-1	1-2	0-1	1-0	5-2	3-5	2-2	2-1	■	0-1
Queen's Island FC	2-3	5-3	1-3	0-0	3-1	3-1	3-3	1-0	0-0	2-1	4-3	■

	Irish League	Pd	Wn	Dw	Ls	GF	GA	Pts
1.	BELFAST CELTIC FC (BELFAST)	22	15	7	-	66	26	37
2.	Queen's Island FC (Belfast)	22	12	6	4	46	34	30
3.	Distillery FC (Belfast)	22	12	5	5	56	36	29
4.	Glentoran FC (Belfast)	22	11	5	6	56	48	27
5.	Ards FC (Newtownards)	22	9	7	6	42	42	25
6.	Larne FC (Larne)	22	10	4	8	55	50	24
7.	Linfield FC (Belfast)	22	8	6	8	41	35	22
8.	Portadown FC (Portadown)	22	7	4	11	50	48	18
9.	Cliftonville FC (Belfast)	22	7	3	12	32	40	17
10.	Newry Town FC (Newry)	22	6	5	11	39	48	17
11.	Glenavon FC (Lurgan)	22	4	3	15	33	57	11
12.	Barn FC (Carrickfergus)	22	2	3	17	35	87	7
		264	103	58	103	551	551	264

Elected: Bangor FC (Bangor), Coleraine FC (Coleraine)

The league was extended to 14 clubs for next season

IRISH CUP FINAL   (The Oval, Belfast – 26/03/1927)

ARDS FC (NEWTOWNARDS)	3-2	Cliftonville FC (Belfast)
Croft, McGee 2		*Mortished, Hughes*

Ards: McMullan, McKeown, Wilson, Smyth, Risk, Gamble, Bothwell, Patton, McGee, Croft, McIlreavy.
Cliftonville: Gardiner, Jones, McGuire, Simpson, Cooke, Addis, Davis, Gowdy, Hughes, Mortished, Ferguson.

Semi-finals

Belfast Celtic FC (Belfast)	1-3	Ards FC (Newtownards)
Crusaders FC (Belfast)	2-4	Cliftonville FC (Belfast)

Quarter-finals

Belfast Celtic FC (Belfast)	4-0	Linfield Rangers FC (Belfast)
Glenavon FC (Lurgan)	1-2	Ards FC (Newtownards)
Larne FC (Larne)	1-2	Crusaders FC (Belfast)
Cliftonville FC (Belfast) received a bye		

1927-28

Irish League 1927-28	Ards	Bangor	Barn	Belfast Celtic	Cliftonville	Coleraine	Distillery	Glenavon	Glentoran	Larne	Linfield	Newry Town	Portadown	Queen's Island
Ards FC		1-1	3-1	1-4	3-1	0-1	3-3	4-3	5-2	1-2	1-1	0-0	3-1	7-1
Bangor FC	4-3		3-1	2-6	2-3	3-1	1-1	5-1	0-2	4-3	1-5	2-1	2-4	2-4
Barn FC	1-3	2-0		0-8	2-1	2-6	2-1	2-4	3-2	1-1	1-1	1-3	1-2	5-3
Belfast Celtic FC	8-3	5-3	6-0		5-1	2-1	2-2	4-0	6-2	7-0	1-1	3-2	1-1	3-3
Cliftonville FC	0-2	1-1	3-2	0-2		2-0	0-2	1-4	0-2	3-3	1-3	0-2	2-1	2-1
Coleraine FC	3-0	1-3	6-1	3-2	4-1		0-3	5-3	5-4	3-2	1-4	1-2	5-2	2-0
Distillery FC	2-0	3-0	6-1	0-3	3-2	4-0		1-3	1-1	2-2	3-2	1-1	1-2	2-3
Glenavon FC	2-0	2-4	3-3	3-4	7-1	2-2	2-1		2-2	4-3	3-5	0-0	1-1	0-2
Glentoran FC	0-0	5-4	4-0	0-2	5-2	3-1	4-1	3-2		2-1	1-5	1-1	3-1	3-2
Larne FC	5-2	3-2	7-1	1-3	2-0	0-2	3-0	4-2	3-2		1-3	2-0	4-3	2-1
Linfield FC	8-4	8-4	2-0	2-2	5-1	7-0	0-0	3-0	6-1	3-4		3-0	2-1	1-0
Newry Town FC	5-3	2-2	6-2	0-1	3-0	4-0	4-0	3-5	6-1	0-0	1-0		4-1	4-1
Portadown FC	7-2	0-1	5-1	4-5	5-0	1-1	2-0	3-2	2-4	3-2	1-4	0-1		2-4
Queen's Island FC	3-0	1-1	2-2	0-6	1-1	3-3	1-2	2-3	4-4	1-3	1-4	0-0	2-6	

	Irish League	Pd	Wn	Dw	Ls	GF	GA	Pts	
1.	BELFAST CELTIC FC (BELFAST)	26	20	5	1	101	35	45	
2.	Linfield FC (Belfast)	26	18	5	3	88	34	41	
3.	Newry Town FC (Newry)	26	13	7	6	55	30	33	
4.	Larne FC (Larne)	26	13	4	9	63	55	30	
5.	Glentoran FC (Belfast)	26	12	5	9	63	65	29	
6.	Coleraine FC (Coleraine)	26	12	3	11	57	60	27	
7.	Distillery FC (Belfast)	26	9	7	10	45	44	25	
8.	Portadown FC (Portadown)	26	10	3	13	61	58	23	
9.	Glenavon FC (Lurgan)	26	9	5	12	63	68	23	
10.	Bangor FC (Bangor)	26	9	5	12	57	69	23	
11.	Ards FC (Newtownards)	26	8	5	13	54	69	21	
12.	Queen's Island FC (Belfast)	26	5	7	14	46	70	17	
13.	Barn FC (Carrickfergus)	26	5	4	17	38	91	14	#
14.	Cliftonville FC (Belfast)	26	5	3	18	29	72	13	
		364	148	68	148	820	820	364	

Barn FC (Carrickfergus) were not re-elected to the league for the next season.

Elected: Ballymena FC (Ballymena)

IRISH CUP FINAL (Windsor Park, Belfast – 31/03/1928)

WILLOWFIELD FC (BELFAST)　　　　　　1-1　　　　　　　　　　Larne FC (Larne)
Kimlin　　　　　　　　　　　　　　　　　　　　　　　　　　　　　　　　　　　*Crooks*

Willowfield: McFarlane, Mallon, Vance, Conway, Kirkwood, McClure, Aiken, Young, Hume, Kimlin, Shaw.
Larne: Irvine, McCambridge, Fulton, Horner, Fergie, Rodgers, White, Crooks, Houston, Snodden, Gunning.

IRISH CUP FINAL REPLAY (Windsor Park, Belfast – 25/04/1928)

WILLOWFIELD FC (BELFAST)　　　　　　1-0　　　　　　　　　　Larne FC (Larne)
Aiken

Willowfield: McFarlane, Mallon, Vance, Conway, Kirkwood, McClure, Aiken, Young, Hume, Kimlin, Shaw.
Larne: Irvine, Fergie, Fulton, Horner, Gamble, Rodgers, McLean, Crooks, Houston, McCambridge, Gunning.

Semi-finals

Larne FC (Larne)	2-1	Portadown FC (Portadown)
Willowfield FC (Belfast)	1-1, 2-1	Belfast Celtic FC (Belfast)

Quarter-finals

Belfast Celtic FC (Belfast)	2-1	Cliftonville FC (Belfast)
Larne FC (Larne)	2-0	Distillery FC (Belfast)
Portadown FC (Portadown)	2-1	Coleraine FC (Coleraine)
Willowfield FC (Belfast)	4-2	Barn FC (Carrickfergus)

1928-29

Irish League 1928-29	Ards	Ballymena	Bangor	Belfast Celtic	Cliftonville	Coleraine	Distillery	Glenavon	Glentoran	Larne	Linfield	Newry Town	Portadown	Queen's Island
Ards FC	■	1-2	2-1	2-6	4-1	5-1	0-1	1-1	4-3	4-0	2-4	1-1	1-2	3-2
Ballymena FC	4-2	■	1-2	0-3	4-0	3-3	5-3	2-2	3-0	2-0	4-2	0-1	1-3	7-3
Bangor FC	3-0	2-2	■	0-0	2-1	2-2	3-1	3-3	1-3	2-1	1-3	4-2	4-2	2-0
Belfast Celtic FC	3-0	3-2	7-2	■	4-0	3-2	6-1	1-1	6-0	7-1	5-0	7-1	6-0	5-0
Cliftonville FC	1-1	3-2	0-1	0-5	■	1-3	0-1	0-1	2-4	3-4	1-5	2-2	1-2	4-2
Coleraine FC	2-2	0-0	2-1	1-4	4-2	■	5-3	4-1	5-2	1-2	2-0	1-2	3-1	4-3
Distillery FC	6-3	5-1	1-0	0-1	2-0	2-1	■	3-2	2-3	2-1	2-3	4-1	7-3	5-0
Glenavon FC	3-2	1-1	2-2	1-3	5-1	2-0	3-4	■	3-4	0-1	2-3	3-2	3-1	5-4
Glentoran FC	3-1	2-2	4-0	2-2	4-1	2-3	2-2	7-3	■	4-5	2-1	5-1	1-2	10-3
Larne FC	2-3	2-2	4-4	2-7	2-2	2-0	1-3	2-2	2-3	■	0-4	4-3	3-4	2-3
Linfield FC	6-1	6-0	4-1	2-2	3-0	0-2	3-2	4-1	4-3	1-2	■	3-1	5-1	8-1
Newry Town FC	1-2	2-2	2-1	1-3	1-2	3-0	6-3	1-1	0-1	2-1	3-4	■	2-0	4-2
Portadown FC	1-4	3-5	3-4	0-7	2-1	2-3	3-3	3-2	2-4	2-1	1-2	1-0	■	2-2
Queen's Island FC	4-4	0-7	2-1	2-10	3-3	3-9	2-3	4-8	2-4	2-4	2-8	1-2	1-6	■

	Irish League	Pd	Wn	Dw	Ls	GF	GA	Pts	
1.	BELFAST CELTIC FC (BELFAST)	26	22	4	-	116	23	48	
2.	Linfield FC (Belfast)	26	19	1	6	88	44	39	
3.	Glentoran FC (Belfast)	26	15	3	8	82	62	33	
4.	Distillery FC (Belfast)	26	15	2	9	71	58	32	
5.	Coleraine FC (Coleraine)	26	13	4	9	63	53	30	
6.	Ballymena FC (Ballymena)	26	10	8	8	64	54	28	
7.	Bangor FC (Bangor)	26	10	6	10	49	54	26	
8.	Glenavon FC (Lurgan)	26	8	8	10	61	63	24	
9.	Ards FC (Newtownards)	26	9	5	12	55	64	23	
10.	Newry Town FC (Newry)	26	9	4	13	47	58	22	
11.	Portadown FC (Portadown)	26	10	2	14	52	76	22	
12.	Larne FC (Larne)	26	8	4	14	51	72	20	
13.	Cliftonville FC (Belfast)	26	3	4	19	32	73	10	
14.	Queen's Island FC (Belfast)	26	2	3	21	53	130	7	#
		364	153	58	153	884	884	364	

\# Queen's Island FC (Belfast) were not re-elected to the league for the next season.

Elected: Derry City FC (Londonderry)

IRISH CUP FINAL   (Solitude, Belfast – 30/03/1929)

BALLYMENA FC (BALLYMENA)   2-1   Belfast Celtic FC (Belfast)
Shiels, McCambridge   *J. Mahood*

Ballymena: Gough, McNinch, McDiarmid, J. Reid, D. Reid, Howard, Clarke, Mitchell, Shiels, McCambridge, Cassidy.
Belfast: Diffen, Wallace, Fulton, Moore, Hamill, Pollock, Gallagher, Curran, S. Mahood, J. Mahood.

Semi-finals

Ballymena FC (Ballymena)	3-0	Coleraine FC (Coleraine)
Belfast Celtic FC (Belfast)	3-0	Linfield FC (Belfast)

Quarter-finals

Ballymena FC (Ballymena)	4-1	Broadway United FC
Belfast Celtic FC (Belfast)	3-3, 7-1	Glenavon FC (Lurgan)
Coleraine FC (Coleraine)	3-0	Portadown FC (Portadown)
Linfield FC (Belfast)	6-2	Cliftonville FC (Belfast)

1929-30

Irish League 1929-30	Ards	Ballymena	Bangor	Belfast Celtic	Cliftonville	Coleraine	Derry City	Distillery	Glenavon	Glentoran	Larne	Linfield	Newry Town	Portadown
Ards FC	■	0-2	4-4	1-2	2-1	2-3	1-2	1-1	3-5	1-5	2-1	1-3	3-2	4-2
Ballymena FC	1-3	■	4-0	1-1	7-1	0-1	4-0	6-3	5-0	2-1	3-1	1-4	3-0	2-2
Bangor FC	2-0	3-1	■	3-1	6-3	1-1	0-3	2-1	3-3	2-3	2-3	1-0	2-0	4-3
Belfast Celtic FC	6-1	4-3	1-2	■	7-2	1-1	4-0	1-5	4-3	1-2	4-1	2-5	1-4	5-1
Cliftonville FC	2-3	0-2	0-0	1-1	■	4-2	4-2	1-2	2-5	2-3	1-2	0-3	1-5	4-3
Coleraine FC	6-1	2-1	2-0	3-5	3-0	■	1-2	2-5	5-1	1-2	7-5	0-0	4-1	8-0
Derry City FC	2-2	1-1	3-2	3-1	4-3	0-0	■	1-1	2-0	1-2	2-1	2-6	2-0	5-2
Distillery FC	6-3	3-1	0-2	2-3	3-1	2-0	4-2	■	2-0	2-5	3-0	2-5	4-3	3-3
Glenavon FC	4-1	3-1	5-2	4-4	1-0	1-3	2-3	2-3	■	2-1	3-1	7-1	6-1	2-2
Glentoran FC	6-1	1-2	6-6	4-0	5-2	4-0	2-0	4-3	2-1	■	4-3	3-3	5-2	3-3
Larne FC	3-3	1-2	2-5	1-3	1-2	2-4	2-2	3-1	1-2	0-1	■	1-5	3-1	3-1
Linfield FC	2-2	4-7	3-1	3-1	1-0	7-1	2-0	4-2	5-3	3-1	7-1	■	6-1	3-3
Newry Town FC	3-1	2-0	1-3	0-2	2-3	1-0	2-3	2-0	3-1	3-2	2-2	2-4	■	5-0
Portadown FC	1-1	5-3	5-3	1-3	2-0	1-3	6-5	4-2	3-4	4-4	5-3	1-5	5-3	■

	Irish League	Pd	Wn	Dw	Ls	GF	GA	Pts
1.	LINFIELD FC (BELFAST)	26	19	4	3	94	46	42
2.	Glentoran FC (Belfast)	26	16	4	6	79	53	36
3.	Coleraine FC (Coleraine)	26	14	4	8	66	47	32
4.	Belfast Celtic FC (Belfast)	26	13	4	9	68	57	30
5.	Ballymena FC (Ballymena)	26	13	3	10	65	46	29
6.	Bangor FC (Bangor)	26	12	5	9	61	58	29
7.	Derry City FC (Londonderry)	26	12	5	9	52	55	29
8.	Glenavon FC (Lurgan)	26	12	3	11	70	63	27
9.	Distillery FC (Belfast)	26	12	3	11	65	61	27
10.	Portadown FC (Portadown)	26	7	7	12	68	90	21
11.	Newry Town FC (Newry)	26	9	1	16	51	66	19
12.	Ards FC (Newtownards)	26	6	6	14	47	77	18
13.	Larne FC (Larne)	26	5	3	18	47	77	13
14.	Cliftonville FC (Belfast)	26	5	2	19	40	77	12
		364	155	54	155	873	873	364

No clubs promoted or relegated

IRISH CUP FINAL   (Celtic Park, Belfast – 29/03/1930)

LINFIELD FC (BELFAST)	4-3	Ballymena FC (Ballymena)
Bambrick 4		*Shiels 2, Reid*

Linfield: Lawson, Brown, Watson, McCleery, Jones, Sloan, Houston, McCracken, Bambrick, Grice, McCaw.
Ballymena: Gough, McNinch, McDiarmid, Baskett, Reid, Howard, Kilpatrick, Cassidy, Shiels, Gilmore, Murphy.

Semi-finals

Ballymena FC (Ballymena)	3-2	Newry Town FC (Newry)
Linfield FC (Belfast)	2-1	Glentoran FC (Belfast)

Quarter-finals

Belfast Celtic FC (Belfast)	2-3	Ballymena FC (Ballymena)
Coleraine FC (Coleraine)	0-1	Linfield FC (Belfast)
Glentoran FC (Belfast)	2-2, 4-2	Larne FC (Larne)
Newry Town FC (Newry)	2-1	Glenavon FC (Lurgan)

1930-31

Irish League 1930-31	Ards	Ballymena	Bangor	Belfast Celtic	Cliftonville	Coleraine	Derry City	Distillery	Glenavon	Glentoran	Larne	Linfield	Newry Town	Portadown
Ards FC	■	3-6	5-4	1-3	2-3	3-3	4-4	3-1	6-1	1-4	0-0	5-1	6-2	5-4
Ballymena FC	5-1	■	1-4	4-1	2-2	2-3	4-1	4-0	6-1	2-4	3-1	2-2	6-1	1-3
Bangor FC	3-3	2-6	■	3-4	2-1	3-2	1-2	3-3	4-4	0-3	2-2	1-6	5-0	6-2
Belfast Celtic FC	3-2	4-1	3-1	■	1-1	4-3	1-3	3-1	4-1	2-4	6-0	4-4	5-2	3-2
Cliftonville FC	5-2	4-3	4-2	0-5	■	1-4	3-0	4-3	3-1	0-5	2-0	0-1	1-4	3-2
Coleraine FC	1-4	1-1	2-3	0-1	2-0	■	0-2	3-3	7-0	0-2	2-2	1-2	5-3	1-1
Derry City FC	0-1	1-2	3-3	1-2	5-0	2-0	■	2-3	5-2	4-4	0-0	6-2	1-0	1-0
Distillery FC	1-0	1-2	3-1	2-1	2-1	4-3	9-0	■	5-1	2-3	3-1	3-3	9-1	5-0
Glenavon FC	3-4	1-1	2-1	0-2	2-1	2-0	4-2	1-4	■	1-5	2-1	0-1	6-1	1-1
Glentoran FC	4-2	2-2	3-1	4-3	5-2	2-0	4-1	2-0	3-2	■	6-2	1-1	5-3	4-3
Larne FC	1-2	4-0	2-0	2-2	4-6	5-2	0-3	2-4	4-2	0-9	■	2-3	2-1	3-2
Linfield FC	7-2	2-1	2-1	1-2	4-1	3-0	3-0	1-1	3-1	0-2	3-1	■	4-1	7-1
Newry Town FC	0-1	0-1	5-1	5-5	2-4	1-3	2-0	1-8	0-1	1-5	2-2	1-5	■	2-1
Portadown FC	0-0	1-7	2-5	4-1	5-2	0-0	7-1	0-2	1-5	4-1	7-1	2-2	8-4	■

	Irish League	Pd	Wn	Dw	Ls	GF	GA	Pts
1.	GLENTORAN FC (BELFAST)	26	22	3	1	96	39	47
2.	Linfield FC (Belfast)	26	16	6	4	73	42	38
3.	Belfast Celtic FC (Belfast)	26	16	4	6	75	52	36
4.	Distillery FC (Belfast)	26	15	4	7	82	46	34
5.	Ballymena FC (Ballymena)	26	13	5	8	75	50	31
6.	Ards FC (Newtownards)	26	11	5	10	68	69	27
7.	Derry City FC (Londonderry)	26	10	4	12	50	61	24
8.	Cliftonville FC (Belfast)	26	11	2	13	54	70	24
9.	Portadown FC (Portadown)	26	7	5	14	63	73	19
10.	Bangor FC (Bangor)	26	7	5	14	62	75	19
11.	Glenavon FC (Lurgan)	26	8	3	15	47	75	19
12.	Coleraine FC (Coleraine)	26	6	6	14	48	56	18
13.	Larne FC (Larne)	26	6	6	14	44	74	18
14.	Newry Town FC (Newry)	26	4	2	20	45	100	10
		364	152	60	152	882	882	364

No clubs promoted or relegated

IRISH CUP FINAL   (The Oval, Belfast – 28/03/1931)

LINFIELD FC (BELFAST)   3-0   Ballymena FC (Ballymena)

Hewitt, Houston, McCracken

Linfield: Higgs, Pyper, Curran, McCleery, Jones, Sloan, Houston, McCracken, Hewitt, Grice, McCaw.
Ballymena: McKeen, McNinch, McCandless, Reid, Stewart, Dalrymple, Cassidy, Gilmore, Shiels, Murphy.

Semi-finals

Ballymena FC (Ballymena)	2-1	Derry City FC (Londonderry)
Linfield FC (Belfast)	5-1	Glentoran FC (Belfast)

Quarter-finals

Ballymena FC (Ballymena)	2-2, 2-0	Bangor FC (Bangor)
Belfast Celtic FC (Belfast)	1-2	Linfield FC (Belfast)
Derry City FC (Londonderry)	5-0	Glenavon FC (Lurgan)
Glentoran FC (Belfast)	6-2	Coleraine FC (Coleraine)

1931-32

Irish League 1931-32	Ards	Ballymena	Bangor	Belfast Celtic	Cliftonville	Coleraine	Derry City	Distillery	Glenavon	Glentoran	Larne	Linfield	Newry Town	Portadown
Ards FC		1-1	2-2	2-1	2-2	3-4	1-2	3-1	4-1	3-2	4-1	2-5	2-0	3-4
Ballymena FC	6-2		6-4	6-0	3-5	7-0	0-0	4-0	4-1	5-0	2-0	2-0	6-2	2-3
Bangor FC	3-0	2-3		1-3	0-1	1-3	1-4	2-4	0-1	3-3	0-0	1-5	1-4	5-3
Belfast Celtic FC	3-0	2-1	0-0		4-6	2-2	0-1	3-0	7-1	4-0	5-1	4-2	3-2	0-0
Cliftonville FC	9-2	1-1	3-1	0-2		4-1	0-1	3-0	4-2	0-5	1-1	0-3	3-0	3-2
Coleraine FC	4-0	4-1	2-5	1-0	3-1		1-1	6-3	2-1	3-3	4-1	2-2	3-1	8-4
Derry City FC	6-3	2-2	4-1	1-0	6-1	1-0		3-2	5-1	1-2	6-0	1-1	1-0	2-1
Distillery FC	1-1	2-0	1-1	0-0	4-3	2-2	4-4		4-2	3-3	5-2	2-3	2-1	3-2
Glenavon FC	3-2	0-4	1-1	0-2	1-4	1-4	1-4	1-0		2-2	4-2	2-3	2-2	2-0
Glentoran FC	6-2	3-0	3-1	2-1	1-1	3-2	1-1	5-2	3-1		8-2	0-1	2-3	3-1
Larne FC	5-4	3-0	5-4	1-1	1-1	1-4	2-1	4-7	2-4	2-2		1-6	4-1	2-2
Linfield FC	4-1	2-0	4-1	0-1	2-0	4-1	3-0	4-2	3-1	4-3	6-0		4-1	2-0
Newry Town FC	4-0	1-1	1-0	2-4	3-1	1-1	0-2	4-1	1-1	2-5	1-2	3-1		1-0
Portadown FC	2-3	1-0	2-0	3-4	4-2	1-0	2-1	2-2	5-5	4-3	2-2	3-3	1-2	

Irish League	Pd	Wn	Dw	Ls	GF	GA	Pts
1. LINFIELD FC (BELFAST)	26	19	3	4	77	34	41
2. Derry City FC (Londonderry)	26	16	6	4	61	30	38
3. Belfast Celtic FC (Belfast)	26	14	5	7	56	35	33
4. Coleraine FC (Coleraine)	26	13	6	7	67	54	32
5. Glentoran FC (Glentoran)	26	12	7	7	73	54	31
6. Ballymena FC (Ballymena)	26	12	5	9	67	41	29
7. Cliftonville FC (Belfast)	26	11	5	10	59	55	27
8. Distillery FC (Belfast)	26	8	7	11	57	68	23
9. Portadown FC (Portadown)	26	8	6	12	54	63	22
10. Newry Town FC (Newry)	26	9	4	13	43	53	22
11. Larne FC (Larne)	26	6	7	13	47	85	19
12. Ards FC (Newtownards)	26	7	4	15	52	82	18
13. Glenavon FC (Lurgan)	26	6	5	15	42	74	17
14. Bangor FC (Bangor)	26	3	6	17	41	68	12
	364	144	76	144	796	796	364

No clubs promoted or relegated

IRISH CUP FINAL   (Celtic Park, Belfast – 26/03/1932)

GLENTORAN FC (BELFAST)　　　　2-1　　　　　　　　　　　Linfield FC (Belfast)

McKenzie, Burnison pen.　　　　　　　　　　　　　　　　　　　　　　　　*Burns*

Glentoran: Bennett, Allen, Gibson, Turnbull, Mathieson, McClements, Morgan, Geary, Roberts, Borland, Lucas.
Linfield: Lawson, Pyper, Curran, Buchanan, Jones, McCleery, Houston, McCracken, Bambrick, Donnelly, McCaw.

Semi-finals

| Glentoran FC (Belfast) | 2-1 | Portadown FC (Portadown) |
| Linfield FC (Belfast) | 2-2, 2-2, 2-1 | Belfast Celtic FC (Belfast) |

Quarter-finals

Bangor FC (Bangor)	2-3	Portadown FC (Portadown)
Belfast Celtic FC (Belfast)	3-3, 3-1	Derry City FC (Londonderry)
Glentoran FC (Belfast)	2-2, 3-1	Ballymena FC (Ballymena)
Linfield FC (Belfast)	5-2	Ards FC (Newtownards)

1932-33

Irish League 1932-33	Ards	Ballymena	Bangor	Belfast Celtic	Cliftonville	Coleraine	Derry City	Distillery	Glenavon	Glentoran	Larne	Linfield	Newry Town	Portadown
Ards FC		0-4	2-1	1-1	2-2	1-2	1-0	5-6	3-2	4-4	2-3	1-1	6-0	1-1
Ballymena FC	8-2		1-3	1-1	1-1	2-1	3-1	1-3	3-1	2-3	2-1	0-1	2-1	5-1
Bangor FC	1-4	5-3		1-3	3-1	3-2	0-1	0-1	1-1	0-3	3-2	1-1	6-1	1-2
Belfast Celtic FC	4-0	7-2	4-1		5-1	3-2	5-1	4-1	2-1	4-1	1-3	1-2	5-1	6-2
Cliftonville FC	3-4	6-1	2-6	1-3		2-2	0-4	1-1	1-2	5-2	4-2	4-2	5-5	5-1
Coleraine FC	5-0	3-0	4-2	1-1	3-1		0-2	2-1	3-2	1-2	4-1	4-5	1-2	11-1
Derry City FC	2-0	1-0	0-1	1-3	3-1	3-0		3-7	2-1	2-2	4-0	2-0	8-0	1-0
Distillery FC	5-0	2-2	5-3	2-0	2-1	1-0	2-1		6-4	3-4	2-0	2-1	5-3	5-1
Glenavon FC	2-1	0-1	3-1	2-3	4-1	4-4	2-3	2-4		1-1	4-1	1-2	5-1	1-2
Glentoran FC	7-5	6-1	2-5	2-4	4-0	0-2	3-5	1-1	2-1		5-0	1-5	7-1	2-1
Larne FC	6-3	2-2	5-6	2-6	3-2	4-3	0-1	1-3	4-3	2-4		1-4	9-2	0-5
Linfield FC	6-0	2-0	1-2	1-2	4-0	2-2	4-1	4-0	4-3	4-2	9-0		6-1	5-0
Newry Town FC	4-1	3-5	2-3	0-3	3-3	4-4	2-1	1-5	2-3	1-2	3-1	2-2		1-0
Portadown FC	3-2	1-4	0-1	1-0	2-1	1-3	2-6	2-0	1-1	1-2	1-2	1-5	4-1	

	Irish League	Pd	Wn	Dw	Ls	GF	GA	Pts
1.	BELFAST CELTIC FC (BELFAST)	26	19	3	4	81	34	41
2.	Distillery FC (Belfast)	26	18	3	5	75	47	39
3.	Linfield FC (Belfast)	26	17	4	5	83	34	38
4.	Derry City FC (Londonderry)	26	16	1	9	59	39	33
5.	Glentoran FC (Belfast)	26	14	4	8	74	61	32
6.	Bangor FC (Bangor)	26	13	2	11	60	56	28
7.	Coleraine FC (Coleraine)	26	11	5	10	69	50	27
8.	Ballymena FC (Ballymena)	26	11	4	11	56	58	26
9.	Glenavon FC (Lurgan)	26	7	4	15	56	59	18
10.	Portadown FC (Portadown)	26	8	2	16	37	72	18
11.	Larne FC (Larne)	26	8	1	17	55	88	17
12.	Ards FC (Newtownards)	26	6	5	15	51	83	17
13.	Cliftonville FC (Belfast)	26	5	6	15	54	74	16
14.	Newry Town FC (Newry)	26	5	4	17	47	102	14
		364	158	48	158	857	857	364

No clubs promoted or relegated

IRISH CUP FINAL   (Windsor Park, Belfast – 08/04/1933)

GLENTORAN FC (BELFAST)   1-1   Distillery FC (Belfast)
Roberts   *Storer*

Glentoran: Harris, Little, Gibson, Turnbull, Craig, Leathem, McNeill, Crooks, Roberts, Doherty, Hutchinson.
Distillery: Newlands, Smith, Gillespie, Gray, Jones, Mitchell, Storer, Sinnamon, McAdam, McLarnon, Kirby.

IRISH CUP FINAL REPLAY   (Windsor Park, Belfast – 12/04/1933)

GLENTORAN FC (BELFAST)   1-1   Distillery FC (Belfast)
McNeill   *Kirby*

Glentoran: Harris, Little, Gibson, Turnbull, Craig, Leathem, McNeill, Crooks, Roberts, Doherty, Hutchinson.
Distillery: Newlands, Smith, Gillespie, Gray, Jones, Mitchell, Storer, O'Neill, McAdam, McLarnon, Kirby.

IRISH CUP FINAL 2ND REPLAY   (Windsor Park, Belfast – 28/04/1933)

GLENTORAN FC (BELFAST)   3-1   Distillery FC (Belfast)
Doherty, Roberts, Crooks   *McLarnon*

Glentoran: Harris, Lyttle, Gibson, Turnbull, Craig, Arrigan, Doherty, Crooks, Roberts, Leatham, Fitzsimmons.
Distillery: Newlands, Smith, Gillespie, Gray, Lawless, Jones, Storer, McLarnon, McAdam, Mitchell, Kirby.

Semi-finals

Distillery FC (Belfast)	2-0	Cliftonville FC (Belfast)
Glentoran FC (Belfast)	2-1	Coleraine FC (Coleraine)

Quarter-finals

Cliftonville FC (Belfast)	1-0	Belfast Celtic FC (Belfast)
Coleraine FC (Coleraine)	1-1, 3-1	Linfield FC (Belfast)
Derry City FC (Londonderry)	1-2	Distillery FC (Belfast)
Glentoran FC (Belfast)	4-1	Portadown FC (Portadown)

1933-34

Irish League 1933-34	Ards	Ballymena	Bangor	Belfast Celtic	Cliftonville	Coleraine	Derry City	Distillery	Glenavon	Glentoran	Larne	Linfield	Newry Town	Portadown
Ards FC	■	2-1	2-0	2-2	3-2	2-0	2-2	3-2	4-0	0-2	1-0	1-4	5-1	2-0
Ballymena FC	2-2	■	5-0	2-1	1-4	4-2	2-1	4-2	3-3	3-1	4-2	2-4	7-0	1-0
Bangor FC	3-2	2-3	■	2-2	3-4	1-2	1-1	3-5	2-1	3-2	2-2	1-4	3-0	3-2
Belfast Celtic FC	3-3	3-2	0-1	■	5-1	5-2	3-2	3-0	2-0	4-0	6-1	2-5	3-2	3-1
Cliftonville FC	0-2	0-3	2-1	2-4	■	2-1	4-1	0-4	3-2	0-2	2-1	0-6	2-3	4-2
Coleraine FC	2-1	0-0	3-2	2-3	4-2	■	2-1	2-4	1-2	1-3	4-2	2-2	4-1	0-1
Derry City FC	2-0	2-2	2-0	0-1	5-1	1-0	■	0-1	3-3	2-1	1-0	2-0	1-2	2-3
Distillery FC	2-1	1-0	1-0	1-2	5-1	3-3	3-0	■	2-2	0-1	3-1	1-2	6-1	0-1
Glenavon FC	2-1	7-2	1-0	3-2	1-2	5-1	0-1	1-6	■	2-1	0-0	0-2	3-1	2-1
Glentoran FC	6-2	1-1	5-2	4-2	5-2	3-1	1-0	3-0	1-0	■	4-0	0-3	3-0	3-3
Larne FC	1-3	0-3	3-2	1-5	2-4	4-1	0-0	2-4	1-2	1-4	■	3-3	5-3	2-2
Linfield FC	5-0	3-0	2-1	3-1	3-0	2-0	2-1	3-0	8-1	0-1	8-1	■	1-0	5-0
Newry Town FC	1-1	2-2	0-3	0-6	6-2	3-0	1-1	2-2	2-1	1-1	1-2	0-2	■	1-1
Portadown FC	1-0	1-0	2-2	0-1	6-1	2-0	3-3	0-3	2-1	0-4	2-0	1-6	4-3	■

	Irish League	Pd	Wn	Dw	Ls	GF	GA	Pts	
1.	LINFIELD FC (BELFAST)	26	22	2	2	88	21	46	
2.	Belfast Celtic FC (Belfast)	26	17	3	6	74	42	37	
3.	Glentoran FC (Belfast)	26	16	3	7	59	36	35	
4.	Distillery FC (Belfast)	26	14	3	9	61	41	31	
5.	Ballymena FC (Ballymena)	26	12	6	8	59	46	30	#
6.	Ards FC (Newtownards)	26	11	5	10	47	46	27	
7.	Portadown FC (Portadown)	26	10	5	11	41	52	25	
8.	Glenavon FC (Lurgan)	26	10	4	12	45	54	24	
9.	Derry City FC (Londonderry)	26	8	7	11	37	38	23	
10.	Cliftonville FC (Belfast)	26	11	-	15	50	78	22	
11.	Bangor FC (Bangor)	26	7	4	15	43	58	18	
12.	Coleraine FC (Coleraine)	26	7	3	16	40	61	17	
13.	Newry Town FC (Newry)	26	5	6	15	37	71	16	
14.	Larne FC (Larne)	26	4	5	17	37	74	13	
		364	154	56	154	718	718	364	

Ballymena FC (Ballymena) were suspended by the Irish League for refusing to submit their financial records to inspection by the management committee. Ballymena Crusaders FC (Ballymena) applied for the vacant league position but were rejected. They then merged with Ballymena FC as Ballymena United FC (Ballymena), applied once more and were elected to the league, playing home games at the same venue and with the same nucleus of players/officials as the former Ballymena FC (Ballymena).

No clubs were promoted or relegated

IRISH CUP FINAL (The Oval, Belfast – 14/04/1934)

LINFIELD FC (BELFAST)　　　　5-0　　　　Cliftonville FC (Belfast)
Bambrick, Caiels, Mackie, Donnelly, McCracken

Linfield: Eckersley, Richmond, Richardson, Edwards, Jones, McCleery, Mackie, McCracken, Bambrick, Donnelly, Caiels.
Cliftonville: Hill, Haire, McGuire, McNeill, Leckey, Mitchell, Billingsley, Millar, Hewitt, Wishart, McCaw.

Semi-finals

Glentoran FC (Belfast)　　　　2-4　　　　Cliftonville FC (Belfast)
Linfield FC (Belfast)　　　　7-0　　　　Belfast Celtic FC (Belfast)

Quarter-finals

Ballymena FC (Ballymena)　　　　1-4　　　　Belfast Celtic FC (Belfast)
Bangor FC (Bangor)　　　　0-2　　　　Glentoran FC (Belfast)
Cliftonville FC (Belfast)　　　　4-0　　　　Derry City FC (Londonderry)
Linfield FC (Belfast)　　　　2-0　　　　Portadown FC (Portadown)

1934-35

Irish League 1934-35	Ards	Ballymena U.	Bangor	Belfast Celtic	Cliftonville	Coleraine	Derry City	Distillery	Glenavon	Glentoran	Larne	Linfield	Newry Town	Portadown
Ards FC		2-2	8-1	1-4	2-5	2-0	0-3	1-3	2-2	3-4	1-2	0-4	5-2	4-4
Ballymena United FC	5-1		4-4	0-3	5-1	3-1	0-2	1-4	5-1	0-3	1-1	1-3	5-2	1-3
Bangor FC	1-4	1-4		0-7	1-2	4-0	1-5	3-2	1-1	2-7	2-2	0-4	0-3	1-2
Belfast Celtic FC	9-0	3-0	8-1		6-2	5-1	4-1	5-2	1-1	3-1	2-3	1-2	8-2	1-1
Cliftonville FC	8-2	4-1	0-0	1-4		1-3	2-1	1-1	1-4	3-2	2-2	0-1	3-2	0-5
Coleraine FC	3-0	2-1	0-0	1-2	3-1		1-3	0-2	2-1	0-2	3-4	1-1	4-1	2-4
Derry City FC	4-2	7-3	5-3	2-1	3-0	5-2		3-1	2-1	2-2	2-1	1-2	3-0	2-0
Distillery FC	2-1	3-2	0-0	1-7	0-1	3-1	1-1		1-3	2-0	1-0	1-1	2-1	0-1
Glenavon FC	1-0	1-1	5-0	2-3	2-1	4-2	0-1	2-2		2-2	1-3	1-3	4-2	0-2
Glentoran FC	6-0	1-1	5-3	3-2	4-1	2-1	2-1	1-3	3-1		4-1	2-2	4-3	2-1
Larne FC	3-0	4-0	3-0	0-0	4-2	3-2	1-1	0-5	3-2	0-4		2-5	2-1	1-2
Linfield FC	6-0	6-0	7-1	2-1	5-0	5-2	0-0	2-1	3-0	1-0	2-1		3-0	3-1
Newry Town FC	2-3	2-0	7-3	2-5	2-1	5-2	2-3	5-4	8-0	1-3	4-1	2-1		0-2
Portadown FC	5-1	0-2	3-3	4-1	4-2	2-4	0-1	1-0	1-1	3-1	3-1	0-2	2-2	

	Irish League	Pd	Wn	Dw	Ls	GF	GA	Pts
1.	LINFIELD FC (BELFAST)	26	21	4	1	76	19	46
2.	Derry City FC (Londonderry)	26	18	4	4	64	32	40
3.	Belfast Celtic FC (Belfast)	26	17	3	6	96	36	37
4.	Glentoran FC (Belfast)	26	16	4	6	70	42	36
5.	Portadown FC (Portadown)	26	14	5	7	56	38	33
6.	Distillery FC (Belfast)	26	11	5	10	47	44	27
7.	Larne FC (Larne)	26	11	5	10	48	52	27
8.	Glenavon FC (Lurgan)	26	7	7	12	43	55	21
9.	Newry Town FC (Newry)	26	9	1	16	63	73	19
10.	Ballymena United FC (Ballymena)	26	7	5	14	48	65	19
11.	Cliftonville FC (Belfast)	26	8	3	15	45	69	19
12.	Coleraine FC (Coleraine)	26	7	2	17	43	66	16
13.	Ards FC (Newtownards)	26	5	3	18	45	91	13
14.	Bangor FC (Bangor)	26	2	7	17	36	98	11
		364	153	58	153	780	780	364

No clubs promoted or relegated

IRISH CUP FINAL   (Windsor Park, Belfast – 06/04/1935)

GLENTORAN FC (BELFAST)   0-0   Larne FC (Larne)

Glentoran: Lewis, Millar, McCaw, Arrigan, Beck, Leathem, Goodwin, Aicken, McNeill, Tyson, Smith.
Larne: Kenny, Craigie, McIlveen, Swann, Mathieson, Gemmell, McGuffie, Dodds, Byrne, Lyness, Thompson.

IRISH CUP FINAL REPLAY   (Windsor Park, Belfast – 10/04/1935)

GLENTORAN FC (BELFAST)   0-0   Larne FC (Larne)

Glentoran: Lewis, Millar, McDiarmid, Arrigan, Leathem, McCaw, Goodwin, Aicken, Neill, Duncan, Smith.
Larne: Kenny, Craigie, McIlveen, Swann, Mathieson, Gemmell, McGuffie, Dodds, Byrne, Lyness, Thompson.

IRISH CUP FINAL 2ND REPLAY (Windsor Park, Belfast – 30/04/1935)

GLENTORAN FC (BELFAST) 1-0 Larne FC (Larne)
Goodwin

Glentoran: Lewis, Millar, McDiarmid, Arrigan, Beck, Leathem, Goodwin, Aitken, McNeill, Duncan, Smith.
Larne: Kenny, Craigie, McIlveen, Swann, Mathieson, Gemmell, McGuffie, Dodds, Byrne, Lyness, Thomson.

Semi-finals

Glentoran FC (Belfast)	3-0	Ballymena United FC (Ballymena)
Larne FC (Larne)	1-0	Belfast Celtic FC (Belfast)

Quarter-finals

Distillery FC (Belfast)	2-3	Ballymena United FC (Ballymena)
Glentoran FC (Belfast)	4-2	Linfield FC (Belfast)
Larne FC (Larne)	4-4, 2-2, 2-0	Newry Town FC (Newry)
Portadown FC (Portadown)	0-2	Belfast Celtic FC (Belfast)

1935-36

Irish League 1935-36	Ards	Ballymena U.	Bangor	Belfast Celtic	Cliftonville	Coleraine	Derry City	Distillery	Glenavon	Glentoran	Larne	Linfield	Newry Town	Portadown
Ards FC	■	1-5	5-1	0-3	2-3	2-1	0-2	2-7	3-1	2-1	3-3	0-4	2-3	2-2
Ballymena United FC	1-1	■	4-3	1-3	2-1	1-0	2-2	1-0	2-1	2-4	3-2	1-1	2-3	2-2
Bangor FC	0-3	2-1	■	1-3	1-2	1-2	1-1	1-2	2-1	3-2	0-2	1-1	2-2	8-2
Belfast Celtic FC	2-1	2-0	4-1	■	4-2	1-0	2-6	2-0	2-0	4-0	9-1	2-1	5-1	2-0
Cliftonville FC	6-0	5-4	2-1	0-4	■	0-1	2-4	0-0	3-3	2-4	0-0	1-7	5-1	2-0
Coleraine FC	6-0	1-0	2-3	0-2	0-0	■	2-4	0-0	2-2	0-1	0-0	0-2	1-2	2-4
Derry City FC	8-1	1-0	5-0	0-0	4-0	1-1	■	6-0	4-2	3-0	2-1	2-0	2-1	1-0
Distillery FC	4-0	1-0	0-3	0-1	4-2	3-2	3-2	■	5-2	4-2	6-0	2-2	2-1	3-5
Glenavon FC	3-1	2-0	3-4	0-4	4-1	1-0	1-1	1-1	■	1-2	0-4	0-3	0-2	0-1
Glentoran FC	9-6	2-2	1-2	0-1	1-3	4-0	2-3	1-1	1-0	■	6-0	1-2	2-5	1-1
Larne FC	3-2	3-1	3-2	3-0	4-1	4-1	2-4	4-1	1-6	1-2	■	2-1	2-2	1-0
Linfield FC	5-1	3-2	7-0	2-2	2-1	3-0	8-1	4-1	2-0	0-1	2-1	■	4-3	2-0
Newry Town FC	7-1	5-1	8-1	2-2	2-3	2-1	4-0	6-1	3-3	2-3	5-0	2-1	■	4-2
Portadown FC	4-3	8-1	4-3	1-0	2-2	1-3	1-2	2-0	2-3	0-4	6-2	1-3	2-2	■

	Irish League	Pd	Wn	Dw	Ls	GF	GA	Pts
1.	BELFAST CELTIC FC (BELFAST)	26	20	3	3	66	23	43
2.	Derry City FC (Londonderry)	26	18	5	3	71	36	41
3.	Linfield FC (Belfast)	26	17	4	5	72	28	38
4.	Newry Town FC (Newry)	26	14	5	7	80	50	33
5.	Glentoran FC (Belfast)	26	12	3	11	57	50	27
6.	Distillery FC (Belfast)	26	11	5	10	51	52	27
7.	Larne FC (Larne)	26	11	4	11	49	65	26
8.	Portadown FC (Portadown)	26	9	5	12	53	58	23
9.	Cliftonville FC (Belfast)	26	9	5	12	49	61	23
10.	Ballymena United FC (Ballymena)	26	7	5	14	41	59	19
11.	Bangor FC (Bangor)	26	8	3	15	47	72	19
12.	Glenavon FC (Lurgan)	26	6	5	15	40	56	17
13.	Coleraine FC (Coleraine)	26	5	5	16	28	44	15
14.	Ards FC (Newtownards)	26	5	3	18	44	94	13
		364	152	60	152	748	748	364

No clubs promoted or relegated

IRISH CUP FINAL   (Celtic Park, Belfast – 04/04/1936)

LINFIELD FC (BELFAST)   0-0   Derry City FC (Londonderry)

Linfield: Frame, Hare, Richardson, Edwards, Bowden, McCleery, Foye, Donnelly, Hume, Baird, McCormick.
Derry: Wallace, Hobson, Ross, Doherty, Carlyle, Martin, Smith, Grant, Renfrew, Duffy, Kelly.

IRISH CUP FINAL REPLAY   (Celtic Park, Belfast – 08/04/1936)

LINFIELD FC (BELFAST)   2-1   Derry City FC (Londonderry)
Baird, McCormick   *Kelly*

Derry: Wallace, Hobson, Ross, Doherty, Carlisle, Martin, Smith, Grant, Renfrew, Duffy, Kelly.
Linfield: Frame, Haire, Richardson, Edwards, Bowden, McCleery, Foye, Donnelly, Hume, Baird, McCormick.

Semi-finals

Derry City FC (Londonderry)	3-0	Glentoran FC (Belfast) 2nd XI
Linfield FC (Belfast)	1-0	Belfast Celtic FC (Belfast)

Quarter-finals

Belfast Celtic FC (Belfast)	1-1, 1-1, 0-0, 5-1	Newry Town FC (Newry)
Distillery FC (Belfast)	1-3	Glentoran FC (Belfast) 2nd XI
Glentoran FC (Belfast)	0-4	Derry City FC (Londonderry)
Linfield FC (Belfast)	0-0, 3-1	Portadown FC (Portadown)

1936-37

Irish League 1936-37	Ards	Ballymena U.	Bangor	Belfast Celtic	Cliftonville	Coleraine	Derry City	Distillery	Glenavon	Glentoran	Larne	Linfield	Newry Town	Portadown
Ards FC		6-1	0-1	0-5	3-1	1-1	4-5	3-1	0-4	2-0	5-0	2-6	0-2	1-3
Ballymena United FC	4-1		2-5	0-2	1-3	1-0	1-4	3-1	1-3	4-4	1-3	0-7	1-3	1-3
Bangor FC	1-1	2-0		0-3	1-1	2-1	1-6	4-0	4-3	1-4	1-3	1-7	2-1	1-3
Belfast Celtic FC	10-0	4-0	5-0		4-2	5-0	4-2	2-1	1-0	2-2	2-1	4-0	4-1	1-3
Cliftonville FC	4-2	4-1	0-2	0-1		3-1	2-2	7-4	3-0	3-3	5-3	0-2	2-6	3-3
Coleraine FC	0-2	1-0	0-0	0-6	2-0		1-1	1-0	1-1	0-1	2-2	0-3	2-1	2-1
Derry City FC	3-1	2-0	5-2	2-1	4-0	4-0		5-2	5-2	4-1	4-1	2-1	6-1	4-0
Distillery FC	2-1	2-2	2-1	1-2	1-1	1-2	1-3		4-1	1-0	2-3	0-4	0-3	1-3
Glenavon FC	1-2	5-2	4-0	1-5	4-6	3-2	3-1	4-1		0-1	5-0	2-3	3-1	2-0
Glentoran FC	2-1	8-2	6-1	2-4	1-0	5-3	4-5	0-5	5-2		2-4	2-3	4-2	2-3
Larne FC	9-1	1-2	4-3	1-1	3-4	4-0	0-2	2-1	3-1	4-2		0-3	4-1	3-0
Linfield FC	3-1	4-0	7-2	1-2	2-0	4-1	2-2	5-0	3-0	5-1	2-0		4-0	1-2
Newry Town FC	4-1	5-3	5-1	0-0	7-1	7-0	1-0	3-1	3-2	1-2	0-3	0-0		1-2
Portadown FC	0-1	4-1	2-1	1-1	1-1	3-1	1-2	0-1	2-0	3-1	5-2	1-3	0-0	

	Irish League	Pd	Wn	Dw	Ls	GF	GA	Pts
1.	BELFAST CELTIC FC (BELFAST)	26	20	4	2	86	21	44
2.	Derry City FC (Londonderry)	26	20	3	3	85	37	43
3.	Linfield FC (Belfast)	26	20	2	4	85	25	42
4.	Portadown FC (Portadown)	26	14	4	8	49	38	32
5.	Larne FC (Larne)	26	13	2	11	63	57	28
6.	Newry Town FC (Newry)	26	12	3	11	59	48	27
7.	Glentoran FC (Belfast)	26	11	3	12	65	65	25
8.	Cliftonville FC (Belfast)	26	9	6	11	56	64	24
9.	Glenavon FC (Lurgan)	26	10	1	15	56	59	21
10.	Bangor FC (Bangor)	26	8	3	15	40	80	19
11.	Ards FC (Newtownards)	26	8	2	16	42	73	18
12.	Coleraine FC (Coleraine)	26	6	5	15	24	61	17
13.	Distillery FC (Belfast)	26	6	2	18	36	65	14
14.	Ballymena United FC (Ballymena)	26	4	2	20	34	87	10
		364	161	42	161	780	780	364

No clubs promoted or relegated

IRISH CUP FINAL   (The Oval, Belfast – 10/04/1937)

BELFAST CELTIC FC (BELFAST)   3-0   Linfield FC (Belfast)

Turnbull 3

Belfast: McAlinden, McMillan, Lavery, H. Walker, Leathem, J. Walker, Kernaghan, McArdle, Turnbull, Bruce, McIlroy.

Linfield: Doak, Haire, Richardson, Miles, Bowden, McCleery, Houston, Donnelly, Ramsay, Brownlow, McCormick.

Semi-finals

Belfast Celtic FC (Belfast)	1-1, 3-0	Ballymena United FC (Ballymena)
Linfield FC (Belfast)	2-2, 2-0	Newry Town FC (Newry)

Quarter-finals

Ballymena United FC (Ballymena)	1-0	Derry City FC (Londonderry)
Cliftonville FC (Belfast)	0-1	Belfast Celtic FC (Belfast)
Linfield FC (Belfast)	0-0, 6-1	Glentoran FC (Belfast)
Newry Town FC (Newry)	2-2, 4-3	Portadown FC (Portadown)

1937-38

Irish League 1937-38	Ards	Ballymena U.	Bangor	Belfast Celtic	Cliftonville	Coleraine	Derry City	Distillery	Glenavon	Glentoran	Larne	Linfield	Newry Town	Portadown
Ards FC	■	1-3	2-1	1-4	6-0	2-1	2-5	1-1	1-3	3-4	3-0	0-3	6-2	2-2
Ballymena United FC	1-4	■	2-1	1-0	3-1	6-2	5-0	5-1	7-2	0-1	3-2	2-2	2-2	1-1
Bangor FC	1-3	0-3	■	1-2	3-2	2-1	1-2	3-3	1-2	2-1	4-3	1-2	2-0	1-2
Belfast Celtic FC	6-0	3-1	4-0	■	8-0	4-1	6-1	3-3	6-0	6-1	5-1	2-1	1-1	4-0
Cliftonville FC	1-1	1-3	1-3	1-4	■	3-0	1-2	1-3	1-1	1-3	4-3	0-2	1-1	0-8
Coleraine FC	3-1	3-6	1-1	0-3	8-2	■	1-2	2-0	2-2	2-4	3-2	0-4	2-2	0-2
Derry City FC	3-0	9-1	4-1	1-0	4-0	4-0	■	3-0	2-0	3-0	7-1	7-1	3-1	3-0
Distillery FC	3-1	4-4	3-2	1-0	0-0	4-1	1-3	■	2-1	3-1	5-2	1-5	1-2	2-1
Glenavon FC	4-1	2-0	3-2	1-1	2-2	0-3	1-4	2-1	■	0-4	3-4	1-3	2-4	0-2
Glentoran FC	2-0	1-2	1-5	1-4	3-2	1-1	3-3	5-3	2-0	■	3-2	2-0	4-2	1-2
Larne FC	1-1	2-6	3-0	0-4	3-1	1-1	2-3	4-2	1-1	3-8	■	0-4	2-1	3-2
Linfield FC	6-0	1-1	4-1	0-2	1-1	8-0	6-1	2-3	3-2	5-2	6-3	■	4-1	2-5
Newry Town FC	4-1	5-2	5-0	3-3	6-0	5-0	4-1	1-2	4-1	2-3	4-0	0-2	■	0-0
Portadown FC	2-0	4-2	3-0	3-3	5-0	4-2	2-1	6-0	2-0	1-3	3-0	1-1	4-1	■

Play-off

Derry City FC (Londonderry)	2-2, 1-3	BELFAST CELTIC FC (BELFAST)

	Irish League	**Pd**	**Wn**	**Dw**	**Ls**	**GF**	**GA**	**Pts**
1.	Belfast Celtic FC (Belfast)	26	18	5	3	88	24	41
1.	Derry City FC (Londonderry)	26	20	1	5	81	40	41
3.	Portadown FC (Portadown)	26	16	5	5	67	32	37
4.	Linfield FC (Belfast)	26	16	5	5	78	38	37
5.	Ballymena United FC (Ballymena)	26	14	5	7	72	55	33
6.	Glentoran FC (Belfast)	26	15	2	9	64	57	32
7.	Newry Town FC (Newry)	26	10	6	10	63	49	26
8.	Distillery FC (Belfast)	26	10	6	10	51	61	26
9.	Ards FC (Newtownards)	26	7	4	15	43	66	18
10.	Glenavon FC (Lurgan)	26	6	5	15	36	65	17
11.	Bangor FC (Bangor)	26	7	2	17	39	62	16
12.	Larne FC (Larne)	26	6	3	17	48	87	15
13.	Coleraine FC (Coleraine)	26	5	5	16	40	75	15
14.	Cliftonville FC (Belfast)	26	2	6	18	27	86	10
		364	152	60	152	797	797	364

No clubs promoted or relegated

IRISH CUP FINAL   (Solitude, Belfast – 09/04/1938)

BELFAST CELTIC FC (BELFAST)   0-0   Bangor FC (Bangor)

Belfast: K. McAlinden, Lavery, Fulton, O'Connor, Leathem, Walker, Kernaghan, Walker, Turnbull, Bruce, McIlroy.

Bangor: Hewitt, Graham, Clayton, Jones, Fullerton, Yeats, Morrow, Couser, Russell, Robinson, McCartney.

IRISH CUP FINAL REPLAY   (Solitude, Belfast – 07/05/1938)

BELFAST CELTIC FC (BELFAST)   2-0   Bangor FC (Bangor)

J. McAlinden, Bruce

Bangor: Hewitt, John Graham, Clayton, Jones, Fullerton, Yeates, Morrow, James Graham, Russell, Robinson, McCartney.

Belfast: K. McAlinden, Lavery, Fulton, H. Walker, Leathem, J. Walker, Kernaghan, J. McAlinden, Kelly, Bruce, McIlroy.

Semi-finals

Bangor FC (Bangor)	2-2, 3-1	Derry City FC (Londonderry)
Belfast Celtic FC (Belfast)	1-1, 3-1	Glentoran FC (Belfast)

Quarter-finals

Bangor FC (Bangor)	2-0	Linfield Swifts FC (Linfield)
Belfast Celtic FC (Belfast)	0-0, 0-0, 1-0	Ballymena United FC (Ballymena)
Derry City FC (Londonderry)	2-1	Newry Town FC (Newry)
Glentoran FC (Belfast)	1-1, 0-0, 2-1	Glenavon FC (Lurgan)

1938-39

Irish League 1938-39	Ards	Ballymena U.	Bangor	Belfast Celtic	Cliftonville	Coleraine	Derry City	Distillery	Glenavon	Glentoran	Larne	Linfield	Newry Town	Portadown
Ards FC	■	2-6	2-0	2-3	5-2	4-4	3-1	4-2	4-2	2-1	3-2	4-1	4-2	3-3
Ballymena United FC	1-1	■	2-3	0-8	7-2	4-0	1-0	3-0	1-1	1-0	7-3	2-1	1-0	2-4
Bangor FC	1-1	3-3	■	1-3	3-0	0-0	1-5	1-1	2-2	2-4	0-0	3-2	2-3	4-3
Belfast Celtic FC	8-1	1-2	10-1	■	3-0	8-1	3-4	2-0	3-1	4-3	6-1	1-2	4-1	2-1
Cliftonville FC	4-3	0-3	1-2	1-10	■	5-2	1-5	3-2	2-3	4-3	1-4	0-3	0-0	0-2
Coleraine FC	2-5	1-2	2-0	0-1	0-4	■	1-3	1-2	4-1	3-5	2-3	2-4	1-1	3-1
Derry City FC	5-0	3-5	8-0	2-2	2-1	4-1	■	5-0	3-2	4-0	5-0	1-1	0-0	6-2
Distillery FC	2-0	0-0	7-1	1-0	2-1	5-2	1-4	■	1-2	4-5	6-0	0-2	3-3	2-2
Glenavon FC	2-4	7-0	1-1	2-1	2-1	5-2	3-2	5-1	■	2-3	4-3	6-2	2-2	5-2
Glentoran FC	2-1	1-3	3-2	1-6	4-2	4-0	4-2	2-0	4-3	■	3-1	3-2	0-0	2-9
Larne FC	2-2	2-2	1-0	1-1	4-0	4-3	4-2	0-2	3-0	2-5	■	1-4	0-1	3-2
Linfield FC	1-0	1-2	4-1	1-2	0-0	4-0	2-4	1-0	3-2	2-1	5-0	■	4-1	5-0
Newry Town FC	1-1	3-1	1-2	0-2	4-3	3-1	4-3	1-5	1-2	5-1	3-1	1-0	■	2-2
Portadown FC	6-2	7-2	2-1	2-3	3-0	5-2	5-1	6-4	2-0	3-1	4-0	3-1	3-0	■

	Irish League	Pd	Wn	Dw	Ls	GF	GA	Pts
1.	BELFAST CELTIC FC (BELFAST)	26	19	2	5	97	32	40
2.	Ballymena United FC (Ballymena)	26	15	5	6	63	54	35
3.	Derry City FC (Londonderry)	26	15	3	8	84	47	33
4.	Portadown FC (Portadown)	26	15	3	8	84	56	33
5.	Linfield FC (Belfast)	26	14	2	10	58	40	30
6.	Glentoran FC (Belfast)	26	14	1	11	65	69	29
7.	Glenavon FC (Lurgan)	26	12	4	10	67	57	28
8.	Ards FC (Newtownards)	26	11	6	9	63	66	28
9.	Newry Town FC (Newry)	26	9	8	9	43	48	26
10.	Distillery FC (Belfast)	26	9	4	13	53	56	22
11.	Larne FC (Larne)	26	8	4	14	45	73	20
12.	Bangor FC (Bangor)	26	6	7	13	37	71	19
13.	Cliftonville FC (Belfast)	26	5	2	19	38	81	12
14.	Coleraine FC (Coleraine)	26	3	3	20	40	87	9
		364	155	54	155	837	837	364

No clubs promoted or relegated

IRISH CUP FINAL (Solitude, Belfast – 29/04/1939)

LINFIELD FC (BELFAST)   2-0   Ballymena United FC (Ballymena)

Finlay, Marshall

Linfield: Doak, Thompson, Richardson, Waddell, Perry, Rosbotham, Brownlow, Donnelly, Marshall, Finlay, McCormick.

Ballymena: Redmond, Vincent, McDaid, Wallace, McCartney, Surgenor, Kirby, Horner, Sclater, Olphert, Moore.

Semi-finals

Ballymena United FC (Ballymena)	3-2	Portadown FC (Portadown)
Linfield FC (Belfast)	4-0	Cliftonville FC (Belfast)

Quarter-finals

Ballymena United FC (Ballymena)	3-1	Belfast Celtic FC (Belfast)
Bangor FC (Bangor)	2-4	Portadown FC (Portadown)
Cliftonville FC (Belfast)	3-0	Glenavon FC (Lurgan)
Linfield FC (Belfast)	3-1	Newry Town FC (Newry)

1939-40

Irish League 1939-40	Ards	Ballymena U.	Bangor	Belfast Celtic	Cliftonville	Coleraine	Derry City	Distillery	Glenavon	Glentoran	Larne	Linfield	Newry Town	Portadown
Ards FC		0-2	3-1	3-3	3-1	5-0	1-3	1-4	0-1	2-1	7-1	2-3	1-1	5-4
Ballymena United FC	5-0		6-0	1-5	4-3	6-1	4-1	4-0	2-2	2-3	5-1	2-1	8-2	2-1
Bangor FC	2-5	2-2		1-3	3-1	4-2	1-3	1-0	5-1	0-4	4-1	2-0	4-1	1-2
Belfast Celtic FC	3-0	3-3	6-0		6-2	6-1	3-0	4-0	4-2	4-2	0-0	5-0	12-0	0-0
Cliftonville FC	1-3	0-1	2-3	0-7		1-2	2-1	7-2	1-2	0-3	3-3	1-6	3-2	2-4
Coleraine FC	3-1	2-4	5-1	1-3	4-1		2-1	5-4	1-4	3-7	3-1	0-4	3-1	2-1
Derry City FC	6-2	5-2	5-2	0-0	6-1	0-0		2-1	9-0	3-2	6-0	1-2	4-1	3-5
Distillery FC	1-2	3-3	3-1	1-3	4-1	1-3	1-3		4-2	2-3	5-2	1-3	7-0	1-1
Glenavon FC	5-1	4-2	6-2	0-3	8-1	3-0	0-1	2-1		4-3	3-2	3-3	2-0	2-3
Glentoran FC	8-1	4-2	5-1	0-3	8-2	4-1	6-1	6-2	6-1		6-2	3-2	6-1	0-3
Larne FC	4-0	2-4	1-1	0-2	1-0	0-1	2-8	4-1	0-5	0-2		1-1	2-1	2-7
Linfield FC	4-0	2-1	1-1	0-2	5-1	3-1	1-0	3-1	5-5	1-2	3-1		3-0	0-5
Newry Town FC	2-0	1-3	3-0	0-1	3-1	1-1	2-0	1-1	3-2	1-9	1-1	3-4		1-1
Portadown FC	3-1	4-2	6-1	1-0	6-2	1-0	3-1	3-2	6-0	2-2	4-2	3-3	7-0	

	Irish League	Pd	Wn	Dw	Ls	GF	GA	Pts
1.	BELFAST CELTIC FC (BELFAST)	26	20	5	1	91	18	45
2.	Portadown FC (Portadown)	26	18	5	3	86	37	41
3.	Glentoran FC (Belfast)	26	19	1	6	104	46	39
4.	Ballymena United FC (Ballymena)	26	15	4	7	82	52	34
5.	Linfield FC (Belfast)	26	14	5	7	63	47	33
6.	Derry City FC (Londonderry)	26	14	2	10	73	46	30
7.	Glenavon FC (Lurgan)	26	13	3	10	69	68	29
8.	Coleraine FC (Coleraine)	26	11	2	13	47	68	24
9.	Ards FC (Newtownards)	26	9	2	15	49	72	20
10.	Bangor FC (Bangor)	26	8	3	13	44	77	19
11.	Distillery FC (Belfast)	26	6	3	17	53	70	15
12.	Newry Town FC (Newry)	26	5	5	16	32	86	15
13.	Larne FC (Larne)	26	4	5	17	36	83	13
14.	Cliftonville FC (Belfast)	26	3	1	22	40	99	7
		364	159	46	159	869	869	364

The Irish League was suspended from 1940-41 to 1946-47 due to World War 2. However, some regional leagues were contested during this period with the Irish League re-starting for season 1947-48.

IRISH CUP FINAL   (Windsor Park, Belfast – 20/04/1940)

BALLYMENA UNITED FC (BALLYMENA)   2-0   Glenavon FC (Lurgan)

Moore, Sclater

Ballymena: Redmond, Vincent, Swann, Barr, McCartney, Rosbotham, Grant, Olphert, Sclater, Weir, Moore.
Glenavon: Kelly, Weir, Hoy, Magill, Clayton, Fraham, Holbeach, Robinson, Craig, Duffy, McCunnie.

Semi-finals

Ballymena United FC (Ballymena)	2-0	Belfast Celtic FC (Belfast)
Glenavon FC (Lurgan)	2-0	Linfield FC (Belfast)

Quarter-finals

Ballymena United FC (Ballymena)	3-2	Dundela FC (Belfast)
Belfast Celtic FC (Belfast)	3-0	Derry City FC (Londonderry)
Belfast Celtic FC (Belfast) 2nd XI	0-3	Glenavon FC (Lurgan)
Larne FC (Larne)	1-2	Linfield FC (Belfast)

1940-41

Belfast & District League 1940-41	Belfast Celtic	Cliftonville	Derry City	Distillery	Glenavon	Glentoran	Linfield	Portadown
Belfast Celtic FC	■	9-1	1-2	4-0	13-0	1-2	5-2	6-0
	■	3-1	8-2	3-2	5-2	8-2	2-4	3-1
Cliftonville FC	0-1	■	2-5	1-3	3-2	1-3	0-5	0-8
	1-3	■	4-5	1-7	1-1	0-4	3-4	2-5
Derry City FC	0-4	2-1	■	1-2	5-3	0-4	0-4	2-2
	0-1	2-1	■	1-4	2-3	2-2	2-2	2-5
Distillery FC	2-7	7-1	6-0	■	5-0	6-3	5-1	2-2
	0-0	5-1	5-2	■	2-2	2-3	2-3	1-2
Glenavon FC	1-5	1-2	6-1	2-1	■	1-0	---	0-4
	0-3	6-3	3-4	0-1	■	1-1	1-1	1-4
Glentoran FC	1-1	6-2	5-0	5-0	8-0	■	1-2	4-2
	3-3	6-3	4-0	6-1	1-2	■	3-1	7-4
Linfield FC	1-0	2-1	7-2	1-1	2-0	1-4	■	2-0
	0-2	3-1	1-2	1-3	6-1	3-3	■	3-4
Portadown FC	---	5-1	6-2	3-1	8-0	6-5	1-4	■
	2-2	4-2	4-0	1-1	3-1	4-3	3-3	■

	Belfast & District League	**Pd**	**Wn**	**Dw**	**Ls**	**GF**	**GA**	**Pts**	
1.	BELFAST CELTIC FC (BELFAST)	27	19	4	4	104	32	42	
2.	Portadown FC (Portadown)	27	17	4	6	92	58	38	#
3.	Glentoran FC (Belfast)	28	16	5	7	99	57	37	
4.	Linfield FC (Belfast)	27	14	4	9	67	51	32	
5.	Distillery FC (Belfast)	28	13	5	10	77	57	31	
6.	Derry City FC (Londonderry)	28	8	3	17	48	100	19	
7.	Glenavon FC (Lurgan)	28	6	4	17	40	95	16	#
8.	Cliftonville FC (Belfast)	28	2	1	25	40	117	5	
		220	95	30	95	567	567	220	

Note: The matches Glenavon FC vs Linfield FC and Portadown FC vs Belfast Celtic FC were not played.

\# Glenavon FC (Lurgan) and Portadown FC (Portadown) resigned from the league which was reduced to 6 clubs for the next season.

IRISH CUP FINAL   (Windsor Park, Belfast – 26/04/1941)

BELFAST CELTIC FC (BELFAST)　　　　　1-0　　　　　　　　　　　Linfield FC (Belfast)

O'Connor

Belfast: Breen, McMillan, Fulton, Walker, Vernon, Leathem, Kernaghan, Kelly, O'Connor, McAlinden, McIlroy.
Linfield: Redmond, Kirkwood, McNickle, McKeown, Brolly, Wright, Donnelly, Barker, Marshall, Sheen, Baird.

Semi-finals

Belfast Celtic FC (Belfast)	5-2	Glenavon FC (Lurgan)
Linfield FC (Belfast)	3-3, 5-2	Distillery FC (Belfast)

Quarter-finals

Belfast Celtic FC (Belfast)	3-2	Bangor FC (Bangor)
Derry City FC (Londonderry)	0-1	Distillery FC (Belfast)
Glenavon FC (Lurgan)	3-3, 5-0	Cliftonville FC (Belfast)
Portadown FC (Portadown)	0-3	Linfield FC (Belfast)

1941-42

Belfast & District League 1941-42	Belfast Celtic	Cliftonville	Derry City	Distillery	Glentoran	Linfield
Belfast Celtic FC		3-1	1-0	5-2	4-0	0-0
		9-0	10-1	1-1	2-1	0-3
Cliftonville FC	2-4		2-2	2-0	0-5	5-5
	0-2		6-1	1-2	1-3	1-4
Derry City FC	0-0	1-0		2-0	1-1	2-2
	1-4	2-1		1-4	0-2	1-2
Distillery FC	0-2	1-1	3-3		5-1	2-2
	1-1	4-1	8-2		1-1	0-2
Glentoran FC	4-1	3-1	7-0	2-1		0-3
	1-3	4-1	7-1	4-2		3-4
Linfield FC	2-2	3-1	9-1	1-2	3-7	
	3-3	6-2	4-1	3-2	3-3	

	Belfast & District League	**Pd**	**Wn**	**Dw**	**Ls**	**GF**	**GA**	**Pts**
1.	BELFAST CELTIC FC (BELFAST)	20	12	6	2	57	23	30
2.	Linfield FC (Belfast)	20	11	7	2	64	38	29
3.	Glentoran FC (Belfast)	20	11	3	6	59	37	25
4.	Distillery FC (Belfast)	20	6	6	8	41	38	18
5.	Derry City FC (Londonderry)	20	3	5	12	23	73	11
6.	Cliftonville FC (Belfast)	20	2	3	15	29	64	7
		120	45	30	45	273	273	120

No clubs promoted or relegated

IRISH CUP FINAL   (Celtic Park, Belfast – 18/04/1942)

LINFIELD FC (BELFAST)   3-1   Glentoran FC (Belfast)
Thompson 2, Peppitt   *Keddie*

Linfield: Redmond, Kirkwood, Feeney, McKeown, Mould, Brolly, Thompson, Wright, Peppitt, Ormiston, Baker.
Glentoran: Hinton, Gager, Aston, McDermott, Bray, Kirkham, Wright, Keddie, Robinson, Matthias, Douglas.

Semi-finals

Ards FC (Newtownards)	0-2	Glentoran FC (Belfast)
Linfield FC (Belfast)	6-0	Distillery FC (Belfast)

Quarter-finals

Bangor FC (Bangor) 2nd XI	1-2, 1-4	Ards FC (Newtownards)
Cliftonville FC (Belfast)	0-3, 0-4	Distillery FC (Belfast)
Glentoran FC (Belfast)	4-0, 0-2	Royal Irish Fusiliers Regiment
Linfield FC (Belfast)	5-1, 4-1	Inniskilling Fusiliers Regiment

1942-43

Belfast & District League 1942-43	Belfast Celtic	Cliftonville	Derry City	Distillery	Glentoran	Linfield
Belfast Celtic FC		6-1	4-0	5-1	3-0	1-4
		4-0	4-0	1-1	2-1	2-1
Cliftonville FC	1-3		3-0	0-4	4-2	0-4
	0-2		1-1	2-1	2-2	0-1
Derry City FC	0-1	4-2		3-2	4-2	1-4
	0-0	1-1		2-0	2-6	0-2
Distillery FC	3-2	4-2	3-2		2-1	2-0
	1-2	4-1	1-2		5-2	0-0
Glentoran FC	3-4	9-3	3-3	2-1		2-1
	2-1	6-2	3-2	1-3		1-3
Linfield FC	2-2	5-1	6-2	2-0	4-3	
	1-0	5-0	3-2	2-4	5-3	

	Belfast & District League	**Pd**	**Wn**	**Dw**	**Ls**	**GF**	**GA**	**Pts**
1.	LINFIELD FC (BELFAST)	20	14	2	4	55	26	30
2.	Belfast Celtic FC (Belfast)	20	13	3	4	50	22	29
3.	Distillery FC (Belfast)	20	10	2	8	42	34	22
4.	Glentoran FC (Belfast)	20	7	2	11	54	56	16
5.	Derry City FC (Londonderry)	20	6	3	11	32	51	15
6.	Cliftonville FC (Belfast)	20	3	2	15	26	70	8
		120	53	14	53	259	259	120

No clubs promoted or relegated

IRISH CUP FINAL (Windsor Park, Belfast – 17/04/1943)

BELFAST CELTIC FC (BELFAST)   1-0   Glentoran FC (Belfast)

Hollinger

Belfast: Kelly, McMillan, Fulton, Walker, Vernon, Douglas, Kernaghan, O'Connor, Byrne, Townsend, Hollinger.
Glentoran: Beale, Hickman, Henderson, McDermott, Dykes, Stevenson, Wright, Beattie, Kelly, Grant, Douglas.

Semi-finals

Belfast Celtic FC (Belfast)	4-2	Larne FC (Larne)
Glentoran FC (Belfast)	4-2	Ards FC (Newtownards)

Quarter-finals

Alexander Works FC	1-2, 2-3	Belfast Celtic FC (Belfast)
Ards FC (Newtownards)	2-1, 5-0	Infantry Training Centre
Glentoran FC (Belfast)	7-2, 8-0	Royal Irish Fusiliers Regiment
Larne FC (Larne) received a bye		

1943-44

Belfast & District League 1943-44	Belfast Celtic	Cliftonville	Derry City	Distillery	Glentoran	Linfield
Belfast Celtic FC		3-0	9-0	4-3	3-1	3-1
		7-1	4-0	1-1	5-3	0-2
Cliftonville FC	0-5		2-1	3-1	4-2	0-2
	1-1		7-0	0-5	3-5	0-3
Derry City FC	1-1	2-1		3-5	2-1	---
	1-2	1-0		3-4	4-2	2-6
Distillery FC	1-1	1-0	5-3		1-3	2-2
	3-2	0-2	3-1		3-1	6-1
Glentoran FC	0-1	3-1	5-4	4-2		2-2
	0-1	3-1	5-0	3-1		1-3
Linfield FC	---	2-1	5-2	8-1	4-1	
	2-2	4-2	3-5	2-4	5-5	

	Belfast & District League	**Pd**	**Wn**	**Dw**	**Ls**	**GF**	**GA**	**Pts**
1.	BELFAST CELTIC FC (BELFAST)	19	12	5	2	55	21	29
2.	Linfield FC (Belfast)	18	11	3	4	57	38	25
3.	Distillery FC (Belfast)	20	10	3	7	52	47	23
4.	Glentoran FC (Belfast)	20	8	1	11	49	50	17
5.	Cliftonville FC (Belfast)	20	5	1	14	29	51	11
6.	Derry City FC (Londonderry)	19	5	1	13	35	70	11
		116	51	14	51	277	277	116

The matches Linfield FC vs Glentoran FC and Derry City FC vs Linfield FC were not played.

No clubs promoted or relegated

IRISH CUP FINAL   (Windsor Park, Belfast – 22/04/1944)

BELFAST CELTIC FC (BELFAST)　　　　　3-1　　　　　　　　　　Linfield FC (Belfast)

Bonnar, McAlinden, A. Kelly　　　　　　　　　　　　　　　　　　　　　　　　　*Cochrane*

Belfast: H. Kelly, McMillan, Cullen, Walker, Vernon, O'Connor, Collins, McAlinden, Byrne, A. Kelly, Bonnar.
Linfield: Twoomey, Bryson, Feeney, H. Walsh, Stark, McWilliams, Cochrane, McCrory, D. Walsh, Pearson, Lockhart.

Semi-finals

Belfast Celtic FC (Belfast)	3-0	Infantry Training Centre
Linfield FC (Belfast)	0-0, 2-0	Cliftonville FC (Belfast)

Quarter-finals

Bangor FC (Bangor) 2nd XI	0-1, 2-2	Infantry Training Centre
Belfast Celtic FC (Belfast)	3-0, 4-1	Distillery FC (Belfast)
Cliftonville FC (Belfast)	2-2, 3-0	Ards FC (Newtownards)
Linfield FC (Belfast)	4-2, 4-1	Larne FC (Larne)

1944-45

Belfast & District League 1944-45	Belfast Celtic	Cliftonville	Derry City	Distillery	Glentoran	Linfield
Belfast Celtic FC		1-0	3-1	4-2	4-1	1-1
		2-0	2-2	6-2	7-3	3-0
Cliftonville FC	1-2		1-4	1-3	2-3	0-6
	0-2		2-3	0-1	2-1	0-4
Derry City FC	1-0	2-3		3-1	2-1	0-2
	3-3	3-1		0-5	4-0	0-5
Distillery FC	2-2	4-2	4-2		3-5	0-4
	1-5	3-1	0-1		5-0	1-3
Glentoran FC	1-2	9-3	6-2	2-1		1-2
	1-2	6-2	6-3	3-4		1-5
Linfield FC	2-2	6-0	5-2	7-1	3-3	
	3-1	4-2	3-3	7-1	9-2	

	Belfast & District League	**Pd**	**Wn**	**Dw**	**Ls**	**GF**	**GA**	**Pts**
1.	LINFIELD FC (BELFAST)	20	15	4	1	81	24	34
2.	Belfast Celtic FC (Belfast)	20	13	5	2	54	27	31
3.	Derry City FC (Londonderry)	20	8	3	9	41	53	19
4.	Distillery FC (Belfast)	20	8	1	11	44	58	17
5.	Glentoran FC (Belfast)	20	7	1	12	55	67	15
6.	Cliftonville FC (Belfast)	20	2	-	18	23	69	4
		120	53	14	53	298	298	120

No clubs promoted or relegated

IRISH CUP FINAL   (Celtic Park, Belfast – 14/04/1945)

LINFIELD FC (BELFAST)   4-2   Glentoran FC (Belfast)

McCrory 2, Lockhart, Cochrane   *Hill, McIlvenny*

Linfield: Breen, Henderson, Feeney, H. Walsh, Bryson, McWilliams, Cochrane, McCrory, D. Walsh, Robinson, Lockhart.

Glentoran: Vernon, McIlroy, Gilmore, McDermott, Dykes, Wright, McIlvenny, Hill, Nimmick, Langton, Deakin.

Semi-finals

Glentoran FC (Belfast)	3-0	Distillery FC (Belfast)
Linfield FC (Belfast)	4-0	Derry City FC (Londonderry)

Quarter-finals

Derry City FC (Londonderry)	5-0, 3-2	Cliftonville FC (Belfast)
Distillery FC (Belfast)	4-1, 3-4	Belfast Celtic FC (Belfast)
Larne FC (Larne)	3-4, 3-5	Glentoran FC (Belfast)
Linfield FC (Belfast)	8-0, 2-0	Ards FC (Newtownards)

1945-46

Belfast & District League 1945-46	Belfast Celtic	Cliftonville	Derry City	Distillery	Glentoran	Linfield
Belfast Celtic FC		4-1	2-1	5-0	3-1	3-0
		5-0	5-0	4-3	2-2	0-2
Cliftonville FC	0-4		4-1	1-1	1-1	2-3
	0-3		3-2	0-6	2-3	1-3
Derry City FC	2-2	8-2		1-0	1-2	1-4
	1-4	5-2		4-1	4-3	3-5
Distillery FC	1-3	1-1	8-4		3-3	3-2
	0-0	4-2	2-1		4-1	1-6
Glentoran FC	2-5	5-0	5-4	1-3		0-3
	2-2	1-1	9-2	2-2		1-7
Linfield FC	0-1	8-1	4-3	8-2	5-0	
	2-1	5-0	5-0	3-2	4-2	

	Belfast & District League	**Pd**	**Wn**	**Dw**	**Ls**	**GF**	**GA**	**Pts**
1.	LINFIELD FC (BELFAST)	20	17	-	3	79	27	34
2.	Belfast Celtic FC (Belfast)	20	14	4	2	58	20	32
3.	Distillery FC (Belfast)	20	7	5	8	47	52	19
4.	Glentoran FC (Belfast)	20	5	6	9	46	58	16
5.	Derry City FC (Londonderry)	20	5	1	14	48	72	11
6.	Cliftonville FC (Belfast)	20	2	4	14	24	73	8
		120	50	20	50	302	302	120

Elected: Coleraine FC (Coleraine), Ballymena United FC (Ballymena)

The league was extended to 8 clubs for next season

IRISH CUP FINAL (Celtic Park, Belfast – 13/04/1946)

LINFIELD FC (BELFAST)   3-0   Distillery FC (Belfast)

Walsh 2, McCrory

Linfield: Breen, Henderson, Feeney, Jones, Bryson, McWilliams, McKenna, McCrory, Walsh, Russell, Lockhart.
Distillery: Smyth, Crossley, McAuley, Collins, Bowler, Currie, O'Connor, Kernaghan, Lonsdale, Brennan, Walker.

Semi-finals

Distillery FC (Belfast)	0-0, 1-0	Belfast Celtic FC (Belfast) 2nd XI
Linfield FC (Belfast)	2-0	Belfast Celtic FC (Belfast)

Quarter-finals

Belfast Celtic FC (Belfast) 2nd XI	0-0, 3-1	Cliftonville FC (Belfast)
Derry City FC (Londonderry)	0-3, 2-7	Glentoran FC (Belfast)
Distillery FC (Belfast)	2-1, 2-0	Linfield Swifts FC (Belfast)
Linfield FC (Belfast)	2-0, 3-3	Ards FC (Newtownards)

1946-47

Belfast & District League 1946-47	Ballymena U.	Belfast Celtic	Cliftonville	Coleraine	Derry City	Distillery	Glentoran	Linfield
Ballymena United FC	■	2-4	4-3	3-0	3-3	2-0	3-5	3-5
	■	1-1	5-1	1-1	3-2	1-0	1-1	0-1
Belfast Celtic FC	1-1	■	4-1	2-3	2-0	6-1	1-3	2-3
	10-1	■	6-1	3-2	8-1	4-0	2-1	2-0
Cliftonville FC	2-2	1-2	■	1-2	1-0	0-6	2-5	3-5
	5-5	0-2	■	3-3	1-2	3-4	0-5	1-0
Coleraine FC	3-0	0-2	2-1	■	4-0	1-3	0-0	2-2
	1-0	3-6	4-3	■	4-2	2-0	0-2	2-4
Derry City FC	2-1	0-2	4-1	3-0	■	4-2	2-3	0-2
	3-4	2-9	6-2	4-1	■	1-0	0-3	3-1
Distillery FC	6-1	2-4	10-1	3-4	2-2	■	2-1	0-3
	0-2	1-2	2-3	2-2	4-1	■	2-1	2-1
Glentoran FC	3-1	3-0	5-2	7-2	2-1	3-1	■	1-2
	5-1	4-2	9-3	6-1	4-3	4-1	■	2-4
Linfield FC	6-0	1-2	5-0	2-0	7-1	5-1	2-3	■
	2-1	2-3	5-1	10-5	4-1	5-2	4-2	■

	Belfast & District League	**Pd**	**Wn**	**Dw**	**Ls**	**GF**	**GA**	**Pts**
1.	BELFAST CELTIC FC (BELFAST)	28	21	2	5	95	40	44
2.	Glentoran FC (Belfast)	28	20	2	6	93	46	42
3.	Linfield FC (Belfast)	28	20	1	7	93	45	41
4.	Coleraine FC (Coleraine)	28	10	5	13	54	75	25
5.	Ballymena United FC (Ballymena)	28	8	7	13	52	76	23
6.	Distillery FC (Belfast)	28	9	2	17	59	69	20
7.	Derry City FC (Londonderry)	28	9	2	17	53	80	20
8.	Cliftonville FC (Belfast)	28	3	3	22	46	114	9
		224	100	24	100	545	545	224

The Irish League restarted the next season with the above 8 clubs plus the following elected clubs:
Ards FC (Newtownards), Bangor FC (Bangor), Glenavon FC (Lurgan), Portadown FC (Portadown)

IRISH CUP FINAL (Windsor Park, Belfast – 26/04/1947)

BELFAST CELTIC FC (BELFAST)　　　　　1-0　　　　　　　　　Glentoran FC (Belfast)

Tully

Belfast: K. McAlinden, McMillan, Aherne, Walker, Currie, R. Lawler, Campbell, Tully, McMorran, Denver, Douglas.
Glentoran: McKee, Kane, Neill, Blanchflower, Waters, Hughes, Wright, Kelly, McCormack, J. Lawler, Lavery.

Semi-finals

Belfast Celtic FC (Belfast)	1-0	Linfield FC (Belfast)
Glentoran FC (Belfast)	1-1, 1-1, 2-1	Ballymena United FC (Ballymena)

Quarter-finals

Cliftonville FC (Belfast)	0-2, 0-3	Ballymena United FC (Ballymena)
Coleraine FC (Coleraine)	4-1, 0-3, 0-3	Linfield FC (Belfast)
Derry City FC (Londonderry)	0-1, 2-5	Belfast Celtic FC (Belfast)
Distillery FC (Belfast)	1-0, 0-1, 1-2	Glentoran FC (Belfast)

1947-48

Irish League 1947-48	Ards	Ballymena U.	Bangor	Belfast Celtic	Cliftonville	Coleraine	Derry City	Distillery	Glenavon	Glentoran	Linfield	Portadown
Ards FC		2-2	1-2	2-5	1-3	3-2	4-1	1-2	2-4	1-1	2-1	3-0
Ballymena United FC	0-1		2-0	4-3	5-2	3-2	6-0	2-1	4-2	1-1	1-2	5-2
Bangor FC	1-2	3-7		2-5	1-1	2-2	4-0	3-2	2-5	2-3	1-4	1-3
Belfast Celtic FC	6-0	2-0	3-2		3-0	5-2	5-1	5-0	3-1	0-0	3-0	6-2
Cliftonville FC	3-4	1-1	2-3	2-4		0-1	3-0	2-0	3-3	2-1	0-0	2-1
Coleraine FC	1-1	4-0	3-0	1-8	4-0		3-0	0-2	2-2	2-2	1-2	5-2
Derry City FC	6-2	1-1	0-2	1-5	1-3	2-5		0-2	1-2	2-3	0-7	1-0
Distillery FC	2-0	2-2	3-1	0-2	3-0	0-2	2-0		2-0	2-2	0-4	1-0
Glenavon FC	1-1	1-2	1-1	1-3	3-2	2-2	4-0	0-2		0-5	1-1	5-1
Glentoran FC	4-1	2-2	4-0	1-3	3-1	3-0	4-0	0-2	1-2		0-2	1-1
Linfield FC	3-1	3-1	1-1	3-1	3-1	2-2	2-0	4-1	4-1	1-1		3-0
Portadown FC	4-2	1-1	1-2	1-4	2-3	5-2	1-1	2-4	1-2	1-2	0-3	

	Irish League	Pd	Wn	Dw	Ls	GF	GA	Pts
1.	BELFAST CELTIC FC (BELFAST)	22	19	1	2	84	26	39
2.	Linfield FC (Belfast)	22	15	5	2	55	19	35
3.	Ballymena United FC (Ballymena)	22	10	7	5	52	38	27
4.	Distillery FC (Belfast)	22	12	2	8	35	32	26
5.	Glentoran FC (Belfast)	22	9	8	5	44	29	26
6.	Coleraine FC (Coleraine)	22	8	6	8	48	46	22
7.	Glenavon FC (Lurgan)	22	8	6	8	45	45	22
8.	Ards FC (Newtownards)	22	7	4	11	37	54	18
9.	Cliftonville FC (Belfast)	22	7	4	11	36	47	18
10.	Bangor FC (Bangor)	22	6	4	12	36	55	16
11.	Portadown FC (Portadown)	22	3	3	16	31	60	9
12.	Derry City FC (Londonderry)	22	2	2	18	18	70	6
		264	106	52	106	521	521	264

Top goalscorer 1947-48

1) James JONES   (Belfast Celtic FC)   28

Note: The match Bangor FC 2-5 Celtic FC was abandoned after 76 minutes, but the result was allowed to stand.

No clubs promoted or relegated

IRISH CUP FINAL   (Celtic Park, Belfast)

LINFIELD FC (BELFAST)   3-0   Coleraine FC (Coleraine)

Thompson, O'Connor o.g., Simpson

Linfield: A. Russell, McCune, McMichael, Liggett, Bryson, Walsh, Thompson, Bardsley, Simpson, J. Russell, McKenna.

Coleraine: K. McAlinden, O'Connor, Gilmore, Masters, McCavana, Doherty, O'Reilly, Nolan, Clarke, McDowell, Mahood.

Semi-finals

| Coleraine FC (Coleraine) | 3-3, 3-2 | Belfast Celtic FC (Belfast) |
| Linfield FC (Belfast) | 5-1 | Glenavon FC (Lurgan) |

Quarter-finals

Belfast Celtic FC (Belfast)	4-1	Brantwood FC (Belfast)
Coleraine FC (Coleraine)	1-0	Derry City FC (Londonderry)
Glenavon FC (Lurgan)	3-0	Distillery FC (Belfast)
Linfield FC (Belfast)	3-2	Bangor FC (Bangor)

1948-49

Irish League 1948-49	Ards	Ballymena U.	Bangor	Belfast Celtic	Cliftonville	Coleraine	Derry City	Distillery	Glenavon	Glentoran	Linfield	Portadown
Ards FC	■	8-0	2-4	4-4	1-2	7-0	3-1	0-1	0-2	2-1	0-4	2-2
Ballymena United FC	1-0	■	1-1	0-5	3-4	5-2	3-2	7-5	0-0	1-1	0-3	1-1
Bangor FC	2-3	2-2	■	0-1	2-1	1-0	4-1	5-2	1-1	3-0	3-3	2-3
Belfast Celtic FC	4-3	3-2	3-0	■	4-3	4-0	8-0	10-2	3-1	0-3	0-1	5-1
Cliftonville FC	3-2	1-1	2-2	2-5	■	6-0	1-1	2-1	5-2	1-0	1-3	5-0
Coleraine FC	4-1	1-2	3-1	1-0	3-0	■	1-2	0-6	1-1	1-3	0-2	2-4
Derry City FC	2-3	1-2	3-1	4-3	2-1	7-1	■	2-2	1-2	0-1	1-3	3-2
Distillery FC	2-1	6-2	5-0	1-2	0-1	2-0	2-3	■	2-0	2-1	3-2	2-2
Glenavon FC	1-2	2-2	4-2	1-0	2-2	4-1	4-1	2-2	■	1-2	0-3	2-2
Glentoran FC	2-0	4-2	2-1	0-0	2-0	3-2	2-2	4-1	7-1	■	1-4	2-1
Linfield FC	5-1	4-2	1-2	1-1	0-0	3-1	3-0	5-2	1-1	2-0	■	3-1
Portadown FC	2-1	2-0	2-4	2-4	2-1	2-1	0-1	5-0	3-1	1-4	1-2	■

	Irish League	Pd	Wn	Dw	Ls	GF	GA	Pts	
1.	LINFIELD FC (BELFAST)	22	16	4	2	58	21	36	
2.	Belfast Celtic FC (Belfast)	22	14	3	5	69	32	31	#
3.	Glentoran FC (Belfast)	22	13	3	6	45	28	29	
4.	Cliftonville FC (Belfast)	22	9	5	8	44	38	23	
5.	Bangor FC (Bangor)	22	8	5	9	43	45	21	
6.	Distillery FC (Belfast)	22	9	3	10	51	56	21	
7.	Portadown FC (Portadown)	22	8	4	10	41	48	20	
8.	Glenavon FC (Lurgan)	22	6	8	8	35	43	20	
9.	Derry City FC (Londonderry)	22	8	3	11	40	52	19	
10.	Ballymena United FC (Ballymena)	22	6	7	9	39	58	19	
11.	Ards FC (Newtownards)	22	7	2	13	46	49	16	
12.	Coleraine FC (Coleraine)	22	4	1	17	25	66	9	
		264	108	48	108	536	536	624	

\# Belfast Celtic FC (Belfast) resigned from the league as a result of "trouble" at some of their matches, including the Boxing Day match in which Celtic player Jimmy Jones had his leg broken after being attacked by spectators.

Top goalscorer 1948-49

1) William SIMPSON   (Linfield FC)   19

Elected: Crusaders FC (Belfast)

IRISH CUP FINAL   (Windsor Park, Belfast – 16/04/1949)

DERRY CITY FC (LONDONDERRY)   3-1   Glentoran FC (Belfast)

Colvan, Cannon, Hermon   *Peacock*

Derry: Muir, Cully, Brennan, Doherty, Ferris, McCreary, Hermon, Aitken, Cannon, Colvan, Kelly.
Glentoran: Moore, Neill, McCarthy, Ferran, Hughes, Blanchflower, Nimmick, Peacock, McFarlane, Kerr, Feeney.

Semi-finals

Derry City FC (Londonderry)	2-0	Distillery FC (Belfast)
Glentoran FC (Belfast)	2-2, 1-1, 3-0	Portadown FC (Portadown)

Quarter-finals

Cliftonville FC (Belfast)	1-3	Glentoran FC (Belfast)
Derry City FC (Londonderry)	1-1, 3-3, 1-1, 1-0	Bangor FC (Bangor)
Distillery FC (Belfast)	2-1	Coleraine FC (Coleraine)
Portadown FC (Portadown)	3-1	Glenavon FC (Lurgan)

1949-50

Irish League 1949-50	Ards	Ballymena U.	Bangor	Cliftonville	Coleraine	Crusaders	Derry City	Distillery	Glenavon	Glentoran	Linfield	Portadown
Ards FC	■	1-1	2-2	0-0	3-1	5-2	0-1	2-2	0-2	3-4	0-2	1-1
Ballymena United FC	0-0	■	1-2	6-0	4-1	1-3	1-1	0-3	1-1	1-5	1-3	1-2
Bangor FC	1-2	3-0	■	1-3	2-1	1-2	2-3	2-3	0-1	0-4	0-2	7-0
Cliftonville FC	6-0	2-2	1-2	■	1-3	2-7	0-3	1-4	2-4	0-6	1-4	3-3
Coleraine FC	1-0	0-1	2-4	3-0	■	2-2	3-6	1-3	6-4	0-5	2-3	3-2
Crusaders FC	2-6	0-1	0-4	0-5	2-2	■	0-4	1-1	4-1	0-4	2-2	2-3
Derry City FC	1-3	5-1	2-0	3-0	0-0	2-0	■	2-4	0-1	1-1	2-2	1-0
Distillery FC	1-2	2-1	1-1	4-1	3-1	2-1	1-2	■	5-1	1-4	0-2	1-0
Glenavon FC	3-0	3-1	0-1	2-2	4-0	9-0	6-2	3-2	■	2-3	1-2	1-1
Glentoran FC	2-1	5-0	1-0	4-2	2-1	4-2	2-0	2-3	3-1	■	2-3	2-1
Linfield FC	3-1	6-1	4-2	2-1	7-2	4-1	1-2	1-0	2-0	1-1	■	2-2
Portadown FC	0-2	1-3	1-1	2-1	3-3	4-4	1-1	0-2	1-1	2-4	3-6	■

Play-off

LINFIELD FC (BELFAST)	2-0	Glentoran FC (Belfast)

	Irish League	Pd	Wn	Dw	Ls	GF	GA	Pts
1.	Linfield FC (Belfast)	22	17	4	1	64	27	38
1.	Glentoran FC (Belfast)	22	18	2	2	70	25	38
3.	Distillery FC (Belfast)	22	13	3	6	48	31	29
4.	Derry City FC (Londonderry)	22	12	5	5	44	29	29
5.	Glenavon FC (Lurgan)	22	10	4	8	51	38	24
6.	Ards FC (Newtownards)	22	7	6	9	34	38	20
7.	Bangor FC (Bangor)	22	8	3	11	38	36	19
8.	Ballymena United FC (Ballymena)	22	5	5	12	29	49	15
9.	Portadown FC (Portadown)	22	3	9	10	33	52	15
10.	Coleraine FC (Coleraine)	22	5	4	13	38	61	14
11.	Crusaders FC (Belfast)	22	4	5	13	37	69	13
12.	Cliftonville FC (Belfast)	22	3	4	15	34	65	10
		264	105	54	105	520	520	264

No club promoted or relegated

Top goalscorer 1949-50
1) Samuel HUGHES (Glentoran FC) 23

IRISH CUP FINAL (Windsor Park, Belfast – 22/04/1950)
LINFIELD FC (BELFAST) 2-1 Distillery FC (Belfast)
Thompson, McDowell *Mycock*

Linfield: Russell, McCune, Houston, Smyth, Hamill, Walsh, Thompson, Currie, Simpson, McDowell, Dickson.
Distillery: Smyth, Wilson, Mills, Casement, Lonsdale, Gray, Dodds, Mulholland, McClinton, Mycock, Kelly.

Semi-finals
Distillery FC (Belfast)	5-1	Linfield Swifts FC (Belfast)
Linfield FC (Belfast)	1-0	Derry City FC (Londonderry)

Quarter-finals
Crusaders FC (Belfast)	1-7	Distillery FC (Belfast)
Derry City FC (Londonderry)	2-0	Ards FC (Newtownards)
Linfield FC (Belfast)	3-0	Glentoran FC (Belfast)
Linfield Swifts FC (Belfast)	3-0	Bangor FC (Bangor)

1950-51

Irish League 1950-51	Ards	Ballymena U.	Bangor	Cliftonville	Coleraine	Crusaders	Derry City	Distillery	Glenavon	Glentoran	Linfield	Portadown
Ards FC		1-1	3-0	3-0	1-3	1-2	1-2	3-5	1-2	1-5	0-3	3-2
Ballymena United FC	4-2		0-2	4-0	2-3	1-2	2-1	2-2	1-5	0-2	3-2	0-2
Bangor FC	1-1	4-1		4-3	1-5	0-3	2-2	1-2	0-1	1-6	3-5	1-4
Cliftonville FC	3-1	2-0	4-0		2-3	3-2	2-0	2-3	1-0	0-4	0-2	4-4
Coleraine FC	5-0	3-0	3-1	6-1		6-1	4-1	0-3	1-1	1-0	1-0	2-0
Crusaders FC	8-1	3-3	1-2	4-4	4-2		3-2	1-1	1-4	1-1	1-1	1-0
Derry City FC	3-2	3-1	1-1	3-2	1-0	0-1		1-1	0-3	1-2	0-6	1-0
Distillery FC	2-1	1-2	6-0	2-3	2-2	2-0	3-1		1-4	1-5	0-1	3-1
Glenavon FC	4-0	4-0	2-0	4-2	6-2	4-0	1-1	6-2		1-3	1-1	2-7
Glentoran FC	7-2	2-0	2-1	5-3	3-2	4-1	4-1	2-1	3-0		1-1	3-0
Linfield FC	3-0	1-1	3-2	3-0	2-1	6-0	3-2	4-2	3-1	2-1		4-2
Portadown FC	1-0	7-2	4-1	3-1	3-0	3-2	6-0	3-0	1-2	0-2	2-1	

	Irish League	Pd	Wn	Dw	Ls	GF	GA	Pts
1.	GLENTORAN FC (BELFAST)	22	18	2	2	66	21	38
2.	Linfield FC (Belfast)	22	15	4	3	57	24	34
3.	Glenavon FC (Lurgan)	22	14	3	5	58	31	31
4.	Coleraine FC (Coleraine)	22	13	2	7	55	35	28
5.	Portadown FC (Portadown)	22	12	1	9	55	35	25
6.	Distillery FC (Belfast)	22	9	4	9	45	44	22
7.	Crusaders FC (Belfast)	22	8	5	9	42	51	21
8.	Cliftonville FC (Belfast)	22	7	2	13	42	60	16
9.	Derry City FC (Londonderry)	22	6	4	12	27	50	16
10.	Ballymena United FC (Ballymena)	22	5	4	13	30	54	14
11.	Bangor FC (Bangor)	22	4	3	15	28	62	11
12.	Ards FC (Newtownards)	22	3	2	17	28	66	8
		264	114	36	114	533	533	264

Top goalscorers 1950-51

1) Walter ALLEN (Portadown FC) 23
   Samuel HUGHES (Glentoran FC) 23

No clubs promoted or relegated

IRISH CUP FINAL   (Windsor Park, Belfast – 28/04/1951)

GLENTORAN FC (BELFAST)   3-1   Ballymena United FC (Ballymena)

S. Hughes 2, Williamson   *Currie*

Glentoran: Moore, Dunlop, McCarthy, Mulholland, T. Hughes, Ferran, Cunningham, Ewing, S. Hughes, Williamson, Feeney.

Ballymena: Rodgers, Trevorrow, Barr, Gray, Murphy, Douglas, Morrison, Anderson, Ewart, O'Hara, Currie.

Semi-finals

Ballymena United FC (Ballymena)	2-1	Portadown FC (Portadown)
Glentoran FC (Belfast)	3-1	Linfield FC (Belfast)

Quarter-finals

Ards FC (Newtownards)	0-1	Portadown FC (Portadown)
Cliftonville FC (Belfast)	2-2, 0-1	Ballymena United FC (Ballymena)
Glentoran FC (Belfast)	3-0	Brantwood FC (Belfast)
Linfield FC (Belfast)	0-0, 3-2	Crusaders FC (Belfast)

1951-52

Irish League 1951-52	Ards	Ballymena U.	Bangor	Cliftonville	Coleraine	Crusaders	Derry City	Distillery	Glenavon	Glentoran	Linfield	Portadown
Ards FC	■	4-1	1-2	0-0	3-5	3-0	4-1	2-2	3-4	1-3	3-1	1-2
Ballymena United FC	3-1	■	4-0	2-1	1-1	3-1	2-1	3-3	0-1	2-2	2-0	0-2
Bangor FC	2-3	5-4	■	2-1	1-1	0-2	1-1	0-0	0-3	1-1	1-6	3-2
Cliftonville FC	4-3	2-2	1-0	■	1-3	2-1	2-2	1-2	1-4	2-3	0-1	2-1
Coleraine FC	0-1	5-1	4-2	3-1	■	7-2	2-1	2-1	1-1	2-1	1-0	1-3
Crusaders FC	1-3	1-1	5-2	1-0	1-1	■	3-0	0-1	0-3	0-1	0-5	2-1
Derry City FC	4-0	2-2	0-1	3-0	3-2	2-3	■	0-2	0-3	3-1	2-1	2-1
Distillery FC	4-3	2-2	2-0	1-1	0-0	1-2	2-2	■	1-0	3-0	2-2	2-1
Glenavon FC	1-1	2-1	1-0	6-2	5-0	5-0	5-0	1-2	■	8-3	5-0	2-2
Glentoran FC	8-1	1-3	6-0	3-1	3-2	4-1	4-0	3-0	1-2	■	4-3	2-2
Linfield FC	0-0	2-2	1-2	1-0	0-1	1-1	1-1	1-1	0-3	1-0	■	1-1
Portadown FC	1-2	5-0	2-2	3-2	1-0	5-5	2-3	2-1	1-2	1-3	2-1	■

	Irish League	**Pd**	**Wn**	**Dw**	**Ls**	**GF**	**GA**	**Pts**	
1.	GLENAVON FC (LURGAN)	22	17	3	2	67	19	37	
2.	Coleraine FC (Coleraine)	22	11	5	6	44	33	27	PO
3.	Distillery FC (Belfast)	22	9	9	4	35	28	27	PO
4.	Glentoran FC (Belfast)	22	12	3	7	57	39	27	PO
5.	Ballymena United FC (Ballymena)	22	7	8	7	41	44	22	
6.	Portadown FC (Portadown)	22	8	5	9	43	39	21	
7.	Ards FC (Newtownards)	22	8	4	10	43	40	20	
8.	Derry City FC (Londonderry)	22	7	5	10	33	44	19	
9.	Crusaders FC (Belfast)	22	7	4	11	32	51	18	
10.	Linfield FC (Belfast)	22	5	7	10	29	34	17	
11.	Bangor FC (Bangor)	22	6	5	11	27	51	17	
12.	Cliftonville FC (Belfast)	22	4	4	14	27	47	12	
		264	101	62	101	478	478	264	

2nd Place Play-off

Distillery FC (Belfast)   1-1   Coleraine FC (Coleraine)
(Coleraine took 2nd place on better goal-average in the league)
Glentoran FC (Belfast)   1-2   Distillery FC (Belfast)
Coleraine FC (Coleraine) received a bye

Top goalscorer 1951-52

1) James JONES   (Glenavon FC)   27

No clubs promoted or relegated

IRISH CUP FINAL (Windsor Park, Belfast – 26/04/1952)

ARDS FC (NEWTOWNARDS)   1-0   Glentoran FC (Belfast)

Thompson

Ards: O'Connell, Moore, Hamill, Tucker, Robinson, Corbett, Lawther, Thompson, Drake, McDowell, Walker.
Glentoran: Clarke, Lucas, King, Neill, T. Hughes, McFarlane, Lowry, Ewing, S. Hughes, Williamson, Feeney.

Semi-finals

Ards FC (Newtownards)	1-0	Ballymena United FC (Ballymena)
Glentoran FC (Belfast)	0-0, 2-2, 0-0, 1-0	Linfield FC (Belfast)

Quarter-finals

Brantwood FC (Belfast)	0-1	Ards FC (Newtownards)
Cliftonville FC (Belfast)	2-2, 0-3	Ballymena United FC (Ballymena)
Glentoran FC (Belfast)	3-3, 1-1, 3-0	Glenavon FC (Lurgan)
Linfield FC (Belfast)	4-0	Portadown FC (Portadown)

1952-53

Irish League 1952-53	Ards	Ballymena U.	Bangor	Cliftonville	Coleraine	Crusaders	Derry City	Distillery	Glenavon	Glentoran	Linfield	Portadown
Ards FC		1-3	2-1	3-1	6-4	1-1	3-0	0-1	1-0	1-1	1-1	0-0
Ballymena United FC	4-0		3-1	6-1	1-1	5-3	3-0	4-0	4-1	0-1	2-2	4-0
Bangor FC	2-2	1-2		1-2	0-3	0-3	0-0	1-0	2-5	0-2	2-1	3-2
Cliftonville FC	2-1	1-4	4-1		3-2	3-1	1-0	3-2	2-1	2-4	1-4	1-4
Coleraine FC	2-2	2-1	3-1	4-0		1-1	0-3	1-2	2-1	2-5	0-2	2-1
Crusaders FC	2-1	1-2	5-2	4-2	2-2		4-0	3-0	1-2	4-2	1-1	2-2
Derry City FC	1-3	3-1	4-1	2-2	0-2	3-0		2-2	2-4	2-3	1-3	3-0
Distillery FC	0-0	2-4	3-0	0-0	3-1	2-0	2-0		0-2	1-1	0-1	1-0
Glenavon FC	4-3	5-2	3-0	4-4	0-2	2-0	5-1	0-1		0-3	2-2	3-2
Glentoran FC	3-0	4-1	6-0	7-1	2-2	2-0	2-0	1-3	1-1		3-1	4-1
Linfield FC	2-0	3-0	5-1	3-0	6-1	0-0	4-0	2-0	2-0	1-1		1-1
Portadown FC	0-1	1-1	1-0	3-1	1-1	1-1	2-0	1-1	2-4	2-1	1-0	

	Irish League	Pd	Wn	Dw	Ls	GF	GA	Pts
1.	GLENTORAN FC (BELFAST)	22	14	5	3	59	25	33
2.	Linfield FC (Belfast)	22	12	7	3	47	18	31
3.	Ballymena United FC (Ballymena)	22	13	3	6	57	34	29
4.	Glenavon FC (Lurgan)	22	11	3	8	49	39	25
5.	Distillery FC (Belfast)	22	9	5	8	26	27	23
6.	Coleraine FC (Coleraine)	22	8	6	8	40	43	22
7.	Crusaders FC (Belfast)	22	7	7	8	39	36	21
8.	Ards FC (Newtownards)	22	7	7	8	32	35	21
9.	Cliftonville FC (Belfast)	22	8	3	11	37	61	19
10.	Portadown FC (Portadown)	22	6	7	9	28	35	19
11.	Derry City FC (Londonderry)	22	5	3	14	27	47	13
12.	Bangor FC (Bangor)	22	3	2	17	20	61	8
		264	103	58	103	461	461	264

Top goalscorer 1952-53

1) Samuel HUGHES   (Glentoran FC)   28

No clubs promoted or relegated

IRISH CUP FINAL   (Solitude, Belfast)

LINFIELD FC (BELFAST)   5-0   Coleraine FC (Coleraine)
Thompson 2, Walker, McDowell, Dickson
Linfield: Russell, Keith, Lewis, G. Nixon, Hamill, McMillan, Thompson, McDowell, Walker, Dickson, Lunn.
Coleraine: Watt, Montgomery, Canning, Brolly, McCavana, McDermott, Cuneen, Colvan, O'Kane, Doherty, McCormick.

Semi-finals

Coleraine FC (Coleraine)	5-0	Glentoran FC (Belfast) 2nd XI
Linfield FC (Belfast)	2-1	Glentoran FC (Belfast)

Quarter-finals

Ards FC (Newtownards)	4-5	Glentoran FC (Belfast)
Crusaders FC (Belfast)	0-1	Coleraine FC (Coleraine)
Glentoran FC (Belfast) 2nd XI	2-0	Bangor FC (Bangor)
Portadown FC (Portadown)	1-2	Linfield FC (Belfast)

1953-54

Irish League 1953-54	Ards	Ballymena U.	Bangor	Cliftonville	Coleraine	Crusaders	Derry City	Distillery	Glenavon	Glentoran	Linfield	Portadown
Ards FC	■	1-2	1-3	4-2	1-4	3-2	3-2	1-0	3-4	0-4	1-2	4-1
Ballymena United FC	2-0	■	2-0	2-0	5-1	1-2	5-2	1-1	4-4	1-4	2-2	1-4
Bangor FC	0-2	2-1	■	1-0	5-1	4-2	2-1	1-0	1-3	2-0	1-1	3-0
Cliftonville FC	3-2	0-3	4-2	■	1-6	2-3	2-3	1-3	1-5	1-6	1-4	0-2
Coleraine FC	1-1	1-2	1-1	5-2	■	3-3	2-1	3-2	3-0	1-1	1-1	3-2
Crusaders FC	2-0	1-1	4-0	4-0	0-6	■	5-3	3-0	1-3	1-3	4-5	4-2
Derry City FC	6-1	1-3	2-0	1-1	4-2	1-3	■	1-1	0-0	2-3	0-2	3-1
Distillery FC	2-2	4-0	6-0	1-2	5-2	3-3	3-2	■	5-2	2-3	0-1	2-2
Glenavon FC	4-2	1-2	3-1	2-0	6-1	2-4	5-1	0-1	■	5-3	4-2	4-0
Glentoran FC	2-0	4-1	3-2	5-1	4-1	5-3	1-0	2-1	5-3	■	0-2	4-1
Linfield FC	4-0	3-3	3-0	1-1	4-0	1-1	3-0	2-1	2-1	3-2	■	2-1
Portadown FC	1-0	2-3	2-3	2-1	1-1	1-4	2-0	1-2	3-7	1-3	2-6	■

	Irish League	Pd	Wn	Dw	Ls	GF	GA	Pts
1.	LINFIELD FC (BELFAST)	22	15	6	1	56	26	36
2.	Glentoran FC (Belfast)	22	17	1	4	67	34	35
3.	Glenavon FC (Lurgan)	22	13	2	7	68	45	28
4.	Ballymena United FC (Ballymena)	22	11	5	6	47	40	27
5.	Crusaders FC (Belfast)	22	11	4	7	60	49	26
6.	Bangor FC (Bangor)	22	10	2	10	34	42	22
7.	Coleraine FC (Coleraine)	22	8	6	8	49	52	22
8.	Distillery FC (Belfast)	22	8	5	9	45	36	21
9.	Ards FC (Newtownards)	22	6	2	14	32	53	14
10.	Derry City FC (Londonderry)	22	5	3	14	36	50	13
11.	Portadown FC (Portadown)	22	5	2	15	34	60	12
12.	Cliftonville FC (Belfast)	22	3	2	17	26	67	8
		264	112	40	112	554	554	264

Top goalscorer 1953-54

1) James JONES   (Glenavon FC)   32

No clubs promoted or relegated

IRISH CUP FINAL   (Windsor Park, Belfast – 24/04/1954)

DERRY CITY FC (LONDONDERRY)   2-2   Glentoran FC (Belfast)

Delaney, Brady   *Cunningham, Feeney*

IRISH CUP FINAL REPLAY   (Windsor Park, Belfast – 29/04/1954)

DERRY CITY FC (LONDONDERRY)   0-0   Glentoran FC (Belfast)

IRISH CUP FINAL 2ND REPLAY   (Windsor Park, Belfast – 10/05/1954)

DERRY CITY FC (LONDONDERRY)   1-0   Glentoran FC (Belfast)

O'Neill

Derry: Heffron, Wilson, Houston, Brolly, Curran, Smyth, Brady, Delaney, Forsythe, Toner, O'Neill.
Glentoran: Bond, McCarthy, King, Neill, Murdough, Lewis, Lowry, Scott, Hughes, Cunningham, Feeney.

Semi-finals

| Derry City FC (Londonderry) | 2-2, 2-1 | Linfield FC (Belfast) |
| Glentoran FC (Belfast) | 2-1 | Distillery FC (Belfast) |

Quarter-finals

Coleraine FC (Coleraine)	2-2, 0-1	Distillery FC (Belfast)
Derry City FC (Londonderry)	1-1, 2-0	Bangor FC (Bangor)
Glentoran FC (Belfast)	4-1	Ards FC (Newtownards)
Linfield FC (Belfast)	2-0	Ballymena United FC (Ballymena)

1954-55

Irish League 1954-55	Ards	Ballymena U.	Bangor	Cliftonville	Coleraine	Crusaders	Derry City	Distillery	Glenavon	Glentoran	Linfield	Portadown
Ards FC		4-3	5-1	4-5	6-1	4-0	4-2	4-0	0-1	3-1	1-3	3-3
Ballymena United FC	2-2		1-3	2-3	4-2	2-0	2-1	2-2	2-3	0-4	2-3	3-3
Bangor FC	1-1	2-2		0-5	2-2	3-1	2-1	2-1	1-4	2-3	2-2	2-0
Cliftonville FC	1-1	1-0	5-1		1-2	0-1	5-1	2-0	0-4	1-2	1-1	3-3
Coleraine FC	4-1	3-0	2-5	3-2		3-0	4-2	4-0	1-3	1-1	2-1	2-0
Crusaders FC	2-2	1-3	2-3	1-4	1-2		0-0	5-1	0-4	1-5	2-3	2-0
Derry City FC	0-1	1-1	2-1	2-1	5-2	0-2		1-0	1-2	2-1	1-2	1-1
Distillery FC	2-3	3-1	0-2	2-1	1-3	5-3	4-0		2-2	1-3	1-1	3-1
Glenavon FC	4-0	3-1	4-2	1-1	1-0	0-1	7-4	3-1		3-1	1-1	5-3
Glentoran FC	3-2	4-1	5-3	1-3	3-1	1-2	6-1	1-4	2-5		1-2	4-2
Linfield FC	2-2	2-0	3-2	2-0	2-1	3-0	1-0	0-0	2-0	3-0		5-2
Portadown FC	4-0	2-1	2-1	4-5	5-1	0-2	0-3	0-2	1-1	3-2	0-2	

Play-off

LINFIELD FC (BELFAST)　　　　　　　2-0　　　　　　　Glenavon FC (Lurgan)

	Irish League	Pd	Wn	Dw	Ls	GF	GA	Pts
1.	Linfield FC (Belfast)	22	15	6	1	46	21	36
1.	Glenavon FC (Lurgan)	22	16	4	2	61	27	36
3.	Cliftonville FC (Belfast)	22	10	4	8	50	38	24
4.	Ards FC (Newtownards)	22	9	6	7	53	45	24
5.	Coleraine FC (Coleraine)	22	11	2	9	46	46	24
6.	Glentoran FC (Belfast)	22	11	1	10	54	46	23
7.	Bangor FC (Bangor)	22	8	4	10	43	53	20
8.	Distillery FC (Belfast)	22	7	4	11	35	44	18
9.	Crusaders FC (Belfast)	22	7	2	13	29	48	16
10.	Portadown FC (Portadown)	22	5	5	12	39	53	15
11.	Derry City FC (Londonderry)	22	6	3	13	31	49	15
12.	Ballymena United FC (Ballymena)	22	4	5	13	35	52	13
		264	109	46	109	522	522	264

Top goalscorer 1954-55

1) Fay COYLE　　　　　　(Coleraine FC)　　　　20

No clubs promoted or relegated

IRISH CUP FINAL   (Windsor Park, Belfast – 23/04/1955)

DUNDELA FC (BELFAST)　　　　　　　3-0　　　　　　　Glenavon FC (Lurgan)

Ervine 2, Greenwood

Dundela: J. Smyth, R. Smyth, Stewart, McAuley, Lynch, Millar, Greenwood, Reid, Ervine, Kavanagh, Gourley.
Glenavon: Durkan, Greer, Armstrong, Corr, Liggett, Cush, Masters, Denver, Jones, Campbell, McVeigh.

Semi-finals

Dundela FC (Belfast)	2-1	Crusaders FC (Belfast)
Glenavon FC (Lurgan)	5-0	Glentoran FC (Belfast)

Quarter-finals

Crusaders FC (Belfast)	2-1	Linfield FC (Belfast)
Dundela FC (Belfast)	1-0	Cliftonville FC (Belfast)
Glenavon FC (Lurgan)	1-1, 1-1, 1-0	Ards FC (Newtownards)
Glentoran FC (Belfast)	2-0	Portadown FC (Portadown)

1955-56

Irish League 1955-56	Ards	Ballymena U.	Bangor	Cliftonville	Coleraine	Crusaders	Derry City	Distillery	Glenavon	Glentoran	Linfield	Portadown
Ards FC	■	4-3	2-4	3-2	1-1	5-2	1-2	3-2	1-0	2-3	0-1	4-0
Ballymena United FC	3-2	■	2-3	1-2	0-4	2-1	1-3	3-1	1-4	4-1	1-3	1-4
Bangor FC	1-1	6-2	■	4-2	4-4	8-3	4-1	2-2	4-6	4-2	0-4	2-3
Cliftonville FC	1-6	3-1	0-1	■	1-2	1-1	3-2	1-4	1-7	0-1	0-4	0-0
Coleraine FC	1-0	5-1	3-4	4-1	■	1-2	3-1	2-1	1-2	2-3	1-1	4-2
Crusaders FC	3-0	6-0	1-1	1-1	2-2	■	3-2	0-1	2-1	2-3	2-5	1-0
Derry City FC	3-1	1-2	2-1	5-2	2-2	4-1	■	2-2	1-4	1-2	1-2	1-1
Distillery FC	1-2	5-1	2-2	0-3	5-2	3-0	2-1	■	2-1	0-0	1-3	2-2
Glenavon FC	6-0	3-1	3-1	1-2	9-6	5-1	5-2	3-1	■	4-4	0-1	4-0
Glentoran FC	2-1	2-3	2-3	3-4	0-1	2-1	4-2	0-0	4-2	■	1-1	0-1
Linfield FC	2-1	1-2	4-3	4-1	2-1	3-0	3-1	5-0	1-0	1-0	■	2-0
Portadown FC	2-4	5-1	3-7	6-2	2-4	3-1	5-1	2-2	1-7	1-4	0-3	■

	Irish League	Pd	Wn	Dw	Ls	GF	GA	Pts
1.	LINFIELD FC (BELFAST)	22	19	2	1	56	16	40
2.	Glenavon FC (Lurgan)	22	14	1	7	77	38	29
3.	Bangor FC (Bangor)	22	11	5	6	69	54	27
4.	Coleraine FC (Coleraine)	22	10	5	7	56	46	25
5.	Glentoran FC (Belfast)	22	10	4	8	43	40	24
6.	Distillery FC (Belfast)	22	7	7	8	39	40	21
7.	Ards FC (Newtownards)	22	9	2	11	44	45	20
8.	Portadown FC (Portadown)	22	7	4	11	43	57	18
9.	Derry City FC (Londonderry)	22	6	4	12	42	54	16
10.	Crusaders FC (Belfast)	22	6	4	12	36	53	16
11.	Cliftonville FC (Belfast)	22	5	4	13	33	62	14
12.	Ballymena United FC (Ballymena)	22	7	-	15	36	69	14
		264	111	42	111	574	574	264

Top goalscorer 1955-56

1) James JONES (Glenavon FC) 26

No clubs promoted or relegated

IRISH CUP FINAL   (Windsor Park, Belfast – 21/04/1956)

DISTILLERY FC (BELFAST)　　　　　　2-2　　　　　　Glentoran FC (Belfast)

McEvoy, Curry　　　　　　　　　　　　　　　　　　　　　　　　*Fogarty, Nolan*

IRISH CUP FINAL REPLAY   (Windsor Park, Belfast – 26/04/1956)

DISTILLERY FC (BELFAST)　　　　　　1-1　　　　　　Glentoran FC (Belfast)

Tait　　　　　　　　　　　　　　　　　　　　　　　　　　　　　　*Nolan*

IRISH CUP FINAL 2ND REPLAY   (Windsor Park, Belfast – 30/04/1956)

DISTILLERY FC (BELFAST)　　　　　　1-0　　　　　　Glentoran FC (Belfast)

Curry

Distillery: Beare, Magee, Brennan, Twinem, Watters, Tait, Curry, Hepburn, Dugan, Dougan, Hamilton.
Glentoran: McMahon, McCarthy, Lucas, Neill, Murdough, Dubois, Lowry, Fogarty, Mulvey, Bruce, Nolan.

Semi-finals

Distillery FC (Belfast)	1-0	Cliftonville FC (Belfast)
Glentoran FC (Belfast)	4-0	Portadown FC (Portadown)

Quarter-finals

Ards FC (Newtownards)	1-2	Cliftonville FC (Belfast)
Crusaders FC (Belfast)	0-4	Distillery FC (Belfast)
Linfield FC (Belfast)	1-2	Portadown FC (Portadown)
Linfield Swifts FC (Belfast)	0-3	Glentoran FC (Belfast)

1956-57

Irish League 1956-57	Ards	Ballymena U.	Bangor	Cliftonville	Coleraine	Crusaders	Derry City	Distillery	Glenavon	Glentoran	Linfield	Portadown
Ards FC	■	2-1	5-4	4-3	5-1	3-1	4-2	8-1	1-2	3-3	1-1	4-1
Ballymena United FC	0-5	■	2-3	4-3	1-1	5-2	1-2	2-4	0-4	1-3	1-6	6-1
Bangor FC	0-3	1-1	■	3-0	2-3	1-1	5-0	6-1	0-4	1-1	4-2	1-1
Cliftonville FC	0-7	2-1	2-6	■	3-4	0-2	4-1	1-6	1-1	2-4	1-4	1-3
Coleraine FC	2-1	4-1	4-2	2-2	■	2-5	2-1	2-3	5-2	3-1	3-3	4-2
Crusaders FC	1-0	3-1	0-1	4-1	2-3	■	3-1	0-2	2-1	3-1	0-5	4-2
Derry City FC	0-2	3-0	1-1	4-1	2-0	4-1	■	4-1	2-2	2-1	3-4	2-2
Distillery FC	3-1	5-1	3-2	2-0	1-5	2-2	2-0	■	1-3	2-2	1-4	2-2
Glenavon FC	1-0	5-0	3-0	6-1	4-0	2-0	7-1	8-1	■	3-1	3-2	5-0
Glentoran FC	1-0	7-2	3-1	2-1	3-2	3-1	4-0	3-0	2-1	■	1-3	5-4
Linfield FC	2-2	3-1	2-1	5-1	3-1	4-0	3-2	1-1	1-1	2-2	■	3-2
Portadown FC	4-4	3-3	2-2	4-1	2-1	2-1	2-4	5-3	1-3	2-3	0-4	■

	Irish League	Pd	Wn	Dw	Ls	GF	GA	Pts
1.	GLENAVON FC (LURGAN)	22	16	3	3	71	22	35
2.	Linfield FC (Belfast)	22	14	6	2	67	32	34
3.	Glentoran FC (Belfast)	22	13	4	5	56	39	30
4.	Ards FC (Newtownards)	22	12	4	6	65	34	28
5.	Coleraine FC (Coleraine)	22	11	3	8	54	51	25
6.	Distillery FC (Belfast)	22	9	4	9	47	62	22
7.	Bangor FC (Bangor)	22	7	6	9	47	44	20
8.	Crusaders FC (Belfast)	22	9	2	11	38	46	20
9.	Derry City FC (Londonderry)	22	8	3	11	41	52	19
10.	Portadown FC (Portadown)	22	5	6	11	47	66	16
11.	Ballymena United FC (Ballymena)	22	3	3	16	35	72	9
12.	Cliftonville FC (Belfast)	22	2	2	18	31	79	6
		264	109	46	109	599	599	264

Top goalscorer 1956-57

1) James JONES   (Glenavon FC)   33

No clubs promoted or relegated

IRISH CUP FINAL   (Windsor Park, Belfast – 13/04/1957)

GLENAVON FC (LURGAN)   2-0   Derry City FC (Londonderry)

Houston o.g., Jones

Glenavon: Rea, Armstrong, Lyske, Corr, Davis, Cush, Wilson, McVeigh, Jones, Campbell, Elwood.
Derry: Heffron, Kinnen, Houston, Brolly, Travers, Smyth, Wright, Crossan, Campbell, P. Coyle, Nash.

Semi-finals

| Derry City FC (Londonderry) | 0-0, 1-0 | Linfield FC (Belfast) |
| Glenavon FC (Lurgan) | 1-0 | Distillery FC (Belfast) |

Quarter-finals

Derry City FC (Londonderry)	3-0	Ards FC (Newtownards)
Distillery FC (Belfast)	1-1, 4-4, +:-	Portadown FC (Portadown)
Glentoran FC (Belfast)	2-2, 1-2	Linfield FC (Belfast)
Newry Town FC (Newry)	1-4	Glentoran FC (Belfast)

1957-58

Irish League 1957-58	Ards	Ballymena U.	Bangor	Cliftonville	Coleraine	Crusaders	Derry City	Distillery	Glenavon	Glentoran	Linfield	Portadown
Ards FC		3-0	5-2	7-2	3-4	6-1	2-1	2-2	3-4	5-1	3-0	3-2
Ballymena United FC	1-1		1-3	4-0	2-2	4-2	2-1	3-2	3-2	5-1	3-1	1-0
Bangor FC	1-2	0-2		5-1	2-1	1-1	4-0	2-1	1-2	2-9	1-2	2-0
Cliftonville FC	3-4	2-4	1-1		4-4	4-3	0-2	3-2	0-1	2-6	1-7	1-2
Coleraine FC	1-3	4-2	6-1	2-1		1-3	1-0	1-2	2-8	2-1	4-3	2-3
Crusaders FC	1-4	5-2	1-2	4-2	2-4		2-4	2-3	1-0	0-1	2-6	0-3
Derry City FC	0-1	1-2	4-1	6-1	2-2	2-1		2-2	2-3	0-1	3-2	2-2
Distillery FC	1-1	0-5	2-3	3-2	2-2	0-1	2-2		2-4	1-3	1-0	0-6
Glenavon FC	0-3	2-1	5-0	6-3	2-1	1-0	7-1	3-0		5-1	2-3	5-2
Glentoran FC	0-1	3-1	3-0	7-0	5-1	5-2	5-1	3-2	0-1		0-2	2-1
Linfield FC	4-4	5-1	5-3	4-1	3-3	2-3	0-2	3-3	4-1	3-1		3-4
Portadown FC	1-2	1-2	3-3	2-1	5-3	0-1	1-2	0-3	2-3	1-1	1-1	

	Irish League	Pd	Wn	Dw	Ls	GF	GA	Pts
1.	ARDS FC (NEWTOWNARDS)	22	16	4	2	68	32	36
2.	Glenavon FC (Lurgan)	22	17	-	5	67	35	34
3.	Ballymena United FC (Ballymena)	22	13	2	7	51	41	28
4.	Glentoran FC (Belfast)	22	12	1	9	50	38	25
5.	Linfield FC (Belfast)	22	11	3	8	68	48	25
6.	Bangor FC (Bangor)	22	9	3	10	40	48	21
7.	Coleraine FC (Coleraine)	22	8	5	9	53	59	21
8.	Derry City FC (Londonderry)	22	8	4	10	40	44	20
9.	Portadown FC (Portadown)	22	7	3	12	43	48	17
10.	Distillery FC (Belfast)	22	5	6	11	36	53	16
11.	Crusaders FC (Belfast)	22	7	1	14	38	57	15
12.	Cliftonville FC (Belfast)	22	2	2	18	35	86	6
		264	115	34	115	589	589	264

Top goalscorer 1957-58

1) Jackie MILBURN   (Linfield FC)   29

No clubs promoted or relegated

IRISH CUP FINAL   (The Oval, Belfast)

BALLYMENA UNITED FC (BALLYMENA)   2-0   Linfield FC (Belfast)

McGhee, Russell

Ballymena: Bond, Trevorrow, Johnston, Brown, Lowry, Cubitt, Egan, Forsyth, McGhee, McCrae, Russell.
Linfield: Russell, Gilliland, Graham, Rodgers, Hamill, Fletcher, Robinson, Parke, Milburn, Dickson, Braithwaite.

Semi-finals

Ballymena United FC (Ballymena)	3-0	Derry City FC (Londonderry)
Linfield FC (Belfast)	4-2	Glenavon FC (Lurgan)

Quarter-finals

Ballymena United FC (Ballymena)	3-1	Ards FC (Newtownards)
Bangor FC (Bangor)	2-3	Derry City FC (Londonderry)
Glenavon FC (Lurgan)	3-1	Linfield Swifts FC (Belfast)
Linfield FC (Belfast)	6-4	Portadown FC (Portadown)

1958-59

Irish League 1958-59	Ards	Ballymena U.	Bangor	Cliftonville	Coleraine	Crusaders	Derry City	Distillery	Glenavon	Glentoran	Linfield	Portadown
Ards FC	■	1-4	1-0	7-0	5-3	1-2	3-1	3-5	2-3	2-3	0-3	1-0
Ballymena United FC	3-3	■	2-0	5-0	4-2	4-1	2-3	4-2	0-0	2-3	2-1	1-3
Bangor FC	2-3	0-2	■	1-0	5-0	0-3	3-0	1-1	0-2	3-2	2-3	4-3
Cliftonville FC	1-5	4-1	2-4	■	0-3	1-3	0-3	3-1	2-5	0-2	0-4	1-8
Coleraine FC	1-2	4-0	3-3	6-1	■	4-0	2-0	2-2	2-1	1-1	4-0	1-2
Crusaders FC	5-1	0-2	3-0	3-0	0-1	■	2-5	4-4	2-3	2-1	3-2	3-1
Derry City FC	0-6	1-4	1-0	1-1	0-1	2-1	■	1-3	1-6	0-4	1-4	2-1
Distillery FC	1-1	3-4	2-0	5-1	4-4	2-2	3-1	■	1-2	2-6	2-3	0-3
Glenavon FC	2-3	3-1	2-1	6-0	3-0	1-1	2-2	7-0	■	7-1	3-6	2-3
Glentoran FC	1-1	4-0	3-1	8-3	3-2	3-3	2-0	3-3	1-2	■	2-1	0-1
Linfield FC	5-1	5-0	4-0	9-0	3-1	1-2	2-0	3-0	2-0	4-2	■	1-0
Portadown FC	6-1	3-4	5-0	2-0	6-0	1-1	3-2	5-3	1-4	1-1	2-3	■

	Irish League	**Pd**	**Wn**	**Dw**	**Ls**	**GF**	**GA**	**Pts**
1.	LINFIELD FC (BELFAST)	22	17	-	5	69	27	34
2.	Glenavon FC (Lurgan)	22	14	3	5	66	32	31
3.	Glentoran FC (Belfast)	22	11	5	6	56	41	27
4.	Portadown FC (Portadown)	22	12	2	8	60	35	26
5.	Ballymena United FC (Ballymena)	22	12	2	8	51	46	26
6.	Crusaders FC (Belfast)	22	10	5	7	46	40	25
7.	Ards FC (Newtownards)	22	10	3	9	53	51	23
8.	Coleraine FC (Coleraine)	22	9	4	9	47	45	22
9.	Distillery FC (Belfast)	22	5	7	10	49	63	17
10.	Bangor FC (Bangor)	22	6	2	14	30	47	14
11.	Derry City FC (Londonderry)	22	6	2	14	27	55	14
12.	Cliftonville FC (Belfast)	22	2	1	19	20	92	5
		264	114	36	114	574	574	264

Top goalscorer 1958-59

1) Jackie MILBURN   (Linfield FC)   26

No clubs promoted or relegated

IRISH CUP FINAL   (Windsor Park, Belfast – 18/04/1959)

GLENAVON FC (LURGAN)   1-1   Ballymena United FC (Ballymena)
Jones   *Lowry pen.*

Glenavon: Rea, Armstrong, Cummings, Lawther, Forde, Hughes, Wilson, Magee, Jones, Campbell, McVeigh.
Ballymena: Bond, Trevorrow, Johnston, Brown, Lowry, Cubitt, Walsh, McCrae, McGhee, Russell, Clarke

IRISH CUP FINAL REPLAY   (Windsor Park, Belfast – 29/04/1959)

GLENAVON FC (LURGAN)   2-0   Ballymena United FC (Ballymena)
Wilson, Magee

Ballymena: Bond, Trevorrow, Johnston, Brown, Lowry, Cubitt, Walsh, McCrae, McGhee, Russell, Clarke.
Glenavon: Rea, Armstrong, Cummings, Masters, Forde, Hughes, Wilson, Magee, Jones, Campbell, McVeigh.

Semi-finals

Ballymena United FC (Ballymena)	2-1	Linfield FC (Belfast)
Glenavon FC (Lurgan)	5-1	Distillery FC (Belfast)

Quarter-finals

Distillery FC (Belfast)	1-0	Derry City FC Londonderry)
Glenavon FC (Lurgan)	2-0	Glentoran FC (Belfast)
Linfield FC (Belfast)	4-2	Ards FC (Newtownards)
Portadown FC (Portadown)	1-1, 0-1	Ballymena United FC (Ballymena)

1959-60

Irish League 1959-60	Ards	Ballymena U.	Bangor	Cliftonville	Coleraine	Crusaders	Derry City	Distillery	Glenavon	Glentoran	Linfield	Portadown
Ards FC		1-1	1-4	4-1	2-0	4-1	2-1	4-5	2-0	1-2	2-5	2-0
Ballymena United FC	2-1		2-0	3-1	4-4	1-2	2-0	1-3	0-4	5-3	2-4	2-2
Bangor FC	5-1	1-0		3-2	1-2	2-2	3-3	0-2	1-3	2-2	3-2	1-2
Cliftonville FC	2-0	0-4	1-3		1-0	0-1	0-4	0-1	0-1	0-5	3-7	0-2
Coleraine FC	1-3	2-5	4-3	4-3		3-2	1-0	1-3	0-6	1-2	1-1	2-4
Crusaders FC	2-2	3-2	1-0	4-1	5-0		3-0	1-1	1-3	1-3	5-1	1-1
Derry City FC	1-4	6-1	2-4	5-0	1-2	5-2		1-0	0-2	0-2	1-3	2-2
Distillery FC	3-0	1-2	0-0	5-2	5-2	2-3	3-2		3-5	1-2	4-4	4-1
Glenavon FC	4-0	1-4	5-2	5-1	4-2	5-0	2-4	1-2		0-0	2-1	1-0
Glentoran FC	5-1	2-0	3-1	3-1	4-1	3-0	2-2	1-2	3-4		7-3	1-1
Linfield FC	2-0	4-1	2-0	7-1	2-1	1-1	2-0	3-3	2-5	3-2		1-1
Portadown FC	0-0	1-5	3-0	4-2	1-1	4-2	2-1	2-2	0-4	1-3	1-3	

Irish League	Pd	Wn	Dw	Ls	GF	GA	Pts
1. GLENAVON FC (LURGAN)	22	17	1	4	67	28	35
2. Glentoran FC (Belfast)	22	14	4	4	60	31	32
3. Distillery FC (Belfast)	22	12	5	5	55	38	29
4. Linfield FC (Belfast)	22	12	5	5	63	46	29
5. Ballymena United FC (Ballymena)	22	10	3	9	49	46	23
6. Crusaders FC (Belfast)	22	9	5	8	43	44	23
7. Portadown FC (Portadown)	22	7	8	7	35	40	22
8. Ards FC (Newtownards)	22	8	3	11	37	47	19
9. Bangor FC (Bangor)	22	7	4	11	39	45	18
10. Derry City FC (Londonderry)	22	6	3	13	41	44	15
11. Coleraine FC (Coleraine)	22	6	3	13	35	62	15
12. Cliftonville FC (Belfast)	22	2	-	20	22	75	4
	264	110	44	110	546	546	264

Top goalscorer 1959-60

1) James JONES   (Glenavon FC)   29

No clubs promoted or relegated

IRISH CUP FINAL   (The Oval, Belfast)

LINFIELD FC (BELFAST)   5-1   Ards FC (Newtownards)
Ferguson 2, Milburn 2, Gough   *Welsh*

Linfield: Irvine, Gilliland, Graham, Wilson, Hamill, Gough, Stewart, Dickson, Milburn, Ferguson, Braithwaite.
Ards: Moffatt, Patterson, Hunter, McCullough, Reynolds, Hamill, Humphries, Welsh, McCrory, Ewing, Boyd.

Semi-finals

Ards FC (Newtownards)	1-0	Derry City FC (Londonderry)
Linfield FC (Belfast)	5-2	Distillery FC (Belfast)

Quarter-finals

Distillery FC (Belfast)	5-2	Ballymena United FC (Ballymena)
Glentoran FC (Belfast)	1-1, 2-3	Derry City FC (Londonderry)
Linfield FC (Belfast)	5-3	Glenavon FC (Lurgan)
Portadown FC (Portadown) 2nd XI	2-4	Ards FC (Newtownards)

1960-61

Irish League 1960-61	Ards	Ballymena U.	Bangor	Cliftonville	Coleraine	Crusaders	Derry City	Distillery	Glenavon	Glentoran	Linfield	Portadown
Ards FC		1-1	4-2	6-3	7-2	2-0	5-1	3-0	3-2	2-1	1-4	0-2
Ballymena United FC	1-1		5-2	8-2	1-3	1-1	3-0	1-5	6-0	2-1	2-1	3-3
Bangor FC	1-6	2-0		6-4	5-5	1-4	2-3	1-4	1-2	1-4	0-3	3-3
Cliftonville FC	1-5	1-3	4-2		2-4	3-1	0-1	1-6	2-3	0-3	1-4	1-3
Coleraine FC	1-3	0-1	4-7	5-0		1-1	2-1	1-5	2-3	1-1	3-5	1-2
Crusaders FC	1-2	1-0	1-1	2-1	2-1		4-1	1-0	0-0	1-2	0-0	1-3
Derry City FC	3-6	1-3	0-5	0-2	2-3	1-3		1-0	1-1	2-1	2-4	1-5
Distillery FC	3-2	3-4	2-2	9-2	5-3	1-1	7-2		0-2	1-7	5-4	0-4
Glenavon FC	3-4	1-1	3-2	10-2	2-0	1-2	1-3	5-2		3-2	5-1	1-1
Glentoran FC	2-0	4-0	3-0	7-0	4-1	3-0	5-3	1-3	2-0		0-1	1-0
Linfield FC	2-2	1-2	3-0	3-0	5-3	1-1	5-1	8-1	3-1	3-2		3-1
Portadown FC	3-1	4-3	2-2	2-1	4-0	3-2	1-1	5-1	2-2	2-2	1-1	

Play-off
LINFIELD FC (BELFAST)   3-2   Portadown FC (Portadown)

	Irish League	Pd	Wn	Dw	Ls	GF	GA	Pts
1.	Linfield FC (Belfast)	22	14	4	4	65	34	32
1.	Portadown FC (Portadown)	22	12	8	2	56	31	32
3.	Ards FC (Newtownards)	22	14	3	5	66	39	31
4.	Glentoran FC (Belfast)	22	13	2	7	58	26	28
5.	Ballymena United FC (Ballymena)	22	11	5	6	51	38	27
6.	Glenavon FC (Lurgan)	22	10	5	7	51	42	25
7.	Crusaders FC (Belfast)	22	8	7	7	30	29	23
8.	Distillery FC (Belfast)	22	10	2	10	63	61	22
9.	Bangor FC (Bangor)	22	4	5	13	48	69	13
10.	Coleraine FC (Coleraine)	22	5	3	14	46	68	13
11.	Derry City FC (Londonderry)	22	5	2	15	31	68	12
12.	Cliftonville FC (Belfast)	22	3	-	19	33	93	6
		264	109	46	109	598	598	264

Top goalscorer 1960-61
1) Trevor THOMPSON   (Glentoran FC)   22

IRISH CUP FINAL   (Solitude, Belfast – 22/04/1961)
GLENAVON FC (LURGAN)   5-1   Linfield FC (Belfast)
Campbell 3, Jones 2   *Ferguson*

Glenavon: Kinkead, Hughes, Armstrong, Dugan, McKinstry, Magee, Wilson, Johnston, Jones, Campbell, Weatherup.

Linfield: Irvine, Gilliland, Graham, Wilson, Parke, Gough, Stewart, Ferguson, Walker, Dickson, Braithwaite.

Semi-finals

Glenavon FC (Lurgan)	3-2	Crusaders FC (Belfast)
Linfield FC (Belfast)	4-2	Ballyclare Comrades FC (Ballyclare)

Quarter-finals

Ards FC (Newtownards)	0-4	Glenavon FC (Lurgan)
Ballymena United FC (Ballymena)	1-3	Ballyclare Comrades FC (Ballyclare)
Distillery FC (Belfast)	1-1, 2-2, 1-3	Crusaders FC (Belfast)
Linfield FC (Belfast)	5-1	Bangor FC (Bangor)

1961-62

Irish League 1961-62	Ards	Ballymena U.	Bangor	Cliftonville	Coleraine	Crusaders	Derry City	Distillery	Glenavon	Glentoran	Linfield	Portadown
Ards FC	■	1-1	1-1	5-1	3-2	4-1	2-0	3-1	4-3	4-2	2-4	2-1
Ballymena United FC	1-2	■	2-1	7-0	1-1	1-1	2-0	3-2	3-3	1-1	4-2	1-3
Bangor FC	2-0	0-4	■	2-0	1-3	3-2	3-3	4-5	1-3	4-1	0-1	2-6
Cliftonville FC	1-3	1-3	0-0	■	0-0	1-2	2-2	4-5	1-1	1-2	0-5	0-4
Coleraine FC	0-1	0-1	4-0	2-1	■	4-1	4-2	2-3	1-2	1-1	2-0	1-1
Crusaders FC	3-0	1-2	3-0	6-0	3-1	■	1-0	2-1	1-3	1-0	3-2	3-4
Derry City FC	0-0	0-0	1-0	5-0	0-1	1-1	■	2-2	2-2	0-1	0-2	0-1
Distillery FC	2-2	1-4	2-4	6-0	4-2	2-3	2-3	■	2-2	4-3	4-6	2-1
Glenavon FC	5-1	2-2	5-2	2-2	7-2	1-1	4-0	5-1	■	2-3	2-1	3-4
Glentoran FC	1-0	1-2	2-0	6-0	2-1	0-1	5-1	3-0	4-4	■	1-1	2-2
Linfield FC	3-2	6-1	4-1	3-1	4-3	9-0	0-0	2-2	2-0	3-1	■	2-1
Portadown FC	3-3	3-1	4-0	2-1	1-0	4-2	3-0	2-3	2-1	2-3	2-0	■

Play-off

LINFIELD FC (BELFAST)   3-1   Portadown FC (Portadown)

	Irish League	Pd	Wn	Dw	Ls	GF	GA	Pts
1.	Linfield FC (Belfast)	22	14	3	5	62	32	31
1.	Portadown FC (Portadown)	22	14	3	5	56	32	31
3.	Ballymena United FC (Ballymena)	22	11	7	4	47	32	29
4.	Ards FC (Newtownards)	22	11	5	6	46	38	27
5.	Glenavon FC (Lurgan)	22	9	8	5	62	43	26
6.	Crusaders FC (Belfast)	22	11	3	8	42	43	25
7.	Glentoran FC (Belfast)	22	10	5	7	45	35	25
8.	Distillery FC (Belfast)	22	8	4	10	56	62	20
9.	Coleraine FC (Coleraine)	22	7	4	11	37	39	18
10.	Derry City FC (Londonderry)	22	3	8	11	22	38	14
11.	Bangor FC (Bangor)	22	5	3	14	31	56	13
12.	Cliftonville FC (Belfast)	22	-	5	17	17	73	5
		264	103	58	103	523	523	264

Top goalscorer 1961-62

1) Michael LYNCH   (Ards FC)   20

IRISH CUP FINAL   (The Oval, Belfast)

LINFIELD FC (BELFAST)　　　　　　　　4-0　　　　　　　　Portadown FC (Portadown)

Dickson 2, Barr, Braithwaite

Linfield: Irvine, Gilliland, Graham, Wilson, Hatton, Parke, Stewart, Ferguson, Barr, Dickson, Braithwaite.
Portadown: Kydd, Burke, Loughlin, Cush, Beattie, Campbell, Gillespie, McMillen, Gorman, Wilson, Callan.

Semi-finals

Linfield FC (Belfast)	3-1	Bangor FC (Bangor)
Portadown FC (Portadown)	3-1	Glenavon FC (Lurgan)

Quarter-finals

Bangor FC (Bangor)	1-0	Glentoran FC (Belfast)
Cliftonville FC (Belfast)	2-4	Linfield FC (Belfast)
Crusaders FC (Belfast)	3-3, 0-2	Portadown FC (Portadown)
Glenavon FC (Lurgan)	2-1	Coleraine FC (Coleraine)

1962-63

Irish League 1962-63	Ards	Ballymena U.	Bangor	Cliftonville	Coleraine	Crusaders	Derry City	Distillery	Glenavon	Glentoran	Linfield	Portadown
Ards FC	■	2-2	3-0	1-4	1-2	1-2	1-5	2-3	1-0	1-6	0-1	0-0
Ballymena United FC	0-0	■	4-2	5-1	2-2	2-1	5-2	3-1	1-1	4-3	1-1	2-2
Bangor FC	1-3	2-2	■	2-1	3-1	0-3	1-2	1-3	0-3	0-5	2-5	2-2
Cliftonville FC	3-4	0-1	3-1	■	0-3	1-5	1-2	0-3	0-0	0-3	0-2	0-4
Coleraine FC	1-2	3-0	0-0	2-2	■	3-2	2-2	2-1	0-0	2-1	0-3	0-1
Crusaders FC	4-1	4-1	4-0	3-2	3-2	■	4-0	0-3	4-3	1-4	0-3	0-1
Derry City FC	3-2	1-1	2-0	1-1	1-2	1-1	■	0-1	1-0	0-1	1-1	3-1
Distillery FC	5-3	6-1	9-1	4-1	0-0	1-0	3-1	■	1-2	1-1	4-2	2-2
Glenavon FC	2-0	1-1	6-1	6-2	3-3	2-3	4-1	0-2	■	0-1	3-2	3-0
Glentoran FC	2-1	5-1	2-2	1-1	2-3	1-1	0-2	5-1	2-1	■	1-1	1-3
Linfield FC	3-1	1-1	1-0	2-0	0-0	2-0	3-2	2-2	2-3	1-1	■	2-2
Portadown FC	5-0	1-1	1-1	1-1	4-1	8-2	3-1	1-1	3-1	0-1	0-0	■

	Irish League	**Pd**	**Wn**	**Dw**	**Ls**	**GF**	**GA**	**Pts**
1.	DISTILLERY FC (BELFAST)	22	13	5	4	57	30	31
2.	Linfield FC (Belfast)	22	10	9	3	40	24	29
3.	Portadown FC (Portadown)	22	9	10	3	45	25	28
4.	Glentoran FC (Belfast)	22	11	6	5	49	27	28
5.	Ballymena United FC (Ballymena)	22	7	11	4	41	42	25
6.	Crusaders FC (Belfast)	22	11	2	9	47	42	24
7.	Coleraine FC (Coleraine)	22	8	8	6	34	33	24
8.	Glenavon FC (Lurgan)	22	9	5	8	44	31	23
9.	Derry City FC (Londonderry)	22	8	5	9	34	38	21
10.	Ards FC (Newtownards)	22	5	3	14	30	54	13
11.	Cliftonville FC (Belfast)	22	2	5	15	24	56	9
12.	Bangor FC (Bangor)	22	2	5	15	22	65	9
		264	95	74	95	467	467	264

Top goalscorer 1962-63

1) Joe MELDRUM   (Distillery FC)   27

No clubs promoted or relegated

IRISH CUP FINAL   (The Oval, Belfast – 20/04/1963)

LINFIELD FC (BELFAST)   2-1   Distillery FC (Belfast)
Cairns, Braithwaite   *Kennedy*

Linfield: Irvine, Parke, Graham, Andrews, Hatton, Gough, Stewart, Ferguson, Cairns, Dickson, Braithwaite.
Distillery: Kennedy, D. Meldrum, Ellison, Kennedy, White, Gregg, Welsh, Curley, J. Meldrum, Scott, Hamilton.

Semi-finals

Distillery FC (Belfast)	3-1	Ballymena United FC (Ballymena)
Linfield FC (Belfast)	3-1	Crusaders FC (Belfast)

Quarter-finals

Ballymena United FC (Ballymena)	3-1	Glentoran FC (Belfast)
Bangor FC (Bangor)	2-6	Crusaders FC (Belfast)
Coleraine FC (Coleraine)	1-3	Linfield FC (Belfast)
Distillery FC (Belfast)	4-2	Ards FC (Newtownards)

1963-64

Irish League 1963-64	Ards	Ballymena U.	Bangor	Cliftonville	Coleraine	Crusaders	Derry City	Distillery	Glenavon	Glentoran	Linfield	Portadown
Ards FC	■	2-3	4-0	5-0	1-3	4-2	4-3	2-2	2-4	2-2	3-1	0-1
Ballymena United FC	3-3	■	1-2	6-0	2-1	3-2	1-3	2-1	3-2	0-3	1-4	4-2
Bangor FC	0-2	2-3	■	3-3	0-3	2-6	1-3	2-7	4-1	1-5	0-2	1-2
Cliftonville FC	0-6	1-3	3-1	■	1-2	2-1	0-4	3-4	2-5	0-2	0-2	0-4
Coleraine FC	3-0	1-0	2-1	4-3	■	2-1	0-1	4-1	2-1	2-2	1-4	2-1
Crusaders FC	3-1	0-2	3-0	4-0	0-2	■	3-1	1-5	1-2	3-1	2-2	2-1
Derry City FC	6-1	5-5	1-1	3-0	0-0	3-1	■	2-1	5-2	5-0	1-0	3-1
Distillery FC	6-1	5-2	6-1	3-3	2-2	2-0	0-3	■	4-0	3-3	0-1	2-2
Glenavon FC	6-0	5-3	4-1	5-1	1-3	0-1	2-1	4-3	■	0-1	2-1	1-3
Glentoran FC	2-0	3-2	4-0	5-0	0-0	3-2	4-3	3-1	1-1	■	3-2	4-0
Linfield FC	5-2	1-3	4-2	2-0	3-0	1-1	4-2	3-1	6-2	1-8	■	2-2
Portadown FC	3-0	4-3	7-0	5-2	0-1	2-1	2-1	2-4	2-1	1-0	2-2	■

Irish League	Pd	Wn	Dw	Ls	GF	GA	Pts
1. GLENTORAN FC (BELFAST)	22	14	5	3	59	29	33
2. Coleraine FC (Coleraine)	22	14	4	4	40	25	32
3. Derry City FC (Londonderry)	22	13	3	6	59	33	29
4. Linfield FC (Belfast)	22	12	4	6	53	38	28
5. Portadown FC (Portadown)	22	12	3	7	49	36	27
6. Ballymena United FC (Ballymena)	22	11	2	9	55	52	24
7. Distillery FC (Belfast)	22	9	5	8	63	46	23
8. Glenavon FC (Lurgan)	22	10	1	11	51	50	21
9. Crusaders FC (Belfast)	22	8	2	12	40	41	18
10. Ards FC (Newtownards)	22	7	3	12	45	58	17
11. Bangor FC (Bangor)	22	2	2	18	26	76	6
12. Cliftonville FC (Belfast)	22	2	2	18	24	80	6
	264	114	36	114	564	564	264

Top goalscorer 1963-64

1) Trevor THOMPSON   (Glentoran FC)   21

Note: The Distillery FC 4-0 Glenavon FC match was abandoned after 78 minutes but the result was allowed to stand.

No club promoted or relegated

IRISH CUP FINAL   (Windsor Park, Belfast – 25/04/1964)

DERRY CITY FC (LONDONDERRY)   2-0   Glentoran FC (Belfast)

Wilson, Doherty

Derry: Mahon, Campbell, Cathcart, McGeogh, Crossan, Wood, McKenzie, Doherty, Coyle, Wilson, Seddon.
Glentoran: Finlay, Creighton, Borne, Byrne, McCullough, Bruce, Pavis, Curley, Thompson, Brannigan, Green.

Semi-finals

Derry City FC (Londonderry)	3-0	Banbridge Town FC (Banbridge)
Glentoran FC (Belfast)	2-0	Coleraine FC (Coleraine)

Quarter-finals

Banbridge Town FC (Banbridge)	3-0	Cliftonville FC (Belfast)
Coleraine FC (Coleraine)	3-1	Portadown FC (Portadown)
Crusaders FC (Belfast)	2-2, 0-2	Glentoran FC (Belfast)
Derry City FC (Londonderry)	5-0	Distillery FC (Belfast)

1964-65

Irish League 1964-65	Ards	Ballymena U.	Bangor	Cliftonville	Coleraine	Crusaders	Derry City	Distillery	Glenavon	Glentoran	Linfield	Portadown
Ards FC	■	2-3	1-1	4-2	1-5	1-4	3-3	0-4	2-0	1-4	0-1	3-0
Ballymena United FC	4-1	■	3-0	3-1	0-4	1-0	3-5	1-1	3-1	0-2	3-2	0-1
Bangor FC	1-1	4-2	■	7-0	1-3	2-0	0-2	2-4	2-3	2-2	3-4	4-3
Cliftonville FC	1-2	2-8	1-3	■	0-5	0-3	1-3	0-4	0-10	0-4	1-5	0-4
Coleraine FC	2-1	2-2	4-1	4-1	■	4-2	1-2	2-1	3-0	0-0	3-1	1-1
Crusaders FC	1-1	0-0	1-0	5-0	2-0	■	4-1	3-1	2-1	1-0	1-8	1-1
Derry City FC	5-1	3-3	2-1	10-1	1-0	3-1	■	2-2	6-1	2-0	2-0	4-3
Distillery FC	2-1	1-2	1-3	6-1	0-2	0-6	2-3	■	1-4	1-2	4-2	2-0
Glenavon FC	7-2	1-2	3-0	3-2	3-1	2-4	3-0	3-1	■	6-0	1-1	4-0
Glentoran FC	2-2	3-2	1-1	0-3	3-2	2-1	0-1	2-0	3-2	■	1-1	1-1
Linfield FC	3-3	5-2	2-1	6-0	1-4	2-2	4-2	0-3	0-3	4-1	■	2-0
Portadown FC	0-1	3-3	1-3	1-0	2-2	2-2	1-1	3-0	0-0	5-0	1-3	■

	Irish League	**Pd**	**Wn**	**Dw**	**Ls**	**GF**	**GA**	**Pts**
1.	DERRY CITY FC (LONDONDERRY)	22	15	5	2	62	32	35
2.	Coleraine FC (Coleraine)	22	13	4	5	54	26	30
3.	Crusaders FC (Belfast)	22	11	5	6	46	32	27
4.	Glenavon FC (Lurgan)	22	12	2	8	61	35	26
5.	Linfield FC (Belfast)	22	10	5	7	54	40	25
6.	Ballymena United FC (Ballymena)	22	10	5	7	50	44	25
7.	Glentoran FC (Belfast)	22	9	6	7	33	38	24
8.	Bangor FC (Bangor)	22	7	4	11	42	44	18
9.	Distillery FC (Belfast)	22	8	2	12	41	44	18
10.	Portadown FC (Portadown)	22	5	8	9	33	37	18
11.	Ards FC (Newtownards)	22	5	6	11	34	55	16
12.	Cliftonville FC (Belfast)	22	1	-	21	17	100	2
		264	106	52	106	527	527	264

Note: The Linfield FC 0-3 Distillery FC match was abandoned after 83 minutes but the result was allowed to stand.

Top goalscorers 1964-65

1) Dennis GUY   (Glenavon FC)   19
   Kenneth HALLIDAY (Coleraine FC)   19

No clubs promoted or relegated

IRISH CUP FINAL   (Windsor Park, Belfast – 24/04/1965)

COLERAINE FC (COLERAINE)   2-1   Glenavon FC (Lurgan)
Dunlop, Irwin   *Johnston*

Coleraine: V. Hunter, McCurdy, Campbell, Murray, A. Hunter, Peacock, Kinsella, Curley, Halliday, Dunlop, Irwin.
Glenavon: McNally, Murphy, E. Johnston, Magee, Lowry, Hughes, Watson, E. Magee, Guy, W. Johnston, Weatherup.

Semi-finals

Coleraine FC (Coleraine)	1-0	Glentoran FC (Belfast)
Glenavon FC (Lurgan)	3-3, 3-2	Linfield FC (Belfast)

Quarter-finals

Crusaders FC (Belfast)	0-1	Coleraine FC (Coleraine)
Derry City FC (Londonderry)	2-2, 0-0, 1-2	Linfield FC (Belfast)
Glenavon FC (Lurgan)	6-1	Banbridge Town FC (Banbridge)
Glentoran FC (Belfast)	4-0	Portadown FC (Portadown)

1965-66

Irish League 1965-66	Ards	Ballymena U.	Bangor	Cliftonville	Coleraine	Crusaders	Derry City	Distillery	Glenavon	Glentoran	Linfield	Portadown
Ards FC	■	1-2	1-1	1-1	0-0	2-2	0-3	1-0	1-3	2-3	1-3	1-4
Ballymena United FC	2-2	■	2-0	8-0	1-2	5-2	3-4	3-0	5-5	2-1	0-0	1-0
Bangor FC	2-2	0-0	■	3-1	0-3	1-1	1-0	1-3	2-5	0-4	1-4	4-1
Cliftonville FC	2-1	1-5	1-3	■	3-3	0-4	1-1	0-3	1-6	3-5	0-10	0-6
Coleraine FC	5-1	1-3	6-0	6-2	■	2-2	3-1	3-0	2-0	0-1	0-0	1-1
Crusaders FC	6-1	1-3	4-1	7-1	4-2	■	1-2	1-0	2-1	0-1	2-3	5-0
Derry City FC	4-1	5-1	4-1	4-1	3-2	5-0	■	3-1	1-3	3-2	0-0	5-0
Distillery FC	2-2	1-1	3-1	2-2	3-1	1-2	2-5	■	2-4	0-4	3-3	3-3
Glenavon FC	1-2	0-1	3-1	6-1	2-4	4-1	1-2	2-1	■	8-2	0-1	4-1
Glentoran FC	2-3	0-0	3-1	2-0	2-0	2-1	0-1	7-3	0-0	■	2-0	2-0
Linfield FC	5-1	5-2	3-0	3-0	4-1	6-1	3-2	3-3	1-1	1-2	■	3-0
Portadown FC	0-2	2-1	0-0	7-2	3-5	4-0	5-3	0-3	4-3	1-3	1-2	■

	Irish League	Pd	Wn	Dw	Ls	GF	GA	Pts
1.	LINFIELD FC (BELFAST)	22	14	6	2	68	23	34
2.	Derry City FC (Londonderry)	22	15	2	5	61	33	32
3.	Glentoran FC (Belfast)	22	15	2	5	50	29	32
4.	Ballymena United FC (Ballymena)	22	11	6	5	51	33	28
5.	Glenavon FC (Lurgan)	22	11	3	8	61	28	25
6.	Coleraine FC (Coleraine)	22	10	5	7	52	36	25
7.	Crusaders FC (Belfast)	22	9	3	10	49	47	21
8.	Portadown FC (Portadown)	22	7	3	12	43	53	17
9.	Distillery FC (Belfast)	22	5	6	11	39	52	16
10.	Ards FC (Newtownards)	22	4	6	12	29	54	14
11.	Bangor FC (Bangor)	22	5	4	13	26	59	14
12.	Cliftonville FC (Belfast)	22	1	4	17	23	96	6
		264	107	50	107	553	553	264

Top goalscorer 1965-66

1) Samuel PAVIS (Linfield FC) 28

No clubs promoted or relegated

IRISH CUP FINAL (The Oval, Belfast – 23/04/1966)

GLENTORAN FC (BELFAST)   2-0   Linfield FC (Belfast)

Conroy 2

Glentoran: Finlay, Creighton, Borne, McCullough, Byrne, Bruce, Conroy, Stewart, Thompson, McDonnell, McAlinden.

Linfield: McFaul, Gilliland, White, Gregg, Hatton. Leishman, Ferguson, Thomas, Pavis, Scott, McCambley.

Semi-finals

Glentoran FC (Belfast)	1-1, 5-0	Coleraine FC (Coleraine)
Linfield FC (Belfast)	2-0	Crusaders FC (Belfast)

Quarter-finals

Ards FC (Newtownards)	1-3	Crusaders FC (Belfast)
Ballymena United FC (Ballymena)	1-2	Coleraine FC (Coleraine)
Distillery FC (Belfast)	1-2	Glentoran FC (Belfast)
Linfield FC (Belfast)	5-1	Brantwood FC (Belfast)

1966-67

Irish League 1966-67	Ards	Ballymena U.	Bangor	Cliftonville	Coleraine	Crusaders	Derry City	Distillery	Glenavon	Glentoran	Linfield	Portadown
Ards FC	■	1-2	2-2	3-1	1-0	3-1	2-3	3-0	1-1	1-3	1-1	3-3
Ballymena United FC	1-1	■	5-1	2-1	4-4	7-3	1-2	4-0	2-0	2-3	2-4	4-1
Bangor FC	1-4	0-2	■	3-1	4-3	0-5	1-2	0-11	1-4	2-4	1-3	5-2
Cliftonville FC	0-1	1-1	3-2	■	1-1	0-0	0-2	2-2	0-2	2-5	2-4	1-9
Coleraine FC	4-2	1-2	4-1	2-0	■	3-2	1-0	2-2	4-1	1-2	0-3	2-2
Crusaders FC	3-2	4-3	5-1	3-2	1-6	■	6-3	3-1	2-1	1-3	4-4	2-1
Derry City FC	0-2	2-1	4-4	4-0	4-1	9-4	■	0-2	2-2	1-0	5-2	1-1
Distillery FC	1-1	1-1	8-3	3-2	2-5	3-1	1-1	■	0-5	2-4	1-4	0-2
Glenavon FC	2-0	4-4	10-0	3-1	2-2	2-5	0-1	0-1	■	1-2	2-1	3-2
Glentoran FC	2-2	5-2	6-0	5-0	2-3	3-2	4-4	2-0	2-2	■	2-2	2-2
Linfield FC	6-2	2-1	2-2	7-2	4-2	2-0	4-1	5-1	2-3	1-1	■	4-1
Portadown FC	1-0	4-1	5-1	4-1	0-2	2-6	3-0	3-2	4-0	2-5	1-3	■

	Irish League	Pd	Wn	Dw	Ls	GF	GA	Pts
1.	GLENTORAN FC (BELFAST)	22	14	6	2	67	35	34
2.	Linfield FC (Belfast)	22	14	5	3	70	37	33
3.	Derry City FC (Londonderry)	22	11	5	6	51	42	27
4.	Coleraine FC (Coleraine)	22	10	5	7	53	42	25
5.	Crusaders FC (Belfast)	22	11	2	9	63	60	24
6.	Glenavon FC (Lurgan)	22	9	5	8	50	39	23
7.	Ballymena United FC (Ballymena)	22	9	5	8	54	45	23
8.	Ards FC (Newtownards)	22	7	7	8	37	38	21
9.	Portadown FC (Portadown)	22	8	4	10	46	48	20
10.	Distillery FC (Belfast)	22	6	5	11	44	53	17
11.	Bangor FC (Bangor)	22	3	3	16	35	95	9
12.	Cliftonville FC (Belfast)	22	2	4	16	23	59	8
		264	104	56	104	593	593	264

Top goalscorer 1966-67

1) Samuel PAVIS   (Linfield FC)   25

No clubs promoted or relegated

IRISH CUP FINAL   (Windsor Park, Belfast – 02/04/1967)

CRUSADERS FC (BELFAST)   3-1   Glentoran FC (Belfast)
Trainor, McNeill, McCullough   *Thompson*

Crusaders: Nicholson, Paterson, Lewis, McPolin, Campbell, S. McCullough, Law, Trainer, Meldrum, McNeill, Wilson.

Glentoran: Finlay, Creighton, McKeag, Jackson, W.McCullough, Stewart, Morrow, Bruce, Thompson, Ross, Weatherup.

Semi-finals

Crusaders FC (Belfast)	3-2	Bangor FC (Bangor)
Glentoran FC (Belfast)	1-0	Linfield FC (Belfast)

Quarter-finals

Bangor FC (Bangor)	4-1	Portadown FC (Portadown)
Cliftonville FC (Belfast)	1-4	Linfield FC (Belfast)
Crusaders FC (Belfast)	1-0	Coleraine FC (Coleraine)
Glentoran FC (Belfast)	3-1	Distillery FC (Belfast)

1967-68

Irish League 1967-68	Ards	Ballymena U.	Bangor	Cliftonville	Coleraine	Crusaders	Derry City	Distillery	Glenavon	Glentoran	Linfield	Portadown
Ards FC	■	3-1	2-0	5-0	1-1	2-1	6-1	5-1	2-1	1-6	0-2	1-2
Ballymena United FC	3-1	■	3-1	5-2	3-7	2-2	0-1	3-1	4-3	2-5	4-5	5-2
Bangor FC	1-5	4-4	■	3-2	0-5	4-4	2-4	0-1	2-3	0-5	0-4	3-2
Cliftonville FC	0-1	1-5	6-4	■	0-4	1-3	4-2	0-3	2-8	0-5	1-4	2-2
Coleraine FC	3-1	7-2	2-3	5-1	■	2-2	1-2	3-1	4-1	1-0	5-5	7-1
Crusaders FC	3-5	3-1	5-5	6-2	1-5	■	3-1	3-3	2-2	0-2	1-3	10-3
Derry City FC	2-3	5-1	4-3	6-0	1-2	1-1	■	4-1	2-1	1-4	4-1	4-2
Distillery FC	2-4	0-2	3-1	2-1	3-4	2-1	0-1	■	2-5	1-3	1-5	0-3
Glenavon FC	0-1	3-1	3-1	3-1	0-0	4-4	5-1	0-1	■	0-2	1-6	2-1
Glentoran FC	3-0	2-2	10-1	5-0	2-2	2-1	4-2	4-1	4-2	■	2-2	4-1
Linfield FC	1-1	3-1	11-1	3-0	1-3	5-0	8-1	8-3	1-1	3-1	■	1-0
Portadown FC	0-1	2-1	1-0	1-0	2-3	2-1	2-1	2-1	1-3	1-4	1-3	■

	Irish League	Pd	Wn	Dw	Ls	GF	GA	Pts
1.	GLENTORAN FC (BELFAST)	22	17	3	2	79	24	37
2.	Linfield FC (Belfast)	22	16	4	2	85	32	36
3.	Coleraine FC (Coleraine)	22	15	5	2	76	33	35
4.	Ards FC (Newtownards)	22	14	2	6	51	34	30
5.	Derry City FC (Londonderry)	22	11	1	10	51	54	23
6.	Glenavon FC (Lurgan)	22	9	4	9	51	45	22
7.	Ballymena United FC (Ballymena)	22	8	3	11	55	63	19
8.	Crusaders FC (Belfast)	22	5	8	9	57	59	18
9.	Portadown FC (Portadown)	22	8	1	13	34	57	17
10.	Distillery FC (Belfast)	22	6	1	15	33	62	13
11.	Bangor FC (Bangor)	22	3	3	16	39	89	9
12.	Cliftonville FC (Belfast)	22	2	1	19	26	85	5
		264	114	36	114	637	637	264

Top goalscorer 1967-68

1) Samuel PAVIS   (Linfield FC)   30

No clubs promoted or relegated

IRISH CUP FINAL   (The Oval, Belfast – 27/04/1968)

CRUSADERS FC (BELFAST)   2-0   Linfield FC (Belfast)

Meldrum 2

Crusaders: Nicholson, Anderson, Cathcart, Campbell, McFarlane, McPolin, Brush, Trainor, Meldrum, Jamison, Wilson,

Linfield: McGonigal, Gilliland, Patterson, Andrews, Hatton, Wood, Ferguson, Hamilton, Pavis, Scott, Cathcart (Millen).

Semi-finals

Crusaders FC (Belfast)	1-1, 3-2	Derry City FC (Londonderry)
Linfield FC (Belfast)	2-1	Ards FC (Newtownards)

Quarter-finals

Ballyclare Comrades FC (Ballyclare)	0-1	Ards FC (Newtownards)
Bangor FC (Bangor)	0-5	Linfield FC (Belfast)
Crusaders FC (Belfast)	0-0, 2-2, 4-3	Portadown FC (Portadown)
Glentoran FC (Belfast)	2-2, 2-2, 0-1	Derry City FC (Londonderry)

1968-69

Irish League 1968-69	Ards	Ballymena U.	Bangor	Cliftonville	Coleraine	Crusaders	Derry City	Distillery	Glenavon	Glentoran	Linfield	Portadown
Ards FC	■	4-3	2-0	1-0	3-1	1-1	2-1	3-1	4-1	1-2	1-2	5-2
Ballymena United FC	1-4	■	3-0	2-1	5-0	1-3	5-3	2-1	1-1	2-2	1-2	3-2
Bangor FC	0-3	1-1	■	0-1	2-4	1-3	0-2	4-3	2-3	0-2	0-2	2-1
Cliftonville FC	3-3	0-3	2-2	■	0-5	1-3	2-2	1-2	0-4	1-3	0-2	0-2
Coleraine FC	3-3	1-6	2-0	2-0	■	1-1	1-2	5-2	2-0	2-1	0-1	4-0
Crusaders FC	3-3	2-1	2-0	2-2	0-1	■	4-1	1-2	1-0	1-1	0-4	3-1
Derry City FC	3-0	5-1	3-0	6-0	0-1	4-1	■	3-2	4-1	2-1	2-1	4-0
Distillery FC	1-2	2-2	5-1	1-1	2-2	3-6	0-4	■	3-0	1-2	3-7	3-0
Glenavon FC	1-2	2-2	1-2	3-5	2-1	2-4	0-2	4-0	■	1-2	1-5	3-0
Glentoran FC	1-1	2-1	1-2	4-0	0-1	0-2	1-1	1-0	7-1	■	2-1	2-0
Linfield FC	3-0	3-1	4-1	4-1	0-1	3-0	3-1	0-0	3-0	1-3	■	8-1
Portadown FC	1-0	0-1	1-2	2-3	0-3	1-4	1-2	0-2	0-1	0-2	0-2	■

	Irish League	Pd	Wn	Dw	Ls	GF	GA	Pts
1.	LINFIELD FC (BELFAST)	22	17	1	4	61	19	35
2.	Derry City FC (Londonderry)	22	15	2	5	57	27	32
3.	Glentoran FC (Belfast)	22	13	4	5	42	22	30
4.	Coleraine FC (Coleraine)	22	13	3	6	43	30	29
5.	Ards FC (Newtownards)	22	12	5	5	48	34	29
6.	Crusaders FC (Belfast)	22	12	5	5	47	34	29
7.	Ballymena United FC (Ballymena)	22	9	5	8	48	41	23
8.	Distillery FC (Belfast)	22	6	4	12	39	51	16
9.	Glenavon FC (Lurgan)	22	6	2	14	32	52	14
10.	Bangor FC (Bangor)	22	5	2	15	22	51	12
11.	Cliftonville FC (Belfast)	22	3	5	14	24	58	11
12.	Portadown FC (Portadown)	22	2	-	20	15	59	4
		264	113	38	113	478	478	264

Top goalscorer 1968-69

1) Daniel HALE   (Derry City FC)   21

No clubs promoted or relegated

IRISH CUP FINAL (Windsor Park, Belfast – 19/04/1969)

ARDS FC (NEWTOWNARDS)   0-0   Distillery FC (Belfast)

Ards: Kydd, Johnston, Crothers, Bell, Stewart, Nixon, Cochrane, McAvoy, Brown, Humphries, Shields.
Distillery: Young, Meldrum, Pike, Kennedy, Conlon, McCarroll, Rafferty, McCaffrey, O'Halloran, Brannigan, Lennox.

IRISH CUP FINAL REPLAY (Windsor Park, Belfast – 23/04/1969)

ARDS FC (NEWTOWNARDS)   4-2   Distillery FC (Belfast)

McAvoy 4   *McCaffrey, Conlon*

Distillery: Young, Patterson, Pike, Kennedy, Conlon, McCarroll, Rafferty, McCafferty, O'Halloran, Brannigan, Lennox.

Ards: Kydd, Johnston, Crothers, Bell, Stewart, Nixon, Shields (Sands), McAvoy, Brown, Humphries, Mowat.

Semi-finals

Ards FC (Newtownards)	1-0	Coleraine FC (Coleraine)
Distillery FC (Belfast)	1-1, 0-0, 2-1	Glentoran FC (Belfast)

Quarter-finals

Ards FC (Newtownards)	4-1	Crusaders FC (Belfast)
Ballymena United FC (Ballymena)	1-2	Distillery FC (Belfast)
Bangor FC (Bangor)	0-1	Coleraine FC (Coleraine)
Glentoran FC (Belfast)	3-2	Derry City FC (Londonderry)

1969-70

Irish League 1969-70	Ards	Ballymena U.	Bangor	Cliftonville	Coleraine	Crusaders	Derry City	Distillery	Glenavon	Glentoran	Linfield	Portadown
Ards FC	■	4-1	2-1	3-1	1-1	2-1	4-0	1-0	0-1	2-3	2-3	4-1
Ballymena United FC	1-2	■	2-2	1-1	1-5	2-0	3-4	0-0	3-1	0-3	0-4	1-3
Bangor FC	2-2	3-4	■	3-1	0-1	3-4	1-1	3-1	1-0	1-1	3-2	2-0
Cliftonville FC	0-2	0-1	0-1	■	3-1	0-2	2-3	1-3	3-3	0-3	1-5	1-2
Coleraine FC	2-1	3-0	2-2	1-0	■	2-1	1-1	6-1	1-3	2-0	3-1	2-3
Crusaders FC	1-1	1-1	1-0	8-3	0-7	■	0-3	2-1	4-1	2-0	1-3	6-2
Derry City FC	3-2	0-2	2-1	2-0	0-1	1-0	■	4-1	0-1	0-0	1-1	0-4
Distillery FC	0-0	1-0	1-1	1-1	0-3	4-3	2-4	■	5-0	0-5	0-1	2-0
Glenavon FC	0-2	3-0	1-1	2-1	4-2	1-1	1-1	0-0	■	2-2	5-2	0-2
Glentoran FC	1-1	0-0	2-0	2-0	2-1	7-2	1-0	3-0	2-0	■	2-2	2-1
Linfield FC	2-2	1-0	4-1	1-1	4-2	4-1	2-4	3-0	1-1	0-2	■	0-3
Portadown FC	1-1	1-1	2-0	1-0	3-1	4-1	1-4	4-2	2-2	1-3	1-2	■

	Irish League	**Pd**	**Wn**	**Dw**	**Ls**	**GF**	**GA**	**Pts**
1.	GLENTORAN FC (BELFAST)	22	14	6	2	46	17	34
2.	Coleraine FC (Coleraine)	22	12	3	7	50	31	27
3.	Ards FC (Newtownards)	22	10	7	3	41	26	27
4.	Linfield FC (Belfast)	22	11	5	6	48	36	27
5.	Derry City FC (Londonderry)	22	11	5	6	38	31	27
6.	Portadown FC (Portadown)	22	11	3	8	42	37	25
7.	Glenavon FC (Lurgan)	22	7	8	7	32	36	22
8.	Bangor FC (Bangor)	22	6	7	9	32	36	19
9.	Crusaders FC (Belfast)	22	8	3	11	42	52	19
10.	Ballymena United FC (Ballymena)	22	5	6	11	24	42	16
11.	Distillery FC (Belfast)	22	5	5	12	25	45	15
12.	Cliftonville FC (Belfast)	22	1	4	17	20	51	6
		264	101	62	101	440	440	264

Top goalscorer 1969-70

1) Des DICKSON   (Coleraine FC)   21

No clubs promoted or relegated

IRISH CUP FINAL   (Windsor Park, Belfast – 04/04/1970)

LINFIELD FC (BELFAST)   2-1   Ballymena United FC (Ballymena)
Scott 2   *Fleming*

Linfield: Stewart, Gilliland, Patterson, Andrews, Hatton, Bowyer, Viollet, Hamilton, Millen, Scott, Pavis.
Ballymena: Platt, Erwin, Richardson, Torrens, Averell, Russell, Porter, McGowan, Fleming, Martin, McFall.

Semi-finals

Ballymena United FC (Ballymena)	2-0	Coleraine FC (Coleraine)
Linfield FC (Belfast)	2-1	Derry City FC (Londonderry)

Quarter-finals

Ballymena United FC (Ballymena)	2-1	Crusaders FC (Belfast)
Derry City FC (Londonderry)	1-1, 0-0, 3-2	Cliftonville FC (Belfast)
Glenavon FC (Lurgan)	2-4	Coleraine FC (Coleraine)
Linfield FC (Belfast)	2-0	Newry Town FC (Newry)

1970-71

Irish League 1970-71	Ards	Ballymena U.	Bangor	Cliftonville	Coleraine	Crusaders	Derry City	Distillery	Glenavon	Glentoran	Linfield	Portadown
Ards FC	■	0-1	1-2	2-0	0-2	1-1	3-2	1-4	4-2	2-2	2-1	3-2
Ballymena United FC	0-1	■	4-0	2-1	1-2	1-1	3-1	2-2	4-2	0-2	1-2	1-1
Bangor FC	0-0	1-1	■	1-0	2-1	0-3	2-1	3-3	3-6	0-3	0-1	2-0
Cliftonville FC	3-3	2-2	1-3	■	0-0	0-2	1-1	1-4	3-1	1-5	3-1	4-2
Coleraine FC	2-1	0-2	2-0	3-1	■	6-0	4-2	1-0	4-2	3-1	1-3	3-2
Crusaders FC	0-0	1-0	0-0	4-1	2-1	■	1-0	0-4	3-4	0-4	0-4	3-1
Derry City FC	3-1	2-2	1-0	5-2	4-2	4-0	■	1-3	3-3	0-3	3-3	4-1
Distillery FC	2-1	1-1	0-0	3-0	2-0	3-0	2-1	■	3-0	1-2	2-5	6-3
Glenavon FC	1-3	2-1	3-0	1-1	4-2	2-2	3-4	0-1	■	1-2	0-2	1-3
Glentoran FC	4-0	0-2	1-0	5-0	1-1	1-0	2-0	4-1	4-1	■	0-3	3-0
Linfield FC	3-0	3-0	1-0	2-0	2-1	7-0	3-1	2-0	2-0	1-1	■	5-0
Portadown FC	0-1	1-3	1-2	1-1	0-2	1-1	2-2	1-4	1-0	0-2	1-2	■

	Irish League	Pd	Wn	Dw	Ls	GF	GA	Pts	
1.	LINFIELD FC (BELFAST)	22	18	2	2	58	16	38	
2.	Glentoran FC (Belfast)	22	16	3	3	52	17	35	
3.	Distillery FC (Belfast)	22	13	4	5	51	29	30	**
4.	Coleraine FC (Coleraine)	22	12	2	8	43	32	26	
5.	Ballymena United FC (Ballymena)	22	8	7	7	34	28	23	
6.	Ards FC (Newtownards)	22	8	5	9	30	37	21	
7.	Crusaders FC (Belfast)	22	7	6	9	24	45	20	
8.	Bangor FC (Bangor)	22	7	5	10	21	34	19	
9.	Derry City FC (Londonderry)	22	7	5	10	45	46	19	**
10.	Glenavon FC (Lurgan)	22	5	3	14	39	55	13	
11.	Cliftonville FC (Belfast)	22	3	6	13	26	53	12	
12.	Portadown FC (Portadown)	22	2	4	16	24	55	8	
		264	106	52	106	447	447	264	

** Due to the "civil unrest" in the country, Distillery FC (Belfast) and Derry City FC (Londonderry) were ordered to play several "home" games on neutral ground for security reasons. At the end of the season Distillery FC moved from their traditional home ground, "Grosvenor Park", to share with Crusaders FC (Belfast) at "Seaview Ground" and Derry City FC moved from their home ground "Brandywell Park" in Londonderry to share with Coleraine FC at "The Showgrounds" in Coleraine.

Top goalscorer 1970-71

1) Bryan HAMILTON (Linfield FC) 18

No clubs promoted or relegated

IRISH CUP FINAL   (Windsor Park, Belfast – 03/04/1971 – 6,000)

DISTILLERY FC (BELFAST) 3-0 Derry City FC (Londonderry)
O'Neill 2, Savage
Distillery: McDonald, McCarroll, Meldrum, Brannigan, Rafferty, Donnelly, Law, Watson, Savage, O'Neill, Lennox.
Derry: McKibbin, Duffy, McLaughlin, McDowell, White, Wood, Rowland, O'Halloran, Ward, Hale, Smith (Hill 49').

Semi-finals

Derry City FC (Londonderry)	1-0	Linfield FC (Belfast)
Distillery FC (Belfast)	1-1, 2-1	Coleraine FC (Coleraine)

Quarter-finals

Coleraine FC (Coleraine)	2-0	Ballymena United FC (Ballymena)
Derry City FC (Londonderry)	2-1	Chimney Corner FC (Antrim)
Glenavon FC (Lurgan)	0-2	Distillery FC (Belfast)
Linfield FC (Belfast)	4-1	Crusaders FC (Belfast)

1971-72

Irish League 1971-72	Ards	Ballymena U.	Bangor	Cliftonville	Coleraine	Crusaders	Derry City	Distillery	Glenavon	Glentoran	Linfield	Portadown
Ards FC	■	1-0	3-1	8-1	4-2	1-0	1-2	2-4	1-0	2-0	1-1	4-3
Ballymena United FC	1-1	■	2-1	2-0	3-2	4-2	1-1	0-0	2-3	1-2	2-1	1-6
Bangor FC	2-4	0-1	■	2-2	2-2	0-0	4-4	2-4	0-4	1-2	0-7	0-1
Cliftonville FC	0-2	0-0	2-1	■	0-4	0-1	2-2	2-1	2-3	0-6	0-5	0-2
Coleraine FC	1-1	4-2	4-0	3-0	■	5-5	2-0	1-4	4-1	2-1	1-1	3-2
Crusaders FC	4-0	2-1	3-2	3-0	1-0	■	4-7	2-0	1-1	0-0	2-1	1-5
Derry City FC	0-4	0-5	4-4	4-2	2-2	1-3	■	0-0	3-3	2-2	1-3	1-3
Distillery FC	1-4	2-0	2-4	4-4	3-3	0-0	2-0	■	1-1	0-6	2-1	0-3
Glenavon FC	2-2	1-4	3-0	2-1	1-2	0-1	4-3	4-1	■	0-1	0-2	1-1
Glentoran FC	2-1	1-0	4-0	4-0	1-0	2-0	1-0	2-2	5-0	■	4-0	0-0
Linfield FC	1-1	2-2	3-0	2-1	3-3	4-1	0-2	3-0	2-1	2-2	■	2-2
Portadown FC	2-1	2-0	1-2	3-0	3-1	1-0	3-2	0-1	1-1	4-2	1-2	■

	Irish League	Pd	Wn	Dw	Ls	GF	GA	Pts	
1.	GLENTORAN FC (BELFAST)	22	14	5	3	50	17	33	
2.	Portadown FC (Portadown)	22	13	4	5	49	25	30	
3.	Ards FC (Newtownards)	22	12	5	5	49	30	29	
4.	Linfield FC (Belfast)	22	10	7	5	48	29	27	
5.	Crusaders FC (Belfast)	22	10	5	7	36	35	25	
6.	Coleraine FC (Coleraine)	22	9	7	6	51	40	25	
7.	Ballymena United FC (Ballymena)	22	8	5	9	34	34	21	
8.	Distillery FC (Belfast)	22	7	7	8	34	44	21	**
9.	Glenavon FC (Lurgan)	22	7	6	9	36	40	20	
10.	Derry City FC (Londonderry/Coleraine)	22	4	8	10	41	55	16	**
11.	Bangor FC (Bangor)	22	2	5	15	28	62	9	
12.	Cliftonville FC (Belfast)	22	2	4	16	19	64	8	
		264	98	68	98	475	475	264	

** Due to the "civil unrest" in the country Distillery FC played their "home" games at the ground of Crusaders FC and Derry City FC played "sensitive" home games at Coleraine. During the match between Derry City FC and Ballymena United at Brandywell Park in Londonderry the Ballymena team bus was hijacked, driven away and set on fire by "terrorists".

Top goalscorers 1971-72

1) Des DICKSON (Coleraine FC) 15
   Peter WATSON (Distillery FC) 15

IRISH CUP FINAL   (Windsor Park, Belfast – 22/04/1972 – 8,000)

COLERAINE FC (COLERAINE)   2-1   Portadown FC (Portadown)
Dickson, Murray   *Anderson*

Coleraine: Crossan, McCurdy, Gordon, Curley, Jackson, Murray, Dunlop, Mullan, Healey, Dickson, Jennings.
Portadown: Carlisle, Strain, McFall, Malcolmson, Lunn, Hutton, R.Morrison, McGowan, Anderson, B.Morrison, Fleming.

Semi-finals

Ards FC (Newtownards)	1-1, 0-1	Coleraine FC (Coleraine)
Portadown FC (Portadown)	2-0	Derry City FC (Londonderry)

Quarter-finals

Crusaders FC (Belfast)	1-1, 0-3	Ards FC (Newtownards)
Glentoran FC (Belfast)	2-3	Coleraine FC (Coleraine)
Portadown FC (Portadown)	2-0	Linfield FC (Belfast)
Queen's University FC (Belfast)	2-4	Derry City FC (Londonderry)

1972-73

Irish League 1972-73	Ards	Ballymena U.	Bangor	Cliftonville	Coleraine	Crusaders	Distillery	Glenavon	Glentoran	Larne	Linfield	Portadown
Ards FC	■	3-1	3-1	7-0	1-1	5-2	1-1	1-3	2-3	2-0	1-1	4-0
Ballymena United FC	0-2	■	1-0	2-1	2-4	1-1	2-1	1-1	4-1	2-2	0-0	3-1
Bangor FC	1-1	1-0	■	1-0	1-2	1-1	2-5	1-1	2-3	6-0	0-1	1-3
Cliftonville FC	0-4	1-0	1-1	■	0-5	0-1	2-3	3-1	0-5	1-3	1-2	1-5
Coleraine FC	0-1	2-1	0-0	1-0	■	0-3	4-0	4-0	4-1	6-1	4-2	1-3
Crusaders FC	2-1	3-0	2-0	3-0	2-1	■	1-0	2-0	2-0	6-1	2-0	1-1
Distillery FC	0-2	1-2	2-4	4-2	4-1	0-8	■	1-0	4-2	1-0	2-2	1-1
Glenavon FC	1-2	4-1	0-0	3-0	0-3	1-0	2-0	■	4-0	4-1	2-0	2-0
Glentoran FC	0-1	0-1	3-0	9-0	1-3	2-2	3-3	4-0	■	3-2	0-2	1-1
Larne FC	0-2	2-2	1-1	2-3	2-4	2-5	3-2	2-4	1-5	■	0-2	2-3
Linfield FC	4-2	2-0	1-3	2-1	3-1	5-1	2-3	1-0	0-1	2-1	■	3-1
Portadown FC	1-1	2-0	1-1	2-1	3-0	1-0	1-2	1-0	2-1	1-0	3-1	■

	Irish League	Pd	Wn	Dw	Ls	GF	GA	Pts	
1.	CRUSADERS FC (BELFAST)	22	14	4	4	50	22	32	
2.	Ards FC (Newtownards)	22	13	5	4	49	22	31	
3.	Portadown FC (Portadown)	22	12	5	5	37	27	29	
4.	Coleraine FC (Coleraine0	22	13	2	7	51	31	28	
5.	Linfield FC (Belfast)	22	12	3	7	38	29	27	
6.	Glenavon FC (Lurgan)	22	10	3	9	33	28	23	
7.	Distillery FC (Belfast)	22	9	4	9	40	47	22	**
8.	Glentoran FC (Belfast)	22	9	3	10	48	40	21	
9.	Ballymena United FC (Ballymena)	22	7	5	10	26	35	19	
10.	Bangor FC (Bangor)	22	5	8	9	28	32	18	
11.	Cliftonville FC (Belfast)	22	2	1	18	18	66	7	
12.	Larne FC (Larne)	22	2	3	17	28	67	7	**
		264	109	46	109	446	446	264	

** Derry City FC (Londonderry) resigned from the league in November 1972 due to the refusal of other clubs to play at Brandywell Park because of the security risks caused by the "civil unrest" in the country.

Distillery FC (Belfast) continued to play "home" games at the ground of Crusaders FC (Belfast) and would continue to do so until moving to the town of Lisburn in 1979.

Top goalscorer 1972-73
1) Des DICKSON　　　　　　　　　(Coleraine FC)　　　　23

Elected: Larne FC (Larne) to replace Derry City FC (Londonderry).

IRISH CUP FINAL   (Windsor Park, Belfast – 28/04/1973 – 10,000)
GLENTORAN FC (BELFAST)　　　　　3-2　　　　　　　　Linfield FC (Belfast)
Feeney 2 (1 pen.), Jamison　　　　　　　　　　　　　　　　　　　　*Malone, Magee*

Glentoran: A. Patterson, Hill, McKeag, Stewart (Walker 45'), Murray, McCreary, Weatherup, Anderson, Hall, Jamison, Feeney.

Linfield: Barclay, Fraser, J. Patterson, Sinclair, McAllister, Bowyer, Nixon, Magee, Millen, Malone, Cathcart (Larmour 45').

Semi-finals
Coleraine FC (Coleraine)	1-2	Linfield FC (Belfast)
Glentoran FC (Belfast)	1-0	Glenavon FC (Lurgan)

Quarter-finals
Coleraine FC (Coleraine)	2-1	Portadown FC (Portadown)
Crusaders FC (Belfast)	1-2	Glentoran FC (Belfast)
Glenavon FC (Lurgan)	3-1	Bangor FC (Bangor)
Larne FC (Larne)	2-2, 0-2	Linfield FC (Belfast)

1973-74

Irish League 1973-74	Ards	Ballymena U.	Bangor	Cliftonville	Coleraine	Crusaders	Distillery	Glenavon	Glentoran	Larne	Linfield	Portadown
Ards FC	■	1-0	2-1	4-1	2-2	3-4	3-1	3-2	3-0	4-3	2-2	0-1
Ballymena United FC	1-0	■	1-2	2-2	1-3	1-0	6-0	0-1	1-2	2-0	1-0	1-1
Bangor FC	3-2	1-2	■	8-2	2-0	1-4	4-0	3-1	1-1	2-0	1-2	0-1
Cliftonville FC	1-4	1-1	0-2	■	1-2	2-1	1-1	0-1	2-1	0-1	0-4	1-2
Coleraine FC	1-0	3-2	1-0	2-1	■	1-0	4-1	2-0	3-2	5-1	1-1	2-0
Crusaders FC	4-3	2-1	2-1	2-0	2-0	■	5-2	2-0	1-1	5-2	1-4	1-1
Distillery FC	1-1	1-5	0-4	2-3	0-1	0-2	■	2-3	3-0	1-4	1-1	1-6
Glenavon FC	1-0	0-1	1-0	2-1	1-2	1-3	4-2	■	2-1	3-1	1-1	0-0
Glentoran FC	1-0	0-2	0-1	1-0	0-2	0-3	4-2	4-0	■	2-3	3-2	1-0
Larne FC	2-2	1-0	1-1	2-0	1-3	1-3	0-1	4-3	1-3	■	0-0	1-7
Linfield FC	4-1	2-3	1-1	8-1	1-0	2-0	3-0	2-3	5-1	0-1	■	1-0
Portadown FC	1-2	3-0	4-1	3-0	1-1	5-1	6-2	1-3	2-0	3-1	3-0	■

	Irish League	Pd	Wn	Dw	Ls	GF	GA	Pts
1.	COLERAINE FC (COLERAINE)	22	16	3	3	41	20	35
2.	Portadown FC (Portadown)	22	13	4	5	51	20	30
3.	Crusaders FC (Belfast)	22	14	2	6	48	32	30
4.	Linfield FC (Belfast)	22	10	6	6	46	25	26
5.	Glenavon FC (Lurgan)	22	11	2	9	33	35	24
6.	Ballymena United FC (Ballymena)	22	10	3	9	34	26	23
7.	Bangor FC (Bangor)	22	10	3	9	40	28	23
8.	Ards FC (Newtownards)	22	9	4	9	42	37	37
9.	Glentoran FC (Belfast)	22	8	2	12	28	39	18
10.	Larne FC (Larne)	22	7	3	12	31	50	17
11.	Cliftonville FC (Belfast)	22	3	3	16	20	56	9
12.	Distillery FC (Belfast)	22	2	3	17	24	70	7
		264	113	38	113	438	438	264

Note: Distillery FC (Belfast) continued to play "home" games at the ground of Crusaders FC (Belfast).

Top goalscorer 1973-74

1) Des DICKSON   (Coleraine FC)   24

No clubs promoted or relegated

IRISH CUP FINAL   (Windsor Park, Belfast – 27/04/1974 – 7,000)

ARDS FC (NEWTOWNARDS)   2-1   Ballymena United FC (Ballymena)
Guy, McAvoy   *Sloan*

Ards: Matthews, Patton, Patterson, Mowat, McCoy, Nixon, McAteer, McAvoy, Guy, Humphries, Cathcart (Graham 60').
Ballymena: McKenzie, Gowdy, McAuley, Stewart, Averell, Brown, Donald, Sloan, Erwin (Todd 82'), McFall, Frickleton.

Semi-finals

Ards FC (Newtownards)	4-2	Glenavon FC (Lurgan)
Ballymena United FC (Ballymena)	1-1, 2-2 (aet)	Larne FC (Larne)
	(Ballymena United won 4-3 on penalties)	

Quarter-finals

Ards FC (Newtownards)	4-2	Bangor FC (Bangor)
Ballymena United FC (Ballymena)	7-1	Crusaders FC (Belfast)
Chimney Corner FC (Antrim)	0-3	Larne FC (Larne)
Coleraine FC (Coleraine)	0-2	Glenavon FC (Lurgan)

1974-75

Irish League 1974-75	Ards	Ballymena U.	Bangor	Cliftonville	Coleraine	Crusaders	Distillery	Glenavon	Glentoran	Larne	Linfield	Portadown
Ards FC	■	0-0	1-0	3-2	1-3	0-1	3-0	4-1	1-2	1-4	2-6	1-1
Ballymena United FC	1-2	■	1-2	4-0	2-1	0-0	2-0	8-0	1-2	4-2	1-1	2-0
Bangor FC	1-1	2-2	■	2-2	2-5	3-1	2-0	4-1	3-1	0-1	3-4	1-1
Cliftonville FC	0-2	3-3	2-4	■	0-3	0-4	3-1	1-0	0-4	1-0	0-1	0-0
Coleraine FC	2-0	3-1	2-3	3-0	■	3-0	3-0	6-1	3-1	2-0	2-0	2-3
Crusaders FC	1-3	1-2	4-2	6-1	2-2	■	2-1	5-0	2-3	2-1	0-2	2-0
Distillery FC	2-0	1-1	0-1	1-1	2-2	2-4	■	0-2	0-3	1-2	0-2	1-2
Glenavon FC	3-1	2-3	2-1	3-2	0-2	0-0	3-3	■	2-4	1-4	2-3	3-1
Glentoran FC	4-0	1-1	0-0	4-0	3-1	1-4	5-1	0-0	■	5-1	1-0	2-0
Larne FC	4-0	0-1	1-1	2-0	2-3	1-2	0-2	4-2	2-3	■	0-2	2-0
Linfield FC	3-1	2-1	2-0	3-1	2-1	1-1	5-1	2-1	4-1	4-2	■	2-2
Portadown FC	2-1	0-2	1-0	1-0	0-4	2-2	5-1	4-2	4-2	0-3	0-2	■

	Irish League	Pd	Wn	Dw	Ls	GF	GA	Pts
1.	LINFIELD FC (BELFAST)	22	17	3	2	53	23	37
2.	Coleraine FC (Coleraine)	22	15	2	5	58	25	32
3.	Glentoran FC (Belfast)	22	14	3	5	52	30	31
4.	Ballymena United FC (Ballymena)	22	10	7	5	43	25	27
5.	Crusaders FC (Belfast)	22	11	5	6	46	30	27
6.	Bangor FC (Bangor)	22	8	6	8	37	35	22
7.	Portadown FC (Portadown)	22	8	5	9	29	37	21
8.	Larne FC (Larne)	22	9	1	12	38	37	19
9.	Ards FC (Newtownards)	22	7	3	12	28	43	17
10.	Glenavon FC (Lurgan)	22	5	3	14	31	62	13
11.	Cliftonville FC (Belfast)	22	3	4	15	19	54	10
12.	Distillery FC (Belfast)	22	2	4	16	20	53	8
		264	109	46	109	454	454	264

Note: Distillery FC (Belfast) continued to play "home" games at the ground of Crusaders FC (Belfast).

Top goalscorer 1974-75

1) Martin MALONE   (Portadown FC)   19

No clubs promoted or relegated

IRISH CUP FINAL   (Showgrounds, Ballymena – 19/04/1975 – 5,600)

COLERAINE FC (COLERAINE)   1-1   Linfield FC (Belfast)
Smith 32'   *Graham 65'*

Coleraine: V. Magee, McCurdy, Gordon, Beckett, Jackson, Murray, Tweed, Jennings, Guy, Smith, Simpson.
Linfield: Barclay, Fraser, McVeigh, E. Magee, Rafferty, Bowyer, Patterson (Campbell 60'), M. Malone, P. Malone, Graham, McKee.

IRISH CUP FINAL REPLAY   (Showgrounds, Ballymena – 23/04/1975 – 5,400)

COLERAINE FC (COLERAINE)　　　　　　　0-0　　　　　　　　　　Linfield FC (Belfast)

Linfield: Barclay, Fraser, McVeigh, E. Magee, Rafferty, Bowyer, Campbell, M. Malone (Bell 66'), P. Malone, Graham, Hunter.

Coleraine: V. Magee, McCurdy, Gordon, Beckett, Jackson, Murray, McNutt, Jennings, Guy, Smith, Cochrane.

IRISH CUP FINAL 2ND REPLAY   (Showgrounds, Ballymena – 29/04/1975 – 5,200)

COLERAINE FC (COLERAINE)　　　　　　　1-0　　　　　　　　　　Linfield FC (Belfast)

Smith 17'

Coleraine: V. Magee, McCurdy, McNutt, Beckett, Jackson, Murray, Cochrane, Jennings, Smith, Dickson, Gordon.

Linfield: Barclay, Fraser, McVeigh, E. Magee, Rafferty, Bowyer, Campbell (Bell 70'), Patterson, P. Malone, Graham, Hunter.

Semi-finals

Brantwood FC (Belfast)	0-6	Coleraine FC (Coleraine)
Carrick Rangers FC (Carrickfergus)	0-6	Linfield FC (Belfast)

Quarter-finals

Brantwood FC (Belfast)	2-1	Glentoran FC (Belfast)
Carrick Rangers FC (Carrickfergus)	2-1	Distillery FC (Belfast)
Cliftonville FC (Belfast)	1-1, 0-5	Coleraine FC (Coleraine)
Linfield FC (Belfast)	3-0	Larne FC (Larne)

1975-76

Irish League 1975-76	Ards	Ballymena U.	Bangor	Cliftonville	Coleraine	Crusaders	Distillery	Glenavon	Glentoran	Larne	Linfield	Portadown
Ards FC	■	1-1	1-2	4-3	3-1	0-3	1-2	2-2	0-3	3-1	1-3	2-4
Ballymena United FC	0-1	■	4-1	1-0	5-1	2-3	1-0	4-1	1-2	3-2	1-1	1-1
Bangor FC	0-0	1-1	■	2-1	1-0	2-2	3-1	2-2	2-0	3-0	0-2	3-1
Cliftonville FC	2-2	2-0	0-0	■	0-1	0-2	2-1	1-1	2-4	1-0	1-5	2-4
Coleraine FC	3-0	4-2	1-1	1-1	■	3-1	1-0	2-1	0-1	2-1	3-0	7-2
Crusaders FC	1-1	2-0	1-0	4-1	0-0	■	2-2	4-0	2-2	1-1	3-2	2-1
Distillery FC	0-2	1-3	1-1	5-2	2-3	0-7	■	1-1	0-5	1-2	0-1	2-0
Glenavon FC	1-3	1-1	0-1	0-3	0-1	1-5	3-1	■	1-1	4-1	0-5	2-1
Glentoran FC	2-3	5-2	3-0	4-1	2-2	0-1	3-0	2-0	■	1-1	3-1	1-0
Larne FC	3-0	0-1	2-3	1-4	1-2	0-2	5-3	3-2	2-1	■	2-4	0-1
Linfield FC	3-0	2-1	3-0	2-0	2-2	0-1	1-1	0-0	1-2	2-3	■	1-1
Portadown FC	3-2	3-1	1-0	2-3	1-2	1-2	5-0	0-1	0-2	1-1	1-2	■

	Irish League	Pd	Wn	Dw	Ls	GF	GA	Pts
1.	CRUSADERS FC (BELFAST)	22	15	6	1	51	19	36
2.	Glentoran FC (Belfast)	22	14	4	4	48	22	32
3.	Coleraine FC (Coleraine)	22	13	5	4	42	27	31
4.	Linfield FC (Belfast)	22	11	5	6	43	25	27
5.	Bangor FC (Bangor)	22	9	7	6	28	27	25
6.	Ballymena United FC (Ballymena)	22	8	5	9	36	35	21
7.	Ards FC (Newtownards)	22	7	5	10	32	43	19
8.	Portadown FC (Portadown)	22	7	3	12	34	39	17
9.	Cliftonville FC (Belfast)	22	6	4	12	32	46	16
10.	Larne FC (Larne)	22	6	3	13	32	45	15
11.	Glenavon FC (Lurgan)	22	4	7	11	24	44	15
12.	Distillery FC (Belfast)	22	3	4	15	24	54	10
		264	103	58	103	426	426	264

Note: Distillery FC (Belfast) continued to play "home" games at the ground of Crusaders FC (Belfast).

Top goalscorer 1975-76

1) Des DICKSON   (Coleraine FC)   23

No clubs promoted or relegated

IRISH CUP FINAL   (The Oval, Belfast – 10/04/1976 – 9,500)

CARRICK RANGERS FC 2-1 Linfield FC (Belfast)
Prenter 25', 64' *Malone 50 seconds*

Carrick: Cowan, Hamilton, Macklin, Matchett, Whiteside, Brown, Cullen, Connor, McKenzie, Prenter, Allen.
Linfield: Barclay, Fraser, McVeigh, Coyle, Rafferty, Bowyer, Nixon, Lemon (McKee 45'), Bell, M. Malone, Magee.

Semi-finals

Glentoran FC (Belfast)	0-2	Linfield FC (Belfast)
Larne FC (Larne)	3-3, 2-3	Carrick Rangers FC (Carrickfergus)

Quarter-finals

Ards FC (Newtownards)	1-1, 1-7	Linfield FC (Belfast)
Coleraine FC (Coleraine)	1-1, 3-3, 1-2	Carrick Rangers FC (Carrickfergus)
Glentoran FC (Belfast)	2-1	Cliftonville FC (Belfast)
Larne FC (Larne)	+:-	Crusaders FC (Belfast)

1976-77

Irish League 1976-77	Ards	Ballymena U.	Bangor	Cliftonville	Coleraine	Crusaders	Distillery	Glenavon	Glentoran	Larne	Linfield	Portadown
Ards FC		2-0	3-2	2-1	4-2	2-1	1-0	2-3	0-1	3-5	3-1	2-1
Ballymena United FC	1-0		0-2	0-1	2-3	0-2	2-0	1-0	0-4	4-1	1-1	2-4
Bangor FC	0-2	1-1		4-2	3-2	2-2	1-2	0-2	1-4	3-3	0-3	1-0
Cliftonville FC	0-1	0-1	1-1		0-0	0-3	0-2	1-3	1-3	2-1	2-1	1-2
Coleraine FC	2-0	3-2	2-0	3-1		3-0	0-0	3-2	0-0	3-0	1-3	3-1
Crusaders FC	4-3	4-1	1-1	6-2	0-2		1-1	1-2	2-0	2-1	0-2	2-1
Distillery FC	0-0	0-0	1-0	4-1	2-4	2-5		0-2	3-4	2-3	1-6	1-2
Glenavon FC	4-1	1-0	3-1	1-2	2-0	1-1	3-2		1-0	1-1	2-1	3-2
Glentoran FC	3-0	3-1	1-0	5-0	4-2	2-1	3-0	1-0		3-1	2-0	3-1
Larne FC	2-0	1-0	3-0	2-1	1-0	3-0	0-1	5-1	2-2		1-2	3-2
Linfield FC	3-1	0-0	2-0	4-0	1-0	0-0	1-1	0-3	3-0	0-1		4-2
Portadown FC	3-2	1-1	3-0	2-1	1-2	2-1	5-0	0-0	0-2	1-2	0-1	

	Irish League	Pd	Wn	Dw	Ls	GF	GA	Pts
1.	GLENTORAN FC (BELFAST)	22	17	2	3	50	19	36
2.	Glenavon FC (Lurgan)	22	14	3	5	40	25	31
3.	Linfield FC (Belfast)	22	12	4	6	39	21	28
4.	Coleraine FC (Coleraine)	22	12	3	7	40	29	27
5.	Larne FC (Larne)	22	12	3	7	42	33	27
6.	Crusaders FC (Belfast)	22	9	5	8	39	33	23
7.	Ards FC (Newtownards)	22	10	1	11	34	39	21
8.	Portadown FC (Portadown)	22	8	2	12	36	37	18
9.	Ballymena United FC (Ballymena)	22	5	5	12	20	34	15
10.	Distillery FC (Belfast)	22	5	5	12	25	44	15
11.	Bangor FC (Bangor)	22	4	5	13	23	43	13
12.	Cliftonville FC (Belfast)	22	4	2	16	20	51	10
		264	112	40	112	408	408	624

Note: Distillery FC (Belfast) continued to play "home" games at the ground of Crusaders FC (Belfast).

Top goalscorer 1976-77

1) Ronald McATEER   (Crusaders FC)   20

No clubs promoted or relegated

IRISH CUP FINAL   (The Oval, Belfast – 10,000)

COLERAINE FC (COLERAINE)   4-1   Linfield FC (Belfast)
Beckett, Dickson, Moffatt, Guy   *Lemon*

Coleraine: V. Magee, Hutton, McNutt, Beckett, Jackson, Connell, Porter, Jennings, Guy, Dickson, Moffatt.
Linfield: Barclay, Parkes, Garrett, Coyle, Rafferty, Lemon, Nixon, Dornan, Bell, Martin, E. Magee.

Semi-finals

Coleraine FC (Coleraine)	0-0, 3-0	Distillery FC (Belfast)
Linfield FC (Belfast)	1-1, 3-2	Larne FC Larne)

Quarter-finals

Ards FC (Newtownards)	0-6	Linfield FC (Belfast)
Crusaders FC (Belfast)	0-1	Coleraine FC (Coleraine)
Glenavon FC (Lurgan)	0-3	Distillery FC (Belfast)
Portadown FC (Portadown)	1-3	Larne FC (Larne)

1977-78

Irish League 1977-78	Ards	Ballymena U.	Bangor	Cliftonville	Coleraine	Crusaders	Distillery	Glenavon	Glentoran	Larne	Linfield	Portadown
Ards FC		2-1	1-2	1-2	3-0	3-1	1-2	2-0	1-1	1-0	0-1	3-2
Ballymena United FC	1-3		1-0	1-2	2-0	2-1	3-1	0-1	0-2	2-3	0-3	1-3
Bangor FC	1-2	2-2		1-1	1-0	4-1	0-1	0-1	0-4	2-3	1-1	2-1
Cliftonville FC	1-1	3-0	2-0		1-4	1-0	3-2	0-4	3-1	0-1	1-3	2-1
Coleraine FC	2-0	3-0	2-1	1-2		1-2	3-1	3-2	1-1	1-0	0-4	3-3
Crusaders FC	1-2	2-1	2-0	2-2	1-1		1-2	0-5	3-3	1-0	0-3	2-0
Distillery FC	2-2	2-2	0-3	1-3	3-1	5-2		1-2	0-5	3-1	1-4	1-1
Glenavon FC	5-2	2-1	1-1	1-1	2-0	1-0	4-1		2-1	2-1	0-4	3-1
Glentoran FC	4-2	2-0	6-1	5-0	4-1	4-0	2-2	2-0		1-0	2-3	2-1
Larne FC	3-1	2-1	1-0	3-2	4-3	0-1	4-0	2-0	0-1		1-2	0-4
Linfield FC	6-4	2-1	2-0	3-0	4-2	3-1	7-1	4-2	1-2	1-0		2-2
Portadown FC	3-1	3-0	1-0	2-2	0-1	3-0	4-0	3-1	1-4	2-2	1-2	

	Irish League	Pd	Wn	Dw	Ls	GF	GA	Pts
1.	LINFIELD FC (BELFAST)	22	19	2	1	65	22	40
2.	Glentoran FC (Belfast)	22	15	4	3	59	22	34
3.	Glenavon FC (Lurgan)	22	13	2	7	41	30	28
4.	Cliftonville FC (Belfast)	22	10	5	7	34	38	25
5.	Portadown FC (Portadown)	22	8	5	9	42	34	21
6.	Larne FC (Larne)	22	10	1	11	31	31	21
7.	Ards FC (Newtownards)	22	9	3	10	38	41	21
8.	Coleraine FC (Coleraine)	22	8	3	11	34	41	19
9.	Distillery FC (Belfast)	22	6	4	12	32	59	16
10.	Crusaders FC (Belfast)	22	6	3	13	24	46	15
11.	Bangor FC (Bangor)	22	5	4	13	22	36	14
12.	Ballymena United FC (Ballymena)	22	4	2	16	22	44	10
		264	113	38	113	444	444	264

Note: Distillery FC (Belfast) continued to play "home" games at the ground of Crusaders FC (Belfast).

Top goalscorer 1977-78

1) Warren FEENEY   (Glentoran FC)   17

IRISH CUP FINAL (The Oval, Belfast – 29/04/1978 – 12,000)

LINFIELD FC (BELFAST)　　　　　　　3-1　　　　　　　Ballymena United FC (Ballymena)

Dornan 14', Garrett 39', Rafferty 83'　　　　　　　　　　　　　　　　　　　*Nelson 67'*

Linfield: Barclay, Fraser, Parks, Coyle, Rafferty, Dornan, Nixon, Garrett, Martin, Hamilton, Murray.
Ballymena: Rafferty, Donald, Spence, McCullough, Jackson, Simpson, Nelson, T. Sloan, Johnston, J.Sloan, McLean.

Semi-finals

Ballymena United FC (Ballymena)	1-1, 1-1, 1-1	Crusaders FC (Belfast)(aet 4-1 pen)
Linfield FC (Belfast)	2-1	Portadown FC (Portadown)

Quarter-finals

Ballymena United FC (Ballymena)	1-0	Ards FC (Newtownards)
Bangor FC (Bangor)	0-6	Portadown FC (Portadown)
Crusaders FC (Belfast)	1-0	Larne FC (Larne)
Linfield FC (Belfast)	4-3	Glentoran FC (Belfast)

1978-79

Irish League 1978-79	Ards	Ballymena U.	Bangor	Cliftonville	Coleraine	Crusaders	Distillery	Glenavon	Glentoran	Larne	Linfield	Portadown
Ards FC		3-3	1-2	3-2	2-2	3-2	2-0	3-0	4-4	3-2	0-2	3-0
Ballymena United FC	1-3		1-1	1-1	1-1	0-0	2-0	0-2	5-1	1-3	1-2	1-0
Bangor FC	2-5	0-0		0-0	3-1	2-0	2-0	2-6	0-0	1-3	0-2	1-3
Cliftonville FC	2-1	5-0	3-0		2-0	1-0	3-0	1-3	2-4	0-1	0-3	1-1
Coleraine FC	1-2	1-2	1-1	1-1		5-0	0-1	4-3	0-0	0-3	0-0	3-0
Crusaders FC	1-0	4-0	2-2	2-2	1-0		5-2	1-0	0-2	2-2	1-4	1-2
Distillery FC	0-3	4-2	2-2	2-3	1-2	0-3		1-4	1-3	1-3	0-1	1-4
Glenavon FC	3-1	3-2	0-1	2-0	3-0	1-1	1-1		3-2	2-1	0-0	1-1
Glentoran FC	1-0	2-0	3-2	1-1	2-1	3-2	2-2	2-2		0-2	1-1	1-0
Larne FC	3-3	2-1	2-1	2-0	0-1	1-1	2-0	1-2	1-1		3-4	3-5
Linfield FC	1-2	6-1	2-2	2-1	2-3	1-1	2-0	0-0	2-1	3-1		3-1
Portadown FC	0-0	2-0	3-1	0-0	0-2	0-0	1-0	5-1	2-0	3-1	2-3	

	Irish League	Pd	Wn	Dw	Ls	GF	GA	Pts	
1.	LINFIELD FC (BELFAST)	22	14	6	2	46	21	34	
2.	Glenavon FC (Lurgan)	22	11	6	5	42	30	28	
3.	Ards FC (Newtownards)	22	11	5	6	47	34	27	
4.	Glentoran FC (Belfast)	22	9	8	5	36	33	26	
5.	Portadown FC (Portadown)	22	10	5	7	35	27	25	
6.	Larne FC (Larne)	22	10	4	8	42	35	24	
7.	Cliftonville FC (Belfast)	22	7	7	8	31	29	21	
8.	Coleraine FC (Coleraine)	22	7	6	9	29	30	20	
9.	Crusaders FC (Belfast)	22	6	8	8	30	33	20	
10.	Bangor FC (Bangor)	22	5	8	9	28	40	18	
11.	Ballymena United FC (Ballymena)	22	4	6	12	25	46	14	
12.	Distillery FC (Belfast)	22	2	3	17	19	52	7	**
		264	96	72	96	410	410	264	

** Distillery FC (Belfast), who had playing "home" games at the ground of Crusaders FC (Belfast) since 1971 because of the "civil unrest" in the country moved out of Belfast to a new stadium "New Grosvenor Park", Ballyskeagh Road, Lambeg, Lisburn, County Down for the next season.

Top goalscorer 1978-79

1) Thomas ARMSTRONG   (Ards FC)   21

No clubs promoted or relegated

IRISH CUP FINAL   (Windsor Park, Belfast – 15,000)

CLIFTONVILLE FC (BELFAST)   3-2   Portadown FC (Portadown)
Platt 32', Adair 46', Bell 89'   *Campbell 02', Alexander 77'*

Cliftonville: Johnston, McGuickan, Largey, Flanagan, M. Quinn, McCurry, T. Bell, McCusker, Mills (O'Connor 66'), Platt, Adair.

Portadown: McCullum, Smyth, Douglas, Wilson, Kilburn, Cleary, Gordon, Magee (J. Bell 66'), Alexander, Campbell, Quinn.

Semi-finals

Larne FC (Larne)	2-2, 0-1	Cliftonville FC (Belfast)
Portadown FC (Portadown)	2-1	Glenavon FC (Lurgan)

Quarter-finals

Ballymena United FC (Ballymena)	0-0, 1-2	Portadown FC (Portadown)
Coleraine FC (Coleraine)	2-3	Cliftonville FC (Belfast)
Glenavon FC (Lurgan)	3-2	Banbridge Town FC (Banbridge)
Royal Ulster Constabulary FC (Belfast)	0-1	Larne FC (Larne)

1979-80

Irish League 1979-80	Ards	Ballymena U.	Bangor	Cliftonville	Coleraine	Crusaders	Distillery	Glenavon	Glentoran	Larne	Linfield	Portadown
Ards FC	■	1-3	1-1	0-2	4-1	2-5	0-1	3-0	1-3	1-1	1-1	4-1
Ballymena United FC	2-0	■	2-0	1-1	5-0	2-1	8-0	0-1	1-1	4-0	5-0	2-1
Bangor FC	3-2	2-3	■	0-2	0-5	2-3	0-1	0-0	1-1	4-2	0-2	1-4
Cliftonville FC	2-0	2-1	3-0	■	1-3	1-0	0-1	2-0	2-2	0-0	0-1	0-0
Coleraine FC	2-0	1-1	2-3	1-5	■	5-2	2-2	3-1	1-3	1-0	1-5	2-2
Crusaders FC	2-0	1-1	0-1	1-0	3-1	■	1-2	0-0	1-0	2-0	0-1	2-0
Distillery FC	1-1	1-3	1-2	1-1	1-5	0-4	■	2-0	0-4	2-1	1-2	0-3
Glenavon FC	2-2	1-1	4-1	0-1	0-2	0-1	1-1	■	1-1	2-1	1-2	1-0
Glentoran FC	2-0	2-0	1-1	1-1	2-4	0-2	2-1	3-1	■	1-0	1-2	1-0
Larne FC	0-3	1-1	1-3	1-0	2-2	2-1	1-0	0-1	1-2	■	2-3	0-2
Linfield FC	1-0	4-1	7-0	1-0	2-0	3-0	6-1	2-1	5-0	2-0	■	6-0
Portadown FC	3-0	2-5	3-2	1-3	4-2	1-0	1-2	2-1	1-1	3-1	2-1	■

	Irish League	Pd	Wn	Dw	Ls	GF	GA	Pts
1.	LINFIELD FC (BELFAST)	22	19	1	2	59	17	39
2.	Ballymena United FC (Ballymena)	22	12	6	4	52	23	30
3.	Glentoran FC (Belfast)	22	10	7	5	34	27	27
4.	Cliftonville FC (Belfast)	22	10	6	6	29	16	26
5.	Crusaders FC (Belfast)	22	11	2	9	32	24	24
6.	Portadown FC (Portadown)	22	10	3	9	36	37	23
7.	Coleraine FC (Coleraine)	22	9	4	9	46	48	22
8.	Distillery FC (Lisburn)	22	7	4	11	22	48	18
9.	Glenavon FC (Lurgan)	22	5	6	11	19	30	16
10.	Bangor FC (Bangor)	22	6	4	12	27	50	16
11.	Ards FC (Newtownards)	22	4	5	13	26	39	13
12.	Larne FC (Larne)	22	3	4	15	17	40	10
		264	106	52	106	399	399	264

Top goalscorer 1979-80

1) James MARTIN   (Glentoran FC)   17

No clubs promoted or relegated

IRISH CUP FINAL   (The Oval, Belfast – 26/04/1980 – 10,000)

LINFIELD FC (BELFAST)   2-0   Crusaders FC (Belfast)

McCurdy 12', McKeown 68' pen.

Linfield: Dunlop, Fraser, Hayes, Dornan, Rafferty, McKeown, Nixon (Jameson 74'), McKee, McCurdy, Feeney, Anderson.

Crusaders: McDonald, Thompson, Gorman, Mulhall, Gillespie, McPolin, Kennedy (Patterson 61'), Currie, Byrne, King.

Semi-finals

Linfield FC (Belfast)	1-0	Ballymena United FC (Ballymena)
Royal Ulster Constabulary FC (Belfast)	1-1, 1-2	Crusaders FC (Belfast)

Quarter-finals

Ballymena United FC (Ballymena)	3-2	Portadown FC (Portadown)
Glenavon FC (Lurgan)	0-0, 3-0	Crusaders FC (Belfast)
Linfield FC (Belfast)	4-0	Glentoran FC (Belfast)
Royal Ulster Constabulary FC (Belfast)	1-1, 0-0, 1-0	Coleraine FC (Coleraine)

1980-81

Irish League 1980-81	Ards	Ballymena U.	Bangor	Cliftonville	Coleraine	Crusaders	Distillery	Glenavon	Glentoran	Larne	Linfield	Portadown
Ards FC		0-1	2-2	0-0	4-2	2-0	2-0	2-2	1-1	2-0	1-1	2-0
Ballymena United FC	3-2		5-1	4-3	2-0	1-1	2-0	1-1	1-2	1-0	1-0	2-0
Bangor FC	3-4	3-1		6-1	3-5	0-2	3-1	1-1	2-3	0-2	1-3	1-1
Cliftonville FC	3-0	1-1	1-1		3-2	0-0	1-0	0-2	2-4	2-4	0-2	0-2
Coleraine FC	0-1	0-0	2-0	0-0		0-1	1-1	3-3	1-1	0-0	1-2	2-5
Crusaders FC	8-2	1-0	2-0	1-0	0-1		1-0	3-1	1-1	1-2	2-2	1-1
Distillery FC	1-2	1-2	0-2	1-0	2-2	1-1		3-4	1-7	0-2	0-6	1-2
Glenavon FC	1-1	2-1	2-2	2-2	1-2	4-0	2-1		1-2	2-1	0-3	2-1
Glentoran FC	4-3	2-0	3-2	2-0	1-1	3-1	4-2	3-1		1-1	2-1	2-2
Larne FC	0-2	0-3	3-1	2-0	2-0	0-1	2-0	2-2	0-3		0-2	1-1
Linfield FC	5-0	1-0	7-0	0-1	4-1	4-0	4-2	2-1	1-1	1-0		2-1
Portadown FC	3-0	0-1	3-1	2-0	0-2	1-0	2-0	1-1	1-7	1-2	0-4	

	Irish League	Pd	Wn	Dw	Ls	GF	GA	Pts
1.	GLENTORAN FC (BELFAST)	22	15	7	-	59	26	37
2.	Linfield FC (Belfast)	22	16	3	3	57	15	35
3.	Ballymena United FC (Ballymena)	22	12	4	6	33	21	28
4.	Crusaders FC (Belfast)	22	9	6	7	28	26	24
5.	Ards FC (Newtownards)	22	9	6	7	35	40	24
6.	Glenavon FC (Lurgan)	22	7	8	7	37	37	22
7.	Larne FC (Larne)	22	9	4	9	26	26	22
8.	Portadown FC (Portadown)	22	8	5	9	30	34	21
9.	Coleraine FC (Coleraine)	22	5	8	9	28	36	18
10.	Cliftonville FC (Belfast)	22	5	5	12	20	37	15
11.	Bangor FC (Bangor)	22	4	5	13	35	54	13
12.	Distillery FC (Lisburn)	22	1	3	18	18	54	5
		264	100	64	100	406	406	264

Top goalscorers 1980-81

1) Des DICKSON (Coleraine FC) 18
   Paul MALONE (Ballymena United FC) 18

No clubs promoted or relegated

IRISH CUP FINAL (Windsor Park, Belfast – 02/05/1981 – 8,000)

BALLYMENA UNITED FC (B'MENA)   1-0   Glenavon FC (Lurgan)

McQuiston

Ballymena: Matthews, Beattie, Worthington, Fox, R. McCullough, Smyth, Neill, Sloan, McQuiston, P. Malone, McCusker.

Glenavon: T. McCullough, Fielding, McGuckin, McGuigan, Stitt, Bowyer, Wilson, M. Malone, McDonald, Tully, Dennison.

Semi-finals

Ballymena United FC (Ballymena)	2-2, 2-0	Glentoran FC (Belfast)
Glenavon FC (Lurgan)	1-0	Linfield FC (Belfast)

Quarter-finals

Ards FC (Newtownards)	1-3	Glentoran FC (Belfast)
Cliftonville FC (Belfast)	1-4	Ballymena United FC (Ballymena)
Glenavon FC (Lurgan)	2-1	Carrick Rangers FC (Carrickfergus)
Linfield FC (Belfast)	4-1	Newry Town FC (Newry)

1981-82

Irish League 1981-82	Ards	Ballymena U.	Bangor	Cliftonville	Coleraine	Crusaders	Distillery	Glenavon	Glentoran	Larne	Linfield	Portadown
Ards FC		0-0	2-0	0-1	0-3	0-0	2-0	2-4	1-7	1-0	1-2	0-1
Ballymena United FC	2-1		1-2	1-3	4-2	0-0	1-1	0-0	1-0	2-0	1-1	1-3
Bangor FC	0-1	1-3		1-1	1-5	2-1	3-3	1-2	2-1	0-4	0-5	0-1
Cliftonville FC	4-0	1-1	1-0		2-2	0-1	1-0	2-3	0-1	4-1	0-4	1-0
Coleraine FC	0-1	2-0	3-2	3-1		0-2	3-1	4-0	1-2	0-0	3-1	4-2
Crusaders FC	1-0	2-1	5-1	2-1	3-4		1-3	2-1	3-0	2-3	1-2	2-1
Distillery FC	1-0	2-3	4-0	2-2	1-0	1-2		4-2	0-5	1-0	0-7	3-0
Glenavon FC	2-2	1-1	1-1	2-2	0-3	2-2	3-1		1-3	3-3	0-6	0-2
Glentoran FC	2-0	3-1	4-0	1-2	2-2	6-1	6-1	3-1		4-1	1-2	3-1
Larne FC	2-3	1-1	2-1	0-2	2-5	0-1	1-0	4-0	0-1		2-3	0-3
Linfield FC	5-0	3-0	4-2	1-0	2-1	2-2	1-1	2-1	1-2	2-1		2-0
Portadown FC	1-1	1-0	2-0	2-2	2-4	1-0	1-0	2-1	0-4	3-0	0-1	

	Irish League	Pd	Wn	Dw	Ls	GF	GA	Pts
1.	LINFIELD FC (BELFAST)	22	17	3	2	59	19	37
2.	Glentoran FC (Belfast)	22	16	1	5	61	22	33
3.	Coleraine FC (Coleraine)	22	14	3	5	63	31	31
4.	Crusaders FC (Belfast)	22	11	4	7	36	31	26
5.	Cliftonville FC (Belfast)	22	9	6	7	33	28	24
6.	Portadown FC (Portadown)	22	11	2	9	29	29	24
7.	Ballymena United FC (Ballymena)	22	6	8	8	25	30	20
8.	Distillery FC (Lisburn)	22	7	4	11	30	44	18
9.	Glenavon FC (Lurgan)	22	4	7	11	30	52	15
10.	Ards FC (Newtownards)	22	5	4	13	18	47	14
11.	Larne FC (Larne)	22	5	3	14	27	42	13
12.	Bangor FC (Bangor)	22	3	3	16	20	56	9
		264	108	48	108	431	431	264

Top goalscorer 1981-82

1) Gary BLACKLEDGE (Glentoran FC) 18

No clubs promoted or relegated

IRISH CUP FINAL (The Oval, Belfast – 24/04/1982 – 12,000)

LINFIELD FC (BELFAST) 2-1 Coleraine FC (Coleraine)

McKeown, Murray pen.   *Healey*

Linfield: Dunlop, Mooney, Hayes, Walsh, Gibson, Dornan (Rafferty 61'), McKee, McKeown, McGaughey, Murray, Anderson.

Coleraine: Magee, McDowall, McNutt, O'Kane, Shannon, Mullan, Mahon, Healey, McManus, Dickson, Henry.

Semi-finals

Coleraine FC (Coleraine)	1-0	Cliftonville FC (Belfast)
Linfield FC (Belfast)	2-1	Ards FC (Newtownards)

Quarter-finals

Cliftonville FC (Belfast)	3-2	Royal Ulster Constabulary FC (Belfast)
Distillery FC (Lisburn)	2-2, 0-0, 2-0	Ards FC (Newtownards)
Limavady United FC (Limavady)	0-2	Coleraine FC (Coleraine)
Portadown FC (Portadown)	0-1	Linfield FC (Belfast)

1982-83

Irish League 1982-83	Ards	Ballymena U.	Bangor	Cliftonville	Coleraine	Crusaders	Distillery	Glenavon	Glentoran	Larne	Linfield	Portadown
Ards FC	■	4-0	5-1	2-4	0-3	3-1	1-0	4-2	1-3	1-0	0-1	3-2
Ballymena United FC	4-4	■	1-1	1-0	2-4	0-0	1-2	2-0	1-3	4-2	0-2	0-0
Bangor FC	1-2	0-3	■	0-3	1-3	0-3	0-1	0-0	0-3	1-1	3-6	0-6
Cliftonville FC	0-0	1-0	5-0	■	1-0	1-0	2-0	1-1	1-3	3-2	0-0	0-1
Coleraine FC	2-0	2-4	4-1	3-1	■	5-0	3-3	1-1	3-1	1-0	0-0	1-1
Crusaders FC	0-0	6-0	3-1	2-1	1-3	■	3-1	0-1	2-1	2-1	0-3	2-0
Distillery FC	3-2	2-1	1-2	2-1	2-1	1-6	■	1-0	1-3	1-4	0-4	0-0
Glenavon FC	5-3	1-3	3-1	1-2	0-0	0-3	5-0	■	1-3	0-1	0-3	1-0
Glentoran FC	4-1	1-0	2-1	1-1	0-1	3-0	4-0	4-1	■	5-0	3-0	0-1
Larne FC	2-3	1-2	5-2	0-1	3-2	0-1	2-2	2-1	2-9	■	0-1	2-2
Linfield FC	0-0	4-1	6-0	1-0	2-1	1-0	0-0	3-1	2-2	3-1	■	1-0
Portadown FC	3-1	1-2	2-1	4-1	1-1	0-0	1-0	0-1	1-0	2-0	1-0	■

	Irish League	**Pd**	**Wn**	**Dw**	**Ls**	**GF**	**GA**	**Pts**
1.	LINFIELD FC (BELFAST)	22	15	5	2	43	13	35
2.	Glentoran FC (Belfast)	22	14	2	6	49	21	30
3.	Coleraine FC (Coleraine)	22	11	6	8	44	25	28
4.	Portadown FC (Portadown)	22	10	6	6	29	17	26
5.	Crusaders FC (Belfast)	22	11	3	8	35	26	25
6.	Cliftonville FC (Belfast)	22	10	4	8	30	24	24
7.	Ards FC (Newtownards)	22	9	4	9	40	41	22
8.	Ballymena United FC (Ballymena)	22	8	4	10	32	41	20
9.	Distillery FC (Lisburn)	22	7	4	11	23	46	18
10.	Glenavon FC (Lurgan)	22	6	4	12	26	37	16
11.	Larne FC (Larne)	22	6	3	13	31	40	15
12.	Bangor FC (Bangor)	22	1	3	18	17	68	5
		264	108	48	108	399	399	264

Top goalscorer 1982-83

1) James CAMPBELL   (Ards FC)   15

Elected: Carrick Rangers FC (Carrickfergus), Newry Town FC (Newry)

The league was extended to 14 clubs for next season

IRISH CUP FINAL   (Windsor Park, Belfast – 30/04/1983 – 10,000)

GLENTORAN FC (BELFAST)   1-1   Linfield FC (Belfast)
Mullan   *McKeown pen.*

Glentoran: Patterson, G. Neill, Keeley, Harrison, Connell, Cleary, Jameson, Bowers (Morrison 80'), Manley, Mullan, D. Neill.

Linfield: Dunlop, Hayes, Crawford, Gibson, McKeown, Walsh (Garrett 84'), McKee, Dornan, Doherty, McGaughey, Anderson.

IRISH CUP FINAL REPLAY   (The Oval, Belfast – 07/05/1983 – 8,000)

GLENTORAN FC (BELFAST)   2-1   Linfield FC (Belfast)
Jameson 2   *McGaughey*

Linfield: Dunlop, Hayes, Crawford, Walsh, Gibson, McKeown, McKee, Doherty (Anderson 58'), McGaughey, Dornan, Murray.

Glentoran: Patterson, G. Neill, Connell, Keeley (Morrison 68'), Harrison, Cleary, Jameson, Strain, Manley, Mullan, D. Neill.

Semi-finals

Ards FC (Newtownards)	1-2	Linfield FC (Belfast)
Glentoran FC (Belfast)	3-0	Ballyclare Comrades FC (Ballyclare)

Quarter-finals

Ards FC (Newtownards)	2-1	Larne FC (Larne)
Ballyclare Comrades FC (Ballyclare)	1-1, 1-0	Cliftonville FC (Belfast)
Coleraine FC (Coleraine)	2-3	Glentoran FC (Belfast)
Linfield FC (Belfast)	3-1	Royal Ulster Constabulary FC (Belfast)

1983-84

Irish League 1983-84	Ards	Ballymena U.	Bangor	Carrick R.	Cliftonville	Coleraine	Crusaders	Distillery	Glenavon	Glentoran	Larne	Linfield	Newry Town	Portadown
Ards FC	■	3-0	1-0	2-1	0-0	0-0	1-1	1-0	0-3	0-0	2-0	0-2	2-0	0-0
Ballymena United FC	2-0	■	1-1	2-2	0-0	1-2	2-1	0-2	2-2	1-4	2-1	1-2	2-0	2-1
Bangor FC	2-2	1-2	■	4-1	1-2	0-1	1-0	0-2	0-5	1-3	1-0	1-4	1-2	2-1
Carrick Rangers FC	0-1	1-0	1-1	■	1-2	0-3	2-3	1-2	3-0	0-2	0-3	0-3	2-2	1-3
Cliftonville FC	1-1	0-3	1-0	1-0	■	0-0	0-1	1-0	2-0	0-1	0-3	0-1	3-1	0-1
Coleraine FC	5-3	0-0	3-1	0-3	2-2	■	1-2	4-1	1-1	0-1	4-0	1-2	4-1	0-0
Crusaders FC	0-0	2-1	3-3	1-0	1-4	3-1	■	2-3	1-1	2-3	3-1	3-1	1-2	1-0
Distillery FC	2-1	0-1	0-0	3-2	0-2	2-1	2-0	■	1-4	0-4	3-0	2-7	2-1	2-2
Glenavon FC	2-1	1-3	1-1	2-1	0-0	3-1	2-3	1-1	■	1-3	1-0	0-1	0-1	3-1
Glentoran FC	3-3	0-0	6-0	6-1	1-2	1-0	1-0	1-1	1-1	■	2-2	4-1	5-0	2-0
Larne FC	1-1	0-1	3-1	2-0	2-0	1-4	2-1	0-2	0-3	0-2	■	1-2	2-1	0-1
Linfield FC	1-1	1-0	4-1	3-1	0-1	6-1	6-1	3-1	2-1	3-0	8-0	■	3-0	3-0
Newry Town FC	0-4	2-2	2-0	4-0	2-3	0-3	1-1	2-1	1-2	0-1	2-0	1-3	■	0-1
Portadown FC	0-2	1-1	5-0	2-0	1-1	0-2	0-1	1-0	2-1	0-0	4-1	1-4	0-2	■

	Irish League	Pd	Wn	Dw	Ls	GF	GA	Pts	
1.	LINFIELD FC (BELFAST)	26	22	1	3	76	23	45	
2.	Glentoran FC (Belfast)	26	18	6	2	65	19	42	
3.	Cliftonville FC (Belfast)	26	12	7	7	28	23	31	
4.	Ards FC (Newtownards)	26	9	11	6	32	26	29	
5.	Coleraine FC (Coleraine)	26	11	6	9	44	34	28	
6.	Ballymena United FC (Ballymena)	26	10	8	8	32	30	28	
7.	Glenavon FC (Lurgan)	26	10	7	9	41	33	27	
8.	Crusaders FC (Belfast)	26	11	5	10	38	41	27	
9.	Distillery FC (Lisburn)	26	11	4	11	35	42	26	
10.	Portadown FC (Portadown)	26	9	6	11	28	31	24	
11.	Newry Town FC (Newry)	26	8	3	15	30	48	19	
12.	Bangor FC (Bangor)	26	4	6	16	24	57	14	
13.	Larne FC (Larne)	26	7	1	18	25	58	13	-2
14.	Carrick Rangers FC (Carrickfergus)	26	3	3	20	24	57	9	
		364	145	74	145	522	522	362	

Note: Larne FC (Larne) had 2 points deducted for fielding an ineligible player against Bangor FC (Bangor).

Top goalscorers 1983-84

1) Trevor ANDERSON   (Linfield FC)   15
   Martin McGAUGHEY   (Linfield FC)   15

No clubs promoted or relegated

IRISH CUP FINAL (Windsor Park, Belfast – 05/05/1984 – 5,000)

BALLYMENA UNITED FC (BALLYMENA)   4-1   Carrick Rangers FC (Carrickfergus)

Fox, Crockard, Harrison pen., Speak   *Fellows*

Ballymena: Platt, McCreery, Fox, Harrison, Crockard, Burns, Sloan, Ring, Speak, Guy, Wright.

Carrick: Coburn (Rodgers), Fraser, M. Smyth, Blair, McCullough, Bowyer, Conville, Fellows, Hardy, Thompson, Richardson.

Semi-finals

Ballymena United FC (Ballymena)	2-1	Cliftonville FC (Belfast)
Carrick Rangers FC (Carrickfergus)	2-1	Glentoran FC (Belfast)

Quarter-finals

Ballymena United FC (Ballymena)	2-1	Linfield FC (Belfast)
Cliftonville FC (Belfast)	2-0	P.O.S.C. Belfast (Belfast)
Glentoran FC (Belfast)	1-0	Glenavon FC (Lurgan)
Newry Town FC (Newry)	0-1	Carrick Rangers FC (Carrickfergus)

1984-85

Irish League 1984-85	Ards	Ballymena U.	Bangor	Carrick R.	Cliftonville	Coleraine	Crusaders	Distillery	Glenavon	Glentoran	Larne	Linfield	Newry Town	Portadown
Ards FC		1-2	1-0	4-0	0-1	1-2	1-1	0-0	1-3	3-1	2-1	0-0	1-0	4-1
Ballymena United FC	1-3		1-3	1-1	2-0	2-2	0-0	3-0	3-1	1-3	3-2	0-3	2-2	2-0
Bangor FC	1-3	1-0		2-0	0-3	2-6	1-1	0-0	1-3	0-1	0-2	2-2	2-2	1-1
Carrick Rangers FC	3-2	2-2	1-1		1-2	0-2	2-2	1-3	1-3	0-2	2-0	1-4	0-2	2-1
Cliftonville FC	1-0	0-2	0-1	3-3		2-2	0-0	1-2	2-1	1-1	1-3	0-4	1-1	2-3
Coleraine FC	1-1	3-0	2-0	3-1	1-2		3-0	3-2	1-3	2-2	3-1	0-1	1-1	2-1
Crusaders FC	3-1	0-3	1-1	0-0	3-2	0-6		1-0	3-1	1-1	1-4	0-0	1-2	5-0
Distillery FC	2-1	2-1	0-2	3-1	0-0	2-2	3-2		3-2	0-2	1-1	1-1	7-2	1-3
Glenavon FC	1-1	2-2	2-1	4-0	1-1	1-2	1-1	3-1		0-4	1-0	0-7	0-3	1-2
Glentoran FC	2-0	1-0	1-1	3-0	2-3	2-1	1-3	0-0	5-0		6-0	2-3	3-0	1-1
Larne FC	3-0	0-3	2-0	2-1	1-4	0-1	1-2	0-0	5-2	1-2		1-4	2-1	1-0
Linfield FC	5-0	0-0	2-0	6-1	1-3	1-2	0-2	5-1	3-4	3-1	3-1		2-0	1-0
Newry Town FC	4-1	3-1	1-1	3-0	1-2	3-3	0-1	3-1	0-4	1-4	2-3	0-6		1-2
Portadown FC	1-0	1-0	1-0	2-0	0-0	0-0	3-0	1-0	0-1	1-0	2-0	0-3	6-1	

	Irish League	Pd	Wn	Dw	Ls	GF	GA	Pts
1.	LINFIELD FC (BELFAST)	26	17	5	4	70	22	39
2.	Coleraine FC (Coleraine)	26	14	8	4	56	31	36
3.	Glentoran FC (Belfast)	26	14	6	6	53	26	34
4.	Portadown FC (Portadown)	26	13	4	9	33	29	30
5.	Cliftonville FC (Belfast)	26	10	8	8	37	36	28
6.	Crusaders FC (Belfast)	26	9	10	7	34	37	28
7.	Glenavon FC (Lurgan)	26	11	4	11	45	53	26
8.	Ballymena United FC (Ballymena)	26	9	7	10	37	36	25
9.	Distillery FC (Lisburn)	26	8	8	10	35	41	24
10.	Larne FC (Larne)	26	10	2	14	37	47	22
11.	Ards FC (Newtownards)	26	8	5	13	32	40	21
12.	Newry Town FC (Newry)	26	7	6	13	39	57	20
13.	Bangor FC (Bangor)	26	5	9	12	24	39	19
14.	Carrick Rangers FC (Carrickfergus)	26	3	6	17	24	62	12
		364	138	88	138	556	556	364

Top goalscorer 1984-85

1) Martin McGAUGHEY   (Linfield FC)   34

No clubs promoted or relegated

IRISH CUP FINAL   (Windsor Park, Belfast – 04/05/1985 – 12,000)

GLENTORAN FC (BELFAST)   1-1   Linfield FC (Belfast)
Mullan   *McKeown*

Glentoran: Paterson, Neill, Leeman, Morrison, Dixon, Cleary, Stewart, Bowers, Blackledge, Mullan, Caskey.
Linfield: Dunlop, Mooney, Crawford, Dornan, Gibson, Jeffrey, McKee, Doherty, McClurg, McKeown, Anderson (Murray).

IRISH CUP FINAL REPLAY   (Windsor Park, Belfast – 11/05/1985 – 12,000)

GLENTORAN FC (BELFAST)   1-1, 1-0   Linfield FC (Belfast)
Mooney o.g.

Linfield: Dunlop, Mooney, Crawford, Gibson, Jeffrey, Dornan (Murray), McKee, Doherty, McKeown, McClurg, Anderson.
Glentoran: Paterson, Neill, Leeman, Morrison, Dixon, Cleary, Stewart, Bowers, Blackledge (Jameson), Mullan, Caskey.

Semi-finals

Ballymena United FC (Ballymena)	0-3	Linfield FC (Belfast)
Coleraine FC (Coleraine)	1-2	Glentoran FC (Belfast)

Quarter-finals

Ards FC (Newtownards)	0-1	Ballymena United FC (Ballymena)
Distillery FC (Lisburn)	0-3	Glentoran FC (Belfast)
Glenavon FC (Lurgan)	0-4	Coleraine FC (Coleraine)
Portadown FC (Portadown)	1-2	Linfield FC (Belfast)

1985-86

Irish League 1985-86	Ards	Ballymena U.	Bangor	Carrick R.	Cliftonville	Coleraine	Crusaders	Distillery	Glenavon	Glentoran	Larne	Linfield	Newry Town	Portadown
Ards FC		1-0	2-1	4-1	4-0	1-0	1-3	4-0	2-0	0-0	1-1	2-1	0-1	3-0
Ballymena United FC	1-0		2-1	7-1	4-2	1-2	0-0	3-1	3-3	0-1	0-2	1-1	3-1	0-1
Bangor FC	1-1	0-2		2-0	1-0	2-1	0-1	2-2	1-1	0-3	2-0	0-0	1-1	0-1
Carrick Rangers FC	0-3	0-4	1-1		0-1	0-2	0-1	0-0	0-4	0-2	2-2	0-4	3-1	0-1
Cliftonville FC	0-0	1-0	4-3	0-0		2-1	2-1	1-1	1-1	1-1	3-1	0-1	4-0	0-0
Coleraine FC	1-1	2-1	3-1	2-0	3-1		4-3	0-3	2-2	1-5	7-1	0-2	4-1	4-0
Crusaders FC	2-1	0-0	2-0	1-0	2-1	2-1		4-1	1-1	4-2	2-2	1-3	3-0	2-1
Distillery FC	0-2	1-1	2-1	1-1	1-2	1-1	2-1		4-2	0-1	0-6	0-4	2-1	0-3
Glenavon FC	0-0	0-2	2-1	1-1	1-1	0-1	1-2	0-2		1-0	1-1	0-3	2-2	2-0
Glentoran FC	2-1	2-0	1-4	2-0	3-2	0-2	1-0	1-2	0-1		1-0	2-3	4-0	1-0
Larne FC	2-1	0-0	5-0	5-0	1-1	0-2	3-1	0-1	3-0	0-0		1-1	3-0	1-2
Linfield FC	0-2	5-1	2-1	5-0	2-0	0-1	3-0	5-0	1-0	2-1	3-1		2-1	2-0
Newry Town FC	0-0	1-6	5-1	0-1	0-0	1-2	2-2	3-2	2-0	0-5	2-6	1-3		1-0
Portadown FC	2-0	1-1	1-4	2-1	2-1	0-2	2-1	0-1	0-0	2-1	1-2	0-1	0-1	

	Irish League	Pd	Wn	Dw	Ls	GF	GA	Pts
1.	LINFIELD FC (BELFAST)	26	20	3	3	59	16	43
2.	Coleraine FC (Coleraine)	26	16	3	7	51	31	35
3.	Ards FC (Newtownards)	26	12	7	7	37	19	31
4.	Glentoran FC (Belfast)	26	14	3	9	42	26	31
5.	Crusaders FC (Belfast)	26	13	5	8	42	34	31
6.	Larne FC (Larne)	26	10	8	8	49	34	28
7.	Ballymena United FC (Ballymena)	26	10	7	9	43	30	27
8.	Cliftonville FC (Belfast)	26	8	9	9	31	34	25
9.	Distillery FC (Lisburn)	26	9	6	11	30	49	24
10.	Portadown FC (Portadown)	26	10	3	13	22	32	23
11.	Glenavon FC (Lurgan)	26	5	11	10	26	36	21
12.	Bangor FC (Bangor)	26	6	6	14	31	45	18
13.	Newry Town FC (Newry)	26	6	5	15	28	59	17
14.	Carrick Rangers FC (Carrickfergus)	26	2	6	18	12	58	10
		364	141	82	141	503	503	364

Top goalscorer 1985-86

1) Trevor ANDERSON   (Linfield FC)   14

No clubs promoted or relegated

IRISH CUP FINAL   (Windsor Park, Belfast – 03/05/1986 – 8,000)

GLENTORAN FC (BELFAST)   2-1   Coleraine FC (Coleraine)
Mullan, Millar   *Healy pen.*

Glentoran: Paterson, Neill, Leeman, Connell, More, Cleary, Jameson, Morrison, Manley (Millar 78'), Mullan, Stewart.

Coleraine: Platt, McDowell, Edgar, McIlhinney, Tabb, Wade (Henry 34'), Healey, McQuiston, Campbell, McCreadie, McCoy.

Semi-finals

Coleraine FC (Coleraine)	2-0	Ards FC (Newtownards)
Glentoran FC (Belfast)	3-0	Brantwood FC (Belfast)

Quarter-finals

Brantwood FC (Belfast)	1-0	Portadown FC (Portadown)
Chimney Corner FC (Antrim)	0-4	Coleraine FC (Coleraine)
Carrick Rangers FC (Carrickfergus)	0-1	Ards FC (Newtownards)
Glentoran FC (Belfast)	1-0	Cliftonville FC (Belfast)

1986-87

Irish League 1986-87	Ards	Ballymena U.	Bangor	Carrick R.	Cliftonville	Coleraine	Crusaders	Distillery	Glenavon	Glentoran	Larne	Linfield	Newry Town	Portadown
Ards FC	■	1-1	0-1	4-4	0-0	1-2	3-0	1-0	1-0	1-1	0-5	2-1	4-3	3-1
Ballymena United FC	2-1	■	4-3	3-0	1-1	2-1	2-3	2-0	1-1	2-0	1-1	0-0	1-2	0-0
Bangor FC	0-4	0-1	■	2-0	1-1	0-3	3-2	4-1	1-0	0-2	0-3	0-1	2-2	3-2
Carrick Rangers FC	0-5	3-2	2-1	■	1-0	2-2	2-4	1-0	1-4	0-1	0-2	0-3	2-5	0-0
Cliftonville FC	0-1	3-1	1-2	2-2	■	0-1	2-1	1-0	3-1	2-2	1-1	0-1	4-0	1-1
Coleraine FC	1-3	2-2	5-1	4-2	4-1	■	6-0	4-1	1-1	1-2	1-0	2-0	5-0	1-1
Crusaders FC	1-3	3-3	1-0	1-0	3-2	1-5	■	2-2	2-2	3-1	1-1	1-0	1-3	1-2
Distillery FC	0-2	3-1	3-1	0-1	1-4	2-8	1-3	■	1-3	1-2	1-2	0-5	0-6	1-2
Glenavon FC	1-0	1-2	2-0	2-0	0-0	0-1	1-0	3-1	■	1-1	1-1	1-2	1-3	4-0
Glentoran FC	2-3	7-2	4-1	2-0	2-2	0-1	3-0	5-0	1-1	■	3-0	3-1	2-0	4-0
Larne FC	1-2	1-2	2-0	1-1	1-0	2-0	1-0	0-0	0-0	4-0	■	1-1	3-0	2-0
Linfield FC	2-0	3-0	4-0	2-1	1-0	2-1	3-1	6-0	1-0	1-0	5-0	■	0-1	2-0
Newry Town FC	0-0	1-5	2-0	1-0	0-1	0-0	2-1	4-1	2-1	1-1	2-1	0-2	■	1-1
Portadown FC	2-2	1-2	0-2	0-2	0-2	0-3	1-1	1-1	1-0	2-3	2-2	1-1	1-1	■

	Irish League	Pd	Wn	Dw	Ls	GF	GA	Pts	
1.	LINFIELD FC (BELFAST)	26	18	3	5	50	15	57	
2.	Coleraine FC (Coleraine)	26	16	5	5	65	26	53	
3.	Ards FC (Newtownards)	26	14	6	6	47	31	48	
4.	Larne FC (Larne)	26	11	9	6	38	24	42	
5.	Newry Town FC (Newry)	26	12	6	8	42	40	42	
6.	Ballymena United FC (Ballymena)	26	11	8	7	45	42	41	
7.	Glentoran FC (Belfast)	26	14	6	6	54	30	40	-8
8.	Cliftonville FC (Belfast)	26	8	9	9	34	29	33	
9.	Glenavon FC (Lurgan)	26	8	8	10	32	27	32	
10.	Bangor FC (Bangor)	26	8	2	16	28	52	26	
11.	Crusaders FC (Belfast)	26	8	5	13	37	54	25	-4
12.	Carrick Rangers FC (Carrickfergus)	26	6	5	13	27	53	23	
13.	Portadown FC (Portadown)	26	3	11	12	22	45	20	
14.	Distillery FC (Lisburn)	26	2	3	21	21	74	9	
		364	139	86	139	542	542	491	

From this season onwards a Win was worth 3 points, a Draw was worth 1 point and a Loss was worth 0 points.

Note: Glentoran FC (Belfast) had 8 points deducted and Crusaders FC (Belfast) had 4 points deducted, both for fielding ineligible players in league matches.

Top goalscorers 1986-87

1)	Gary McCARTNEY	(Glentoran FC)	14
	Ray McCOY	(Coleraine FC)	14
3)	BAXTER	(Ards FC)	12
	Martin McGAUGHEY	(Linfield FC)	12
	O'BOYLE	(Linfield FC)	12

No clubs promoted or relegated

IRISH CUP FINAL   (Windsor Park, Belfast – 02/05/1987 – 8,000)

GLENTORAN FC (BELFAST)	1-0	Larne FC (Larne)

Mullan

Glentoran: Paterson, J. Smyth, Stewart, Bowers, Harrison, Cleary, Jameson (Craig 83'), Caskey, Mullan, McCartney, Morrison.

Larne: Magee, McMullan, Huston, Garland, Spiers, Bustard (Campbell 79'), McLoughlin, D. Smyth (Dickey 60'), Guy, Hardy, Sloan.

Semi-finals

Coleraine FC (Coleraine)	1-2	Larne FC (Larne)
Glentoran FC (Belfast)	1-1, 2-1	Newry Town FC (Newry)

Semi-finals

Ards FC (Newtownards)	1-2	Larne FC (Larne)
Bangor FC (Bangor)	1-6	Coleraine FC (Coleraine)
Glentoran FC (Belfast)	3-2	Glenavon FC (Lurgan)
Newry Town FC (Newry)	0-0, 2-0	Cliftonville FC (Belfast)

1987-88

Irish League 1987-88	Ards	Ballymena U.	Bangor	Carrick R.	Cliftonville	Coleraine	Crusaders	Distillery	Glenavon	Glentoran	Larne	Linfield	Newry Town	Portadown
Ards FC		0-1	1-1	1-2	1-0	1-1	1-2	1-1	1-1	0-2	2-3	1-2	0-1	2-0
Ballymena United FC	1-1		1-0	1-0	1-1	2-1	0-0	2-1	1-1	3-2	0-1	1-4	3-4	2-1
Bangor FC	2-4	1-0		2-1	1-3	0-4	1-1	1-6	3-0	0-1	0-2	0-4	1-0	0-0
Carrick Rangers FC	2-1	1-2	0-2		0-2	0-3	1-2	2-0	0-0	0-2	2-2	1-0	1-1	0-1
Cliftonville FC	0-0	1-1	1-2	0-2		0-2	0-0	2-0	2-3	1-1	0-2	0-5	1-1	1-0
Coleraine FC	4-2	5-5	2-1	3-1	3-0		1-1	3-1	1-0	1-2	3-0	1-2	1-3	1-0
Crusaders FC	3-0	0-0	4-1	2-1	2-0	0-1		3-0	1-2	2-3	1-4	1-3	0-3	1-2
Distillery FC	1-3	0-5	0-1	1-1	1-2	1-2	2-0		0-1	0-3	2-1	0-1	0-2	1-2
Glenavon FC	0-1	1-0	1-0	3-2	4-0	3-2	1-0	4-0		1-2	0-1	0-3	0-0	1-2
Glentoran FC	2-2	3-0	3-0	1-1	1-1	2-2	1-0	1-0	1-0		4-0	0-1	1-0	1-0
Larne FC	2-0	1-0	1-2	3-1	0-0	0-4	1-2	2-1	1-0	0-3		1-2	5-1	0-0
Linfield FC	1-0	3-1	3-1	1-0	4-0	0-1	1-1	2-0	3-0	0-2	3-0		1-0	1-1
Newry Town FC	1-0	1-0	1-0	3-1	1-0	1-0	3-0	3-0	0-0	0-2	0-0	1-0		3-2
Portadown FC	2-3	0-0	3-1	4-2	0-1	0-1	2-0	3-0	0-1	0-2	2-1	1-1	3-0	

	Irish League	Pd	Wn	Dw	Ls	GF	GA	Pts
1.	GLENTORAN FC (BELFAST)	26	19	5	2	48	15	62
2.	Linfield FC (Belfast)	26	19	3	4	51	15	60
3.	Coleraine FC (Coleraine)	26	16	4	6	53	28	52
4.	Newry Town FC (Newry)	26	15	5	6	34	22	50
5.	Larne FC (Larne)	26	12	4	10	35	35	40
6.	Glenavon FC (Lurgan)	26	11	5	10	28	27	38
7.	Ballymena United FC (Ballymena)	26	9	9	8	34	34	36
8.	Portadown FC (Portadown)	26	10	5	11	31	27	35
9.	Crusaders FC (Belfast)	26	8	6	12	29	35	30
10.	Cliftonville FC (Belfast)	26	6	8	12	18	38	26
11.	Ards FC (Newtownards)	26	6	7	13	29	38	25
12.	Bangor FC (Bangor)	26	7	4	15	24	47	25
13.	Carrick Rangers FC (Carrickfergus)	26	5	5	16	25	44	20
14.	Distillery FC (Lisburn)	26	3	2	21	19	53	11
		364	146	72	146	458	458	510

On 16/01/1988 the Crusaders FC 1-3 Carrick Rangers FC and Linfield FC 2-1 Glentoran FC matches were both abandoned and replayed at later dates with the results as shown in the above results chart.

Top goalscorers 1987-88

1)	Martin McGAUGHEY	(Linfield FC)	18
2)	David HANNA	(Portadown FC)	10
	Raymond MORRISON	(Glentoran FC)	10
4)	Duncan MacLEOD	(Linfield FC)	9
	Ray McCOY	(Coleraine FC)	9
	Ron MANLEY	(Glentoran FC)	9
	Ricky WADE	(Coleraine FC)	9

No clubs promoted or relegated

IRISH CUP FINAL (Windsor Park, Belfast – 30/04/1988)

GLENTORAN FC (BELFAST)   1-0   Glenavon FC (Lurgan)

Cleary 89' pen.

Glentoran: Smyth, Neill, Stewart, Devine, Moore (Mathieson 75'), Cleary, Morrison, Caskey, McCartney, Mullan (Manley 56'), Jameson.

Glenavon: Beck, McKeown, Russell, Dennison, Byrne, D. Lowry, Denver, McLoughlin, McGroarty, McBride, McCann.

Semi-finals

Glenavon FC (Lurgan)	2-0	Ballymena United FC (Ballymena)
Glentoran FC (Belfast)	3-2	Portadown FC (Portadown)

Semi-finals

Ballymena United FC (Ballymena)	0-0, 3-0	Distillery FC (Lisburn)
Glenavon FC (Lurgan)	2-1	Ards FC (Newtownards)
Glentoran FC (Belfast)	5-0	Newry Town FC (Newry)
Linfield FC (Belfast)	1-1, 0-2	Portadown FC (Portadown)

1988-89

Irish League 1988-89	Ards	Ballymena U.	Bangor	Carrick R.	Cliftonville	Coleraine	Crusaders	Distillery	Glenavon	Glentoran	Larne	Linfield	Newry Town	Portadown
Ards FC	■	0-0	2-3	0-1	0-4	0-2	2-0	1-1	1-5	1-5	3-1	1-3	4-3	0-0
Ballymena United FC	3-2	■	2-1	1-2	3-3	2-0	1-1	3-0	0-3	1-2	0-0	0-4	2-2	3-1
Bangor FC	2-1	1-1	■	1-1	3-1	3-4	1-0	2-0	1-1	2-1	1-1	1-1	2-0	1-1
Carrick Rangers FC	1-0	0-0	2-3	■	2-1	0-1	0-2	1-0	1-3	0-3	3-1	1-3	1-0	1-2
Cliftonville FC	2-2	4-1	0-1	5-1	■	1-1	1-0	4-0	0-1	0-0	0-0	0-3	1-2	1-1
Coleraine FC	1-1	4-1	2-1	0-1	0-0	■	3-1	2-0	0-1	2-3	2-0	0-2	3-2	2-0
Crusaders FC	0-1	0-0	0-3	0-3	1-2	0-3	■	2-1	1-0	0-3	1-1	1-2	3-1	1-3
Distillery FC	2-0	2-2	1-2	0-2	0-4	0-3	2-2	■	2-1	1-3	1-6	1-5	1-2	0-2
Glenavon FC	3-0	2-1	3-2	2-1	3-2	1-2	3-3	3-2	■	2-3	2-2	0-1	0-0	0-2
Glentoran FC	1-0	3-2	2-1	4-0	2-2	1-1	3-0	8-2	2-3	■	3-1	2-3	2-0	0-1
Larne FC	1-1	1-1	1-1	1-2	0-0	0-2	4-0	7-0	1-3	0-1	■	3-2	1-2	1-0
Linfield FC	2-1	1-0	0-1	4-1	2-0	2-0	3-0	3-0	2-1	1-2	2-2	■	1-0	2-1
Newry Town FC	6-1	2-3	1-1	2-0	1-3	0-2	0-3	3-0	1-0	1-1	1-2	0-3	■	1-1
Portadown FC	2-0	0-0	1-1	1-1	0-1	0-0	1-0	0-1	1-1	2-0	4-0	0-1	2-0	■

	Irish League	Pd	Wn	Dw	Ls	GF	GA	Pts
1.	LINFIELD FC (BELFAST)	26	21	2	3	58	19	65
2.	Glentoran FC (Belfast)	26	17	4	5	60	29	55
3.	Coleraine FC (Coleraine)	26	15	5	6	42	23	50
4.	Bangor FC (Bangor)	26	12	9	5	42	30	45
5.	Glenavon FC (Lurgan)	26	13	5	8	47	34	44
6.	Portadown FC (Portadown)	26	10	9	7	29	19	39
7.	Cliftonville FC (Belfast)	26	9	9	8	42	30	36
8.	Carrick Rangers FC (Carrickfergus)	26	11	3	12	29	40	36
9.	Ballymena United FC (Ballymena)	26	6	11	9	33	41	29
10.	Larne FC (Larne)	26	6	10	10	38	38	28
11.	Newry Town FC (Newry)	26	7	5	14	33	43	26
12.	Crusaders FC (Belfast)	26	5	5	16	22	47	20
13.	Ards FC (Newtownards)	26	4	6	16	25	54	18
14.	Distillery FC (Lisburn)	26	3	3	20	20	73	12
		364	139	86	139	520	520	503

Top goalscorers 1988-89

1) Stephen BAXTER   (Linfield FC)   17
2) Gary McCARTNEY   (Glentoran FC)   16
3) Martin MAGEE   (Portadown FC)   15

No clubs promoted or relegated

IRISH CUP FINAL   (The Oval, Belfast – 06/05/1989 – 5,000)

BALLYMENA UNITED FC (BALLYMENA)   1-0   Larne FC (Larne)

Hardy 73'

Ballymena: Grant, Scott, M. Smyth, Garrett, Heron, Young, McKee, Curry, Pyper, Hardy, Doherty (Simpson 64').
Larne: Magee, McMullan, Huston, Garland, Spiers, Bustard, Murphy, Kernoghan, F. Smith (McDonald 49'), Sloan, D. Smyth (Hannan 76').

Semi-finals

Cliftonville FC (Belfast)	1-1, 1-2	Larne FC (Larne)
Linfield FC (Belfast)	1-1, 1-2	Ballymena United FC (Ballymena)

Quarter-finals

Cliftonville FC (Belfast)	0-0, 2-1	Tobermore United FC (Tobermore)
Crusaders FC (Belfast)	2-3	Ballymena United FC (Ballymena)
Glentoran FC (Belfast)	0-3	Linfield FC (Belfast)
Larne FC (Larne)	0-0, 3-2	Carrick Rangers FC (Carrickfergus)

1989-90

Irish League 1989-90	Ards	Ballymena U.	Bangor	Carrick R.	Cliftonville	Coleraine	Crusaders	Distillery	Glenavon	Glentoran	Larne	Linfield	Newry Town	Portadown
Ards FC		0-2	0-2	1-1	3-4	0-4	3-1	5-0	0-1	2-1	0-1	1-2	1-5	0-1
Ballymena United FC	0-0		1-0	3-1	1-2	1-1	0-0	2-1	3-1	1-1	0-0	5-1	1-3	2-3
Bangor FC	3-0	0-1		2-0	1-2	0-1	3-0	2-0	0-0	0-0	0-0	1-0	2-0	1-0
Carrick Rangers FC	2-0	0-1	1-1		3-1	4-0	2-0	2-2	2-2	1-1	4-3	0-3	2-0	1-1
Cliftonville FC	1-2	1-0	1-2	0-2		2-0	2-2	2-2	1-1	0-0	2-2	1-0	3-2	1-3
Coleraine FC	4-0	0-2	3-2	1-0	1-1		1-2	0-3	0-3	1-1	2-1	1-3	0-2	0-0
Crusaders FC	0-3	0-2	2-0	3-2	1-1	1-1		3-3	1-2	0-4	1-2	2-3	2-1	1-2
Distillery FC	2-1	1-1	0-0	1-0	0-3	2-4	2-2		0-5	0-3	2-2	0-7	1-1	0-2
Glenavon FC	0-0	2-1	0-1	1-0	2-2	2-1	1-1	6-0		2-1	4-1	3-1	2-1	2-0
Glentoran FC	0-0	1-0	1-3	2-0	1-0	5-3	6-0	2-0	2-3		2-1	3-2	1-0	2-3
Larne FC	1-0	1-2	3-0	0-2	1-0	2-1	2-2	1-0	0-2	0-0		1-4	0-2	2-0
Linfield FC	0-0	1-2	3-0	3-1	1-4	4-3	2-0	3-1	1-3	1-3	2-0		4-1	1-1
Newry Town FC	2-2	3-3	2-0	2-0	3-0	1-3	2-0	2-4	3-1	1-0	2-0	1-2		0-0
Portadown FC	4-1	1-0	1-0	2-0	3-0	0-0	3-0	2-0	0-3	1-0	0-0	2-2	2-0	3-0	

	Irish League	Pd	Wn	Dw	Ls	GF	GA	Pts
1.	PORTADOWN FC (PORTADOWN)	26	16	7	3	42	17	55
2.	Glenavon FC (Lurgan)	26	16	6	4	52	26	54
3.	Glentoran FC (Belfast)	26	12	8	6	43	24	44
4.	Linfield FC (Belfast)	26	14	2	10	54	40	44
5.	Ballymena United FC (Ballymena)	26	12	7	7	37	25	43
6.	Bangor FC (Bangor)	26	11	5	10	26	22	38
7.	Newry Town FC (Newry)	26	11	4	11	42	37	37
8.	Cliftonville FC (Belfast)	26	9	8	9	37	39	35
9.	Larne FC (Larne)	26	8	7	11	29	38	31
10.	Carrick Rangers FC (Carrickfergus)	26	8	6	12	33	36	30
11.	Coleraine FC (Coleraine)	26	8	6	12	36	44	30
12.	Ards FC (Newtownards)	26	5	6	15	25	44	21
13.	Crusaders FC (Belfast)	26	4	8	14	27	55	20
14.	Distillery FC (Lisburn)	26	4	8	14	27	63	20
		364	138	88	138	510	510	502

Top goalscorers 1989-90

1)	Martin McGAUGHEY	(Linfield FC)	19
2)	Gary McCARTNEY	(Glentoran FC)	17
3)	Oliver RALPH	(Newry Town FC)	14
4)	Gary BLACKLEDGE	(Glenavon FC)	12
	Stephen McBRIDE	(Glenavon FC)	12

Elected: Ballyclare Comrades FC (Ballyclare), Omagh Town FC (Omagh)

The league was extended to 16 clubs for next season

IRISH CUP FINAL (Windsor Park, Belfast – 05/05/1990 – 12,000)
GLENTORAN FC (BELFAST)   3-0   Portadown FC (Portadown)
Neill 60', Douglas 85', Morrison 87'

Glentoran: Smyth, Neill, Moore, Devine, Bowers, McCaffrey, Jameson, Caskey, Campbell (Morrison 49'), McCartney (Totten 46'), Douglas.

Portadown: Keenan, Major, Stewart, Strain, Curliss, Mills (Cunningham 65'), McKeever (Bell 65'), McCreadie, Davidson, Fraser, Cowan.

Semi-finals

Glentoran FC (Belfast)	2-0	Linfield FC (Belfast)
Portadown FC (Portadown)	4-0	Coleraine FC (Coleraine)

Quarter-finals

Banbridge Town FC (Banbridge)	0-1	Coleraine FC (Coleraine)
Larne FC (Larne)	1-2	Linfield FC (Belfast)
Newry Town FC (Newry)	2-3	Glentoran FC (Belfast)
Portadown FC (Portadown)	2-1	Bangor FC (Bangor)

1990-91

Irish League 1990-91	Ards	Ballyclare C.	Ballymena U.	Bangor	Carrick R.	Cliftonville	Coleraine	Crusaders	Distillery	Glenavon	Glentoran	Larne	Linfield	Newry Town	Omagh Town	Portadown
Ards FC	■	4-3	0-0	0-2	2-0	1-1	1-0	0-0	2-1	1-2	2-3	4-1	1-1	1-2	5-1	1-2
Ballyclare Comrades FC	1-0	■	1-5	0-2	1-0	1-3	1-1	2-3	2-0	3-3	0-1	3-3	1-1	0-2	0-3	0-3
Ballymena United FC	4-1	1-1	■	3-0	2-1	1-1	4-0	1-0	1-2	4-3	2-3	4-4	2-2	2-1	2-0	0-2
Bangor FC	1-1	2-0	2-2	■	2-1	4-2	3-1	2-1	2-1	1-2	1-0	2-0	1-0	2-0	3-0	0-1
Carrick Rangers FC	2-5	1-2	2-1	1-3	■	1-3	1-0	2-2	0-2	1-2	2-3	1-1	1-2	0-0	0-3	1-4
Cliftonville FC	2-0	4-0	1-3	2-0	0-2	■	2-0	3-1	2-1	0-2	2-1	4-0	2-2	6-0	3-2	1-2
Coleraine FC	0-1	2-1	0-1	0-4	1-1	2-2	■	1-1	3-4	1-1	1-2	1-0	0-2	2-4	1-4	1-3
Crusaders FC	0-2	1-2	0-0	3-2	3-3	1-1	4-1	■	4-1	1-3	2-0	5-0	2-2	2-1	4-1	2-3
Distillery FC	2-2	4-1	2-0	1-3	2-1	2-2	2-0	1-3	■	3-2	2-3	1-3	2-1	1-3	0-1	0-0
Glenavon FC	1-2	4-0	3-1	2-3	2-0	1-2	5-3	2-2	2-1	■	1-1	2-0	2-1	1-1	3-0	2-1
Glentoran FC	1-1	2-1	2-0	0-1	2-1	3-2	4-0	2-0	3-1	2-0	■	1-0	1-0	2-2	4-1	1-1
Larne FC	0-2	1-1	1-2	0-1	1-0	4-1	2-0	2-2	0-4	0-4	0-1	■	0-1	4-1	3-3	1-3
Linfield FC	1-0	3-1	3-0	2-1	1-0	0-4	2-1	2-0	2-2	0-0	1-1	4-2	■	1-2	0-0	0-1
Newry Town FC	3-1	3-2	3-0	1-1	2-0	0-0	3-1	1-2	3-0	1-0	2-0	1-2	3-1	■	2-1	1-3
Omagh Town FC	2-4	2-1	1-1	0-0	3-4	2-1	2-1	0-1	5-2	2-5	3-1	0-5	0-1	2-1	■	2-5
Portadown FC	1-0	3-1	4-0	2-0	1-0	2-0	3-0	3-1	1-1	0-1	0-0	0-1	1-1	2-1	4-2	■

	Irish League	Pd	Wn	Dw	Ls	GF	GA	Pts
1.	PORTADOWN FC (PORTADOWN)	30	22	5	3	61	22	71
2.	Bangor FC (Bangor)	30	19	4	7	52	29	61
3.	Glentoran FC (Belfast)	30	18	6	6	50	32	60
4.	Glenavon FC (Lurgan)	30	17	6	7	63	38	57
5.	Newry Town FC (Newry)	30	15	5	10	50	42	50
6.	Cliftonville FC (Belfast)	30	14	7	9	59	41	49
7.	Linfield FC (Belfast)	30	12	10	8	40	34	46
8.	Ballymena United FC (Ballymena)	30	12	8	10	49	46	44
9.	Ards FC (Newtownards)	30	12	7	11	47	40	43
10.	Crusaders FC (Belfast)	30	11	9	10	53	46	42
11.	Distillery FC (Lisburn)	30	10	5	15	47	57	35
12.	Omagh Town FC (Omagh)	30	10	4	16	48	66	34
13.	Larne FC (Larne)	30	8	6	16	41	59	30
14.	Ballyclare Comrades FC (Ballyclare)	30	5	6	19	33	68	21
15.	Carrick Rangers FC (Carrickfergus)	30	4	5	21	30	58	17
16.	Coleraine FC (Coleraine)	30	2	5	23	25	70	11
		480	191	98	191	748	748	671

Note: Cliftonville FC 1-2 Portadown FC match was abandoned after 67 minutes due to crowd trouble but the result was allowed to stand and the points were awarded to Portadown FC.

Top goalscorers 1990-91

1)	Stephen McBRIDE	(Glenavon FC)	22
2)	William HAMILTON	(Distillery FC)	19
3)	Steven COWAN	(Portadown FC)	18
	Gary McCARTNEY	(Glentoran FC)	18
5)	Glenn HUNTER	(Crusaders FC)	17

No clubs promoted or relegated

IRISH CUP FINAL (Windsor Park, Belfast – 04/05/1991 – 15,000)

PORTADOWN FC (PORTADOWN)　　　　2-1　　　　　　　　　　Glenavon FC (Lurgan)
Cowan 06', 44'　　　　　　　　　　　　　　　　　　　　　　　　　　　　　　　　　　*Ferguson 46'*

Portadown: Keenan, Major, Strain, Stewart, Curliss, Doolin, Rafferty, Cunningham, Davidson, Cowan, Fraser
Glenavon: Beck, McKeown, McCullough, Byrne, Scrappaticci, McDermott (Davies 69'), Conville, Russell (McCann 80'), McCoy, Ferguson, McBride.

Semi-finals

| Ards FC (Newtownards) | 1-2 | Portadown FC (Portadown) |
| Glenavon FC (Lurgan) | 3-1 | Glentoran FC (Belfast) |

Quarter-finals

Ards FC (Newtownards)	3-2	Linfield FC (Belfast)
Crusaders FC (Belfast)	2-4	Portadown FC (Portadown)
Glenavon FC (Lurgan)	4-0	Ballyclare Comrades FC (Ballyclare)
Larne FC (Larne)	1-1, 1-4	Glentoran FC (Belfast)

1991-92

Irish League 1991-92	Ards	Ballyclare C.	Ballymena U.	Bangor	Carrick R.	Cliftonville	Coleraine	Crusaders	Distillery	Glenavon	Glentoran	Larne	Linfield	Newry Town	Omagh Town	Portadown
Ards FC		0-0	6-1	1-4	1-0	3-0	0-1	1-1	4-4	2-3	1-1	1-1	2-2	2-2	2-0	2-1
Ballyclare Comrades FC	2-1		2-5	1-5	2-2	1-1	4-3	2-1	2-1	1-8	0-2	0-5	0-0	6-1	2-2	1-0
Ballymena United FC	1-2	2-0		2-2	3-3	1-1	1-1	1-3	0-0	1-2	2-1	1-1	2-2	0-2	1-1	0-6
Bangor FC	1-4	2-2	2-0		3-0	0-0	0-2	1-1	4-2	1-0	1-2	0-4	0-2	5-1	1-3	0-2
Carrick Rangers FC	1-1	0-1	1-1	1-1		0-3	2-2	1-3	0-3	1-3	0-3	0-3	0-1	1-1	1-2	1-4
Cliftonville FC	0-0	1-2	0-0	2-0	2-0		1-1	2-2	0-1	1-2	0-0	1-1	0-1	1-0	1-2	0-0
Coleraine FC	1-4	1-0	0-1	3-0	0-2	2-0		0-2	2-0	2-2	1-4	0-0	1-3	0-1	1-1	0-2
Crusaders FC	2-1	2-0	1-2	0-1	6-0	5-1	5-1		0-1	3-1	2-3	2-1	0-2	2-0	3-3	0-2
Distillery FC	1-1	1-1	0-0	0-1	2-2	2-0	1-2	1-3		1-2	0-2	1-2	0-4	1-2	2-1	1-3
Glenavon FC	3-0	2-1	2-0	0-0	2-0	0-2	3-0	2-1	4-0		0-2	0-1	2-1	0-0	4-0	1-2
Glentoran FC	1-1	4-2	4-0	3-1	7-0	1-0	6-1	1-0	3-0	5-1		2-0	3-3	2-1	4-2	1-0
Larne FC	1-0	4-1	3-1	3-1	5-0	1-0	2-2	0-1	2-2	3-2	2-3		2-1	1-0	3-0	0-4
Linfield FC	5-2	0-0	1-0	5-1	4-0	1-0	2-0	0-1	3-2	1-1	0-0	0-0		3-0	2-1	1-2
Newry Town FC	1-2	2-1	1-4	4-3	0-3	1-5	2-2	1-0	2-1	0-2	1-2	1-0	0-1		0-2	0-1
Omagh Town FC	3-0	3-0	0-2	2-3	6-2	1-2	4-3	2-2	3-0	1-0	3-4	1-2	1-7	1-1		0-1
Portadown FC	2-3	3-0	0-2	0-1	3-0	3-0	2-0	3-1	1-0	3-0	1-2	3-1	0-0	3-0	2-1	

	Irish League	Pd	Wn	Dw	Ls	GF	GA	Pts	
1.	GLENTORAN FC (BELFAST)	30	24	5	1	78	26	77	
2.	Portadown FC (Portadown)	30	21	2	7	59	19	65	
3.	Linfield FC (Belfast)	30	17	9	4	58	23	60	
4.	Larne FC (Larne)	30	16	7	7	54	31	55	
5.	Glenavon FC (Lurgan)	30	16	4	10	54	36	52	
6.	Crusaders FC (Belfast)	30	14	5	11	55	37	47	
7.	Ards FC (Newtownards)	30	10	11	9	50	46	41	
8.	Omagh Town FC (Omagh)	30	10	6	14	52	58	36	
9.	Bangor FC (Bangor)	30	11	6	13	45	52	36	-3
10.	Ballymena United FC (Ballymena)	30	8	11	11	37	50	35	
11.	Ballyclare Comrades FC (Ballyclare)	30	8	8	14	37	64	32	
12.	Cliftonville FC (Belfast)	30	7	10	13	27	34	31	
13.	Coleraine FC (Coleraine)	30	7	8	15	35	57	29	
14.	Newry Town FC (Newry)	30	8	5	17	28	57	29	
15.	Distillery FC (Lisburn)	30	5	7	18	31	56	22	
16.	Carrick Rangers FC (Carrickfergus)	30	2	8	20	24	78	14	
		480	184	112	184	724	724	661	

Note: Bangor FC (Bangor) had 3 points deducted as a result of irregularities in the signing of 19 year-old Paul Byrne from Oxford United FC (Oxford) in England.

Top goalscorers 1991-92

1) Stephen McBRIDE (Glenavon FC) 18
   Harold McCOURT (Omagh Town/Ards FC) 18 (15/3)

3)	Justin McBRIDE	(Glentoran FC)	15
4)	Stephen BARNES	(Larne FC)	14
	Robert CAMPBELL	(Ards FC)	14
	Steven COWAN	(Portadown FC)	14
	Martin McGAUGHEY	(Linfield FC)	14

No clubs promoted or relegated

IRISH CUP FINAL (The Oval, Belfast – 02/05/1992 – 14,000)

GLENAVON FC (LURGAN)   2-1   Linfield FC (Belfast)

Ferris 42', McMahon 56'   *McHaughey 13'*

Glenavon: Beck, McCullough, Scrappaticci, Quigley, Byrne, Crawford, McConville, McCoy, McMahon, Ferris (Crowe), Kennedy.

Linfield: Patterson, Dornan, Easton, McConnell, Spiers, Beattie (Hunter), Curry, Doherty (Allen), McGaughey, Baxter, Baillie.

Semi-finals

Glenavon FC (Lurgan)	3-1	Ballymena United FC (Ballymena)
Linfield FC (Belfast)	2-0	Crusaders FC (Belfast)

Quarter-finals

Ballymena United FC (Ballymena)	4-0	Oxford United Stars FC
Glenavon FC (Lurgan)	3-0	Ards FC (Newtownards)
Linfield FC (Belfast)	1-0	Cliftonville FC (Belfast)
Portadown FC (Portadown)	0-1	Crusaders FC (Belfast)

1992-93

Irish League 1992-93	Ards	Ballyclare C.	Ballymena U.	Bangor	Carrick R.	Cliftonville	Coleraine	Crusaders	Distillery	Glenavon	Glentoran	Larne	Linfield	Newry Town	Omagh Town	Portadown
Ards FC	■	1-1	0-0	1-4	2-0	1-0	3-1	2-0	1-1	1-2	0-3	0-0	0-2	1-0	2-2	2-2
Ballyclare Comrades FC	0-1	■	2-3	0-2	0-1	1-1	3-4	1-3	0-2	0-2	2-5	3-2	1-3	2-4	2-2	0-0
Ballymena United FC	3-4	2-2	■	0-1	2-1	0-1	1-1	1-0	4-1	0-5	2-8	2-1	1-2	3-2	0-1	0-2
Bangor FC	4-3	4-1	3-2	■	4-0	3-1	3-1	2-1	1-3	1-3	2-1	5-1	1-0	0-0	1-0	2-2
Carrick Rangers FC	3-2	4-1	3-3	2-4	■	1-2	3-0	0-3	1-5	3-1	1-1	3-1	0-4	0-2	3-1	1-6
Cliftonville FC	1-2	1-0	1-1	0-1	2-3	■	4-0	1-2	1-2	0-2	2-3	3-1	0-4	5-1	3-1	2-0
Coleraine FC	1-3	3-0	1-3	0-2	1-2	1-1	■	1-4	1-2	2-0	2-1	1-4	0-1	1-2	1-2	0-3
Crusaders FC	1-1	1-1	1-0	1-0	2-0	1-2	3-1	■	2-0	3-2	2-1	3-2	1-0	3-0	2-0	0-3
Distillery FC	2-1	4-0	1-0	3-2	3-2	2-1	2-0	0-2	■	1-2	0-3	2-1	1-0	5-0	2-0	3-0
Glenavon FC	0-0	2-1	0-2	1-1	4-1	2-0	0-1	0-2	2-1	■	2-2	1-0	1-2	4-0	3-2	0-3
Glentoran FC	1-1	5-0	1-4	0-2	1-2	3-0	2-2	1-2	1-1	0-0	■	4-0	1-2	6-1	3-0	3-2
Larne FC	1-3	3-1	1-0	0-1	4-1	2-0	1-0	0-1	1-4	1-3	2-4	■	0-0	4-2	4-2	0-1
Linfield FC	1-0	4-0	1-1	0-0	3-0	3-0	2-0	1-0	2-1	1-0	2-0	5-2	■	0-0	1-0	0-3
Newry Town FC	2-3	0-2	0-1	2-1	2-4	1-5	2-0	1-3	2-5	1-1	1-1	0-1	0-2	■	0-1	1-1
Omagh Town FC	1-4	2-1	2-0	0-4	1-3	2-1	2-0	1-2	1-2	3-2	0-4	1-1	1-1	4-0	■	2-2
Portadown FC	6-0	4-0	2-0	3-0	6-2	2-1	2-1	2-2	2-0	1-1	1-1	3-0	0-0	3-1	3-1	■

	Irish League	Pd	Wn	Dw	Ls	GF	GA	Pts
1.	LINFIELD FC (BELFAST)	30	20	6	4	49	15	66
2.	Crusaders FC (Belfast)	30	21	3	6	53	27	66
3.	Bangor FC (Bangor)	30	20	4	6	61	32	64
4.	Portadown FC (Portadown)	30	18	9	3	70	26	63
5.	Distillery FC (Lisburn)	30	20	2	8	61	36	62
6.	Glenavon FC (Lurgan)	30	14	6	10	48	36	48
7.	Glentoran FC (Belfast)	30	13	8	9	70	40	47
8.	Ards FC (Newtownards)	30	12	9	9	45	45	45
9.	Carrick Rangers FC (Carrickfergus)	30	12	2	16	50	73	38
10.	Ballymena United FC (Ballymena)	30	10	6	14	41	51	36
11.	Cliftonville FC (Belfast)	30	10	3	17	42	48	33
12.	Omagh Town FC (Omagh)	30	9	5	16	38	57	32
13.	Larne FC (Larne)	30	9	3	18	41	59	30
14.	Newry Town FC (Newry)	30	5	5	20	30	72	20
15.	Coleraine FC (Coleraine)	30	5	3	22	28	63	18
16.	Ballyclare Comrades FC (Ballyclare)	30	2	6	22	28	75	12
		480	200	80	200	756	756	680

Note: Ballyclare Comrades FC 3-4 Coleraine FC on 14/11/1992 was abandoned after 87 minutes due to a power failure but the result was allowed to stand.

Top goalscorers 1992-93

1)	Steven COWAN	(Portadown FC)	27
2)	David McCALLAN	(Bangor FC)	21
3)	Darren ERSKINE	(Ards FC)	20
4)	Tom CLELLAND	(Distillery FC)	16
	Liam COYLE	(Omagh Town FC)	16
	Sandy FRASER	(Portadown FC)	16
	Gary McCARTNEY	(Glentoran FC)	16
	Tom McCOURT	(Larne FC)	16

No clubs promoted or relegated

IRISH CUP FINAL   (Windsor Park, Belfast – 01/05/1993 – 8,500)

BANGOR FC (BANGOR)   1-1   Ards FC (Newtownards)
Glendinning 88'   *McCourt 86'*

Bangor: Eachus, Canning, Glendinning, Muldoon (Surgeon), Brown, O'Connor, Hill, Magee (McCreadie), McCallan, Byrne, McEvoy.

Ards: Vance, McDonald, Leeman, Mitchell, Jeffrey, Bustard, Beattie, Connell, Erskine, McCourt, Davies.

IRISH CUP FINAL REPLAY   (Windsor Park, Belfast – 08/05/1993 – 6,000)

BANGOR FC (BANGOR)   1-1 (aet)   Ards FC (Newtownards)
Glendinning 35'   *Erskine 02'*

Ards: Vance, McDonald, Leeman, Mitchell, Jeffrey, Bustard, Beattie (Kavanagh), Connell, Erskine, McCourt, Davies (Campbell).

Bangor: Eachus, Canning, Glendinning, Hill, Brown, O'Connor, Surgeon, McCreadie (Magee), McCallan, Byrne, McEvoy (Muldoon).

IRISH CUP FINAL 2ND REPLAY (Windsor Park, Belfast – 11/05/1993 – 5,000)

BANGOR FC (BANGOR)   1-0   Ards FC (Newtownards)

Byrne 89'

Bangor: Eachus, Canning, Glendinning, Muldoon, Brown, O'Connor, Hill, McCreadie, McCallan (Magee), Byrne, McEvoy.

Ards: Vance, McDonald, Leeman, Mitchell, Jeffrey, Bustard, Beattie (Kavanagh), Connell, Erskine, McCourt, Davies (Campbell).

Semi-finals

Ards FC (Newtownards)	3-2	Cliftonville FC (Belfast)
Bangor FC (Bangor)	3-1	Glentoran FC (Belfast)

Quarter-finals

Distillery FC (Lisburn)	0-0, 1-4	Ards FC (Newtownards)
Dundela FC (Belfast)	1-2	Glentoran FC (Belfast)
Larne FC (Larne)	1-1, 0-2	Cliftonville FC (Belfast)
Linfield FC (Belfast)	1-2	Bangor FC (Bangor)

1993-94

Irish League 1993-94	Ards	Ballyclare C.	Ballymena U.	Bangor	Carrick R.	Cliftonville	Coleraine	Crusaders	Distillery	Glenavon	Glentoran	Larne	Linfield	Newry Town	Omagh Town	Portadown
Ards FC		2-0	1-2	5-3	3-3	1-2	3-2	2-4	1-0	4-1	1-0	4-0	0-3	9-0	3-3	1-2
Ballyclare Comrades FC	1-0		1-1	3-0	0-3	0-0	0-1	0-0	2-2	1-1	2-1	1-0	1-2	1-2	4-1	2-0
Ballymena United FC	0-2	2-3		1-2	0-2	2-1	1-0	0-0	1-1	1-3	3-2	2-0	0-1	0-0	1-3	1-1
Bangor FC	0-2	4-2	1-0		5-1	2-1	2-0	2-1	1-2	1-0	0-3	2-1	0-1	3-1	4-2	1-1
Carrick Rangers FC	1-2	2-4	2-5	3-2		1-0	1-1	3-2	2-2	1-5	1-2	2-1	1-2	0-3	0-0	1-6
Cliftonville FC	6-2	0-2	0-2	1-0	3-1		1-2	2-1	1-1	0-1	1-1	0-1	2-2	1-1	1-1	1-1
Coleraine FC	4-0	3-2	5-2	3-1	3-2	0-0		0-2	0-2	0-2	1-1	2-1	2-2	1-1	2-0	0-1
Crusaders FC	3-1	4-0	1-0	4-0	3-0	1-1	2-0		2-2	2-4	3-2	3-1	1-1	2-1	3-0	1-1
Distillery FC	3-2	4-0	4-1	1-2	2-0	1-2	1-2	1-2		1-1	0-2	0-1	2-2	1-0	1-1	1-6
Glenavon FC	1-0	5-2	3-2	3-1	8-0	0-1	2-1	2-0	1-0		2-1	6-1	3-2	5-0	1-0	2-2
Glentoran FC	2-0	3-0	1-1	2-2	3-1	1-4	5-3	0-1	0-2	0-1		0-0	0-2	4-0	3-1	1-3
Larne FC	4-1	1-1	5-1	1-1	1-1	0-3	3-3	1-1	1-2	0-2	2-2		0-2	1-3	4-2	0-5
Linfield FC	2-1	5-0	2-1	1-0	2-1	3-1	5-0	0-1	3-0	0-0	2-0	3-0		1-0	4-1	2-2
Newry Town FC	1-3	2-0	1-2	1-2	2-2	0-3	0-0	0-2	0-1	1-1	1-1	2-0	1-0		1-2	0-2
Omagh Town FC	1-2	2-0	1-2	0-1	3-3	0-1	1-0	0-1	1-2	2-3	1-0	1-3	1-0	1-2		1-2
Portadown FC	1-0	4-0	5-0	2-0	6-1	1-1	4-0	3-0	1-0	3-1	1-0	4-0	0-2	1-1	5-0	

	Irish League	Pd	Wn	Dw	Ls	GF	GA	Pts	
1.	LINFIELD FC (BELFAST)	30	21	7	2	63	22	70	
2.	Portadown FC (Portadown)	30	20	8	2	76	21	68	
3.	Glenavon FC (Lurgan)	30	21	5	4	69	29	68	
4.	Crusaders FC (Belfast)	30	17	7	6	53	30	58	
5.	Bangor FC (Bangor)	30	14	3	13	45	49	45	
6.	Ards FC (Newtownards)	30	13	2	15	59	55	41	
7.	Distillery FC (Lisburn)	30	11	8	11	41	40	41	
8.	Cliftonville FC (Belfast)	30	11	10	9	41	32	40	-3
9.	Glentoran FC (Belfast)	30	10	7	13	46	43	37	
10.	Coleraine FC (Coleraine)	30	10	7	13	41	50	37	
11.	Ballymena United FC (Ballymena)	30	9	6	15	37	55	33	
12.	Ballyclare Comrades FC (Ballyclare)	30	9	6	15	35	57	33	
13.	Carrick Rangers FC (Carrickfergus)	30	6	7	17	42	81	25	
14.	Newry Town FC (Newry)	30	5	9	16	26	52	24	
15.	Omagh Town FC (Omagh)	30	6	5	19	32	58	23	
16.	Larne FC (Larne)	30	5	7	18	30	62	22	
		480	188	104	188	736	736	668	

Note: Cliftonville FC (Belfast) had 3 points deducted for fielding an unregistered player in a league match.

Top goalscorers 1993-94

1)	Darren ERSKINE	(Ards FC)	22
	Stephen McBRIDE	(Glenavon FC)	22
3)	Garry HAYLOCK	(Linfield FC)	21
4)	Trevor SMITH	(Portadown FC)	19
5)	Brian ROBSON	(Carrick Rangers FC)	15

Promotion/relegation was introduced from season 1995-96 when the league was re-structured to a Premier Division and a Division 1 each comprising 8 teams. The top 8 clubs over the 1993-94 and 1994-95 seasons formed the new Premier Division with the remaining 8 clubs forming the new Division 1.

IRISH CUP FINAL   (The Oval, Belfast – 07/05/1994 – 10,000)

LINFIELD FC (BELFAST)	2-0	Bangor FC (Bangor)

Peebles 45', Fenton 90'

Linfield: Lamont, A. Dornan, Easton, Peebles, J. Spiers (Doherty), Beatty, Campbell, Gorman, Haylock, Fenlon, Baillie.

Bangor: Dalton, Canning, Glendinning, E.Spiers, Brown, O'Connor, Hill. McCaffrey, McCallan, Magee (Surgeon), McEvoy.

Semi-finals

Bangor FC (Bangor)	2-0	Portadown FC (Portadown)
Glenavon FC (Lurgan)	0-3	Linfield FC (Belfast)

Quarter-finals

Distillery FC (Lisburn)	2-4	Glenavon FC (Lurgan)
Glentoran FC (Belfast)	0-2	Bangor FC (Bangor)
Linfield FC (Belfast)	0-0, 1-0	Cliftonville FC (Belfast)
Omagh Town FC (Omagh)	1-2	Portadown FC (Portadown)

1994-95

Irish League 1994-95	Ards	Ballyclare C.	Ballymena U.	Bangor	Carrick R.	Cliftonville	Coleraine	Crusaders	Distillery	Glenavon	Glentoran	Larne	Linfield	Newry Town	Omagh Town	Portadown
Ards FC		3-0	4-1	2-0	2-0	1-2	1-2	0-0	2-1	2-2	2-3	3-1	3-1	4-0	1-1	1-4
Ballyclare Comrades FC	1-4		1-3	2-0	1-3	0-2	1-2	1-2	0-4	0-3	0-4	3-0	2-1	2-3	7-2	0-1
Ballymena United FC	1-2	2-2		0-3	2-2	0-1	1-1	0-2	2-3	0-1	3-3	0-0	2-1	1-1	0-2	3-2
Bangor FC	3-1	2-2	2-3		0-0	0-0	3-3	1-1	2-2	1-0	1-3	1-1	0-0	2-2	2-1	0-2
Carrick Rangers FC	4-1	2-1	2-1	0-3		2-1	2-2	2-6	1-3	0-5	2-3	1-2	0-1	2-0	0-4	1-2
Cliftonville FC	1-0	2-2	1-0	1-1	6-1		0-0	2-2	0-3	3-1	1-0	2-0	1-2	2-2	0-1	1-2
Coleraine FC	2-2	1-1	0-0	3-3	3-3	1-2		0-1	0-1	2-1	1-0	4-0	2-1	3-0	1-1	3-1
Crusaders FC	1-2	3-0	2-1	1-0	1-0	1-0	3-3		2-1	1-3	1-2	4-1	1-0	4-0	1-1	2-1
Distillery FC	0-3	2-0	2-1	1-2	2-1	1-1	0-2	0-3		1-3	3-2	2-4	1-1	2-2	1-1	1-4
Glenavon FC	3-0	4-2	3-1	2-2	4-4	2-2	1-4	0-0	3-0		3-1	5-1	4-0	4-0	1-1	1-0
Glentoran FC	4-1	3-1	2-0	1-0	2-2	2-3	1-1	0-2	1-0	1-3		3-1	2-2	2-1	0-0	1-6
Larne FC	0-1	0-0	2-3	0-1	1-2	1-2	0-2	1-3	0-1	0-5	0-4		0-4	1-1	0-2	0-1
Linfield FC	1-1	2-1	3-0	0-5	1-1	0-0	1-2	1-1	0-0	4-0	1-1	6-0		2-0	1-1	2-2
Newry Town FC	1-3	1-3	0-8	1-1	6-1	1-1	4-1	2-5	0-3	2-3	0-0	1-0	0-4		0-2	1-1
Omagh Town FC	1-3	4-2	1-2	0-0	4-1	0-0	1-1	0-1	2-3	3-2	0-0	2-0	0-3	3-2		1-1
Portadown FC	1-0	1-1	2-2	3-1	5-4	3-4	3-0	0-1	2-1	2-4	0-2	0-1	1-2	4-0	2-0	

	Irish League	Pd	Wn	Dw	Ls	GF	GA	Pts
1.	CRUSADERS FC (BELFAST)	30	20	7	3	58	25	67
2.	Glenavon FC (Lurgan)	30	18	6	6	76	40	60
3.	Portadown FC (Portadown)	30	15	5	10	59	41	50
4.	Ards FC (Newtownards)	30	15	5	10	55	42	50
5.	Glentoran FC (Belfast)	30	14	8	8	53	41	50
6.	Cliftonville FC (Belfast)	30	13	11	6	44	32	50
7.	Coleraine FC (Coleraine)	30	12	13	5	52	39	49
8.	Linfield FC (Belfast)	30	11	11	8	48	34	44
9.	Omagh Town FC (Omagh)	30	10	12	8	42	38	42
10.	Distillery FC (Lisburn)	30	12	6	12	45	47	42
11.	Bangor FC (Bangor)	30	8	14	8	42	38	38
12.	Ballymena United FC (Ballymena)	30	7	8	15	43	53	29
13.	Carrick Rangers FC (Carrickfergus)	30	7	7	16	46	75	28
14.	Ballyclare Comrades FC (Ballyclare)	30	5	6	19	39	66	21
15.	Newry Town FC (Newry)	30	4	9	17	34	74	21
16.	Larne FC (Larne)	30	3	4	23	18	69	13
		480	174	132	174	754	754	654

Top goalscorers 1994-95

1)	Glenn FERGUSON	(Glenavon FC)	27
2)	Glenn HUNTER	(Crusaders FC)	19
3)	Darren ERSKINE	(Ards FC)	17
	Stephen McBRIDE	(Glenavon FC)	17
5)	Garry HAYLOCK	(Linfield FC)	15
	Trevor SMITH	(Glentoran FC)	15

The League was split into a Premier Division and Division 1 (8 clubs each) from the next season with automatic promotion and relegation between the divisions to be introduced.

Qualification for the new Premier Division was decided on the top 8 clubs combined "position total" over the 1993-1994 and 1994-95 seasons and not on the actual "points" total.

	Team	1993-94	1994-95	Total	Pts
1.	Glenavon FC (Lurgan)	3	2	5	128
2.	Crusaders FC (Belfast)	4	1	5	125
3.	Portadown FC (Portadown)	2	3	5	118
4.	Linfield FC (Belfast)	1	8	9	114
5.	Ards FC (Newtownards)	6	4	10	91
6.	Cliftonville FC (Belfast)	8	6	14	90
7.	Glentoran FC (Belfast)	9	5	14	87
8.	Bangor FC (Bangor)	5	11	16	83
9.	Coleraine FC (Coleraine)	10	7	17	86
10.	Distillery FC (Lisburn)	7	10	17	83
11.	Ballymena United FC (Ballymena)	11	12	23	62
12.	Omagh Town FC (Omagh)	16	9	25	65
13.	Ballyclare Comrades FC (Ballyclare)	12	14	26	54
14.	Carrick Rangers FC (Carrickfergus)	13	13	26	53
15.	Newry Town FC (Newry)	14	15	29	45
16.	Larne FC (Larne)	15	16	31	35
		136	136	272	1319

As a result of this system Bangor FC finished above Coleraine FC who had actually won more points (86 to 83) and Ballymena United FC finished above Omagh Town FC who had won more actual points (65 to 62).

	Actual Playing Record	Pd	Wn	Dw	Ls	GF	GA	Pts	
1.	Glenavon FC (Lurgan)	60	39	11	10	145	69	128	
2.	Crusaders FC (Belfast)	60	37	14	9	111	55	125	
3.	Portadown FC (Portadown)	60	35	13	12	135	62	118	
4.	Linfield FC (Belfast)	60	32	18	10	111	56	114	
5.	Ards FC (Newtownards)	60	28	7	25	114	97	91	
6.	Cliftonville FC (Belfast)	60	24	21	15	85	64	90	-3
7.	Glentoran FC (Belfast)	60	24	15	21	99	84	87	
8.	Coleraine FC (Coleraine)	60	22	20	18	93	89	86	
9.	Bangor FC (Bangor)	60	22	17	21	87	87	83	
10.	Distillery FC (Lisburn)	60	23	14	23	86	87	83	
11.	Omagh Town FC (Omagh)	60	16	17	27	74	96	65	
12.	Ballymena United FC (Ballymena)	60	16	14	30	80	108	62	
13.	Ballyclare Comrades FC (Ballyclare)	60	14	12	34	74	123	54	
14.	Carrick Rangers FC (Carrickfergus)	60	13	14	33	88	156	53	
15.	Newry Town FC (Newry)	60	9	18	33	60	126	45	
16.	Larne FC (Larne)	60	8	11	41	48	131	35	
		960	362	236	362	1490	1490	1319	

IRISH CUP FINAL   (The Oval, Belfast – 07/05/1995 – 6,000)

LINFIELD FC (BELFAST)   3-1   Carrick Rangers FC (Carrickfergus)

Haylock 18', 56', McCoosh 85'   *Gilmore 40'*

Linfield: Lamont, Dornan, Easton, Peebles (McCoosh 81'), Spiers, Beatty, Campbell, Gorman, Haylock, Fenlon, Baillie.

Carrick: Miskelly, Wilson, Gilmore, Muldoon, Gordon, Coulter, Kirk, McDermott, Donaghey (Doherty 79'), Ferris, MacAuley (Crawford 73').

Semi-finals

Ards FC (Newtownards)	0-0, 1-2	Linfield FC (Belfast)
Carrick Rangers FC (Carrickfergus)	1-0	Portadown FC (Portadown)

Quarter-finals

Ards FC (Newtownards)	3-2	Glenavon FC (Lurgan)
Carrick Rangers FC (Carrickfergus)	2-1	Bangor FC (Bangor)
Linfield FC (Belfast)	1-1, 1-0	Loughgall FC (Loughgall)
Portadown FC (Portadown)	1-1, 1-0	Cliftonville FC (Belfast)

1995-96

Irish League Premier Division 1995-96	Ards	Bangor	Cliftonville	Crusaders	Glenavon	Glentoran	Linfield	Portadown
Ards FC		2-1	2-2	0-1	1-2	0-2	1-2	0-1
		3-0	3-0	0-0	1-1	1-4	2-3	1-1
Bangor FC	0-1		2-3	0-2	1-2	1-1	0-2	0-0
	2-1		3-2	1-2	0-1	1-6	1-2	0-3
Cliftonville FC	1-0	1-1		2-1	0-1	1-0	0-0	0-4
	0-0	2-1		1-4	22	0-0	1-1	0-3
Crusaders FC	2-0	1-0	1-1		1-0	1-3	4-2	3-3
	1-2	2-0	1-0		1-2	2-1	3-0	3-1
Glenavon FC	3-1	0-1	1-1	1-1		1-3	2-2	7-0
	3-0	1-0	1-2	4-0		2-3	0-3	0-1
Glentoran FC	3-1	3-0	2-1	2-2	1-2		3-0	3-3
	3-2	1-1	1-1	3-1	0-2		0-3	1-1
Linfield FC	0-0	2-1	3-1	0-1	2-1	2-0		0-1
	0-0	0-0	0-0	1-2	0-3	0-4		1-0
Portadown FC	1-3	4-3	4-1	1-1	2-1	3-2	1-1	
	3-1	4-2	6-1	1-1	2-1	3-1	3-2	

	Premier Division	Pd	Wn	Dw	Ls	GF	GA	Pts	
1.	PORTADOWN FC (PORTADOWN)	28	16	8	4	61	40	56	
2.	Crusaders FC (Belfast)	28	15	7	6	45	32	52	
3.	Glentoran FC (Belfast)	28	13	7	8	56	38	46	
4.	Glenavon FC (Lurgan)	28	13	5	10	47	32	44	
5.	Linfield FC (Belfast)	28	11	8	9	34	35	41	
6.	Cliftonville FC (Belfast)	28	6	11	11	27	48	29	
7.	Ards FC (Newtownards)	28	6	7	15	29	43	25	
8.	Bangor FC (Bangor)	28	3	5	20	23	54	14	R
		224	83	58	83	322	322	307	

The Premier Division was to be extended to 10 clubs from the 1996-97 season, so the next season (1995-96) the bottom club of the Premier Division automatically entered a play-off against the 3rd placed team in Division 1 for a place in the Premier Division. The top 2 teams of Division 1 were promoted automatically.

Top goalscorers 1995-96

1)	Garry HAYLOCK	(Portadown FC)	19
2)	Stephen BAXTER	(Crusaders FC)	10
	Peter KENNEDY	(Portadown FC)	10
4)	Glenn FERGUSON	(Glenavon FC)	9
	Glenn HUNTER	(Crusaders FC)	9
	Glen LITTLE	(Glentoran FC)	9
	Stephen McBRIDE	(Glenavon FC)	9

Irish League First Division 1995-96	Ballyclare C.	Ballymena U.	Carrick R.	Coleraine	Distillery	Larne	Newry Town	Omagh Town
Ballyclare Comrades FC		0-1	3-2	0-2	0-3	1-1	1-2	0-5
		1-3	2-1	1-0	0-2	2-3	1-1	3-2
Ballymena United FC	2-1		1-2	4-3	1-1	2-2	3-0	2-0
	0-0		3-1	1-2	0-1	0-0	0-0	2-0
Carrick Rangers FC	0-3	0-2		2-5	0-0	1-0	1-0	2-0
	3-0	1-1		0-3	0-0	1-0	3-1	2-3
Coleraine FC	1-3	4-0	5-1		4-2	3-2	5-0	2-1
	2-0	1-1	6-0		2-1	1-0	8-0	5-2
Distillery FC	0-1	1-3	2-1	1-1		0-1	1-1	0-1
	1-2	0-1	3-1	1-1		1-0	2-1	3-2
Larne FC	0-1	0-1	3-1	1-2	3-1		1-1	1-3
	2-0	0-0	0-1	0-2	2-0		1-2	2-2
Newry Town FC	3-0	1-0	1-0	1-2	0-2	2-0		2-2
	2-0	1-2	2-3	1-4	2-5	3-2		1-2
Omagh Town FC	3-0	2-2	6-2	0-4	0-0	1-1	4-0	
	1-3	0-0	1-0	2-2	3-1	1-3	1-0	

	Division 1	Pd	Wn	Dw	Ls	GF	GA	Pts	
1.	Coleraine FC (Coleraine)	28	21	4	3	82	28	67	P
2.	Ballymena United FC (Ballymena)	28	13	10	5	38	25	49	
3.	Omagh Town FC (Omagh)	28	12	7	9	50	43	43	
4.	Distillery FC (Lisburn)	28	10	7	11	35	34	37	
5.	Ballyclare Comrades FC (Ballyclare)	28	10	3	15	29	48	33	
6.	Carrick Rangers FC (Carrickfergus)	28	9	3	16	32	56	30	
7.	Larne FC (Larne)	28	7	7	14	31	36	28	
8.	Newry Town FC (Newry)	28	7	5	16	31	58	26	
		224	89	46	89	330	330	313	

IRISH CUP FINAL   (Windsor Park, Belfast – 04/05/1996 – 10,000)

GLENTORAN FC (BELFAST)	1-0	Glenavon FC (Lurgan)

Little 85'

Glentoran: D. Devine, Nixon, Finlay, Walker, J. Devine, Parker, T. Smith, Little, Coyle, Batey, J. McBride.

Glenavon: Straney, J. Smyth, Glendinning, Murphy, Gould, G. Smyth, Johnston, Shepherd, Ferguson, McBride (McCoy 77'), Shipp.

Semi-finals

Glenavon FC (Lurgan)	1-1, 4-1	Portadown FC (Portadown)
Glentoran FC (Belfast)	2-2, 2-1	Crusaders FC (Belfast)

Quarter-finals

Crusaders FC (Belfast)	2-0	Linfield FC (Belfast)
Glenavon FC (Lurgan)	3-1	Carrick Rangers FC (Carrickfergus)
Glentoran FC (Belfast)	0-0, 4-2	Ballymena United FC (Ballymena)
Portadown FC (Portadown)	2-1	Ards FC (Newtownards)

1996-97

Irish League Premier Division 1996-97	Ards	Cliftonville	Coleraine	Crusaders	Glenavon	Glentoran	Linfield	Portadown
Ards FC		0-1	3-3	1-5	2-2	3-0	4-1	2-2
		0-2	1-4	0-0	0-0	4-3	2-3	2-3
Cliftonville FC	2-1		1-1	0-2	2-0	1-0	0-3	0-0
	0-1		0-1	1-1	0-0	0-2	2-4	1-1
Coleraine FC	0-0	1-1		3-1	1-1	0-0	1-1	0-2
	1-0	0-1		1-0	1-1	3-2	1-3	1-1
Crusaders FC	2-2	3-0	0-0		1-0	1-1	3-0	2-1
	3-1	2-1	1-1		2-2	2-3	0-1	2-0
Glenavon FC	1-1	1-0	1-1	1-2		1-2	3-1	1-2
	2-1	4-0	2-3	0-0		2-1	2-1	1-0
Glentoran FC	2-0	1-1	1-0	4-0	2-1		0-2	2-0
	0-0	1-1	1-0	1-1	2-2		1-1	2-3
Linfield FC	3-1	2-3	0-1	0-0	0-2	0-0		0-2
	0-0	1-1	2-3	0-1	3-0	0-0		1-0
Portadown FC	5-0	1-0	2-3	1-0	1-1	0-1	0-2	
	0-1	4-1	2-2	0-2	2-1	1-1	0-0	

	Premier Division	Pd	Wn	Dw	Ls	GF	GA	Pts	
1.	CRUSADERS FC (BELFAST)	28	12	10	6	39	26	46	
2.	Coleraine FC (Coleraine)	28	10	13	5	37	31	43	
3.	Glentoran FC (Belfast)	28	10	11	7	36	30	41	
4.	Portadown FC (Portadown)	28	10	8	10	36	32	38	
5.	Linfield FC (Belfast)	28	10	8	10	35	33	38	
6.	Glenavon FC (Lurgan)	28	8	11	9	35	34	35	
7.	Cliftonville FC (Belfast)	28	7	9	12	23	38	30	
8.	Ards FC (Newtownards)	28	5	10	13	33	50	25	PO
		224	72	80	72	274	274	296	

Top goalscorers 1996-97

1)	Garry HAYLOCK	(Portadown FC)	16
2)	Glenn FERGUSON	(Glenavon FC)	12
	Glenn HUNTER	(Crusaders FC)	12
4)	Stephen BAXTER	(Crusaders FC)	11
5)	David McCALLAN	(Coleraine FC)	10

Promotion/Relegation Play-off

Bangor FC (Bangor)　　　　　0-1, 0-1　　　　　Ards FC (Newtownards)

The Premier Division was extended to 10 clubs for the next season

Irish League First Division 1996-97	Ballyclare C.	Ballymena U.	Bangor	Carrick R.	Distillery	Larne	Newry Town	Omagh Town
Ballyclare Comrades FC		2-2	0-2	2-0	2-2	4-0	0-2	4-0
		0-1	0-1	1-2	1-0	3-1	0-2	3-1
Ballymena United FC	3-0		0-0	2-1	1-0	1-0	3-1	0-1
	4-1		2-1	1-0	0-1	4-2	2-0	3-1
Bangor FC	3-1	2-1		1-0	0-1	2-0	1-2	3-0
	3-0	0-3		1-0	2-1	1-2	2-2	3-4
Carrick Rangers FC	0-4	0-2	2-1		0-1	2-3	0-2	1-1
	4-2	1-2	0-2		2-4	3-1	1-2	2-5
Distillery FC	0-1	0-1	1-4	1-0		0-0	0-1	0-1
	0-3	1-1	0-1	2-0		1-3	1-2	1-2
Larne FC	1-1	0-1	3-1	0-0	4-4		1-0	1-0
	1-3	1-3	0-1	1-0	2-4		2-1	0-1
Newry Town FC	3-2	1-0	0-1	1-2	1-0	2-2		0-1
	1-2	0-1	1-1	1-1	0-1	1-3		1-2
Omagh Town FC	0-2	0-4	1-0	2-1	1-1	2-0	2-2	
	1-0	0-1	2-2	3-1	2-3	0-1	1-0	

	Division 1	Pd	Wn	Dw	Ls	GF	GA	Pts	
1.	Ballymena United FC (Ballymena)	28	21	2	5	49	17	65	P
2.	Omagh Town FC (Omagh)	28	15	5	8	40	39	50	P
3.	Bangor FC (Bangor)	28	15	4	9	42	29	49	PO
4.	Ballyclare Comrades FC (Ballyclare)	28	11	4	13	44	42	37	
5.	Newry Town FC (Newry)	28	10	5	13	32	35	35	
6.	Distillery FC (Lisburn)	28	10	4	14	31	37	34	
7.	Larne FC (Larne)	28	9	5	14	34	48	32	
8.	Carrick Rangers FC (Carrickfergus)	28	5	3	20	26	51	18	
		224	96	32	96	298	298	320	

Promoted: Dungannon Swifts FC (Dungannon), Limavady United FC (Limavady)

IRISH CUP FINAL (Windsor Park, Belfast – 03/05/1997 – 18,222 – restricted on police advice)

GLENAVON FC (LURGAN)   1-0   Cliftonville FC (Belfast)

Grant 23'

Glenavon: O'Neill, Caffrey, Glendinning, Doherty, Byrne, Smyth, Johnston, McCoy (Murphy 66'), Ferguson, Grant, Gregg (Williamson 78').

Cliftonville: Reece, Hill (Strang 64'), Flynn, Tabb, Davey, O'Neill, McCann, Collins, Small (Toland 78') Stokes, Donnelly.

Semi-finals

Cliftonville FC (Belfast)	3-1	Loughgall FC (Loughgall)
Glenavon FC (Lurgan)	5-0	Omagh Town FC (Omagh)

Quarter-finals

Cliftonville FC (Belfast)	3-1	Crusaders FC (Belfast)
Glenavon FC (Lurgan)	4-0	Coagh United FC (Coagh)
Loughgall FC (Loughgall)	1-1, 1-0	Coleraine FC (Coleraine)
Omagh Town FC (Omagh)	2-2, 1-0	Limavady United FC (Limavady)

1997-98

Irish League Premier Division 1997-98	Ards	Ballymena	Cliftonville	Coleraine	Crusaders	Glenavon	Glentoran	Linfield	Omagh	Portadown
Ards FC		0-2	1-1	1-0	0-1	1-1	0-2	1-5	1-2	0-1
		2-1	2-3	0-0	1-1	3-4	1-1	0-1	2-2	1-1
Ballymena United FC	1-1		4-0	2-2	1-0	2-1	1-2	0-2	2-1	1-2
	3-1		2-0	1-0	2-3	0-0	0-2	1-1	4-2	1-2
Cliftonville FC	2-2	5-2		1-0	0-1	1-0	1-1	0-3	1-0	1-0
	1-0	0-2		3-1	2-2	1-1	0-2	2-1	4-0	3-1
Coleraine FC	2-2	0-0	0-2		0-0	0-1	1-5	0-0	1-1	2-0
	2-1	0-1	5-1		4-0	1-2	2-1	1-0	4-3	0-1
Crusaders FC	1-0	3-4	0-2	3-0		4-1	0-3	1-2	2-2	2-1
	4-0	4-2	2-2	1-3		3-2	0-2	1-0	1-0	1-3
Glenavon FC	0-0	3-3	0-0	4-0	2-2		1-0	2-4	2-4	3-0
	1-2	1-2	0-0	1-1	2-0		1-0	2-3	2-2	1-5
Glentoran FC	2-0	2-2	1-0	3-0	1-1	1-0		1-1	2-0	2-1
	3-0	1-2	0-2	1-0	1-1	0-1		0-3	1-0	1-1
Linfield FC	2-0	1-0	0-1	1-0	0-0	2-0	3-0		0-0	1-1
	4-0	0-0	0-1	1-1	0-0	1-1	2-0		1-1	0-0
Omagh Town FC	2-1	3-0	0-1	1-3	1-2	2-1	0-5	0-3		0-2
	2-4	3-2	0-1	1-3	1-1	2-2	1-1	1-0		1-2
Portadown FC	1-0	4-0	1-2	1-1	3-2	2-0	2-0	0-0	1-1	
	1-0	1-1	0-2	0-1	1-1	2-1	3-2	0-2	3-1	

	Premier Division	**Pd**	**Wn**	**Dw**	**Ls**	**GF**	**GA**	**Pts**	
1.	CLIFTONVILLE FC (BELFAST)	36	20	8	8	49	37	68	
2.	Linfield FC (Belfast)	36	17	13	6	50	19	64	
3.	Portadown FC (Portadown)	36	17	9	10	50	38	60	
4.	Glentoran FC (Belfast)	36	17	8	11	52	34	59	
5.	Crusaders FC (Belfast)	36	13	12	11	51	51	51	
6.	Ballymena United FC (Ballymena)	36	14	9	13	54	55	51	
7.	Coleraine FC (Coleraine)	36	11	10	15	41	47	43	
8.	Glenavon FC (Lurgan)	36	9	12	15	47	56	39	
9.	Omagh Town FC (Omagh)	36	7	10	19	43	68	31	PO
10.	Ards FC (Newtownards)	36	4	11	21	31	63	23	R
		360	129	102	129	468	468	489	

Cliftonville FC 1-1 Glenavon FC on 03/01/1998 was abandoned and replayed on 28/01/1998 with a 1-0 scoreline.
Coleraine FC 1-0 Linfield FC on 29/11/1997 was abandoned after 83minutes but the result was allowed to stand.
Coleraine FC 3-3 Glenavon FC on 17/01/1998 was awarded 0-1 as Coleraine fielded an ineligible player.

Top goalscorers 1997-98

1)	Vinny ARKINS	(Portadown FC)	22	
2)	Tony GRANT	(Glenavon FC)	15	
	Justin McBRIDE	(Glentoran FC)	15	
4)	Glenn FERGUSON	(Glenavon FC/Linfield FC)	14	(6/8)
	Michael McHUGH	(Omagh Town FC)	14	
	Barry O'CONNOR	(Cliftonville FC)	14	
	Barry PATTON	(Ballymena United FC)	14	

Promotion/Relegation Play-off

Bangor FC (Bangor)   0-5, 0-1   Omagh Town FC (Omagh)

Irish League First Division 1997-98	Ballyclare C.	Bangor	Carrick R.	Distillery	Dungannon	Larne	Limavady	Newry Town
Ballyclare Comrades FC	■	2-1	2-0	2-4	3-2	2-0	0-1	2-2
	■	0-1	1-1	0-3	0-1	3-1	3-2	0-2
Bangor FC	2-1	■	2-1	2-2	3-0	1-0	4-0	1-2
	1-2	■	3-2	3-0	1-2	2-0	0-0	1-0
Carrick Rangers FC	2-3	1-2	■	1-2	1-3	2-1	0-3	0-5
	0-1	0-2	■	1-2	0-0	0-1	3-1	1-4
Distillery FC	1-5	1-2	1-0	■	1-2	3-0	0-0	1-0
	2-1	2-1	1-0	■	2-2	0-2	3-0	2-2
Dungannon Swifts FC	3-1	3-4	4-1	0-2	■	4-3	2-1	1-1
	4-5	3-3	2-1	2-2	■	4-2	9-0	0-4
Larne FC	3-2	0-3	1-2	0-1	2-2	■	1-0	0-1
	1-1	1-2	1-0	3-2	1-2	■	3-2	0-2
Limavady United FC	0-2	0-1	1-1	0-1	1-3	1-2	■	1-3
	1-2	0-3	4-0	0-5	1-2	5-1	■	2-0
Newry Town FC	1-0	1-0	3-0	1-1	1-0	6-0	3-1	■
	3-1	0-0	3-0	2-1	2-1	3-0	4-1	■

	Division 1	Pd	Wn	Dw	Ls	GF	GA	Pts	
1.	Newry Town FC (Newry)	28	20	5	3	61	18	65	P
2.	Bangor FC (Bangor)	28	18	4	6	51	26	58	PO
3.	Distillery FC (Lisburn)	28	15	6	7	48	34	51	
4.	Dungannon Swifts FC (Dungannon)	28	14	6	8	63	49	48	
5.	Ballyclare Comrades FC (Ballyclare)	28	13	3	12	47	45	42	
6.	Larne FC (Larne)	28	8	2	18	30	58	26	
7.	Limavady United FC (Limavady)	28	6	2	20	29	61	20	
8.	Carrick Rangers FC (Carrickfergus)	28	3	2	23	21	59	11	
		224	97	30	97	349	349	321	

IRISH CUP FINAL   (Windsor Park, Belfast – 02/05/1998 – 8,250)

GLENTORAN FC (BELFAST)   1-0 (aet)   Glenavon FC (Lurgan)

Kennedy 97'

Glentoran: Russell, Nixon, Kennedy, Walker, Devine, Leeman (Livingstone 97'), Mitchell, Finlay, Kirk, Batey, Hamill.

Glenavon: O'Neill (Welch 108'), Wright (O'Flaherty 102'), Glendinning, Quigley, Cash (Murphy 80'), Smyth, McCoy, Byrne, Shepherd, Grant, Caffrey.

Semi-finals

Crusaders FC (Belfast)	1-3	Glenavon FC (Lurgan)
Glentoran FC (Belfast)	2-1	Linfield FC (Belfast)

Quarter-finals

Crusaders FC (Belfast)	4-0	Institute FC (Londonderry)
Distillery FC (Belfast)	0-2	Glenavon FC (Lurgan)
Glentoran FC (Belfast)	3-1	Armagh City FC (Armagh)
Linfield FC (Belfast)	3-0	Portadown FC (Portadown)

1998-99

Irish League Premier Division 1998-99	Ballymena	Cliftonville	Coleraine	Crusaders	Glenavon	Glentoran	Linfield	Newry Town	Omagh	Portadown
Ballymena United FC		2-2	0-1	1-2	0-1	3-6	4-2	0-0	1-2	2-2
		1-2	1-0	2-0	1-0	1-1	1-0	1-1	0-0	1-0
Cliftonville FC	1-0		0-0	1-1	0-0	0-0	0-1	0-2	2-1	0-0
	0-1		1-1	2-3	2-2	2-4	1-1	1-4	2-1	0-2
Coleraine FC	0-1	3-1		0-2	0-0	0-1	2-1	3-0	1-0	0-2
	2-1	1-1		0-2	1-3	1-3	0-0	2-2	2-1	1-0
Crusaders FC	1-0	1-0	2-0		1-1	0-3	3-2	3-2	2-0	0-0
	2-0	2-1	0-1		1-0	0-0	1-4	2-0	5-0	1-1
Glenavon FC	1-0	0-0	3-1	2-0		0-1	2-2	1-1	6-1	2-2
	0-0	0-1	3-1	3-0		0-1	1-1	1-2	2-0	1-0
Glentoran FC	1-0	1-1	5-0	2-1	1-0		1-2	5-1	2-0	3-1
	2-1	0-1	5-4	1-4	5-2		0-1	1-3	2-0	1-0
Linfield FC	4-1	2-1	1-1	4-2	3-1	1-1		2-1	3-0	3-1
	1-0	1-0	2-1	2-1	2-0	1-1		2-2	2-0	2-2
Newry Town FC	1-0	1-0	1-0	3-0	0-2	1-0	2-1		1-1	1-2
	0-0	2-1	1-1	0-0	1-0	1-2	2-1		0-2	3-2
Omagh Town FC	0-5	1-1	1-1	1-2	0-3	1-4	1-5	2-3		1-0
	1-4	2-2	2-0	0-0	0-3	0-2	1-3	1-3		1-0
Portadown FC	2-1	3-0	1-2	0-0	2-2	1-3	1-1	2-1	3-0	
	1-3	0-1	3-0	0-1	1-1	0-3	0-2	2-3	2-0	

	Premier Division	Pd	Wn	Dw	Ls	GF	GA	Pts	
1.	GLENTORAN FC (BELFAST)	36	24	6	6	74	35	78	
2.	Linfield FC (Belfast)	36	20	10	6	68	39	70	
3.	Crusaders FC (Belfast)	36	18	8	10	48	39	62	
4.	Newry Town FC (Newry)	36	17	9	10	52	46	60	
5.	Glenavon FC (Lurgan)	36	13	12	11	49	35	51	
6.	Ballymena United FC (Ballymena)	36	11	8	17	40	42	41	
7.	Coleraine FC (Coleraine)	36	10	9	17	34	53	39	
8.	Portadown FC (Portadown)	36	9	10	17	41	47	37	
9.	Cliftonville FC (Belfast)	36	7	14	15	31	47	35	PO
10.	Omagh Town FC (Omagh)	36	5	6	25	25	79	21	R
		360	134	92	134	462	462	494	

Note: Glenavon FC 1-0 Portadown FC on 26/12/1998 was abandoned after 60 minutes due to storm. It was replayed on 26/01/1999 and finished with a 2-2 scoreline.

Top goalscorers 1998-99

1)	Vinny ARKINS	(Portadown FC)	19
2)	Des GORMAN	(Newry Town FC)	17
3)	Stephen BAXTER	(Glenavon FC)	16
4)	Glenn FERGUSON	(Linfield FC)	15
5)	Rory HAMILL	(Glentoran FC)	13
	David LARMOUR	(Linfield FC)	13

Promotion/Relegation Play-off

Ards FC (Newtownards)	0-1, 2-4	Cliftonville FC (Belfast)

** Distillery FC (Lisburn) changed their club name to Lisburn Distillery FC (Lisburn) for the next season.

Irish League First Division 1998-99	Ards	Ballyclare C.	Bangor	Carrick R.	Distillery	Dungannon	Larne	Limavady
Ards FC		0-2	1-2	2-4	0-2	1-0	5-1	1-2
		2-1	2-0	1-0	2-0	2-1	1-0	3-0
Ballyclare Comrades FC	2-0		0-1	1-1	3-1	6-0	0-1	4-4
	2-5		3-0	2-1	0-1	1-2	2-0	5-1
Bangor FC	0-0	1-4		2-2	1-0	3-1	1-0	3-4
	1-0	3-2		0-1	2-0	2-1	0-1	0-0
Carrick Rangers FC	1-0	0-2	0-1		2-3	0-1	1-1	4-0
	4-1	3-2	1-2		0-1	3-2	1-0	2-3
Distillery FC	4-3	1-0	2-0	3-2		3-1	0-0	1-0
	0-2	3-3	0-3	0-0		1-1	1-0	3-1
Dungannon Swifts FC	1-2	1-1	1-3	2-0	2-1		1-0	1-2
	2-1	1-0	3-2	2-1	1-5		1-1	2-0
Larne FC	0-2	5-3	2-0	3-2	0-1	0-1		0-0
	0-2	4-1	0-1	1-0	0-1	1-0		4-0
Limavady United FC	0-3	2-2	1-3	2-3	0-1	3-3	1-0	
	2-3	0-1	3-0	1-2	1-5	1-1	3-3	

	Division 1	Pd	Wn	Dw	Ls	GF	GA	Pts	
1.	Distillery FC (Lisburn)	28	17	4	7	44	30	55	P **
2.	Ards FC (Newtownards)	28	16	1	11	47	34	49	PO
3.	Bangor FC (Bangor)	28	15	3	10	37	35	48	
4.	Ballyclare Comrades FC (Ballyclare)	28	11	5	12	55	44	38	
5.	Dungannon Swifts FC (Dungannon)	28	11	5	12	36	46	38	
6.	Carrick Rangers FC (Carrickfergus)	28	10	4	14	41	41	34	
7.	Larne FC (Larne)	28	9	5	14	28	32	32	
8.	Limavady United FC (Limavady)	28	6	7	15	37	63	25	
		224	95	34	95	325	325	319	

Promoted: Armagh City FC (Armagh), Institute FC (Londonderry)

Division 1 was extended to 10 clubs for the next season

IRISH CUP FINAL (not played)

PORTADOWN FC (PORTADOWN)　　　　w/o　　　　　　　Cliftonville FC (Belfast)

The final was not played as Cliftonville FC had fielded Simon Gribben as a substitute in the semi-final match against Linfield FC. Gribben was inelgible to appear as he had played in the competition for an amateur club Kilmore Recreation FC in an earlier round before being signed by Cliftonville FC. Cliftonville were expelled from the competition and the cup was awarded by default to Portadown FC.

Semi-finals

| Cliftonville FC (Belfast) | 1-1, 1-0 | Linfield FC (Belfast) |
| Portadown FC (Portadown) | 2-0 | Ballymena United FC (Ballymena) |

Quarter-finals

Carrick Rangers FC (Carrickfergus)	1-2	Cliftonville FC (Belfast)
Coleraine FC (Coleraine)	1-2	Portadown FC (Portadown)
Distillery FC (Lisburn)	1-1, 1-2	Ballymena United FC (Ballymena)
Linfield FC (Belfast)	0-0, 2-1	Glenavon FC (Lurgan)

1999-2000

Irish League Premier Division 1999-2000	Ballymena	Cliftonville	Coleraine	Crusaders	Glenavon	Glentoran	Linfield	Lisburn Dis.	Newry Town	Portadown
Ballymena United FC		2-2	2-2	2-2	2-0	2-1	0-1	2-1	0-0	2-4
		2-1	0-0	1-1	0-3	0-0	1-3	1-1	2-2	1-1
Cliftonville FC	3-2		0-0	1-1	1-1	2-0	2-3	2-0	0-2	2-0
	1-1		1-4	1-1	1-2	1-2	0-1	0-0	3-2	1-2
Coleraine FC	1-0	0-1		4-2	2-0	1-2	2-1	3-0	4-1	4-0
	1-1	1-1		1-2	.1-1	1-2	0-1	3-0	2-0	4-1
Crusaders FC	2-2	1-1	0-2		0-4	2-2	0-4	2-0	1-0	0-1
	3-0	1-1	1-3		3-1	1-0	1-1	1-2	1-0	2-4
Glenavon FC	2-0	4-0	0-0	1-0		3-3	3-0	1-2	3-0	1-1
	0-0	0-1	0-1	2-1		3-3	0-0	2-0	2-1	3-1
Glentoran FC	3-2	3-0	2-0	1-2	2-1		1-1	2-0	2-1	1-0
	3-1	1-1	3-2	2-0	1-2		1-0	3-1	0-3	5-3
Linfield FC	3-2	1-2	3-0	0-0	1-1	1-2		1-0	3-2	2-1
	3-0	3-1	3-1	0-0	1-0	2-0		3-2	3-1	3-1
Lisburn Distillery FC	2-1	1-0	1-2	0-1	1-2	1-0	1-4		2-3	2-1
	3-4	0-1	1-3	2-2	1-1	2-0	1-2		0-1	2-1
Newry Town FC	2-2	3-2	0-1	2-0	0-2	3-4	0-3	1-1		0-1
	3-1	3-1	3-0	1-1	0-1	1-0	0-3	2-1		1-1
Portadown FC	0-2	3-0	3-2	4-2	2-0	4-0	0-2	3-2	5-0	
	2-2	2-2	3-6	2-1	1-3	1-0	1-1	4-1	0-0	

	Premier Division	**Pd**	**Wn**	**Dw**	**Ls**	**GF**	**GA**	**Pts**	
1.	LINFIELD FC (BELFAST)	36	24	7	5	67	30	79	
2.	Coleraine FC (Coleraine)	36	18	7	11	64	42	61	
3.	Glenavon FC (Lurgan)	36	17	10	9	55	34	61	
4.	Glentoran FC (Belfast)	36	18	7	11	59	51	61	
5.	Portadown FC (Portadown)	36	15	7	14	64	62	52	
6.	Newry Town FC (Newry)	36	11	7	18	44	58	40	
7.	Crusaders FC (Belfast)	36	9	13	14	41	55	40	
8.	Ballymena United FC (Ballymena)	36	6	16	14	45	62	34	
9.	Cliftonville FC (Belfast)	36	7	13	16	38	59	34	PO
10.	Lisburn Distillery FC (Lisburn)	36	9	5	22	39	63	32	R
		360	134	92	134	516	516	494	

Top goalscorers 1999-2000

1) Vinny ARKINS (Portadown FC) 29
2) Tony GRANT (Glenavon FC) 20
   Glenn HUNTER (Ballymena United FC) 20
4) Stuart ELLIOTT (Glentoran FC) 16
5) Darren LARMOUR (Linfield FC) 15

Promotion/Relegation Play-offs

Ards FC (Newtownards)   0-2, 0-1   Cliftonville FC (Belfast)

Irish League First Division 1999-2000	Ards	Armagh	Ballyclare C.	Bangor	Carrick R.	Dungannon	Institute	Larne	Limavady	Omagh Town
Ards FC	■	1-1	2-1	1-1	3-0	2-2	4-2	1-0	1-2	1-1
	■	4-1	4-0	1-1	2-1	0-0	3-1	1-1	2-0	0-1
Armagh City FC	1-2	■	3-4	0-1	0-2	1-2	3-1	1-0	0-0	2-2
	0-4	■	5-0	2-0	0-0	3-3	3-3	6-2	2-0	0-1
Ballyclare Comrades FC	2-2	1-2	■	2-1	0-1	2-1	1-2	1-5	0-1	0-3
	2-2	2-0	■	1-2	3-1	1-2	0-2	0-1	1-3	0-3
Bangor FC	1-1	2-0	2-0	■	2-1	1-0	2-1	0-2	2-0	2-2
	2-2	2-0	3-3	■	1-1	2-0	1-2	3-0	0-3	1-2
Carrick Rangers FC	1-4	4-0	3-0	2-4	■	3-1	2-4	1-2	0-1	1-3
	0-0	0-0	0-2	1-4	■	2-2	0-3	2-1	6-3	0-0
Dungannon Swifts FC	2-2	2-1	1-3	0-1	1-0	■	1-3	1-0	0-3	0-2
	3-1	1-3	1-3	3-4	2-3	■	0-0	3-1	1-2	2-0
Institute FC	0-2	7-0	2-1	0-3	2-0	2-1	■	2-3	3-2	0-0
	0-0	0-1	4-1	3-3	1-1	0-2	■	1-2	2-0	0-0
Larne FC	2-2	1-0	2-2	3-1	2-2	2-0	2-2	■	2-2	0-2
	0-2	1-1	4-0	2-1	3-0	1-1	1-0	■	0-0	3-2
Limavady United FC	1-0	1-1	1-0	2-0	2-2	0-0	3-1	1-2	■	1-2
	1-1	3-2	2-0	3-2	1-1	2-1	0-1	4-1	■	2-3
Omagh Town FC	1-2	0-3	1-0	1-1	3-1	2-0	1-1	3-2	0-2	■
	1-3	2-2	7-0	2-1	2-0	4-1	4-1	2-0	0-0	■

	Division 1	Pd	Wn	Dw	Ls	GF	GA	Pts	
1.	Omagh Town FC (Omagh)	36	20	10	6	65	35	70	P
2.	Ards FC (Newtownards)	36	16	16	4	65	36	64	PO
3.	Limavady United FC (Limavady)	36	17	9	10	54	42	60	
4.	Bangor FC (Bangor)	36	16	9	11	60	49	57	
5.	Larne FC (Larne)	36	15	9	12	56	53	54	
6.	Institute FC (Londonderry)	36	14	9	13	59	53	51	
7.	Armagh City FC (Armagh)	36	10	10	16	50	61	40	
8.	Dungannon Swifts FC (Dungannon)	36	9	8	19	43	62	35	
9.	Carrick Rangers FC (Carrickfergus)	36	8	10	18	45	64	34	
10.	Ballyclare Comrades FC (Ballyclare)	36	8	4	24	39	81	28	
		360	133	94	133	535	535	493	

IRISH CUP FINAL   (Windsor Park, Belfast – 06/05/2000 – 8,355)

GLENTORAN FC (BELFAST)   1-0   Portadown FC (Portadown)

Gilzean 59'

Glentoran: Gough, Nixon, Kennedy, Dickson, McCombe, Young, McCann, Hamill, Russell (Gilzean 54'), Batey, Elliott.

Portadown: Dalton, Brown, O'Hara, Byrne, Strain, Major, Larkin, Clarke, Sheridan, Arkins, Hill (Davidson 65').

Semi-finals

Coleraine FC (Coleraine)	0-0, 0-1	Portadown FC (Portadown)
Glentoran FC (Belfast)	3-2	Linfield FC (Belfast)

Quarter-finals

Coleraine FC (Coleraine)	1-0	Ballymena United FC (Ballymena)
Linfield FC (Belfast)	2-2, 2-1 (aet)	Dungannon Swifts FC (Dungannon)
Lisburn Distillery FC (Lisburn)	0-2	Portadown FC (Portadown)
Newry Town FC (Newry)	1-3	Glentoran FC (Belfast)

2000-2001

Irish League Premier Division 2000-01	Ballymena	Cliftonville	Coleraine	Crusaders	Glenavon	Glentoran	Linfield	Newry Town	Omagh Town	Portadown
Ballymena United FC		2-1	0-1	0-1	1-0	1-3	1-1	0-1	2-1	3-3
		2-2	0-1	2-1	1-2	0-3	1-5	1-0	1-2	1-1
Cliftonville FC	3-1		1-0	0-3	2-1	1-1	1-4	1-0	1-2	0-0
	2-2		1-1	1-1	4-2	1-0	1-3	2-2	2-2	5-3
Coleraine FC	1-0	2-2		1-2	0-2	1-1	1-1	5-2	1-3	1-0
	0-2	3-1		2-2	0-1	5-2	1-0	2-1	0-0	3-3
Crusaders FC	3-1	1-2	2-3		0-2	0-1	1-3	2-2	0-0	2-1
	2-3	0-4	1-1		4-3	1-1	0-2	1-3	2-1	0-1
Glenavon FC	4-0	1-0	2-1	1-0		0-0	0-4	1-0	3-0	3-3
	2-1	1-0	1-1	1-1		3-0	0-1	0-1	3-0	1-2
Glentoran FC	2-1	1-0	0-1	2-0	2-2		2-0	0-0	1-2	4-1
	1-1	4-0	1-1	1-1	1-1		0-1	1-0	2-0	3-1
Linfield FC	2-2	3-0	3-1	3-1	3-0	2-0		1-3	3-2	0-0
	4-1	4-2	0-3	0-0	4-2	1-1		2-0	1-1	4-1
Newry Town FC	0-2	2-1	0-0	2-0	1-4	0-0	0-0		1-0	0-0
	5-2	0-3	2-0	3-2	1-2	1-3	0-2		0-2	4-3
Omagh Town FC	0-1	2-2	3-1	0-2	1-2	1-3	0-0	2-3		2-1
	4-0	0-1	1-2	2-2	1-1	2-1	1-5	2-2		0-0
Portadown FC	3-2	1-1	1-0	3-2	1-2	4-1	1-0	4-0	1-4	
	1-0	0-2	0-1	1-1	0-0	0-3	0-3	2-0	1-2	

	Premier Division	Pd	Wn	Dw	Ls	GF	GA	Pts	
1.	LINFIELD FC (BELFAST)	36	22	9	5	75	31	75	
2.	Glenavon FC (Lurgan)	36	18	8	10	56	42	62	
3.	Glentoran FC (Belfast)	36	15	12	9	52	37	57	
4.	Coleraine FC (Coleraine)	36	14	11	11	48	44	53	
5.	Cliftonville FC (Belfast)	36	12	11	13	53	57	47	
6.	Newry Town FC (Newry)	36	12	8	16	42	55	44	
7.	Omagh Town FC (Omagh)	36	11	10	15	48	54	43	
8.	Portadown FC (Portadown)	36	10	11	15	48	60	41	
9.	Crusaders FC (Belfast)	36	8	11	17	44	59	35	PO
10.	Ballymena United FC (Ballymena)	36	9	7	20	41	68	34	R
		360	131	98	131	507	507	491	

Note: Glenavon FC 0-0 Linfield FC on 12/08/2000 was later awarded 0-1 to Linfield FC as Glenavon FC had fielded Gerard McMahon who was ineligible to play at the time.

Top goalscorers 2000-01

1)	David LARMOUR	(Linfield FC)	17
2)	Glenn FERGUSON	(Linfield FC)	16
	Garry HAYLOCK	(Glenavon FC)	16
4)	Jody TOLAN	(Coleraine FC)	15
5)	Barry CURRAN	(Omagh Town FC)	14
	Tom McCALLION	(Cliftonville FC)	14

Promotion/Relegation Play-off

Lisburn Distillery FC (Lisburn)　　　2-1, 1-3　　　Crusaders FC (Belfast)

Irish League First Division 2000-01	Ards	Armagh	Ballyclare C.	Bangor	Carrick R.	Dungannon	Institute	Larne	Limavady	Lisburn Dis.
Ards FC		2-2	3-1	0-0	3-0	1-0	1-1	0-2	3-0	2-3
		2-2	1-0	1-1	2-0	3-1	2-0	1-1	0-0	3-3
Armagh City FC	2-1		2-2	2-1	2-1	1-3	1-1	2-0	2-0	0-3
	4-0		4-2	1-1	3-0	1-1	3-0	2-2	3-2	1-1
Ballyclare Comrades FC	0-4	1-4		1-1	4-3	1-2	1-0	1-1	0-1	0-3
	1-3	1-2		1-1	2-1	1-1	0-1	1-1	1-2	1-2
Bangor FC	0-2	2-1	2-0		6-1	1-0	2-1	2-0	2-0	0-0
	0-2	3-1	1-0		5-0	3-1	1-4	3-2	1-2	2-1
Carrick Rangers FC	0-3	2-3	2-1	0-3		0-1	2-1	1-0	2-0	0-1
	0-5	0-3	2-2	2-0		1-1	2-3	2-5	2-2	0-1
Dungannon Swifts FC	1-2	3-5	1-0	0-2	1-1		1-2	3-2	0-0	2-3
	1-1	1-2	3-0	1-2	4-1		1-1	0-1	1-1	1-1
Institute FC	0-2	3-1	3-1	1-2	3-2	0-1		1-2	0-0	2-1
	3-1	3-3	3-1	3-1	1-0	1-1		1-2	2-0	1-2
Larne FC	0-3	1-1	2-0	0-1	4-0	2-1	1-2		1-4	2-8
	0-3	2-3	3-2	1-1	3-0	1-3	1-1		1-1	2-4
Limavady United FC	2-2	0-2	0-1	2-2	1-4	1-2	1-6	2-0		1-1
	0-2	1-2	1-2	4-0	1-0	1-0	3-0	0-1		0-0
Lisburn Distillery FC	0-0	2-1	2-2	1-1	3-0	1-0	0-2	1-1	2-1	
	1-3	2-1	1-0	3-0	4-0	1-1	2-1	1-3	1-0	

	Division 1	Pd	Wn	Dw	Ls	GF	GA	Pts	
1.	Ards FC (Newtownards)	36	21	10	5	69	31	73	P
2.	Lisburn Distillery FC (Lisburn)	36	20	11	5	66	37	71	PO
3.	Armagh City FC (Armagh)	36	19	9	8	74	52	66	
4.	Bangor FC (Bangor)	36	18	9	9	56	42	63	
5.	Institute FC (Londonderry)	36	16	7	13	58	48	55	
6.	Larne FC (Larne)	36	12	9	15	53	62	45	
7.	Dungannon Swifts FC (Dungannon)	36	10	11	15	45	48	41	
8.	Limavady United FC (Limavady)	36	9	10	17	37	51	37	
9.	Ballyclare Comrades FC (Ballyclare)	36	5	6	23	35	69	23	
10.	Carrick Rangers FC (Carrickfergus)	36	6	4	26	34	87	22	
		360	136	88	136	527	527	496	

IRISH CUP FINAL   (Windsor Park, Belfast – 05/05/2001 – 14,000)

GLENTORAN FC (BELFAST)   1-0 (aet)   Linfield FC (Belfast)

Halliday 99'

Glentoran: Gough, Nixon, Ferguson, Young, Leeman, Smyth, McCann, Halliday, Fitzgerald, Batey, Lockhart (McBride 62').

Linfield: Robinson, McDonald (Collier 88'), Easton (Morgan 91'), Marks, Murphy, Arthur, Larmour, Scates, Ferguson, Kelly (Beatty 75'), Baillie.

Semi-finals

Glenavon FC (Lurgan)	1-3	Linfield FC (Belfast)
Lisburn Distillery FC (Lisburn)	1-2	Glentoran FC (Belfast)

Quarter-finals

Glenavon FC (Lurgan)	2-1	Ballyclare Comrades FC (Ballyclare)
Institute FC (Londonderry)	1-2	Glentoran FC (Belfast)
Linfield FC (Belfast)	1-0	Bangor FC (Bangor)
Portadown FC (Portadown)	0-1	Lisburn Distillery FC (Lisburn)

2001-2002

Irish League Premier Division 2001-02	Ards	Cliftonville	Coleraine	Crusaders	Glenavon	Glentoran	Linfield	Newry Town	Omagh Town	Portadown
Ards FC		0-0	1-4	2-1	1-2	0-4	2-2	4-2	0-2	0-2
Ards FC		2-1	1-2	0-0	0-0	0-0	2-4	1-4	1-3	1-4
Cliftonville FC	1-0		2-3	3-0	0-1	1-2	3-1	0-2	1-0	0-0
Cliftonville FC	2-0		2-4	1-1	1-0	0-4	1-2	2-2	0-2	0-0
Coleraine FC	5-0	3-2		1-2	4-0	1-0	0-2	1-2	2-1	1-3
Coleraine FC	1-2	0-0		1-0	2-1	2-0	1-0	1-0	2-1	2-4
Crusaders FC	1-1	1-3	2-1		2-0	0-1	1-3	4-3	7-2	1-2
Crusaders FC	3-0	0-2	0-2		3-4	0-2	0-2	1-1	1-2	0-1
Glenavon FC	0-1	2-1	1-2	0-1		1-1	2-0	0-1	3-4	2-3
Glenavon FC	2-1	1-3	1-0	0-2		0-0	0-2	1-1	5-1	1-4
Glentoran FC	1-1	0-0	2-1	6-0	5-1		3-3	2-2	2-0	1-0
Glentoran FC	4-0	2-0	1-0	1-0	1-0		1-0	3-0	4-1	2-2
Linfield FC	2-1	2-0	0-0	0-0	0-0	2-2		4-0	3-2	1-1
Linfield FC	4-0	2-2	3-1	4-0	1-3	0-0		1-1	0-1	0-1
Newry Town FC	1-1	1-4	7-1	0-1	1-1	0-1	0-2		0-1	1-1
Newry Town FC	0-1	1-0	3-1	2-2	1-1	0-1	0-2		1-1	2-2
Omagh Town FC	1-1	1-1	3-2	3-0	2-0	2-1	1-1	0-1		1-2
Omagh Town FC	1-0	0-0	2-2	2-2	1-1	2-2	1-0	4-2		3-0
Portadown FC	3-1	3-1	3-0	3-1	0-0	1-0	0-0	6-1	3-1	
Portadown FC	2-1	1-1	3-4	4-1	4-0	0-1	1-2	4-0	2-0	

	Premier Division	**Pd**	**Wn**	**Dw**	**Ls**	**GF**	**GA**	**Pts**
1.	PORTADOWN FC (PORTADOWN)	36	22	9	5	75	34	75
2.	Glentoran FC (Belfast)	36	21	11	4	63	23	74
3.	Linfield FC (Belfast)	36	17	11	8	64	35	62
4.	Coleraine FC (Coleraine)	36	19	2	15	64	58	59
5.	Omagh Town FC (Omagh)	36	15	9	12	55	55	54
6.	Cliftonville FC (Belfast)	36	9	11	16	37	46	38
7.	Glenavon FC (Lurgan)	36	9	9	18	37	57	36
8.	Newry Town FC (Newry)	36	8	12	16	40	62	36
9.	Crusaders FC (Belfast)	36	9	7	20	41	65	34
10.	Ards FC (Newtownards)	36	6	9	21	30	71	27
		360	135	90	135	506	506	495

Top goalscorers 2001-02

1) Vinny ARKINS   (Portadown FC)   30
2) Chris MORGAN   (Linfield FC)   17
3) Gary HAMILTON   (Portadown FC)   15
4) Andrew CRAWFORD   (Omagh Town FC)   12
   Gerard McMAHON   (Glenavon FC)   12

The Premier Division was extended to 12 clubs and Division 1 was reduced to 8 clubs for the next season.

Irish League First Division 2001-02	Armagh	Ballyclare C.	Ballymena	Bangor	Carrick R.	Dungannon	Institute	Larne	Limavady	Lisburn Dis.
Armagh City FC	■	2-2	0-2	1-1	3-0	0-3	0-3	0-4	0-5	1-4
	■	3-4	0-0	0-0	1-3	0-2	2-1	0-3	4-0	0-2
Ballyclare Comrades FC	1-0	■	3-3	1-3	1-1	2-3	0-0	0-3	0-2	0-4
	0-4	■	2-2	3-2	1-0	4-3	0-1	2-2	0-1	0-1
Ballymena United FC	3-1	2-2	■	1-0	3-2	0-1	2-0	4-4	4-3	1-2
	2-1	2-0	■	3-2	3-1	1-1	2-5	2-1	1-2	0-1
Bangor FC	0-0	1-1	1-1	■	2-1	0-1	0-2	0-0	3-0	0-0
	1-1	1-1	1-3	■	1-1	1-0	0-1	1-3	2-0	0-3
Carrick Rangers FC	1-0	1-0	0-2	2-2	■	0-1	0-3	1-0	2-1	0-1
	2-0	0-0	0-2	0-1	■	1-3	1-1	0-1	1-0	1-5
Dungannon Swifts FC	4-2	3-0	3-1	0-0	0-1	■	1-2	4-2	2-2	3-1
	0-2	4-0	2-2	2-1	1-1	■	1-3	0-1	0-0	0-1
Institute FC	4-1	7-0	2-1	3-1	2-1	1-2	■	2-1	3-0	2-4
	0-1	2-1	1-1	5-1	4-4	3-1	■	3-0	0-0	1-2
Larne FC	2-1	3-1	1-1	0-3	1-0	0-0	1-2	■	7-1	0-1
	1-1	1-1	1-1	1-0	0-0	1-1	1-1	■	0-3	0-1
Limavady United FC	1-3	0-0	1-0	3-1	3-1	0-1	1-4	0-1	■	1-1
	3-3	3-5	2-1	0-3	5-2	1-2	1-1	1-2	■	1-2
Lisburn Distillery FC	2-0	0-1	3-0	0-1	0-1	2-0	0-1	1-2	3-1	■
	1-2	3-1	4-0	1-2	1-1	3-0	0-0	2-1	2-1	■

	Division 1	**Pd**	**Wn**	**Dw**	**Ls**	**GF**	**GA**	**Pts**	
1.	Lisburn Distillery FC (Lisburn)	36	24	4	8	64	26	76	P
2.	Institute FC (Londonderry)	36	22	8	6	76	35	74	P
3.	Dungannon Swifts FC (Dungannon)	36	17	8	11	55	42	59	
4.	Larne FC (Larne)	36	14	11	11	52	42	53	
5.	Ballymena United FC (Ballymena)	36	14	11	11	59	56	53	
6.	Bangor FC (Bangor)	36	10	12	14	40	45	42	
7.	Limavady United FC (Limavady)	36	10	7	19	49	68	37	
8.	Carrick Rangers FC (Carrickfergus)	36	9	9	18	34	55	36	
9.	Ballyclare Comrades FC (Ballyclare)	36	7	12	17	40	73	33	
10.	Armagh City FC (Armagh)	36	8	8	20	40	67	32	
		360	135	90	135	509	509	495	

IRISH CUP FINAL   (Windsor Park, Belfast – 11/05/2002 – 11,129)

LINFIELD FC (BELFAST)   2-1   Portadown FC (Portadown)

Morgan 15', 21'   *Neill 06'*

Linfield: Mannus, Collier, McShane (N. Kelly 80'), Hunter, King (D. Murphy 67'), R. Kelly, Morgan (McBride 56'), Gorman, Ferguson, Marks, Baillie.

Portadown: Keenan, Douglas, O'Hara, McCann, Feeney (Ogden 26'), Major, Clarke (A. Hamilton 63'), Collins, G.Hamilton, Arkins, Neill.

Semi-finals

Linfield FC (Belfast)	4-0	Killyleagh Y.C. (Killyleagh)
Portadown FC (Portadown)	2-0	Coleraine FC (Coleraine)

Quarter-finals

Coleraine FC (Coleraine)	2-0	Dungannon Swifts FC (Dungannon)
Glentoran FC (Belfast)	1-1, 3-4	Portadown FC (Portadown)
Killyleagh Y.C. (Killyleagh)	1-0	Ballyclare Comrades FC (Ballyclare)
Linfield FC (Belfast)	3-0	Glenavon FC (Lurgan)

2002-2003

Irish League Premier Division 2002-03	Ards	Cliftonville	Coleraine	Crusaders	Glenavon	Glentoran	Institute	Linfield	Lisburn D.	Newry T.	Omagh T.	Portadown
Ards FC		0-0	---	0-0	1-0	0-2	1-0	---	1-0	1-0	---	0-3
		1-0	0-1	2-2	1-1	1-2	3-0	1-2	1-0	2-1	0-0	0-2
Cliftonville FC	1-0		---	0-1	2-0	0-2	1-3	---	1-0	1-0	---	---
	0-0		1-1	0-1	3-1	0-1	2-0	2-2	0-2	1-0	2-1	0-3
Coleraine FC	3-1	4-3		---	4-1	2-2	2-1	3-1	2-1	---	0-1	1-1
	2-0	1-1		3-3	3-2	0-0	3-0	3-1	1-4	3-0	0-1	1-0
Crusaders FC	0-0	1-0	0-2		2-0	---	---	0-5	1-1	0-2	2-0	0-5
	0-2	0-0	0-0		0-2	2-4	1-0	1-3	0-2	0-0	0-3	0-4
Glenavon FC	3-0	1-1	---	2-0		0-1	0-2	2-2	0-2	3-2	---	---
	1-1	2-1	2-2	1-1		0-3	3-1	0-0	1-2	3-2	1-3	0-5
Glentoran FC	---	---	1-0	0-1	---		6-1	0-0	---	2-1	0-0	1-0
	3-0	3-0	2-0	4-0	2-0		4-1	3-2	2-0	3-1	2-0	0-1
Institute FC	---	---	0-1	2-1	---	0-4		2-0	---	0-1	3-1	1-0
	2-0	1-1	1-3	2-0	0-0	1-5		1-0	0-1	3-2	0-0	3-3
Linfield FC	1-0	0-0	2-0	---	---	1-1	7-0		---	4-0	1-0	3-2
	3-1	2-2	2-0	2-0	1-1	1-1	2-3		1-4	3-0	3-1	0-1
Lisburn Distillery FC	0-1	1-1	---	0-1	0-0	1-3	1-1	1-2		1-2	---	---
	1-0	0-3	1-1	2-1	0-2	0-1	1-2	0-2		2-1	1-2	2-4
Newry Town FC	1-0	1-1	0-0	3-0	2-2	---	---	0-1			0-1	0-3
	1-3	0-3	0-2	0-3	2-2	0-2	1-0	0-6	1-0		1-4	0-0
Omagh Town FC	0-1	2-1	0-2	---	2-0	0-4	4-1	1-1	0-3	---		3-5
	0-1	2-1	0-3	2-1	3-1	0-2	3-2	1-1	3-0	0-2		1-1
Portadown FC	---	2-1	1-5	---	2-1	3-0	3-3	0-0	1-1	---	5-1	
	1-1	1-0	1-2	1-0	6-0	2-0	4-1	3-1	3-0	4-2	3-1	

	Premier Division (Championship Group)	Pd	Wn	Dw	Ls	GF	GA	Pts	
1.	GLENTORAN FC (BELFAST)	38	28	6	4	78	22	90	
2.	Portadown FC (Portadown)	38	24	8	6	89	36	80	
3.	Coleraine FC (Coleraine)	38	21	10	7	66	38	73	
4.	Linfield FC (Belfast)	38	17	12	9	70	41	63	
5.	Omagh Town FC (Omagh)	38	15	6	17	47	57	51	
6.	Institute FC (Londonderry)	38	12	6	20	44	75	42	
7.	Ards FC (Newtownards)	38	12	10	16	27	39	46	
8.	Lisburn Distillery FC (Lisburn)	38	12	6	20	39	49	42	
9.	Cliftonville FC (Belfast)	38	9	14	15	37	43	41	
10.	Glenavon FC (Lurgan)	38	8	12	18	41	67	36	
11.	Crusaders FC (Belfast)	38	9	9	20	26	61	36	
12.	Newry Town FC (Newry)	38	8	7	23	33	69	31	PO
		456	175	106	175	597	597	631	

	Premier Division (Phase 1)	Pd	Wn	Dw	Ls	GF	GA	Pts
1.	Glentoran FC (Belfast)	33	27	3	3	71	16	84
2.	Portadown FC (Portadown)	33	22	5	6	77	29	71
3.	Coleraine FC (Coleraine)	33	18	8	7	56	33	62
4.	Linfield FC (Belfast)	33	15	10	8	60	37	55
5.	Omagh Town FC (Omagh)	33	14	5	14	40	48	47
6.	Institute FC (Londonderry)	33	12	5	16	39	55	41
7.	Lisburn Distillery FC (Lisburn)	33	12	4	17	37	44	40
8.	Ards FC (Newtownards)	33	10	8	15	25	38	38
9.	Cliftonville FC (Belfast)	33	7	12	14	33	41	33
10.	Crusaders FC (Belfast)	33	8	7	18	24	55	31
11.	Glenavon FC (Lurgan)	33	6	11	16	36	62	29
12.	Newry Town FC (Newry)	33	5	6	22	24	64	21
		396	156	84	156	522	522	552

After 33 matches in the Premier Division the league was split with the top 6 teams playing-off for the championship and the remaining 6 teams playing-off against the promotion/relegation play-off.

Note: Glentoran FC 4-0 Crusaders FC, Glentoran FC 3-1 Newry FC, Glentoran FC 4-1 Institute FC and Cliftonville FC 0-1 Glentoran FC were initially awarded 1-0 to Glentoran FC's opponents as Glentoran had fielded the ineligible player Andrew Kilmartin during these games. This decision was revoked on appeal and the original results were allowed to stand.

Top goalscorers 2002-03

1)	Vinny ARKINS	(Portadown FC)	29
2)	Gary HAMILTON	(Portadown FC)	23
3)	Andrew SMITH	(Glentoran FC)	22
4)	Glenn FERGUSON	(Linfield FC)	18
5)	Mark HOLLAND	(Lisburn Distillery FC)	15

Irish League First Division 2002-03	Armagh	Ballyclare C.	Ballymena	Bangor	Carrick R.	Dungannon	Larne	Limavady
Armagh City FC		3-2	2-2	1-3	0-0	1-2	1-1	1-1
		2-1	2-3	1-3	1-2	0-1	1-2	1-2
Ballyclare Comrades FC	2-0		2-4	2-1	2-5	1-1	1-3	4-4
	3-6		0-3	2-3	3-2	1-1	0-4	3-2
Ballymena United FC	2-3	3-0		1-1	3-2	2-0	1-0	1-3
	2-2	3-0		2-3	6-1	5-2	3-2	4-1
Bangor FC	1-0	2-1	1-1		2-1	1-2	1-1	3-0
	2-0	1-0	0-2		3-3	1-0	0-2	1-1
Carrick Rangers FC	5-3	0-0	1-4	1-0		1-1	1-3	5-6
	4-2	3-2	1-4	0-2		0-4	0-3	0-1
Dungannon Swifts FC	1-0	3-0	2-1	2-1	1-2		2-1	1-0
	3-3	1-0	2-2	4-3	12-1		1-0	2-0
Larne FC	1-0	1-0	2-1	1-0	0-1	1-1		0-1
	2-1	0-1	1-3	0-3	1-0	1-4		1-0
Limavady United FC	3-0	3-1	2-1	2-0	3-1	1-2	1-0	
	2-0	1-2	1-1	3-1	4-1	1-2	1-1	

Division 1

		Pd	Wn	Dw	Ls	GF	GA	Pts	
1.	Dungannon Swifts FC (Dungannon)	28	18	6	4	61	32	60	P
2.	Ballymena United FC (Ballymena)	28	16	6	6	71	40	54	P
3.	Limavady United FC (Limavady)	28	15	5	8	53	37	50	P
4.	Larne FC (Larne)	28	13	4	11	35	30	43	P
5.	Bangor FC (Bangor)	28	12	5	11	40	39	41	
6.	Carrick Rangers FC (Carrickfergus)	28	8	4	16	44	76	28	
7.	Ballyclare Comrades FC (Ballyclare)	28	6	4	18	36	65	22	
8.	Armagh City FC (Armagh)	28	4	6	18	37	58	18	
		224	92	40	92	377	377	316	

Promotion/Relegation Play-off

Bangor FC (Bangor) 0-0, 1-2 Newry Town FC (Newry)

Promoted: Ballinamallard United FC (Ballinamallard), Ballymoney United FC (Ballymoney), Brantwood FC (Belfast), Donegal Celtic FC (Belfast), Harland & Wolff Welders FC (Belfast), Loughgall FC (Loughgall), Lurgan Celtic FC (Lurgan), Moyola Park FC (Castledawson)

At the end of the season, the Irish FA took control of the top tier of football in Northern Ireland and formed the Irish Premier League which was extended to 16 clubs. The Irish League Division 1 continued and was extended to 12 clubs for the next season

IRISH CUP FINAL   (Windsor Park, Belfast – 03/05/2003 – 10,000)

COLERAINE FC (COLERAINE)   1-0   Glentoran FC (Belfast)

Tolan 11'

Coleraine: O'Hare, Clanachan, Flynn, Gaston, McAuley, Beatty, McCoosh, Hamill, Tolan, P. McAllister (Armstrong 87'), Gorman.

Glentoran: Morris, Nixon, Glendinning, Leeman, Young, Smyth, T. McCann, Lockhart (O'Neill 46'), Smith, Armour (Halliday 65'), T.M. McCann (Walker 73').

Semi-finals

Coleraine FC (Coleraine)	5-2	Omagh Town FC (Omagh)
Portadown FC (Portadown)	1-6	Glentoran FC (Belfast)

Quarter-finals

Ards FC (Newtownards)	0-1	Glentoran FC (Belfast)
Coleraine FC (Coleraine)	2-0	Crusaders FC (Belfast)
Omagh Town FC (Omagh)	1-0	Linfield FC (Belfast)
Portadown FC (Portadown)	5-0	Glenavon FC (Lurgan)

2003-2004

Irish Premier League 2003-04	Ards	Ballymena	Cliftonville	Coleraine	Crusaders	Dungannon	Glenavon	Glentoran	Institute	Larne	Limavady	Linfield	Lisburn D.	Newry T.	Omagh T.	Portadown
Ards FC		1-1	0-0	2-2	2-0	0-2	2-4	2-1	2-2	1-1	0-0	0-4	1-1	4-0	2-1	2-1
Ballymena United FC	1-0		0-1	3-1	1-1	1-0	4-0	0-0	2-1	1-1	0-3	0-0	1-4	4-0	3-1	1-4
Cliftonville FC	2-1	0-3		2-0	0-1	1-0	0-1	1-1	1-2	0-0	3-2	1-4	0-0	1-2	1-2	0-1
Coleraine FC	4-1	4-0	1-0		0-1	3-1	2-1	0-1	4-2	0-4	2-1	2-0	0-0	4-3	1-1	3-1
Crusaders FC	0-0	0-0	0-0	0-1		0-1	0-4	0-1	3-1	3-2	2-0	1-3	0-1	2-2	4-1	1-2
Dungannon Swifts FC	2-2	0-0	2-2	3-2	2-1		3-1	1-4	1-1	2-5	1-2	0-4	2-0	3-0	1-0	1-2
Glenavon FC	1-2	0-3	1-1	0-0	2-1	2-2		1-2	0-2	0-4	2-3	0-2	2-2	0-2	0-3	0-3
Glentoran FC	3-0	3-1	1-1	0-1	0-1	1-0	4-0		1-0	1-0	2-1	1-3	0-1	4-0	4-0	1-2
Institute FC	0-1	0-4	2-1	2-2	1-3	1-0	1-0	3-1		4-1	0-4	0-0	0-2	1-1	1-1	0-3
Larne FC	5-1	1-2	2-1	0-2	0-0	0-2	1-0	1-4	2-4		2-1	0-3	0-2	3-3	1-2	2-4
Limavady United FC	0-1	0-1	3-1	3-3	2-3	3-1	2-0	1-0	2-0	0-0		0-2	0-3	1-0	3-2	0-6
Linfield FC	2-2	4-1	1-0	0-0	1-0	2-0	3-1	2-1	6-0	1-0	3-2		3-0	5-0	2-0	0-0
Lisburn Distillery FC	1-0	2-1	2-1	1-1	2-1	2-0	5-0	1-1	3-2	1-0	0-1	1-1		3-2	1-2	1-0
Newry Town FC	0-0	1-1	3-1	0-1	2-1	0-0	4-0	0-0	2-1	3-3	1-1	1-2	1-0		1-0	1-2
Omagh Town FC	1-4	2-0	2-3	1-1	0-3	1-3	1-2	1-4	0-3	0-0	2-0	1-3	3-2	3-0		2-5
Portadown FC	4-0	0-1	5-1	2-1	4-0	5-0	2-0	2-1	0-3	0-0	1-1	4-1	2-0	1-0		

	Irish Premier League	Pd	Wn	Dw	Ls	GF	GA	Pts	
1.	LINFIELD FC (BELFAST)	30	22	7	1	67	16	73	
2.	Portadown FC (Portadown)	30	22	4	4	71	22	70	
3.	Lisburn Distillery FC (Lisburn)	30	16	7	7	45	30	55	
4.	Coleraine FC (Coleraine)	30	14	9	7	48	36	51	
5.	Glentoran FC (Belfast)	30	15	5	10	48	27	50	
6.	Ballymena United FC (Ballymena)	30	13	8	9	41	35	47	
7.	Limavady United FC (Limavady)	30	12	5	13	41	43	41	
8.	Ards FC (Newtownards)	30	9	11	10	36	46	38	
9.	Crusaders FC (Belfast)	30	10	6	14	33	38	36	
10.	Dungannon Swifts FC (Dungannon)	30	10	6	14	36	48	36	
11.	Institute FC (Londonderry)	30	9	7	14	37	53	34	
12.	Newry Town FC (Newry)	30	8	9	13	35	53	33	
13.	Omagh Town FC (Omagh)	30	9	4	17	37	58	31	
14.	Larne FC (Larne)	30	7	8	15	42	51	29	
15.	Cliftonville FC (Belfast)	30	6	8	16	27	45	26	PO
16.	Glenavon FC (Lurgan)	30	4	4	22	24	67	16	R
		480	186	108	186	668	668	666	

Note: Glentoran FC 0-0 Crusaders FC, Limavady FC 0-1 Glentoran FC, Glentoran FC 0-0 Lisburn Distillery FC matches were all awarded as 1-0 wins to Glentoran FC's opponents as Glentoran had fielded the ineligible player Gary Smyth in each match.

Newry FC 1-1 Limavady FC on 17/04/2004 was abandoned after 63 minutes due to a waterlogged pitch but the result stood.

Cliftonville FC vs Glenavon FC on 17/04/2004 was abandoned at half-time due to a waterlogged pitch. The match was replayed on 22/04/2004.

Top goalscorers 2003-04

1)	Glenn FERGUSON	(Linfield FC)	25
2)	Gary HAMILTON	(Portadown FC)	23
3)	Vinny ARKINS	(Portadown FC)	18
4)	Stephen PARKHOUSE	(Institute FC)	15
5)	Chris MORGAN	(Linfield FC)	12

Promotion/Relegation Play-off

Armagh City FC (Armagh) 0-3, 1-1 Cliftonville FC (Belfast)

Irish League First Division 2003-04	Armagh	Ballinamallard	Ballyclare C.	Ballymoney	Bangor	Brantwood	Carrick R.	Donegal Celtic	H & W Welders	Loughgall	Lurgan Celtic	Moyola Park
Armagh City FC		1-0	0-1	1-0	1-1	3-0	4-1	0-0	2-1	2-0	3-1	1-0
Ballinamallard United FC	2-3		1-2	0-1	1-1	1-0	0-1	0-0	1-0	0-1	0-2	3-2
Ballyclare Comrades FC	1-0	0-1		0-0	0-2	0-1	0-1	0-0	2-1	1-2	1-0	2-1
Ballymoney United FC	0-0	1-0	1-3		0-0	0-0	1-0	0-0	2-1	1-4	5-1	1-1
Bangor FC	1-0	4-0	1-3	0-0		2-0	1-2	0-0	1-3	4-0	1-0	1-0
Brantwood FC	0-2	2-2	2-4	1-2	0-4		2-1	2-2	0-1	0-1	1-1	2-1
Carrick Rangers FC	2-0	1-1	1-1	3-3	2-0	2-3		2-2	0-3	0-1	2-3	1-2
Donegal Celtic FC	0-2	2-1	0-2	2-3	1-2	3-0	0-2		1-2	1-2	6-1	2-0
Harland & Wolff Welders FC	0-1	0-0	2-3	2-0	0-4	1-1	2-2	2-1		0-0	1-1	2-1
Loughgall FC	2-1	4-0	1-1	2-1	6-1	1-0	2-2	1-0	0-0		0-0	4-4
Lurgan Celtic FC	0-1	2-2	2-5	2-0	0-3	1-1	1-1	1-1	0-3	0-2		3-3
Moyola Park FC	2-2	1-3	1-2	3-0	1-1	3-0	3-1	2-5	1-2	0-1	2-2	

Division 1

		Pd	Wn	Dw	Ls	GF	GA	Pts	
1.	Loughgall FC (Loughgall)	22	14	6	2	37	20	48	P
2.	Armagh City FC (Armagh)	22	13	4	5	30	15	43	PO
3.	Ballyclare Comrades FC (Ballyclare)	22	13	4	5	34	21	43	
4.	Bangor FC (Bangor)	22	11	6	5	35	20	39	
5.	Harland & Wolff Welders FC (Belfast)	22	9	6	7	29	24	33	
6.	Ballymoney United FC (Ballymoney)	22	7	8	7	22	26	29	
7.	Carrick Rangers FC (Carrickfergus)	22	6	7	9	30	35	25	
8.	Donegal Celtic FC (Belfast)	22	5	8	9	29	27	23	
9.	Ballinamallard United FC (Ballinamallard)	22	5	6	11	20	31	21	
10.	Moyola Park FC (Castledawson)	22	4	6	12	34	41	18	
11.	Lurgan Celtic FC (Lurgan)	22	3	9	10	24	44	18	R
12.	Brantwood FC (Belfast)	22	4	6	12	18	38	18	R
		264	94	76	94	342	342	358	

Note: Carrick Rangers FC vs Brantwood FC on 10/04/2004 was abandoned and replayed on 11/05/2004 with a final scoreline of 2-3.

Lurgan FC vs Ballymoney FC on 20/04/2004 was abandoned after 20 minutes with a 0-0 scoreline after the referee was injured. The match was replayed on 12/05/2004 with a final scoreline of 2-0.

Promoted: Coagh United FC (Coagh), Dundela FC (Belfast)

At the end of the season, the Irish Football League was wound up and the IFA Intermediate League, consisting of two divisions of 12 clubs each was put into place.

IRISH CUP FINAL (Windsor Park, Belfast – 01/05/2004 – 8,300)

GLENTORAN FC (BELFAST) 1-0 Coleraine FC (Coleraine)

M. Halliday 21'

Glentoran: Morris, Nixon, Glendinning, Melaugh, Leeman, G. Smyth, McCann (Kilmartin), Lockhart, Smith, Halliday (Armour), Keegan (McCallion).

Coleraine: O'Hare, Clanachan, Flynn, Gaston, McAuley (Johnson), Beatty, Curran (Armstrong), Hamill, Tolan, Haveron, Gorman.

Semi-finals

Coleraine FC (Coleraine)	3-1	Limavady United FC (Limavady)
Glentoran FC (Belfast)	4-1	Omagh Town FC (Omagh)

Quarter-finals

Ards FC (Newtownards)	1-2	Omagh Town FC (Omagh)
Limavady United FC (Limavady)	2-0	Glenavon FC (Lurgan)
Linfield FC (Belfast)	0-1	Glentoran FC (Belfast)
Newry Town FC (Newry)	1-1, 1-3	Coleraine FC (Coleraine)

2004-2005

Irish Premier League 2004-05	Ards	Ballymena	Cliftonville	Coleraine	Crusaders	Dungannon	Glentoran	Institute	Larne	Limavady	Linfield	Lisburn D.	Loughgall	Newry City	Omagh T.	Portadown
Ards FC		1-1	3-0	1-2	2-2	1-3	0-3	1-2	0-3	0-1	2-2	0-1	0-0	5-1	2-0	0-1
Ballymena United FC	2-2		1-1	2-2	1-1	1-2	0-3	1-1	0-0	2-1	3-4	2-1	2-1	2-1	1-1	2-0
Cliftonville FC	3-1	0-0		1-4	1-0	1-1	0-1	1-0	2-0	0-2	0-0	1-0	1-3	0-1	2-1	0-2
Coleraine FC	3-0	0-2	3-1		1-1	4-2	0-1	2-4	3-0	1-2	0-4	1-3	2-0	6-1	3-4	2-2
Crusaders FC	0-2	2-3	0-2	1-1		0-3	0-2	1-0	1-1	1-0	1-2	0-0	3-2	0-1	3-1	0-1
Dungannon Swifts FC	7-0	1-2	3-1	0-1	0-0		2-0	3-0	3-1	1-1	1-1	1-1	1-0	1-0	2-0	1-3
Glentoran FC	2-0	4-2	4-0	1-0	4-1	5-0		2-0	3-0	2-0	3-2	1-0	2-0	3-1	3-0	1-2
Institute FC	1-1	1-1	1-2	3-1	2-0	3-2	0-1		3-0	0-3	0-1	1-3	3-0	2-1	0-1	2-1
Larne FC	2-2	0-0	0-0	1-5	5-2	3-2	0-5	2-0		0-4	0-2	0-0	2-3	0-1	2-0	2-3
Limavady United FC	0-1	2-1	0-0	0-3	1-1	3-2	2-2	5-1	6-0		0-1	2-2	1-1	3-2	2-0	0-2
Linfield FC	3-0	0-1	3-1	4-1	2-1	2-1	1-1	3-1	1-1	4-1		5-2	3-0	2-0	6-1	0-0
Lisburn Distillery FC	1-1	0-2	3-1	2-2	3-2	2-0	2-1	3-2	2-1	1-1	0-4		3-1	1-3	6-1	2-0
Loughgall FC	3-1	1-0	0-0	1-5	2-0	1-2	1-3	0-1	0-2	1-1	0-4	2-1		1-1	1-3	0-2
Newry City FC	1-0	1-1	4-2	0-1	2-0	0-4	0-4	4-1	1-3	2-2	0-3	0-0	2-5		2-1	0-6
Omagh Town FC	2-1	0-2	0-5	1-3	1-3	1-4	2-3	0-1	3-0	2-5	1-8	2-3	0-2	2-2		1-2
Portadown FC	2-3	-0	3-0	2-0	0-0	1-2	4-3	4-0	3-0	0-1	0-1	2-1	2-2	2-3	9-0	

	Irish Premier League	Pd	Wn	Dw	Ls	GF	GA	Pts	
1.	GLENTORAN FC (BELFAST)	30	24	2	4	73	22	74	
2.	Linfield FC (Belfast)	30	22	6	2	78	23	72	
3.	Portadown FC (Portadown)	30	18	4	8	64	29	58	
4.	Dungannon Swifts FC (Dungannon)	30	15	5	10	57	39	50	
5.	Limavady United FC (Limavady)	30	13	9	8	52	36	48	
6.	Coleraine FC (Coleraine)	30	14	5	11	62	47	47	
7.	Lisburn Distillery FC (Lisburn)	30	13	8	9	49	42	47	
8.	Ballymena United FC (Ballymena)	30	11	12	7	40	37	45	
9.	Institute FC (Londonderry)	30	11	3	16	36	50	36	
10.	Newry City FC (Newry)	30	10	5	15	38	63	35	**
11.	Cliftonville FC (Belfast)	30	9	7	14	29	44	34	
12.	Loughgall FC (Loughgall)	30	8	6	16	34	53	30	
13.	Larne FC (Larne)	30	7	7	16	31	60	28	
14.	Ards FC (Newtownards)	30	6	8	16	33	54	26	
15.	Crusaders FC (Belfast)	30	5	9	16	27	48	24	POR
16.	Omagh Town FC (Omagh)	30	5	2	23	32	88	17	R
		480	191	98	191	735	735	671	

** Newry Town FC (Newry) changed their name in the summer of 2004 to Newry City FC after the town was granted city status.

Top goalscorers 2004-05

1)	Chris MORGAN	(Glentoran FC)	19
2)	Kevin RAMSAY	(Limavady United FC)	18
3)	Jody TOLAN	(Coleraine FC)	16
4)	Vinny ARKINS	(Portadown FC)	15
	Michael HALLIDAY	(Glentoran FC)	15

Promotion/Relegation Play-off

Glenavon FC (Lurgan)   1-1, 2-1 (aet)   Crusaders FC (Belfast)

IFA Intermediate League Division One 2004-05	Armagh	Ballinamallard	Ballyclare C.	Ballymoney	Bangor	Carrick R.	Coagh United	Donegal Celtic	Dundela	Glenavon	H & W Welders	Moyola Park
Armagh City FC	■	3-0	1-0	1-0	3-2	3-0	1-1	2-1	1-1	3-1	1-0	2-0
Ballinamallard United FC	0-2	■	2-0	4-3	1-2	2-0	2-5	0-0	0-3	1-1	0-1	0-0
Ballyclare Comrades FC	1-1	1-0	■	1-1	0-0	0-0	2-1	0-3	1-1	0-1	2-4	2-0
Ballymoney United FC	0-1	1-0	0-4	■	0-2	4-3	4-3	2-1	3-1	0-1	0-1	0-1
Bangor FC	1-1	2-0	0-0	4-0	■	0-2	3-2	0-2	0-1	1-1	1-3	1-0
Carrick Rangers FC	0-0	2-0	1-2	3-1	2-0	■	0-2	1-2	2-3	4-2	1-1	0-1
Coagh United FC	1-2	3-0	1-1	0-3	1-3	2-0	■	1-1	1-1	0-3	2-4	2-0
Donegal Celtic FC	0-0	0-0	1-0	3-1	3-0	5-0	1-3	■	1-2	0-2	3-0	0-0
Dundela FC	1-3	2-0	1-2	3-2	1-4	0-1	2-2	1-2	■	0-3	1-1	0-0
Glenavon FC	0-2	4-0	1-0	4-1	1-2	3-0	6-1	1-1	2-0	■	1-0	3-0
Harland & Wolff Welders FC	1-1	3-2	3-1	3-3	3-3	1-1	2-3	1-0	1-0	0-1	■	1-0
Moyola Park FC	0-1	2-0	1-2	1-0	2-2	3-2	1-2	2-4	1-3	1-1	2-1	■

	Division 1	Pd	Wn	Dw	Ls	GF	GA	Pts	
1.	Armagh City FC (Armagh)	22	15	7	-	35	11	52	P
2.	Glenavon FC (Lurgan)	22	14	4	4	43	17	46	POP
3.	Donegal Celtic FC (Belfast)	22	10	6	6	34	19	36	
4.	Harland & Wolff Welders FC (Belfast)	22	10	6	6	35	29	36	
5.	Bangor FC (Bangor)	22	9	6	7	33	29	33	
6.	Coagh United FC (Coagh)	22	8	5	9	39	42	29	
7.	Ballyclare Comrades FC (Ballyclare)	22	7	7	8	22	24	28	
8.	Dundela FC (Belfast)	22	7	6	9	28	33	27	
9.	Moyola Park FC (Castledawson)	22	6	5	11	18	29	23	
10.	Carrick Rangers FC (Carrickfergus)	22	6	4	12	25	37	22	
11.	Ballymoney United FC (Ballymoney)	22	6	2	14	29	45	20	R
12.	Ballinamallard United FC (Ballinamallard)	22	3	4	15	14	40	13	R
		264	101	62	101	355	355	365	

Promoted: Banbridge Town FC (Banbridge) and Tobermore United FC (Tobermore)

IRISH CUP FINAL (Windsor Park, Belfast – 07/05/2005)

PORTADOWN FC (PORTADOWN)　　　　5-1　　　　　　　　　　　　Larne FC (Larne)

Arkins 15', 59', Convery 34', McCann 36', Kelly 48'　　　　　　　　　　　　*Ogden 03'*

Portadown: Murphy, Feeney, Convery, Kelly, O'Hara, Boyle, Collins, Clarke, Neill, McCann (Hamilton 47'), Arkins.

Larne: Spackman, Small, Murphy, Curran, Hughes, Rodgers, Weir, Ogden, Hamlin, Dickson, Bonner.

Semi-finals

Ballymena United FC (Ballymena)	0-1	Larne FC (Larne)
Portadown FC (Portadown)	0-0, 1-0	Glentoran FC (Belfast)

Quarter-finals

Ards FC (Newtownards)	0-1	Portadown FC (Portadown)
Ballymena United FC (Ballymena)	0-0, 4-0	Harland & Wolff Welders FC (Belfast)
Coleraine FC (Coleraine)	1-2	Glentoran FC (Belfast)
Loughgall FC (Loughgall)	1-1, 0-3	Larne FC (Larne)

2005-2006

Irish Premier League 2005-06	Ards	Armagh	Ballymena	Cliftonville	Coleraine	Dungannon	Glenavon	Glentoran	Institute	Larne	Limavady	Linfield	Lisburn	Loughgall	Newry	Portadown
Ards FC		0-2	1-3	0-1	2-5	3-3	1-0	0-1	1-4	1-3	2-1	0-4	0-1	1-0	1-3	1-2
Armagh City FC	3-0		0-1	1-3	3-0	0-0	0-4	5-2	1-2	1-2	3-3	0-1	1-6	0-1	2-1	2-2
Ballymena United FC	1-1	3-0		0-2	1-0	4-3	2-3	0-4	1-0	1-0	1-3	0-2	1-0	3-2	0-0	2-3
Cliftonville FC	0-1	8-1	2-2		0-1	0-3	2-1	1-1	2-0	2-2	0-1	1-1	2-1	1-0	0-0	0-2
Coleraine FC	2-4	4-0	0-1	0-2		2-0	0-0	0-0	2-5	2-1	0-2	0-1	1-0	1-3	1-3	1-1
Dungannon Swifts FC	4-2	2-1	2-2	1-0	6-1		6-0	2-1	2-1	3-0	3-2	2-3	2-2	3-0	1-1	0-1
Glenavon FC	1-0	1-3	2-2	2-2	1-2	2-2		0-3	0-0	2-3	2-1	0-5	2-2	0-4	1-4	0-1
Glentoran FC	2-1	2-0	1-2	0-0	3-0	3-1	1-0		3-1	5-1	0-1	1-4	0-0	1-0	3-2	5-1
Institute FC	2-1	4-0	0-1	2-3	0-1	3-3	1-2	1-3		1-1	1-1	2-9	0-2	0-0	0-0	1-2
Larne FC	3-1	2-3	1-2	2-4	1-4	1-0	2-2	1-3	1-1		2-3	2-4	3-1	0-0	1-1	2-1
Limavady United FC	1-0	3-0	2-2	1-2	3-3	1-1	1-1	0-2	3-3	1-0		2-2	1-1	0-1	1-4	0-2
Linfield FC	2-0	5-0	3-2	1-0	7-2	1-1	2-1	0-0	2-0	8-1	2-0		1-3	2-0	3-1	4-0
Lisburn Distillery FC	1-0	3-1	2-1	0-0	1-2	0-0	1-2	1-4	4-1	3-1	1-2	0-6		2-3	0-0	1-0
Loughgall FC	2-3	2-1	1-0	2-3	2-3	0-1	1-1	2-3	2-0	1-1	2-1	1-2	0-0		0-3	0-0
Newry City FC	2-1	1-2	2-0	3-1	2-0	2-1	1-2	1-3	5-0	0-0	1-0	1-1	0-3	0-0		0-2
Portadown FC	3-2	1-2	6-1	3-1	2-0	2-3	4-0	0-0	0-1	2-2	5-1	0-0	1-2	2-1	5-1	

	Irish Premier League	Pd	Wn	Dw	Ls	GF	GA	Pts	
1.	LINFIELD FC (BELFAST)	30	23	6	1	88	23	75	
2.	Glentoran FC (Belfast)	30	19	6	5	60	28	63	
3.	Portadown FC (Portadown)	30	16	6	8	56	36	54	
4.	Dungannon Swifts FC (Dungannon)	30	13	10	7	61	41	49	
5.	Cliftonville FC (Belfast)	30	13	8	9	45	35	47	
6.	Newry City FC (Newry)	30	12	9	9	45	35	45	
7.	Ballymena United FC (Ballymena)	30	13	6	11	42	48	45	
8.	Lisburn Distillery FC (Lisburn)	30	12	8	10	44	38	44	
9.	Coleraine FC (Coleraine)	30	11	4	15	40	57	37	
10.	Limavady United FC (Limavady)	30	9	9	12	42	49	36	
11.	Loughgall FC (Loughgall)	30	9	7	14	33	38	34	
12.	Larne FC (Larne)	30	7	9	14	42	63	30	
13.	Glenavon FC (Lurgan)	30	7	9	14	35	59	30	
14.	Armagh City FC (Armagh)	30	9	3	18	38	69	30	
15.	Institute FC (Londonderry)	30	6	8	16	37	58	26	POR
16.	Ards FC (Newtownards)	30	6	2	22	31	62	20	R
		480	185	110	185	739	739	665	

Note: Ards FC 0-3 Glenavon FC played on 28th January 2006 was awarded 1-0 to Ards FC after it was discovered that Glenavon had fielded an ineligible player.

Promotion/Relegation Play-off

Donegal Celtic FC (Belfast)　　　　　　　3-1, 0-0　　　　　　　Institute FC (Londonderry)

Top goalscorers 2005-06

1) Peter THOMPSON   (Linfield FC)   24
2) Glenn FERGUSON   (Linfield FC)   23
3) Timmy ADAMSON   (Dungannon Swifts FC)   13
   Gary BROWNE   (Glentoran FC)   13
   Gary McCUTCHEON   (Larne FC)   13

IFA Intermediate League First Division 2005-06	Ballyclare C.	Ballymoney	Banbridge T.	Bangor	Carrick R.	Coagh Utd.	Crusaders	Donegal C.	Dundela	H & W Welders	Moyola Park	Tobermore U.
Ballyclare Comrades FC	■	3-1	2-2	1-1	1-0	2-2	1-3	0-3	1-2	0-1	2-0	2-2
Ballymoney United FC	1-4	■	1-2	0-4	0-3	2-2	1-3	0-2	1-0	1-0	1-1	0-2
Banbridge Town FC	1-1	1-2	■	1-3	0-1	1-0	0-0	1-1	3-0	3-1	1-2	2-2
Bangor FC	3-2	4-2	2-3	■	0-0	0-2	1-4	3-3	2-0	0-3	5-0	4-0
Carrick Rangers FC	1-0	1-0	2-0	0-2	■	1-3	0-3	2-0	1-1	1-0	2-3	0-2
Coagh United FC	0-1	1-0	1-0	0-1	1-2	■	0-2	0-1	1-1	1-0	1-2	0-1
Crusaders FC	2-0	2-1	2-0	3-1	2-1	1-0	■	4-0	3-1	3-0	3-0	1-0
Donegal Celtic FC	4-1	1-1	1-0	1-0	3-2	4-1	2-3	■	0-2	4-1	1-0	5-1
Dundela FC	2-1	3-0	0-1	2-1	2-2	0-4	2-0	1-1	■	3-1	2-1	1-0
Harland & Wolff Welders FC	3-2	1-1	1-2	1-0	0-0	3-1	0-1	0-1	1-0	■	1-0	0-4
Moyola Park FC	3-2	2-1	3-3	2-4	3-2	0-1	2-3	1-2	2-6	1-1	■	4-3
Tobermore United FC	0-3	2-1	1-2	2-1	3-1	1-3	0-3	1-1	1-1	2-2	3-0	■

	Division 1	Pd	Wn	Dw	Ls	GF	GA	Pts	
1.	Crusaders FC (Belfast)	22	20	1	1	51	13	61	P
2.	Donegal Celtic FC (Belfast)	22	13	5	4	41	25	44	POP
3.	Dundela FC (Belfast)	22	10	5	7	32	28	35	
4.	Bangor FC (Bangor)	22	10	3	9	42	32	33	
5.	Banbridge Town FC (Banbridge)	22	8	6	8	29	29	30	
6.	Tobermore United FC (Tobermore)	22	8	5	9	33	37	29	
7.	Carrick Rangers FC (Carrickfergus)	22	8	4	10	25	29	28	
8.	Coagh United FC (Coagh)	22	8	3	11	25	26	27	
9.	Harland & Wolff Welders FC (Belfast)	22	7	4	11	21	31	25	
10.	Moyola Park FC (Castledawson)	22	7	3	12	32	50	24	
11.	Ballyclare Comrades FC (Ballyclare)	22	6	5	11	32	37	23	R
12.	Ballymoney United FC (Ballymoney)	22	3	4	15	18	44	13	R
		264	108	48	108	381	381	372	

Promoted: Ballinamallard United FC (Ballinamallard) and Portstewart FC (Portstewart)

Note: Omagh Town FC (Omagh) withdrew before the start of the season. As a result Ballymoney United FC (Ballymoney) were re-instated in Division 1 for this season.

IRISH CUP FINAL   (Windsor Park, Belfast – 06/05/2006 – 12,500)

LINFIELD FC (BELFAST)	2-1	Glentoran FC (Belfast)
Thompson 45', 65'		*Halliday 44'*

Linfield: Mannus, Ervin, McShane, Murphy, Bailie, Gault, McAreavey (Hunter 86'), Kearney (McCann 74'), Mouncey, Ferguson, Thompson.

Glentoran: Morris, Melaugh, Nixon, Simpson, Glendinning, Lockhart, Berry (Tolan 77'), McDonagh, Ward, Halliday, Browne (Morgan 69').

Semi-finals

Bangor FC (Bangor)	1-3	Linfield FC (Belfast)
Larne FC (Larne)	0-2	Glentoran FC (Belfast)

Quarter-finals

Glentoran FC (Belfast)	2-0	Portadown FC (Portadown)
Linfield FC (Belfast)	3-0	Glenavon FC (Lurgan)
Lisburn Distillery FC (Lisburn)	0-1	Bangor FC (Bangor)
Newington YC (Belfast)	1-2	Larne FC (Larne)

Round 6

Dungannon Swifts FC (Dungannon)	1-1, 1-3	Portadown FC (Portadown)
Glenavon FC (Lurgan)	3-0	Coleraine FC (Coleraine)
Glentoran FC (Belfast)	1-0	Ballyclare Comrades FC (Ballyclare)
Larne FC (Larne)	3-0	Carrick Rangers FC (Carrickfergus)
Limavady United FC (Limavady)	1-3	Bangor FC (Bangor)
Linfield FC (Belfast)	1-1, 3-1	Loughgall FC (Loughgall)
Lisburn Distillery FC (Lisburn)	0-0, 2-1	Ballymena United FC (Ballymena)
Newington YC (Belfast)	1-0	Portstewart FC (Portstewart)

Round 5

Ards FC (Newtownards)	1-2	Glentoran FC (Belfast)
	(Played in Belfast)	
Ballymena United FC (Ballymena)	4-0	Kilmore Recreation FC (Crossgar)
Ballymoney United FC (Ballymoney)	1-2	Carrick Rangers FC (Carrickfergus)
	(Played in Carrickfergus)	
Ballynure Old Boys FC (Ballynure)	0-4	Ballyclare Comrades FC (Ballyclare)
Banbridge Town FC (Banbridge)	0-0, 2-3	Loughgall FC (Loughgall)
	(Both matches were played in Loughgall)	
Cliftonville FC (Belfast)	1-1, 0-1	Dungannon Swifts FC (Dungannon)
Coleraine FC (Coleraine)	1-1, 0-0 (aet)	Newry City FC (Newry)
	(Coleraine FC won 4-3 on penalties)	
Crusaders FC (Belfast)	2-2, 0-1	Portadown FC (Portadown)
Glenavon FC (Lurgan)	2-1	Dundela FC (Belfast)
Harland & Wolff Welders FC (Belfast)	1-1, 1-3	Bangor FC (Bangor)
	(Both matches were played in Bangor)	
Institute FC (Londonderry)	1-3	Lisburn Distillery FC (Lisburn)
Larne FC (Larne)	1-1, 3-1	Donegal Celtic FC (Belfast)
Linfield FC (Belfast)	5-0	Armagh City FC (Armagh)
Newington YC (Belfast)	1-1, 2-0	Coagh United FC (Coagh)
	(Played in Coagh)	
P.S.N.I. FC (Belfast)	0-5	Limavady United FC (Limavady)
	(Played in Limavady)	
Tobermore United FC (Tobermore)	2-3	Portstewart FC (Portstewart)

2006-2007

Irish Premier League 2006-07	Armagh	Ballymena	Cliftonville	Coleraine	Crusaders	Donegal C.	Dungannon	Glenavon	Glentoran	Larne	Limavady	Linfield	Lisburn	Loughgall	Newry	Portadown
Armagh City FC	■	0-3	1-3	4-3	1-3	1-0	0-1	1-2	0-3	2-1	4-2	0-2	1-2	1-0	1-3	2-3
Ballymena United FC	2-2	■	0-1	2-3	2-1	1-0	2-1	4-2	3-2	3-0	0-0	0-0	0-1	4-1	1-1	2-0
Cliftonville FC	1-0	2-1	■	2-1	4-2	0-0	1-0	0-0	1-2	0-0	0-1	0-0	3-1	2-0	2-1	0-0
Coleraine FC	2-0	0-1	2-1	■	1-3	3-1	2-1	1-3	1-2	4-3	2-4	2-2	2-1	4-2	2-1	1-1
Crusaders FC	6-2	2-2	1-2	0-3	■	4-1	2-1	1-1	1-3	3-1	0-3	2-3	1-1	2-1	1-0	0-3
Donegal Celtic FC	1-2	3-2	0-1	1-3	0-2	■	0-0	2-3	1-0	3-0	2-1	0-1	2-1	1-1	1-1	2-4
Dungannon Swifts FC	4-2	1-0	3-2	1-1	1-2	1-2	■	1-1	2-4	2-1	2-1	1-5	2-3	3-1	3-1	0-1
Glenavon FC	2-3	3-1	0-1	3-3	0-1	3-3	1-2	■	0-3	1-1	0-1	2-4	1-1	2-0	1-2	1-4
Glentoran FC	8-0	2-0	4-1	3-2	1-0	1-1	0-1	2-2	■	6-3	3-0	1-2	3-1	4-0	2-0	2-3
Larne FC	0-1	0-1	1-3	0-1	0-0	2-1	1-0	3-0	0-4	■	2-3	0-0	1-5	3-0	0-4	0-1
Limavady United FC	0-3	1-1	1-1	2-1	0-1	1-1	0-1	3-2	1-2	2-1	■	0-4	0-5	4-1	2-3	1-2
Linfield FC	5-3	2-0	0-3	2-1	1-0	3-0	0-0	0-0	1-1	5-0	3-2	■	3-0	7-0	2-0	0-0
Lisburn Distillery FC	0-1	3-1	0-4	2-0	1-1	4-1	1-0	4-0	3-1	1-3	0-1	0-4	■	3-0	1-1	2-0
Loughgall FC	1-3	3-3	1-2	1-3	0-5	2-2	1-1	1-1	1-3	1-2	1-1	0-6	1-2	■	1-1	0-3
Newry City FC	2-3	1-3	1-2	1-1	2-1	1-1	2-3	3-2	0-4	2-3	3-1	0-4	0-0	1-0	■	0-2
Portadown FC	3-0	2-1	2-2	0-0	1-2	2-0	0-2	2-1	2-0	1-1	3-0	1-2	1-1	0-1	2-0	■

	Irish Premier League	Pd	Wn	Dw	Ls	GF	GA	Pts	
1.	LINFIELD FC (BELFAST)	30	21	8	1	73	19	71	
2.	Glentoran FC (Belfast)	30	20	3	7	76	33	63	
3.	Cliftonville FC (Belfast)	30	18	7	5	47	26	61	
4.	Portadown FC (Portadown)	30	17	7	6	49	26	58	
5.	Lisburn Distillery FC (Lisburn)	30	14	6	10	50	39	48	
6.	Crusaders FC (Belfast)	30	14	5	11	50	42	47	
7.	Coleraine FC (Coleraine)	30	13	6	11	55	50	45	
8.	Dungannon Swifts FC (Dungannon)	30	13	5	12	41	41	44	
9.	Ballymena United FC (Ballymena)	30	12	7	11	46	40	43	
10.	Limavady United FC (Limavady)	30	10	5	15	39	54	35	
11.	Armagh City FC (Armagh)	30	11	2	17	42	66	35	
12.	Newry City FC (Newry)	30	8	7	15	39	54	31	
13.	Donegal Celtic FC (Belfast)	30	6	9	15	33	51	27	
14.	Larne FC (Larne)	30	7	5	18	33	60	26	
15.	Glenavon FC (Lurgan)	30	5	10	15	40	58	25	PO
16.	Loughgall FC (Loughgall)	30	1	8	21	23	77	11	R
		480	190	100	190	736	736	670	

Larne FC had 16 points deducted for fielding the "ineligible" player Padraig Gollogley in 8 games (the results are shown as underlined inthe chart above, each match being awarded 0-1 to their opponents) under league rule 44. However this penalty was revoked on 4th May 2007 with the points being returned to Larne FC and the club receiving a fine of £8,000 instead.

Promotion/Relegation Play-off

Bangor FC (Bangor)   0-1, 1-0 (aet)   Glenavon FC (Lurgan)
(Glenavon won 4-2 on penalties)

Top goalscorers 2006-07

1) Peter THOMPSON　　　　　(Linfield FC)　　29

IFA Intermediate League Division 1 2006-07	Ards	Ballinamallard	Banbridge T.	Bangor	Carrick R.	Coagh United	Dundela	H & W Welders	Institute	Moyola Park	Portstewart	Tobermore U.
Ards FC		2-1	2-0	0-1	1-3	3-1	1-2	4-1	2-2	3-0	2-2	4-1
Ballinamallard United FC	0-0		0-2	0-1	0-1	1-1	1-2	0-0	0-3	2-1	1-3	2-1
Banbridge Town FC	0-3	4-1		2-3	3-2	3-0	3-3	3-2	4-3	6-3	2-0	3-2
Bangor FC	1-3	7-0	0-3		0-0	3-1	1-2	4-1	2-1	4-1	3-2	5-1
Carrick Rangers FC	1-1	2-1	2-1	2-2		2-2	0-0	3-1	0-3	1-0	2-0	2-1
Coagh United FC	0-1	2-1	1-2	0-2	3-1		1-3	0-2	0-0	6-0	2-1	5-4
Dundela FC	1-1	0-2	0-1	1-1	0-3	0-0		2-3	0-4	3-1	4-2	3-2
Harland & Wolff Welders FC	2-1	1-0	0-1	0-2	1-2	3-3	2-1		1-3	1-2	0-1	1-1
Institute FC	2-0	3-0	2-0	1-1	3-0	3-0	1-0	2-0		2-0	2-0	2-1
Moyola Park FC	0-2	4-0	1-1	0-1	0-2	0-1	1-5	1-2	0-2		3-2	0-3
Portstewart FC	3-2	0-1	0-0	0-3	0-3	3-0	2-1	0-1	1-3	2-6		1-2
Tobermore United FC	1-4	2-0	1-1	2-2	4-4	3-3	2-0	0-5	2-3	2-0	1-4	

	Division 1	**Pd**	**Wn**	**Dw**	**Ls**	**GF**	**GA**	**Pts**	
1.	Institute FC (Londonderry)	22	17	3	2	50	14	54	P
2.	Bangor FC (Bangor)	22	14	5	3	49	23	47	PO
3.	Banbridge Town FC (Banbridge)	22	13	4	5	45	31	43	
4.	Carrick Rangers FC (Carrickfergus)	22	12	6	4	38	27	42	
5.	Ards FC (Newtownards)	22	11	5	6	42	25	38	
6.	Dundela FC (Belfast)	22	8	5	9	33	35	29	
7.	Harland & Wolff Welders FC (Belfast)	22	8	3	11	30	36	27	
8.	Coagh United FC (Coagh)	22	6	6	10	32	41	24	
9.	Tobermore United FC (Tobermore)	22	5	5	12	39	54	20	
10.	Portstewart FC (Portstewart)	22	6	2	14	29	44	20	
11.	Ballinamallard United FC (Ballinamallard)	22	4	3	15	14	42	15	R
12.	Moyola Park FC (Castledawson)	22	4	1	17	24	53	13	R
		264	108	48	108	425	425	372	

Carrick Rangers 1-0 Moyola Park played on 2nd December 2006 was abandoned at half-time. The match was replayed on 24th February 2007 and finished with a 1-0 scoreline.

Promoted to Division 1: Ballyclare Comrades FC (Ballyclare) and Lurgan Celtic FC (Lurgan).

IRISH CUP FINAL (Windsor Park, Belfast – 05/05/2007 – 7,600)

LINFIELD FC (BELFAST)	2-2 (aet)	Dungannon Swifts FC (Dungannon)
Dickson 03', Ferguson 38'	*(3-2 on penalties)*	*Hamill 18', MaAnee 40'*

Linfield: Mannus, Ervin, McShane, Murphy, Bailie, McAreavey (Gault 80'), O'Kane (Stewart 72'), Mulgrew, Dickson, Thompson, Ferguson.

Dungannon: Nelson, Wray, J.P. Gallagher (T. Fitzpatrick 105'), Montgomery, McMinn, McCluskey (McConkey 68'), McCabe, McAree, Hamill, McAlister, Scullion (Everaldo 87').

Semi-finals

Cliftonville FC (Belfast)	0-0 (aet)	Dungannon Swifts FC (Dungannon)
	(Dungannon Swifts FC won 5-4 on penalties)	
Linfield FC (Belfast)	4-1	Lisburn Distillery FC (Lisburn)

Quarter-finals

Ballymena United FC (Ballymena)	1-1, 2-4	Linfield FC (Belfast)
Cliftonville FC (Belfast)	3-1	Portadown FC (Portadown)
Dungannon Swifts FC (Dungannon)	2-0	Armagh City FC (Armagh)
Lisburn Distillery FC (Lisburn)	4-1	Crusaders FC (Belfast)

Round 6

Ards FC (Newtownards)	0-5	Linfield FC (Belfast)
Cliftonville FC (Belfast)	2-0	Donegal Celtic FC (Belfast)
Comber Recreation FC (Comber)	0-1	Ballymena United FC (Ballymena)
	(Played in Ballymena)	
Dungannon Swifts FC (Dungannon)	2-1	Newry City FC (Newry)
Glentoran FC (Belfast)	2-2, 1-1 (aet)	Portadown FC (Portadown)
	(Portadown FC won 4-3 on penalties)	
Limavady United FC (Limavady)	0-1	Crusaders FC (Belfast)
Lisburn Distillery FC (Lisburn)	4-1	Glenavon FC (Lurgan)
Loughgall FC (Loughgall)	1-3	Armagh City FC (Armagh)

Round 5

Ards FC (Newtownards)	1-1, 2-1	Dundela FC (Belfast)
Armagh City FC (Armagh)	2-1	Institute FC (Londonderry)
Coleraine FC (Coleraine)	1-2	Lisburn Distillery FC (Lisburn)
Comber Recreation FC (Comber)	0-0, 2-1	Laurelvale FC (Laurelvale)
Crusaders FC (Belfast)	3-1	Lurgan Celtic FC (Lurgan)
Dungannon Swifts FC (Dungannon)	7-1	Coagh United FC (Coagh)
Glenavon FC (Lurgan)	1-0	P.S.N.I. (Belfast)
Glentoran FC (Belfast)	2-1	Ballymoney United FC (Ballymoney)
Harland & Wolff Welders FC (Belfast)	0-1	Ballymena United FC (Ballymena)
Larne FC (Larne)	2-4	Cliftonville FC (Belfast)
Limavady United FC (Limavady)	4-2	Carrick Rangers FC (Carrickfergus)
Linfield FC (Belfast)	3-0	Oxford United Stars FC (Londonderry)
Loughgall FC (Loughgall)	2-1	Ballyclare Comrades FC (Ballyclare)
Newry City FC (Newry)	4-0	Ballynure Old Boys FC (Ballynure)
Portadown FC (Portadown)	6-1	Bangor FC (Bangor)
Tobermore United FC (Tobermore)	1-1, 2-2, 0-1	Donegal Celtic FC (Belfast)
	(The first match was abandoned)	

2007-2008

Irish Premier League 2007-08	Armagh	Ballymena	Cliftonville	Coleraine	Crusaders	Donegal C.	Dungannon	Glenavon	Glentoran	Institute	Larne	Limavady	Linfield	Lisburn	Newry	Portadown
Armagh City FC	■	1-2	0-1	0-1	2-2	1-1	0-1	2-0	0-5	1-1	2-5	1-0	1-3	4-1	1-2	1-1
Ballymena United FC	2-1	■	0-1	2-0	2-2	0-0	0-0	0-4	2-2	3-0	3-0	0-4	2-2	2-1	2-1	
Cliftonville FC	2-1	3-2	■	1-2	0-1	5-1	2-1	3-3	4-2	2-0	1-1	4-1	2-2	2-2	2-0	2-1
Coleraine FC	2-0	1-1	0-3	■	3-3	3-2	2-2	0-1	1-4	2-1	4-1	1-0	1-4	1-4	0-1	1-1
Crusaders FC	1-1	3-0	1-1	3-4	■	2-0	1-0	2-1	0-2	1-0	4-1	2-1	0-3	1-3	4-1	0-2
Donegal Celtic FC	3-0	0-2	0-2	1-1	3-0	■	3-1	2-0	3-3	0-1	4-3	1-0	1-1	1-2	2-3	0-1
Dungannon Swifts FC	5-1	2-1	1-0	4-1	1-1	0-0	■	1-4	0-0	0-1	1-0	0-2	4-0	0-3	4-6	0-3
Glenavon FC	5-0	1-2	1-2	1-0	0-4	0-1	1-2	■	1-2	2-0	2-3	0-3	0-2	2-3	1-0	0-3
Glentoran FC	1-0	2-4	2-1	2-1	3-0	5-1	1-1	3-0	■	4-0	1-0	3-0	1-0	2-2	2-1	3-1
Institute FC	1-1	1-1	1-2	0-0	3-1	1-1	1-0	2-3	1-2	■	0-1	0-0	0-1	0-2	0-2	1-2
Larne FC	0-2	2-1	1-2	1-2	0-3	4-2	3-3	3-4	0-3	1-2	■	2-2	1-5	1-2	3-0	1-2
Limavady United FC	0-3	3-1	3-1	0-0	1-2	0-1	1-1	1-0	1-0	2-2	2-3	■	0-4	1-2	1-3	0-2
Linfield FC	2-1	1-0	0-0	4-0	5-0	2-0	2-1	3-2	0-0	1-0	3-0	3-0	■	2-1	5-0	1-0
Lisburn Distillery FC	1-0	0-2	1-2	1-0	1-0	0-1	1-1	0-0	1-2	0-0	2-0	5-0	0-0	■	1-0	1-0
Newry City FC	3-0	2-2	1-0	0-2	1-1	1-1	3-0	2-1	0-3	2-1	2-2	3-0	0-3	1-4	■	2-1
Portadown FC	2-1	2-1	0-2	1-5	2-0	2-1	0-1	0-1	0-2	2-1	5-1	2-0	2-5	0-1	3-2	■

	Irish Premier League	Pd	Wn	Dw	Ls	GF	GA	Pts	
1.	LINFIELD FC (BELFAST)	30	23	5	2	71	18	74	
2.	Glentoran FC (Belfast)	30	22	5	3	69	24	71	
3.	Cliftonville FC (Belfast)	30	18	6	6	55	32	60	
4.	Lisburn Distillery FC (Lisburn)	30	17	7	6	50	28	58	
5.	Portadown FC (Portadown)	30	15	2	13	44	39	47	R
6.	Ballymena United FC (Ballymena)	30	12	8	10	42	41	44	
7.	Crusaders FC (Belfast)	30	12	7	11	45	47	43	
8.	Newry City FC (Newry)	30	13	4	13	45	62	43	
9.	Coleraine FC (Coleraine)	30	11	7	12	41	50	40	
10.	Dungannon Swifts FC (Dungannon)	30	9	9	12	38	44	36	
11.	Donegal Celtic FC (Belfast)	30	9	8	13	39	47	35	R
12.	Glenavon FC (Lurgan)	30	9	3	18	37	51	30	
13.	Larne FC (Larne)	30	7	4	19	44	71	25	R
14.	Institute FC (Londonderry)	30	5	8	17	23	41	23	
15.	Limavady United FC (Limavady)	30	6	5	19	26	57	23	R
16.	Armagh City FC (Armagh)	30	5	6	19	39	56	21	R
		480	193	94	193	708	708	673	

Lisburn Distillery vs Ballymena United on 1st December 2007 was abandoned after 77 minutes due to floodlight failure when the scoreline stood at 2-1. The match was replayed on 18th December 2007 and finished with a 0-2 scoreline.

The league was reorganised for the 2008-09 season. The Irish Premier League was renamed to the IFA Premiership and reduced to 12 clubs. Membership of the new Premiership was allocated based on a number of ratings including attendances, performance, ground facilities and provision for women/youth football with points being awarded for each category.

The point allocation totals were:

Linfield FC 1339 points, Ballymena United FC 1054 points, Glentoran FC 1016 points, Coleraine FC 965 points, Cliftonville FC 945 points, Dungannon Swifts FC 855 points, Glenavon FC 828 points, Crusaders FC 826 points, Lisburn Distillery FC 815 points, Newry City FC 796 points, Bangor FC 641 points, Institute FC 632 points, Donegal Celtic FC 543 points.

Portadown FC were not considered as their application arrived 14 minutes late on 13th March 2008. Armagh City FC, Larne FC and Limavady United FC were not considered as they did not have the required domestic license. These 4 clubs joined the newly-formed IFA Championship 1.

Top goalscorers 2007-08

1)	Peter THOMPSON	(Linfield FC)	20
	Paul McVEIGH	(Donegal Celtic FC)	20
2)	Gary BROWNE	(Lisburn Distillery FC)	11
3)	Gary HAMILTON	(Glentoran FC)	19
	Kevin KELBIE	(Ballymena United FC)	15
	Glenn FERGUSON	(Linfield FC)	14

IFA Intermediate League Division 1 2007-08	Ards	Ballyclare	Banbridge T.	Bangor	Carrick R.	Coagh Utd.	Dundela	H & W Welders	Loughgall	Lurgan Celtic	Portstewart	Tobermore U.
Ards FC		1-2	1-3	1-2	2-1	3-1	1-2	0-1	2-0	4-0	4-0	0-2
Ballyclare Comrades FC	0-1		1-1	1-0	0-1	2-0	0-1	0-1	1-1	2-0	1-0	2-0
Banbridge Town FC	1-3	0-1		1-6	1-2	2-0	2-4	2-0	1-3	4-1	2-2	3-0
Bangor FC	2-2	0-0	4-3		1-2	2-2	1-0	2-1	1-1	4-0	0-0	2-2
Carrick Rangers FC	2-1	1-0	0-1	3-1		6-0	0-2	0-0	1-2	4-1	2-0	0-1
Coagh United FC	1-0	1-1	4-2	1-2	1-1		1-3	3-0	0-3	3-0	2-1	0-0
Dundela FC	2-2	2-2	1-2	1-1	3-1	2-3		2-0	3-0	2-0	2-1	1-3
Harland & Wolff Welders FC	1-0	0-2	2-1	4-3	1-1	0-0	3-0		1-1	0-0	1-1	1-1
Loughgall FC	2-0	1-0	1-0	3-1	5-1	2-1	1-0	1-0		2-0	2-0	1-4
Lurgan Celtic FC	2-1	1-2	0-1	1-2	1-0	0-1	0-2	3-2	2-2		4-0	1-3
Portstewart FC	0-2	4-4	1-3	3-4	1-3	1-1	0-2	0-0	0-5	1-3		2-1
Tobermore United FC	1-1	0-4	1-2	1-2	5-2	2-1	4-1	4-0	2-3	2-2	2-1	

	Division 1	**Pd**	**Wn**	**Dw**	**Ls**	**GF**	**GA**	**Pts**	
1.	Loughgall FC (Loughgall)	22	15	4	3	42	21	49	
2.	Dundela FC (Belfast)	22	12	3	7	38	28	39	R
3.	Bangor FC (Bangor)	22	10	7	5	43	33	37	P
4.	Ballyclare Comrades FC (Ballyclare)	22	10	6	6	28	17	36	
5.	Tobermore United FC (Tobermore)	22	10	5	7	41	32	35	
6.	Carrick Rangers FC (Carrickfergus)	22	10	3	9	34	30	33	
7.	Banbridge Town FC (Banbridge)	22	10	2	10	38	38	32	
8.	Ards FC (Newtownards)	22	8	3	11	32	28	27	
9.	Coagh United FC (Coagh)	22	7	6	9	27	35	27	
10.	Harland & Wolff Welders FC (Belfast)	22	6	8	8	19	27	26	R
11.	Lurgan Celtic FC (Lurgan)	22	5	3	14	22	44	18	R
12.	Portstewart FC (Portstewart)	22	1	6	15	19	50	9	R
		264	104	56	104	383	383	368	

At the end of the season, the IFA Intermediate League was closed down as part of the reorganisation of top-level football in Northern Ireland. The top division of the Intermediate League became the new IFA Championship.

Dundela FC were relegated as they did not meet the required criteria for the 2008-09 season in the new IFA Championship. Dundela FC duly joined the IFA Interim Intermediate League along with members of the IFA Intermediate League Division 2. Members of this Interim League had one year to make the necessary improvements in order to qualify for entry to the Championship for the 2009-10 season.

Bangor FC were the only Division 1 club to apply for election to the new IFA Premiership for 2008-09.

Promoted: Ballinamallard United FC (Ballinamallard), Ballymoney United FC (Ballymoney), Dergview FC (Castlederg) and Glebe Rangers FC (Ballymoney).

Killymoon Rangers FC (Cookstown) were elected to the new IFA Championship for the next season

IRISH CUP FINAL (Windsor Park, Belfast – 03/05/2008)

LINFIELD FC (BELFAST)	2-1	Coleraine FC (Coleraine)
Thompson 49', 53'		*McLaughlin 18'*

Linfield: Mannus, Lindsay, Murphy, Bailie, O'Kane, Mulgrew, Gault, McAreavey (Dickson 45'), Kearney (Curran 87'), Thompson, Ferguson.

Coleraine: O'Hare, Neill, McVey, P.McLaughlin, Clanachan, Watt (Dooley 74'), Hunter, McCallion, Carson, Patton, Tolan.

Semi-finals

Cliftonville FC (Belfast)	1-2	Linfield FC (Belfast)
Coleraine FC (Coleraine)	1-1, 2-1 (aet)	Donegal Celtic FC (Belfast)

Quarter-finals

Cliftonville FC (Belfast)	4-3	Portadown FC (Portadown)
Glentoran FC (Belfast)	1-2	Donegal Celtic FC (Belfast)
Institute FC (Londonderry)	0-0, 1-5	Coleraine FC (Coleraine)
Newry City FC (Newry)	1-1, 0-4	Linfield FC (Belfast)

Round 6

Ballyclare Comrades FC (Ballyclare)	2-2, 0-2	Institute FC (Londonderry)
Cliftonville FC (Belfast)	1-0	Crusaders FC (Belfast)
Coleraine FC (Coleraine)	5-1	Brantwood FC (Belfast)
Donegal Celtic FC (Belfast)	1-0	Abbey Villa FC (Millisle)
Dungannon Swifts FC (Dungannon)	0-2	Glentoran FC (Belfast)
Linfield FC (Belfast)	3-0	Bangor FC (Bangor)
Newry City FC (Newry)	1-1, 1-0	Dundela FC (Belfast)
Portadown FC (Portadown)	2-1	Downpatrick FC (Downpatrick)

Round 5

Ards FC (Newtownards)	1-1, 0-1	Brantwood FC (Belfast)
Armagh City FC (Armagh)	1-5	Crusaders FC (Belfast)
Ballyclare Comrades FC (Ballyclare)	0-0, 0-1	Ballymoney United FC (Ballymoney)
Banbridge Town FC (Banbridge)	2-3	Abbey Villa FC (Millisle)
Coleraine FC (Coleraine)	1-0	Tobermore United FC (Tobermore)
Donegal Celtic FC (Belfast)	3-0	Carrick Rangers FC (Carrickfergus)
Dundela FC (Belfast)	4-0	Portstewart FC (Portstewart)
Glenavon FC (Lurgan)	1-2	Bangor FC (Bangor)
Glentoran FC (Belfast)	0-0, 3-1	Lisburn Distillery FC (Lisburn)
Institute FC (Londonderry)	6-0	Dunmurry Recreation FC (Dunmurry)
Killyleagh Youth Club FC (Killyleagh)	0-1	Downpatrick FC (Downpatrick)
Larne FC (Larne)	2-3	Cliftonville FC (Belfast)
Limavady United FC (Limavady)	1-1, 1-2	Dungannon Swifts FC (Dungannon)
Loughgall FC (Loughgall)	0-3	Linfield FC (Belfast)
Newry City FC (Newry)	2-2, 0-0 (aet)	Ballymena United FC (Ballymena)
	(Newry City won 4-2 on penalties)	
Portadown FC (Portadown)	1-0	Newington Youth Club FC (Belfast)

2008-2009

IFA Premiership 2008-09	Ballymena	Bangor	Cliftonville	Coleraine	Crusaders	Dungannon	Glenavon	Glentoran	Institute	Linfield	Lisburn	Newry
Ballymena United FC		2-0	1-3	---	---	1-2	1-2	---	1-0	0-3	1-	0-4
		1-2	1-5	2-0	1-0	0-3	0-3	1-1	0-1	2-0	1-2	2-3
Bangor FC	1-1		---	---	1-4	1-3	1-1	---	2-2	0-1	0-0	4-2
	0-3		1-1	4-0	0-5	3-1	1-2	1-2	3-2	0-5	1-0	1-1
Cliftonville FC	---	2-1		0-0	0-0	1-1	2-1	1-3	---	1-2	3-1	---
	0-0	3-2		3-0	1-1	2-2	4-0	0-2	1-1	0-4	0-0	0-0
Coleraine FC	0-1	3-1	0-0		0-1	2-1	2-1	1-2	---	1-2	1-0	---
	1-1	3-1	2-2		2-5	1-0	3-2	1-2	2-1	1-4	1-1	1-0
Crusaders FC	0-0	---	4-2	2-1		2-2	2-2	0-1	---	0-5	1-1	---
	2-0	0-0	3-1	2-1		3-3	2-0	3-0	1-0	2-3	0-1	2-1
Dungannon Swifts FC	4-3	3-2	---	---	---		1-1	0-2	0-1	0-1	1-4	1-2
	2-1	0-2	0-3	0-1	3-6		1-0	1-2	1-1	1-1	0-1	2-2
Glenavon FC	2-1	2-3	---	---	---	3-1		---	1-3	1-4	1-0	2-0
	1-3	0-1	1-0	0-0	1-1	2-2		1-2	0-1	1-0	2-2	1-2
Glentoran FC	1-2	3-1	3-1	1-3	1-1	---	2-0		4-2	1-1	3-3	---
	4-1	1-0	2-1	2-1	1-1	1-1	2-1		1-0	2-0	0-0	2-1
Institute FC	0-0	4-0	0-2	1-0	2-2	3-0	1-1	---		---	---	1-3
	1-1	1-0	0-1	2-1	1-1	2-0	2-1	0-2		1-2	0-2	4-2
Linfield FC	---	---	2-2	0-1	0-0	---	---	1-0	1-0		2-0	1-1
	1-0	0-0	2-1	1-0	1-0	3-1	2-4	3-0	7-0		0-2	1-0
Lisburn Distillery FC	---	---	1-1	2-0	2-0	---	---	0-3	1-2	0-0		3-1
	1-0	1-0	3-1	1-2	1-2	0-1	6-2	1-1	5-2	1-2		1-1
Newry City FC	0-1	2-1	0-1	0-4	0-1	2-2	2-1	0-1	2-1	---	---	
	2-2	0-0	1-0	0-3	3-1	3-2	0-2	0-0	1-1	1-1	2-3	

	IFA Premiership	Pd	Wn	Dw	Ls	GF	GA	Pts	
1.	GLENTORAN FC (BELFAST)	38	24	9	5	63	36	81	
2.	Linfield FC (Belfast)	38	24	8	6	69	28	80	
3.	Crusaders FC (Belfast)	38	16	14	8	63	45	62	
4.	Lisburn Distillery FC (Lisburn)	38	15	11	12	53	41	56	
5.	Coleraine FC (Coleraine)	38	15	6	17	46	51	51	
6.	Cliftonville FC (Belfast)	38	12	14	12	52	48	50	
7.	Institute FC (Londonderry)	38	13	9	16	47	55	48	
8.	Newry City FC (Newry)	38	11	11	16	47	57	44	
9.	Glenavon FC (Lurgan)	38	11	8	19	49	63	41	
10.	Ballymena United FC (Ballymena)	38	11	8	19	39	57	41	
11.	Bangor FC (Bangor)	38	9	9	20	42	67	36	++
12.	Dungannon Swifts FC (Dungannon)	38	8	11	19	49	71	35	PO
		536	169	118	169	619	619	627	

++ Bangor FC withdrew from the professional licensing scheme and were relegated to the 2nd Level. As a result of this decision Dungannon Swifts FC entered the promotion and relegation play-off.

Glentoran 0-0 Glenavon played on 16th August 2008 was abandoned after 13 minutes due to extremely heavy rainfall. The match was replayed on 25th November 2008 and finished with a 2-1 scoreline.

Linfield 1-0 Cliftonville played on 16th August 2008 was abandoned after 32 minutes due to extremely heavy rainfall. The match was replayed on 13th January 2009 and finished with a 2-1 scoreline.

Newry 1-0 Coleraine played on 16th August 2008 was abandoned after 34 minutes due to extremely heavy rainfall. The match was replayed on 9th September 2008 and finished with a 0-3 scoreline.

The League was split after 33 games with the top 6 clubs playing for the championship and the bottom 6 clubs playing against relegation (each 5 games), with Phase 1 records being carried-forward.

Promotion/Relegation Play-off

Donegal Celtic FC (Belfast) 2-1, 0-1 Dungannon Swifts FC (Dungannon)
(Aggregate 2-2. Dungannon Swifts won on the away goals rule to avoid relegation)

Top goalscorers 2008-09

1)	Curtis ALLEN	(Lisburn Distillery FC)	19
2)	Chris SCANNELL	(Cliftonville FC)	18
3)	Timmy ADAMSON	(Dungannon Swifts FC)	17
4)	Mark DICKSON	(Crusaders FC)	16
5)	Glenn FERGUSON	(Linfield FC)	15

IFA Championship 2008-09	Ards	Armagh City	Ball'mallard	Ballyclare	Ballymoney	Banbridge T.	Carrick R.	Coagh Utd.	Dergview	Donegal Cel.	Glebe Ran.	Killymoon R.	Larne	Limavady Utd	Loughgall	Portadown	Tobermore U.
Ards FC	■	1-2	2-1	3-1	1-1	1-0	3-3	0-0	2-0	0-2	2-1	1-0	3-2	2-0	0-0	1-2	8-0
Armagh City FC	2-1	■	1-1	1-1	0-0	3-0	1-1	2-3	1-0	0-4	0-0	0-1	2-2	2-0	1-1	0-7	2-3
Ballinamallard United FC	2-0	3-1	■	3-1	0-2	3-3	3-1	1-0	4-1	2-3	1-0	2-2	2-1	6-4	1-2	1-4	2-0
Ballyclare Comrades FC	0-1	0-1	3-1	■	1-1	0-5	2-2	2-1	1-0	0-2	2-2	1-2	3-3	3-1	3-2	0-5	3-2
Ballymoney United FC	0-3	2-0	0-1	1-0	■	1-1	1-0	0-1	2-1	1-2	0-1	4-0	4-1	4-1	0-2	1-2	2-0
Banbridge Town FC	0-1	5-3	1-3	2-0	1-1	■	2-1	4-6	4-2	1-1	1-0	3-2	2-1	2-1	5-2	1-6	1-0
Carrick Rangers FC	0-1	1-2	1-4	1-0	0-3	4-0	■	0-3	5-1	1-0	4-1	2-1	2-2	4-0	1-3	2-3	1-0
Coagh United FC	2-2	3-2	0-4	4-0	0-2	2-1	1-3	■	1-1	1-0	1-0	2-1	1-3	1-0	1-3	2-1	2-1
Dergview FC	0-2	4-1	0-4	0-1	1-0	4-6	2-3	0-4	■	0-4	0-4	4-3	1-5	0-1	0-7	0-3	2-1
Donegal Celtic FC	1-2	2-1	2-0	2-0	4-2	2-0	2-0	3-2	5-1	■	5-1	3-0	1-0	2-1	2-1	0-2	4-1
Glebe Rangers FC	0-1	3-2	0-1	4-3	0-0	1-4	2-0	0-4	0-4	2-0	■	4-1	0-3	1-2	1-1	1-2	0-0
Killymoon Rangers FC	1-3	1-3	1-1	0-0	0-3	2-3	0-4	1-2	1-0	0-2	1-1	■	1-3	3-3	0-3	1-4	1-4
Larne FC	1-0	1-1	3-3	1-0	2-1	1-2	3-1	0-3	1-0	1-2	1-1	3-1	■	3-4	0-3	1-3	0-0
Limavady United FC	0-2	3-0	1-1	3-0	2-1	4-3	1-1	1-3	1-2	0-2	1-3	0-4	1-2	■	2-3	0-3	3-2
Loughgall FC	0-1	4-2	1-3	4-0	5-0	4-2	2-3	3-0	3-0	2-0	2-0	5-1	3-0	3-0	■	1-0	0-0
Portadown FC	2-0	1-0	2-3	1-0	0-0	5-1	2-1	1-1	2-0	2-0	7-0	6-0	5-0	1-3	0-1	■	2-1
Tobermore United FC	0-3	2-0	4-6	1-3	2-1	0-0	2-2	1-3	2-0	0-1	0-3	2-0	0-3	3-2	0-1	0-2	■

	IFA Championship	Pd	Wn	Dw	Ls	GF	GA	Pts	
1.	Portadown FC (Portadown)	32	25	2	5	88	23	77	P
2.	Donegal Celtic FC (Belfast)	32	24	1	7	65	27	73	PO
3.	Loughgall FC (Loughgall)	32	22	4	6	77	29	70	
4.	Ards FC (Newtownards)	32	20	5	7	53	26	65	
5.	Ballinamallard United FC (Ballinamallard)	32	19	6	7	73	47	63	
6.	Coagh United FC (Coagh)	32	19	4	9	60	43	61	
7.	Banbridge Town FC (Banbridge)	32	15	5	12	66	67	50	
8.	Ballymoney United FC (Ballymoney)	32	12	7	13	41	35	43	
9.	Larne FC (Larne)	32	12	7	13	53	56	43	
10.	Carrick Rangers FC (Carrickfergus)	32	12	6	14	56	53	42	
11.	Glebe Rangers FC (Ballymoney)	32	9	7	16	37	56	34	
12.	Armagh City FC (Armagh)	32	8	8	16	39	61	32	
13.	Limavady United FC (Limavady)	32	9	3	20	46	72	30	
14.	Ballyclare Comrades FC (Ballyclare)	32	8	6	18	34	62	30	
15.	Tobermore United FC (Tobermore)	32	7	5	20	34	64	26	R
16.	Dergview FC (Castlederg)	32	6	1	25	31	84	19	R
17.	Killymoon Rangers FC (Cookstown)	32	4	5	23	33	81	17	R
		544	231	82	231	886	886	775	

Dergview 0-4 Donegal played on 2nd August 2008 was awarded as a 3-0 forfeit win to Dergview as Donegal had fielded ineligible player Liam Watson. However, this decision was later revoked and the original result was reinstated.

The IFA Championship was extended to two divisions for the next season, the IFA Championship 1 and the IFA Championship 2, with normal promotion and relegation to take place between these two divisions.

IRISH CUP FINAL (Windsor Park, Belfast – 09/05/2009 – 7,500)

CRUSADERS FC (BELFAST)   1-0   Cliftonville FC (Belfast)

Dickson 47'

Crusaders: Keenan, McKeown, McBride, Black, G. Smyth, Coates, Owens (Coulter 66'), Doherty, Dickson (Arthurs 72'), Rainey, Donnelly (Caddell 87').

Cliftonville: Connolly, A. Smyth, B. Holland, Johnston, O'Hara, Donaghy, R. Scannell, Catney (Downey 65'), C. Scannell, M. Holland (Hamill 75').

Semi-finals

Cliftonville FC (Belfast)	0-0, 3-2	Linfield FC (Belfast)
Crusaders FC (Belfast)	4-1	Institute FC (Londonderry)

Quarter-finals

Glentoran FC (Belfast)	0-1	Cliftonville FC (Belfast)
Institute FC (Londonderry)	2-1	Newry City FC (Newry)
Linfield FC (Belfast)	3-0	Lisburn Distillery FC (Lisburn)
Portadown FC (Portadown)	2-5	Crusaders FC (Belfast)

Round 5

Ballymena United FC (Ballymena)	0-1	Crusaders FC (Belfast)
Cliftonville FC (Belfast)	2-0	Donegal Celtic FC (Belfast)
Glenavon FC (Lurgan)	1-3	Linfield FC (Belfast)
Glentoran FC (Belfast)	2-1	Coleraine FC (Coleraine)
Institute FC (Londonderry)	1-0	Dungannon Swifts FC (Dungannon)
Lisburn Distillery FC (Lisburn)	1-0	Tobermore United FC (Tobermore)
Newry City FC (Newry)	1-0	Bangor FC (Bangor)
Portadown FC (Portadown)	5-0	Loughgall FC (Loughgall)

Round 4

Ballinamallard United FC (Ballinamallard)	1-1, 0-1	Donegal Celtic FC (Belfast)
(The first match was abandoned at half-time due to high winds)		
Ballyclare Comrades FC (Ballyclare)	0-1, 0-2	Ballymena United FC (Ballymena)
(The first match was abandoned at half-time due to high winds)		
Banbridge Town FC (Banbridge)	0-3	Lisburn Distillery FC (Lisburn)
Bangor FC (Bangor)	1-0, 1-1, 5-1	Carrick Rangers FC (Carrickfergus)
(The first match was abandoned at half-time due to high winds)		
Cliftonville FC (Belfast)	3-1	Warrenpoint Town FC (Warrenpoint)
Coleraine FC (Coleraine)	3-0	Ards FC (Newtownards)
Crusaders FC (Belfast)	1-0	Ballymoney United FC (Ballymoney)
Dungannon Swifts FC (Dungannon)	7-2	Downpatrick FC (Downpatrick)
Glenavon FC (Lurgan)	1-0, 3-1	Newington Youth Club FC (Belfast)
(The first match was abandoned at half-time due to high winds)		
Glentoran FC (Belfast)	1-1, 3-0	Limavady United FC (Limavady)
(The first match was abandoned at half-time due to high winds and loose floodlights)		
Islandmagee FC (Islandmagee)	0-3	Institute FC (Londonderry)
(Played at Drumahoe)		
Larne FC (Larne)	1-3	Loughgall FC (Loughgall)
Linfield FC (Belfast)	0-0, 3-0	P.S.N.I. FC (Belfast)
Newry City FC (Newry)	8-0	Portstewart FC (Portstewart)
Portadown FC (Portadown)	8-1	Dergview FC (Castlederg)
Tobermore United FC (Tobermore)	4-1	Killyleagh Youth Club FC (Killyleagh)

2009-2010

IFA Premiership 2009-10	Ballymena	Cliftonville	Coleraine	Crusaders	Dungannon	Glenavon	Glentoran	Institute	Linfield	Lisburn	Newry	Portadown
Ballymena United FC		2-1	2-4	2-0	---	1-0	---	3-0	---	1-2	0-0	0-1
		0-1	3-2	1-2	0-1	0-3	2-3	1-1	2-0	0-1	1-2	2-1
Cliftonville FC	---		0-1	1-0	4-1	---	1-2	4-1	1-1	1-0	---	2-1
	0-2		0-1	1-2	1-0	3-2	1-2	3-0	4-0	3-0	3-2	2-1
Coleraine FC	3-1	---		---	---	1-0	4-3	1-1	1-3	1-3	2-3	---
	3-2	3-3		4-1	2-1	3-0	0-1	3-1	2-2	2-1	3-0	3-3
Crusaders FC	---	1-2	2-5		2-3	3-0	2-1	---	0-0	---	4-1	3-2
	2-2	2-3	1-0		2-3	3-0	1-1	1-2	0-4	2-0	1-1	3-1
Dungannon Swifts FC	2-1	0-2	1-1	1-1		2-0	---	0-1	--	---	---	4-4
	2-1	1-1	1-0	1-2		4-0	1-1	2-1	2-2	2-1	0-0	2-8
Glenavon FC	1-1	0-2	2-1	---	1-3		1-3	1-2	---	1-3	1-0	0-1
	2-2	3-2	3-2	1-1	3-2		2-2	0-1	1-2	2-1	1-1	2-2
Glentoran FC	3-0	0-3	---	0-0	1-0	---		2-1	2-2	2-0	---	2-0
	1-2	2-1	0-6	0-1	0-0	2-0		1-1	2-2	1-0	0-1	1-0
Institute FC	2-2	---	1-1	1-3	2-0	1-2	---		0-3	2-3	1-1	---
	0-1	1-1	2-2	1-0	0-1	0-1	0-3		1-2	2-1	0-0	1-1
Linfield FC	1-0	1-0	---	2-0	4-1	1-2	3-1	---		---	5-0	5-0
	1-0	1-2	2-4	0-1	1-0	4-1	2-1	2-2		2-0	3-0	1-1
Lisburn Distillery FC	2-2	---	1-1	2-2	2-5	0-0	---	2-1	0-5		3-0	---
	0-2	0-5	3-2	0-1	0-0	2-3	0-4	2-1	1-2		2-4	0-3
Newry City FC	1-0	1-1	2-1	---	4-0	3-2	0-3	0-0	---	2-2		1-5
	3-2	1-2	0-0	0-1	0-1	0-3	1-2	3-1	0-6	0-1		0-0
Portadown FC	---	2-0	3-1	2-2	1-2	---	2-1	3-1	1-0	1-3	---	
	2-0	2-2	4-0	1-2	1-4	2-0	1-2	0-0	0-6	6-1	0-0	

	IFA Premiership	Pd	Wn	Dw	Ls	GF	GA	Pts	
1.	LINFIELD FC (BELFAST)	38	22	8	8	78	37	74	
2.	Cliftonville FC (Belfast)	38	21	6	11	69	42	69	
3.	Glentoran FC (Belfast)	38	19	8	11	58	46	65	
4.	Crusaders FC (Belfast)	38	17	9	12	57	52	60	
5.	Dungannon Swifts FC (Dungannon)	38	16	9	13	56	58	57	
6.	Portadown FC (Portadown)	38	15	10	13	70	55	55	
7.	Coleraine FC (Coleraine)	38	16	9	13	76	62	57	
8.	Glenavon FC (Lurgan)	38	12	7	19	47	67	43	
9.	Newry City FC (Newry)	38	10	12	16	38	63	42	
10.	Ballymena United FC (Ballymena)	38	11	7	20	46	56	40	
11.	Lisburn Distillery FC (Lisburn)	38	11	6	21	45	76	39	
12.	Institute FC (Londonderry)	38	6	13	19	36	62	31	POR
		456	176	104	176	676	676	632	

The League split after 33 games, the top 6 clubs playing for the championship and the bottom 6 clubs playing against relegation (each 5 games), with Phase 1 records being carried forward.

Promotion/Relegation Play-off

Donegal Celtic FC (Belfast)   0-0, 1-0   Institute FC (Londonderry)

Top goalscorers 2009-10

1)	Rory PATTERSON	(Coleraine FC)	30
2)	Darren BOYCE	(Coleraine FC)	17
	George McMULLAN	(Cliftonville FC)	17
4)	Liam BOYCE	(Cliftonville FC)	16
5)	Kevin BRANIFF	(Portadown FC)	14
	Glenn FERGUSON	(Lisburn Distillery FC)	14
	Richard LECKY	(Portadown FC)	14
	David RAINEY	(Crusaders FC)	14

IFA Championship 1 2009-2010	Ards	Armagh City	Ball.mallard	Ballyclare	Ballymoney	Banbridge T.	Bangor	Carrick R.	Coagh Utd.	Donegal Cel.	Glebe Ran.	Larne	Limavady Utd	Loughgall
Ards FC	■	3-0	1-0	5-0	1-0	3-0	1-1	1-2	3-0	4-0	4-0	3-0	0-1	3-1
Armagh City FC	0-3	■	1-1	0-4	1-1	3-0	1-2	0-3	0-0	0-3	0-1	0-2	0-1	0-4
Ballinamallard United FC	1-1	4-1	■	0-2	0-1	0-2	4-3	4-1	0-1	0-0	2-2	2-0	2-3	0-0
Ballyclare Comrades FC	1-1	3-1	0-0	■	0-1	0-3	2-0	1-1	1-1	0-1	6-1	1-2	0-4	1-3
Ballymoney United FC	0-0	2-1	0-1	2-2	■	1-0	2-2	0-1	0-1	2-1	0-1	3-1	0-1	5-4
Banbridge Town FC	0-2	3-1	2-2	0-1	1-3	■	2-6	1-3	2-1	0-2	1-1	1-1	1-2	0-3
Bangor FC	0-1	3-2	0-2	2-1	1-4	2-0	■	2-2	4-3	0-1	1-2	1-3	0-2	0-0
Carrick Rangers FC	2-1	2-0	0-2	1-0	2-2	1-0	4-1	■	1-2	1-0	2-1	3-2	1-1	0-1
Coagh United FC	5-1	3-3	0-1	5-3	2-2	2-3	1-3	3-2	■	0-4	0-2	2-3	1-2	0-3
Donegal Celtic FC	3-3	3-1	4-0	1-0	3-1	2-4	2-1	4-0	2-1	■	4-0	3-0	1-0	3-0
Glebe Rangers FC	3-0	1-3	1-1	1-2	0-3	1-4	2-0	0-0	2-1	1-8	■	1-1	3-4	0-2
Larne FC	1-0	2-1	0-3	2-0	1-1	1-0	1-1	2-0	6-1	1-2	2-0	■	0-1	0-1
Limavady United FC	3-2	4-0	2-0	4-2	2-2	0-2	2-0	5-1	4-2	0-2	3-1	2-0	■	0-1
Loughgall FC	2-0	4-0	1-4	4-1	3-1	4-1	1-0	3-1	5-0	0-1	2-2	4-0	3-2	■

	IFA Championship 1	Pd	Wn	Dw	Ls	GF	GA	Pts	
1.	Loughgall FC (Loughgall)	26	19	3	4	60	24	60	++
2.	Donegal Celtic FC (Belfast)	26	19	2	5	59	21	59	POP
3.	Limavady United FC (Limavady)	26	18	3	5	56	29	57	
4.	Ards FC (Newtownards)	26	13	6	7	49	27	45	
5.	Carrick Rangers FC (Carrickfergus)	26	12	5	9	37	39	41	
6.	Ballinamallard United FC (Ballinamallard)	26	10	8	8	36	29	38	
7.	Ballymoney United FC (Ballymoney)	26	10	8	8	39	33	38	
8.	Larne FC (Larne)	26	11	4	11	34	37	37	
9.	Banbridge Town FC (Banbridge)	26	8	3	15	33	48	27	
10.	Glebe Rangers FC (Ballymoney)	26	7	6	13	30	56	27	
11.	Bangor FC (Bangor)	26	7	5	14	36	48	26	
12.	Ballyclare Comrades FC (Ballyclare)	26	7	5	14	34	46	26	
13.	Coagh United FC (Coagh)	26	6	4	16	38	62	22	R
14.	Armagh City FC (Armagh)	26	2	4	20	20	62	10	R
		364	149	66	149	561	561	513	

++ Loughgall FC were not eligible for promotion as they did not hold the necessary Domestic Club Licence.

IFA Championship 2 2009-2010	Annagh United	Chimney Corner	Dergview	Dundela	Harland & Wolff Welders	Killymoon Rangers	Knockbreda	Lurgan Celtic	Moyola Park	P.S.N.I.	Portstewart	Queen's University	Sport & Leisure Swifts	Tobermore United	Wakehurst
Annagh United FC		3-1	0-3	2-4	2-7	3-2	1-3	0-1	2-1	1-4	0-5	1-2	1-4	1-5	2-0
Chimney Corner FC	0-0		1-6	0-3	0-2	1-4	1-5	2-2	3-3	1-2	0-3	1-4	2-2	0-3	3-3
Dergview FC	3-0	11-0		0-2	1-2	2-1	0-0	1-1	0-1	3-0	5-0	1-0	4-0	4-0	3-2
Dundela FC	2-0	6-2	2-1		2-2	3-2	4-2	4-0	1-1	0-0	2-1	3-1	3-0	2-3	2-1
Harland & Wolff Welders FC	4-0	2-2	0-2	4-2		3-1	2-0	2-1	2-1	4-0	2-1	1-0	0-2	5-1	4-1
Killymoon Rangers FC	1-1	4-1	0-1	2-1	3-4		0-4	2-3	2-1	0-1	1-4	3-0	3-0	0-3	0-1
Knockbreda FC	0-1	2-0	0-4	1-1	0-3	0-0		3-1	2-1	1-2	4-2	0-1	3-1	0-0	2-1
Lurgan Celtic FC	3-0	0-2	3-4	1-1	0-2	3-2	0-1		0-3	1-1	4-0	1-0	2-1	0-4	2-1
Moyola Park FC	1-3	4-1	0-2	1-4	1-2	3-0	0-1	2-0		2-4	1-1	2-2	1-2	3-2	1-0
P.S.N.I. FC	3-1	6-2	2-2	0-3	1-2	3-0	3-4	0-1	1-0		2-1	2-2	1-2	1-2	2-0
Portstewart FC	0-0	2-1	0-1	0-2	3-1	1-2	1-0	1-2	3-0	0-0		2-1	1-1	1-1	1-1
Queen's University FC	1-0	6-0	0-2	1-1	1-3	2-0	1-1	1-0	1-4	1-4	0-1		2-4	2-0	3-0
Sport & Leisure Swifts FC	3-1	3-2	0-3	0-2	2-3	5-1	1-1	3-2	1-1	1-3	1-3	1-6		1-3	0-3
Tobermore United FC	3-0	2-1	1-1	2-2	0-4	2-0	0-2	2-1	0-1	0-2	2-3	2-1	2-0		0-1
Wakehurst FC	0-2	2-2	2-7	1-2	0-1	4-2	0-2	4-2	0-2	3-4	1-1	0-1	1-3	0-2	

	IFA Championship 2	**Pd**	**Wn**	**Dw**	**Ls**	**GF**	**GA**	**Pts**	
1.	Harland & Wolff Welders FC (Belfast)	28	23	2	3	73	30	71	P
2.	Dergview FC (Castlederg)	28	20	4	4	77	20	64	P
3.	Dundela FC (Belfast)	28	18	7	3	66	31	61	
4.	P.S.N.I. FC (Belfast)	28	15	5	8	54	40	50	
5.	Knockbreda FC (Belfast)	28	14	6	8	44	32	48	
6.	Tobermore United FC (Tobermore)	28	14	4	10	47	39	46	
7.	Portstewart FC (Portstewart)	28	11	7	10	42	38	40	
8.	Queen's University FC (Belfast)	28	11	4	13	43	40	37	
9.	Moyola Park FC (Castledawson)	28	10	5	13	42	42	35	
10.	Lurgan Celtic FC (Lurgan)	28	10	4	14	37	49	34	
11.	Sport & Leisure Swifts FC (Belfast)	28	10	4	14	44	60	34	
12.	Annagh United FC (Portadown)	28	7	3	18	28	66	24	
13.	Killymoon Rangers FC (Cookstown)	28	7	2	19	38	60	23	
14.	Wakehurst FC (Castledawson)	28	5	4	19	33	58	19	
15.	Chimney Corner FC (Antrim)	28	1	7	20	32	95	10	
		420	176	68	176	700	700	596	

IRISH CUP FINAL (Windsor Park, Belfast – 08/05/2010 – 7,940)

LINFIELD FC (BELFAST)　　　　　　2-1　　　　　　Portadown FC (Portadown)

Thompson 02', Lowry 10'　　　　　　　　　　　　　　　　　*Braniff 13'*

Linfield: Blayney, Gault, Murphy, Curran, Lowry (Mulgrew 71'), Thompson, Baillie, Burns, Garrett, McAllister (Munster 46'), Gallagher.

Portadown: Miskelly, Redman, Clarke (Taggart 82'), Kelly, Boyle, Braniff, Mouncey, Baker (Lecky 66'), Hunter (McCluskey 57'), Topley, Mackle.

Semi-finals

Linfield FC (Belfast)	4-2	Coleraine FC (Coleraine)
Portadown FC (Portadown)	1-1 (aet)	Ballymena United FC (Ballymena)
	(Portadown FC won 4-3 on penalties)	

Quarter-finals

Coleraine FC (Coleraine)	3-2	Newry City FC (Newry)
Crusaders FC (Belfast)	1-1, 0-1	Portadown FC (Portadown)
Glenavon FC (Lurgan)	3-3, 0-2	Ballymena United FC (Ballymena)
Glentoran FC (Belfast)	1-3	Linfield FC (Belfast)

Round 6

Ballyclare Comrades FC (Ballyclare)	1-2	Glentoran FC (Belfast)
Ballymena United FC (Ballymena)	5-2	Ballinamallard United FC (Ballinamallard)
Coleraine FC (Coleraine)	6-0	Nortel FC (Newtownabbey)
Crusaders FC (Belfast)	4-0	Coagh United FC (Coagh)
Glenavon FC (Lurgan)	2-1	Institute FC (Londonderry)
Linfield FC (Belfast)	4-0	Dungannon Swifts FC (Dungannon)
Loughgall FC (Loughgall)	1-1, 0-1	Newry City FC (Newry)
Portadown FC (Portadown)	2-1	Cliftonville FC (Belfast)

Round 5

Ballyclare Comrades FC (Ballyclare)	5-1	Islandmagee FC (Islandmagee)
Ballymena United FC (Ballymena)	0-0, 1-0	Ards FC (Newtownards)
Carrick Rangers FC (Carrickfergus)	1-1, 0-1	Portadown FC (Portadown)
Coagh United FC (Coagh)	1-0	Tobermore United FC (Tobermore)
Crusaders FC (Belfast)	5-1	Bangor FC (Bangor)
Donegal Celtic FC (Belfast)	0-4	Linfield FC (Belfast)
Dundela FC (Belfast)	0-2	Coleraine FC (Coleraine)
Dungannon Swifts FC (Dungannon)	6-0	Malachians FC (Belfast)
Glebe Rangers FC (Ballymoney)	0-3	Ballinamallard United FC (Ballinamallard)
Glenavon FC (Lurgan)	5-1	Harland & Wolff Welders FC (Belfast)
Glentoran FC (Belfast)	5-0	Omagh United FC (Omagh)
Institute FC (Londonderry)	1-1, 1-0	Ballymoney United FC (Ballymoney)
Lisburn Distillery FC (Lisburn)	0-2	Cliftonville FC (Belfast)
Loughgall FC (Loughgall)	3-1	Ards Rangers FC (Newtownards)
Newry City FC (Newry)	2-1	Larne FC (Larne)
(The match was abandoned after 82 minutes due to mass brawl, but the result was allowed to stand)		
Nortel FC (Newtownabbey)	2-2, 2-2 (aet)	Bryansburn Rangers FC (Bangor)
	(Nortel FC won 5-3 on penalties)	

2010-2011

IFA Premiership 2010-2011	Ballymena Utd	Cliftonville	Coleraine	Crusaders	Donegal Celtic	Dungannon S.	Glenavon	Glentoran	Linfield	Lisburn Dist.	Newry City	Portadown
Ballymena United FC	■	1-1	0-3	0-3	0-2	1-0	2-3			1-0		3-1
	■	1-1	0-1	1-1	0-4	1-1	3-3	0-2	3-3	0-1	1-0	3-1
Cliftonville FC	2-2	■	3-0	2-2	3-2		1-2	2-4	3-2			1-3
	5-0	■	0-2	2-1	4-2	2-0	0-2	2-1	3-1	1-3	2-1	0-1
Coleraine FC	1-1	3-2	■	1-3	2-1		2-1	3-1		1-2	3-1	1-1
	1-0	3-1	■	0-3	4-0	0-3	0-2	1-2	0-2	0-1	2-0	1-3
Crusaders FC		5-0		■	2-1	2-2	1-0	2-1	0-1	4-1		3-1
	2-1	1-3	2-0	■	4-5	1-1	5-4	1-0	2-1	1-2	2-1	3-1
Donegal Celtic FC	3-3		1-1		■	1-2	3-3		2-0		0-0	0-2
	2-3	1-1	2-1	1-3	■	3-4	1-4	0-3	1-3	2-1	0-3	4-4
Dungannon Swifts FC	1-0		1-0		3-1	■	2-2		0-4	1-2	1-0	
	1-2	0-1	3-0	2-3	0-0	■	2-1	1-3	2-1	2-2	0-0	0-1
Glenavon FC	3-1	0-2	1-2		3-0	1-2	■		2-2	0-1	2-1	
	0-2	1-2	1-2	2-1	3-1	2-1	■	0-1	0-1	1-1	2-1	1-0
Glentoran FC		0-0		2-2	4-0	0-0	2-2	■	1-2	2-1		0-1
	1-2	2-0	2-0	3-1	1-0	0-2	4-1	■	0-0	1-3	2-0	1-0
Linfield FC	0-0	1-0	0-1	3-1			3-2		■	2-0	1-1	1-0
	0-0	0-0	1-0	8-1	6-2	1-0	1-0	2-1	■	1-0	4-0	4-0
Lisburn Distillery FC	0-1	4-3		0-1	3-1			0-2	0-4	■		2-1
	1-1	1-1	0-3	2-4	1-3	4-1	2-2	1-6	0-4	■	2-1	2-0
Newry City FC	1-1	0-2	0-2	2-3	0-1	0-1	0-4	3-4		2-1	■	
	0-4	0-1	2-2	1-1	2-1	3-0	2-1	0-0	1-2	1-1	■	4-2
Portadown FC		0-1		0-1		2-1	1-1	2-0	0-4	1-0	2-1	■
	1-3	2-1	2-0	0-2	3-0	2-2	2-2	0-1	1-2	1-0	4-2	■

	IFA Premiership	**Pd**	**Wn**	**Dw**	**Ls**	**GF**	**GA**	**Pts**	
1.	LINFIELD FC (BELFAST)	38	26	7	5	80	29	85	
2.	Crusaders FC (Belfast)	38	23	5	10	78	59	74	
3.	Glentoran FC (Belfast)	38	20	6	12	63	41	66	
4.	Cliftonville FC (Belfast)	38	17	7	14	60	56	58	
5.	Portadown FC (Portadown)	38	15	5	18	49	58	50	
6.	Lisburn Distillery FC (Lisburn)	38	14	6	18	50	66	48	
7.	Coleraine FC (Coleraine)	38	17	5	16	51	50	56	
8.	Dungannon Swifts FC (Dungannon)	38	14	9	15	50	53	51	
9.	Ballymena United FC (Ballymena)	38	12	13	13	48	56	49	
10.	Glenavon FC (Lurgan)	38	12	9	17	60	59	45	
11.	Donegal Celtic FC (Belfast)	38	8	8	22	55	89	32	
12.	Newry City FC (Newry)	38	6	8	24	37	65	26	R

After 33 games, clubs in the bottom half of the table at the split cannot finish in the top half, regardless of the number of points earned during the final 5 matches.

Top goalscorers 2010-11

1) Peter THOMPSON (Linfield FC) 23
2) Paul McVEIGH (Donegal Celtic FC) 19
   Jordan OWENS (Crusaders FC) 19
4) Daryl FORDYCE (Glentoran FC) 17
5) Stuart DALLAS (Crusaders FC) 16

IFA Championship 1 2010-2011	Ards	Ballinamallard	Ballyclare Com.	Ballymoney Utd.	Banbridge Town	Bangor	Carrick Rangers	Dergview	Glebe Rangers	H & W Welders	Institute	Larne	Limavady United	Loughgall
Ards FC		2-2	0-3	3-3	2-1	0-1	0-0	1-1	4-3	2-1	1-1	2-0	1-1	1-2
Ballinamallard United FC	3-1		3-0	0-1	1-1	0-3	1-3	2-1	2-2	4-2	2-0	3-3	0-2	2-0
Ballyclare Comrades FC	0-1	3-2		0-0	1-0	2-1	1-2	0-3	1-3	0-3	1-2	0-4	1-4	2-1
Ballymoney United FC	1-1	2-2	1-1		1-2	2-2	0-1	0-2	3-0	3-2	2-3	0-2	1-1	2-0
Banbridge Town FC	0-1	1-0	1-1	2-0		2-2	3-2	1-2	1-2	1-3	2-3	2-0	0-0	3-1
Bangor FC	2-0	2-3	2-2	2-2	4-1		1-2	4-0	2-1	1-1	3-0	2-0	1-1	2-1
Carrick Rangers FC	3-1	2-1	3-0	3-1	3-1	3-1		2-0	3-1	1-1	3-0	3-0	1-1	3-3
Dergview FC	1-2	0-1	4-2	6-1	2-1	0-0	3-1		4-2	1-2	4-1	1-0	1-0	5-0
Glebe Rangers FC	0-3	1-0	3-3	1-2	1-3	4-0	0-4	0-2		3-2	3-0	1-1	1-2	1-2
Harland & Wolff Welders FC	3-2	2-2	3-2	2-1	3-0	1-1	1-0	1-2	0-0		2-3	2-2	1-2	0-1
Institute FC	2-1	0-2	1-1	2-1	0-0	2-0	0-2	1-0	0-1	0-2		1-3	2-1	0-0
Larne FC	1-3	0-3	2-0	2-1	1-1	7-0	0-2	0-2	0-0	2-3	0-3		3-2	1-3
Limavady United FC	2-1	3-2	2-1	5-0	2-0	0-1	6-2	5-2	1-1	1-0	2-0	0-3		3-0
Loughgall FC	5-1	1-2	4-0	1-0	1-1	1-5	0-3	2-2	1-1	1-2	4-1	1-1	1-4	

	IFA Championship 1	Pd	Wn	Dw	Ls	GF	GA	Pts	
1.	Carrick Rangers FC (Carrickfergus)	26	18	4	4	57	27	58	P
2.	Limavady United FC (Limavady)	26	15	6	5	53	27	51	
3.	Dergview FC (Castlederg)	26	15	3	8	51	32	48	
4.	Bangor FC (Bangor)	26	11	8	7	45	38	41	
5.	Ballinamallard United FC (Ballinamallard)	26	11	6	9	45	38	39	**
6.	Harland & Wolff Welders FC (Belfast)	26	11	6	9	45	38	39	
7.	Ards FC (Bangor)	26	9	7	10	37	42	34	
8.	Institute FC (Londonderry)	26	10	4	12	28	43	34	
9.	Larne FC (Larne)	26	8	6	12	38	41	30	
10.	Loughgall FC (Loughgall)	26	8	6	12	37	48	30	
11.	Banbridge Town FC (Banbridge)	26	7	7	12	31	39	28	
12.	Glebe Rangers FC (Ballymoney)	26	7	7	12	36	46	28	
13.	Ballymoney United FC (Ballymoney)	26	5	8	13	31	48	23	R
14.	Ballyclare Comrades FC (Ballyclare)	26	5	6	15	28	55	21	R
		364	140	84	140	562	562	504	

** Ballinamallard United were placed above Harland & Wolff Welders due to a superior head-to-head record.

The promotion/relegation play-off was not played this season, because Championship runners-up Limavady United were not eligible for promotion as they did not hold the required domestic licence.

IFA Championship 2 2010-2011	Annagh United	Armagh City	Chimney Corner	Coagh United	Dundela	Killymoon Rang.	Knockbreda	Lurgan Celtic	Moyola Park	Portstewart	P.S.N.I.	Queen's Univ.	Sport & Leisure	Tobermore Utd	Wakehurst	Warrenpoint Tn
Annagh United FC		1–2	2–2	0–4	0–2	0–1	2–2	2–1	4–1	1–0	1–7	3–1	1–3	0–2	0–2	0–3
Armagh City FC	2–0		1–0	1–3	1–1	1–1	0–1	1–0	1–2	1–2	1–3	1–5	1–4	0–1	1–1	0–2
Chimney Corner FC	2–3	2–3		0–3	2–4	1–1	3–3	1–3	2–4	3–1	0–0	1–5	1–3	1–4	1–4	2–8
Coagh United FC	3–3	2–4	1–0		2–2	5–0	1–0	4–3	1–0	0–1	2–1	2–1	1–2	1–3	5–1	0–2
Dundela FC	3–1	4–1	7–1	4–1		2–0	0–1	3–0	3–0	3–0	4–2	2–3	3–4	4–3	4–2	1–1
Killymoon Rangers FC	1–2	2–2	1–0	1–2	3–3		2–2	2–2	0–0	5–4	0–3	0–2	7–2	1–3	1–1	0–2
Knockbreda FC	1–2	2–0	3–0	3–4	2–2	2–1		4–1	3–0	2–1	4–1	1–1	4–0	3–0	1–0	2–1
Lurgan Celtic FC	4–0	1–1	2–1	0–1	2–4	2–2	1–3		3–1	5–3	1–1	1–4	1–1	0–1	3–4	1–3
Moyola Park FC	1–0	2–2	3–2	1–5	0–3	2–1	1–2	0–2		0–0	2–3	0–2	4–2	0–3	0–5	1–2
Portstewart FC	4–0	2–1	3–0	2–3	3–0	5–0	1–2	2–1	1–0		0–1	0–2	4–3	0–2	3–1	1–2
P.S.N.I. FC	1–0	3–4	5–0	3–3	1–2	2–0	1–2	1–2	4–2	3–2		1–2	0–0	3–2	2–4	1–3
Queen's University FC	4–4	2–2	3–0	3–1	2–1	1–2	1–0	7–0	1–1	2–3	1–0		1–0	0–2	0–1	0–2
Sport & Leisure Swifts FC	1–0	1–4	7–3	1–1	2–2	1–0	0–1	2–0	2–0	1–1	2–1	0–1		0–4	4–1	1–4
Tobermore United FC	3–1	2–2	3–1	1–1	0–0	1–0	2–1	1–3	4–0	3–2	5–2	0–3	1–0		4–0	2–4
Wakehurst FC	2–0	2–2	7–2	3–3	0–0	4–2	1–2	2–3	2–1	1–0	2–0	3–1	1–1	1–3		2–3
Warrenpoint Town FC	1–1	6–0	4–1	2–1	1–1	5–0	2–0	0–0	2–2	4–0	5–0	1–0	5–2	2–2	2–2	

	IFA Championship 2	Pd	Wn	Dw	Ls	GF	GA	Pts	
1.	Warrenpoint Town FC (Warrenpoint)	30	22	7	1	84	26	73	P
2.	Tobermore United FC (Tobermore)	30	20	4	6	67	36	64	P
3.	Knockbreda FC (Belfast)	30	19	5	6	59	32	62	
4.	Dundela FC (Belfast)	30	16	9	5	74	41	57	
5.	Queen's University FC (Belfast)	30	17	4	9	61	35	55	
6.	Coagh United FC (Coagh)	30	16	6	8	66	48	54	
7.	Wakehurst FC (Castledawson)	30	13	7	10	62	54	46	
8.	Sport & Leisure Swifts FC (Belfast)	30	12	6	12	52	58	42	
9.	Portstewart FC (Portstewart)	30	12	2	16	51	52	38	
10.	P.S.N.I. FC (Belfast)	30	11	4	15	56	58	37	
11.	Lurgan Celtic FC (Lurgan)	30	9	6	15	48	62	33	
12.	Armagh City FC (Armagh)	30	8	9	13	43	60	33	
13.	Annagh United FC (Portadown)	30	7	5	18	34	66	26	
14.	Killymoon Rangers FC (Cookstown)	30	5	9	16	37	64	24	
15.	Moyola Park FC (Castledawson)	30	6	5	19	31	67	23	
16.	Chimney Corner FC (Antrim)	30	1	4	25	35	101	7	
		480	194	92	194	860	860	674	

IRISH CUP FINAL (Windsor Park, Belfast – 07/05/2011 – 8,200)

Crusaders FC (Belfast) 1-2 LINFIELD FC (BELFAST)
Caddell 54', McAllister Goal 87' *Thompson 78'*

Crusaders: Keenan, McKeown, McBride, Magowan, Coates, Dallas, Watson, Morrow (McMaster 86), Caddell, Owens, Halliday (Rainey 79).

Linfield: Blayney, Ervin (Tomelty 75), Douglas, Casement, Curran, Lowry (Mulgrew 63), Gault, Garrett, Carvill, McAllister, Thompson.

Semi-finals

Crusaders FC (Belfast)	3-1	Portadown FC (Portadown)
Linfield FC (Belfast)	2-0	Glentoran FC (Belfast)

Quarter-finals

Ballinamallard United FC (Ballinamallard)	0-5	Crusaders FC (Belfast)
Dungannon Swifts FC (Dungannon)	0-2	Linfield FC (Belfast)
Glentoran FC (Belfast)	1-1, 3-3 (aet)	Coleraine FC (Coleraine)
	(Glentoran FC won 3-2 on penalties)	
Portadown FC (Portadown)	3-3, 3-0	Glenavon FC (Lurgan)

Round 6

Carrick Rangers FC (Carrickfergus)	1-3	Coleraine FC (Coleraine)
Crusaders FC (Belfast)	2-1	Nortel FC (Newtownabbey)
Dungannon Swifts FC (Dungannon)	4-2	Warrenpoint Town FC (Warrenpoint)
Glenavon FC (Lurgan)	2-0	Queen's University FC (Belfast)
Glentoran FC (Belfast)	3-1	Loughgall FC (Loughgall)
Harland & Wolff Welders FC (Belfast)	1-1, 0-1	Portadown FC (Portadown)
Linfield FC (Belfast)	1-1, 3-0	Dunmurry Recreation FC (Dunmurry)
Lisburn Distillery FC (Lisburn)	2-2, 2-4	Ballinamallard United FC (Ballinamallard)

Round 5

Albert Foundry FC (Belfast)	0-2	Nortel FC (Newtownabbey)
Annagh United FC (Portadown)	2-6	Glenavon FC (Lurgan)
Ards FC (Bangor)	2-2, 0-1 (aet)	Harland & Wolff Welders FC (Belfast)
Ballinamallard United FC (Ballinamallard)	3-1	Larne FC (Larne)
Ballymena United FC (Ballymena)	1-1, 2-3 (aet)	Glentoran FC (Belfast)
Carrick Rangers FC (Carrickfergus)	3-3, 6-1	Shankill United FC (Belfast)
Crusaders FC (Belfast)	3-2	Newry City FC (Newry)
Dundela FC (Belfast)	1-4	Lisburn Distillery FC (Lisburn)
Dungannon Swifts FC (Dungannon)	5-1	Ballymoney United FC (Ballymoney)
Dunmurry Recreation FC (Dunmurry)	2-2, 5-0	Kilmore Recreation FC (Crossgar)
Limavady United FC (Limavady)	1-2	Coleraine FC (Coleraine)
Linfield FC (Belfast)	5-1	Institute FC (Londonderry)
Loughgall FC (Loughgall)	3-1	Sport & Leisure Swifts FC (Belfast)
Portadown FC (Portadown)	4-3	Donegal Celtic FC (Belfast)
Queen's University FC (Belfast)	1-0	Crumlin United FC (Crumlin)
Warrenpoint Town FC (Warrenpoint)	1-1, 0-0 (aet)	Cliftonville FC (Belfast)
	(Warrenpoint Town FC won 3-1 on penalties)	

2011-2012

IFA Premiership 2011-2012	Ballymena Utd.	Carrick Rang.	Cliftonville	Coleraine	Crusaders	Donegal Celtic	Dungannon Sw	Glenavon	Glentoran	Linfield	Lisburn Dist.	Portadown
Ballymena United FC	■	3-0	0-1		2-2	1-1	2-2		1-2	2-2	1-2	
	■	0-2	3-7	1-5	0-3	2-0	1-1	3-3	0-3	1-2	1-0	2-4
Carrick Rangers FC	1-3	■		0-4		2-3	0-0	4-4	2-2		2-1	3-1
	0-2	■	3-3	0-2	1-2	1-2	1-1	2-2	3-3	0-4	0-0	2-2
Cliftonville FC		2-1	■	1-1	1-1		2-1	4-3	3-0	1-3		2-3
	3-4	1-0	■	1-2	2-1	2-3	4-1	5-3	2-1	4-2	3-1	0-2
Coleraine FC	2-0		1-0	■		1-0	0-1		3-1	1-1	1-0	4-1
	1-0	4-0	1-1	■	0-0	2-0	3-2	1-1	1-1	1-3	2-3	4-3
Crusaders FC	2-2	3-1	3-2	2-1	■		1-0	2-0	1-1	2-2	0-1	
	3-2	5-1	2-2	1-1	■	1-2	2-0	2-0	1-2	0-1	1-1	0-3
Donegal Celtic FC	0-3	3-5	0-2		1-1	■	3-1	1-1	0-1		2-1	
	2-3	1-2	1-3	0-1	0-2	■	0-2	2-1	0-4	1-5	2-2	1-0
Dungannon Swifts FC	2-4	0-0		1-2	1-2	2-1	■	1-5	2-1		3-2	2-0
	1-1	3-1	1-4	0-0	0-2	2-2	■	1-1	0-5	1-4	0-2	0-3
Glenavon FC	0-2	3-2			4-0	2-2		■	1-0		2-3	0-2
	3-0	1-2	1-2	1-0	3-2	0-1	1-1	■	1-3	1-2	5-2	0-2
Glentoran FC	1-2		1-0	3-3	0-4				■	1-0	1-3	2-2
	2-4	6-1	0-1	1-1	2-2	1-2	2-1	2-0	■	2-0	3-3	0-2
Linfield FC		4-1	2-1	0-0	5-0	4-0	3-0	2-0	0-2	■		2-1
	1-0	3-0	4-1	1-0	2-0	5-0	1-0	1-0	0-1	■	1-1	2-0
Lisburn Distillery FC	2-3	3-1	1-3	3-1		3-0	0-2	3-3		0-3	■	0-2
	1-4	2-3	1-2	1-3	1-2	0-2	1-2	2-1	0-5	2-3	■	0-2
Portadown FC		3-3	2-0	1-2	2-1			0-1	1-1		■	
	2-1	3-0	1-2	1-1	1-3	5-2	2-1	1-0	2-1	2-0	5-1	■

	IFA Premiership	Pd	Wn	Dw	Ls	GF	GA	Pts	
1.	Linfield FC (Belfast)	38	27	4	7	79	29	85	
2.	Portadown FC (Portadown)	38	22	5	11	72	47	71	
3.	Cliftonville FC (Belfast)	38	21	6	11	83	62	69	
4.	Coleraine FC (Coleraine)	38	18	12	8	61	38	66	
5.	Crusaders FC (Belfast)	38	18	10	10	63	47	64	
6.	Glentoran FC (Belfast)	38	16	9	13	67	52	57	
7.	Ballymena United FC (Ballymena)	38	14	8	16	66	71	50	
8.	Donegal Celtic FC (Belfast)	38	12	5	21	44	80	41	
9.	Dungannon Swifts FC (Dungannon)	38	8	11	19	42	71	35	
10.	Glenavon FC (Lurgan)	38	8	10	20	60	71	34	
11.	Lisburn Distillery FC (Lisburn)	38	8	8	22	56	84	32	PO
12.	Carrick Rangers FC (Carrickfergus)	38	7	10	21	50	91	31	R
		456	179	98	179	743	743	635	

After 33 games, clubs in the bottom half of the table at the split cannot finish in the top half, regardless of the number of points earned during the final 5 matches.

Promotion/Relegation Play-off

Lisburn Distillery FC (Lisburn)   0-0, 3-2   Newry City FC (Newry)
(Lisburn Distillery FC won 3-2 on aggregate to avoid relegation)

Top goalscorers 2011-12

1) Gary McCUTCHEON   (Ballymena United FC)   27
2) Matthew TIPTON   (Portadown FC)   24
3) Gary LIGGETT   (Lisburn Distillery FC)   22
4) Curtis ALLEN   (Coleraine FC)   20
5) Kevin BRANIFF   (Portadown FC)   17
   Chris SCANNELL   (Cliftonville FC)   17

IFA Championship 1 2011-2012	Ards	Ballinamallard	Banbridge Town	Bangor	Dergview	Glebe Rangers	H & W Welders	Institute	Larne	Limavady United	Loughgall	Newry City	Tobermore Utd	Warrenpoint Tn
Ards FC		0-5	2-0	2-0	1-2	3-0	1-1	2-0	1-1	0-2	2-3	0-0	2-0	5-1
Ballinamallard United FC	1-0		5-1	3-2	1-1	2-0	3-0	1-1	2-1	2-1	3-0	0-2	2-1	2-0
Banbridge Town FC	2-3	2-7		3-4	2-1	3-0	0-2	0-1	3-0	1-2	3-2	0-6	1-3	1-1
Bangor FC	0-1	1-2	4-0		1-1	0-0	2-0	2-0	1-1	1-0	2-2	3-2	5-0	1-0
Dergview FC	2-0	0-0	5-1	1-4		1-1	0-0	1-0	0-1	2-1	3-1	1-3	1-1	2-2
Glebe Rangers FC	0-3	1-3	0-3	2-2	2-2		4-1	0-0	0-3	1-4	3-5	0-3	1-2	0-1
Harland & Wolff Welders FC	2-2	1-3	1-1	0-2	0-2	0-1		2-1	3-1	3-0	1-0	1-2	1-0	3-1
Institute FC	2-0	0-3	2-1	3-4	1-0	3-2	0-1		1-0	0-2	2-1	1-1	3-2	4-3
Larne FC	0-2	3-2	1-1	0-2	5-2	4-2	0-2	0-2		4-2	2-3	2-0	2-1	1-1
Limavady United FC	3-1	0-1	9-0	3-1	2-1	3-2	3-1	0-2	3-0		0-0	1-0	2-4	0-4
Loughgall FC	2-1	1-4	2-0	4-0	1-1	0-1	2-0	3-4	1-1	2-2		3-2	4-0	0-2
Newry City FC	0-0	3-1	3-0	2-0	4-1	1-1	2-1	0-3	5-0	2-0	2-0		3-3	1-0
Tobermore United FC	1-4	1-2	1-1	2-1	1-1	1-1	0-2	2-0	3-1	4-2	0-2	0-0		0-0
Warrenpoint Town FC	1-1	1-2	3-0	0-0	1-4	3-0	2-1	1-1	2-3	4-1	0-1	0-2	0-1	

	IFA Championship 1	Pd	Wn	Dw	Ls	GF	GA	Pts	
1.	Ballinamallard United FC (Ballinamallard)	26	20	3	3	62	24	63	P
2.	Newry City FC (Newry)	26	15	6	5	51	22	51	PO
3.	Institute FC (Londonderry)	26	13	4	9	37	34	43	
4.	Bangor FC (Bangor)	26	12	6	8	45	34	42	
5.	Ards FC (Bangor)	26	11	6	9	39	31	39	
6.	Limavady United FC (Limavady)	26	12	2	12	48	43	38	
7.	Loughgall FC (Loughgall)	26	11	5	10	45	41	38	
8.	Dergview FC (Castlederg)	26	8	10	8	38	37	34	
9.	Harland & Wolff Welders FC (Belfast)	26	10	4	12	30	35	34	
10.	Larne FC (Larne)	26	9	5	12	37	47	32	
11.	Tobermore United FC (Tobermore)	26	8	7	11	34	44	31	
12.	Warrenpoint Town FC (Warrenpoint)	26	7	7	12	34	37	28	
13.	Banbridge Town FC (Banbridge)	26	5	4	17	30	70	19	R
14.	Glebe Rangers FC (Ballymoney)	26	3	7	16	25	56	16	R
		364	144	76	144	555	555	508	

IFA Championship 2 2011-2012	Annagh United	Armagh City	Ballyclare Com.	Ballymoney Utd	Chimney Corner	Coagh United	Dundela	Killymoon Rang	Knockbreda	Lurgan Celtic	Moyola Park	Portstewart	P.S.N.I.	Queen's University	Sport & Leisure	Wakehurst
Annagh United FC		1-1	1-2	1-0	2-0	2-1	1-1	4-2	0-2	2-6	1-0	2-0	2-0	5-2	2-1	5-2
Armagh City FC	3-3		0-4	0-1	4-0	2-2	2-3	0-1	1-4	0-3	1-0	2-0	3-1	0-1	2-1	0-3
Ballyclare Comrades FC	2-0	2-2		2-1	3-1	1-3	2-0	3-0	3-1	1-3	0-2	0-1	3-0	2-1	2-3	3-2
Ballymoney United FC	1-2	5-0	2-3		6-1	1-1	2-1	1-0	2-0	0-1	5-0	0-2	4-3	0-2	5-3	2-3
Chimney Corner FC	1-2	2-1	0-2	1-0		2-6	0-6	4-2	0-1	1-0	2-4	1-0	1-1	1-5	1-4	0-5
Coagh United FC	2-2	3-0	3-1	3-0	7-0		3-3	2-0	2-2	2-3	5-1	2-4	2-0	4-0	1-0	4-2
Dundela FC	2-5	4-0	4-5	2-1	2-0	3-4		3-0	2-1	4-0	4-1	4-0	3-2	4-1	1-0	3-0
Killymoon Rangers FC	3-3	1-4	1-3	3-2	3-1	3-0	1-2		0-4	1-1	4-2	3-2	0-2	0-3	1-1	0-2
Knockbreda FC	3-0	1-0	4-2	3-1	4-0	1-2	1-0	4-0		2-4	3-0	2-3	4-0	0-1	3-1	1-1
Lurgan Celtic FC	4-1	0-0	2-1	2-0	5-1	2-1	2-3	4-0	4-4		6-1	2-1	2-2	1-1	0-2	0-1
Moyola Park FC	0-4	0-4	1-1	1-2	1-0	1-4	1-2	2-0	0-1	0-5		3-1	5-0	0-3	1-0	1-3
Portstewart FC	1-5	3-0	1-2	2-1	1-1	2-2	2-4	4-1	1-1	1-0	1-0		0-4	0-1	2-2	2-1
PSNI FC	2-0	2-1	2-2	1-1	2-1	0-2	2-1	0-1	0-4	2-7	1-1	3-2		1-3	2-1	0-4
Queen's University FC	3-0	0-1	2-1	1-2	6-1	2-3	4-0	2-1	1-2	1-2	5-0	1-2	4-1		1-2	1-0
Sport & Leisure Swifts FC	1-1	0-4	0-0	0-2	3-1	0-1	1-3	5-2	0-5	3-1	1-2	3-1	2-0	2-4		2-6
Wakehurst FC	3-0	1-1	3-2	1-1	2-1	1-4	2-5	2-0	0-2	1-1	2-3	3-1	1-0	0-1	2-2	

	IFA Championship 2	Pd	Wn	Dw	Ls	GF	GA	Pts	
1.	Coagh United FC (Coagh)	30	19	6	5	81	41	63	P
2.	Dundela FC (Belfast)	30	20	2	8	79	46	62	P
3.	Knockbreda FC (Belfast)	30	19	4	7	70	31	61	
4.	Lurgan Celtic FC (Lurgan)	30	17	6	7	73	40	57	
5.	Queen's University FC (Belfast)	30	18	1	11	63	38	55	
6.	Ballyclare Comrades FC (Ballyclare)	30	16	4	10	60	46	52	
7.	Annagh United FC (Portadown)	30	15	6	9	59	51	51	
8.	Wakehurst FC (Castledawson)	30	14	5	11	59	48	47	
9.	Ballymoney United FC (Ballymoney)	30	12	3	15	51	45	39	
10.	Portstewart FC (Portstewart)	30	11	4	15	43	56	37	
11.	Armagh City FC (Armagh)	30	9	6	15	39	52	33	
12.	Sport & Leisure Swifts FC (Belfast)	30	9	5	16	46	59	32	
13.	P.S.N.I. FC (Belfast)	30	8	5	17	36	67	29	
14.	Moyola Park FC (Castledawson)	30	9	2	19	34	71	29	
15.	Killymoon Rangers FC (Cookstown)	30	7	3	20	34	72	24	
16.	Chimney Corner FC (Antrim)	30	5	2	23	26	90	17	
		480	208	64	208	853	853	688	

IRISH CUP FINAL (Windsor Park, Belfast – 05/05/2012 – 7,325)

Crusaders FC (Belfast)	1-4	LINFIELD FC (BELFAST)
Coates 56'		*McAllister 28', 41', Carvill 60', Mulgrew 83'*

Crusaders: O'Neill, McKeown (Leeman 45), McBride (Watson 81), Magowan, Coates, Dallas, Morrow, Adamson, Rainey, Caddell, Dallas, McMaster (Owens 45).

Linfield: Blayney, Curran, Murphy, Watson, Ervin, Carvill, Garrett (Casement 71), Mulgrew (BJ Burns 89), Lowry, McAllister (Fordyce 92), Thompson.

Semi-finals

Dungannon Swifts FC (Dungannon)	0-1	Crusaders FC (Belfast)
Newry City FC (Newry)	0-7	Linfield FC (Belfast)

Quarter-finals

Coleraine FC (Coleraine)	0-2	Crusaders FC (Belfast)
Donegal Celtic FC (Belfast)	1-1, 0-1	Dungannon Swifts FC (Dungannon)
Linfield FC (Belfast)	4-0	Coagh United FC (Coagh)
Newry City FC (Newry)	1-2	Ballymena United FC (Ballymena)

Ballymena United FC were subsequently ejected from the competition after it was discovered that they had fielded an ineligible player. Newry City FC were reinstated and entered the semi-final stage. Ballymena United FC appealed the decision, but the appeal was rejected.

Round 6

Ballymena United FC (Ballymena)	3–1	Derriaghy Cricket Club FC (Derriaghy)
Ballymoney United FC (Ballymoney)	1–6	Newry City FC (Newry)
Coagh United FC (Coagh)	1-1, 4-1	Newbuildings United FC (Newbuildings)
Coleraine FC (Coleraine)	3–0	Ballinamallard United FC (Ballinamallard)
Donegal Celtic FC (Belfast)	1–0	Cliftonville FC (Belfast)
Dungannon Swifts FC (Dungannon)	3–0	Newington Youth Club FC (Belfast)
Glenavon FC (Lurgan)	0–4	Crusaders FC (Belfast)
Linfield FC (Belfast)	5–1	Carrick Rangers FC (Carrickfergus)

Round 5

Banbridge Town FC (Banbridge)	0-1	Newry City FC (Newry)
Bangor FC (Bangor)	2-4	Ballymoney United FC (Ballymoney)
Cliftonville FC (Belfast)	2-0	Ards FC (Bangor)
Coagh United FC (Coagh)	2-2, 2-1	Loughgall FC (Loughgall)
Coleraine FC (Coleraine)	3-2	Larne Technical Old Boys FC (Larne)
Crusaders FC (Belfast)	3-0	Warrenpoint Town FC (Warrenpoint)
Dergview FC (Castlederg)	0-1	Derriaghy Cricket Club FC (Derriaghy)
Dundela FC (Belfast)	0-3	Ballinamallard United FC (Ballinamallard)
Dungannon Swifts FC (Dungannon)	3-1	Larne FC (Larne)
Glenavon FC (Lurgan)	2-1	Portadown FC (Portadown)
Glentoran FC (Belfast)	0-1	Newington Youth Club FC (Belfast)
Institute FC (Londonderry)	1-1, 0-1	Donegal Celtic FC (Belfast)
Killymoon Rangers FC (Cookstown)	1-3	Carrick Rangers FC (Carrickfergus)
Linfield FC (Belfast)	7-1	Ballyclare Comrades FC (Ballyclare)
Lisburn Distillery FC (Lisburn)	1-2	Ballymena United FC (Ballymena)
Newbuildings United FC (Newbuildings)	4-1	Dunmurry Recreation FC (Dunmurry)

2012-2013

IFA Premiership 2012-2013	Ballinamallard	Ballymena Utd	Cliftonville	Coleraine	Crusaders	Donegal Celtic	Dungannon Sw	Glenavon	Glentoran	Linfield	Lisburn Dist.	Portadown
Ballinamallard United FC	■	0–1	1-1	1-3		4-0	3-1	0-0	0–0			0–1
		0–0	1-3	1–0	0-2	0–0	2-2	2-1	1-4	1-3	2-0	2-0
Ballymena United FC	3-0	■		0–1		2-2	1-2	0-2	0–0		3-3	6-1
	1-1		0-8	0-2	2-1	3-3	1-1	2-1	1-1	2-0	2-0	1-2
Cliftonville FC	2-1	5-0	■		5-0	3-1	2-1	2-0		4-1	3-2	4-0
	0-1	2-1		3-1	1-0	3-1	4-1	2-1	1-1	3-0	4-0	3-2
Coleraine FC	0-0		0-2	■		1-3	0-0		1-1	1-1	3-1	
	1-5	4-1	1-5		3-1	2-1	2-0	0-2	1-0	3-2	2-1	1-1
Crusaders FC	3-1	5-1	3-0	2-1	■		1-1		3-2	3-0		1-0
	2-1	0–0	3-1	1-1		2-0	2-1	5-1	2-0	2-2	3-1	2-0
Donegal Celtic FC	1-0	1-4		0-3		■	2-1	1-0		1-4	0-3	1-2
	0-3	1-0	0-1	1-3	2-5		1-1	1-1	2-1	0-3	0-3	1-1
Dungannon Swifts FC		0–0		1-3		0–0	■	2-3		1-4	1-0	2-0
	0–1	1-3	1-1	1-1	2-0	3–0		2-1	1-3	1-1	1-1	1-1
Glenavon FC		7–0	1-3	1-1	2-3	3-1	3–1	■		0-3	7-0	1-3
	0–1	4–1	0-2	1-1	1-0	4-2	0–1		1-1	2-3	4-1	2-2
Glentoran FC	3-0		3-0	1-1	4-5	5-0	2-3	2-1	■	1-1		
	2-1	1-2	1-1	0-0	1-1	3-1	2-1	2-1		1-1	3-0	0-1
Linfield FC	0-1	2-2	3-1	5-2	1-2			1-0		■	1-1	2-0
	1-3	2-1	1-2	0-0	1-2	4-0	2-1	1-1	2-1		4-0	1-0
Lisburn Distillery FC	0–2	0-2			0–2	0-1	0-1	2-1	0-3		■	1-1
	0–5	0-4	1-2	1-1	1-3	3-3	2-1	0-1	0-2	1-1		0-5
Portadown FC		0–0	1-3	2-0		1-0	1-1	3-1	0-1		1-0	■
	2-1	2-2	3-3	3-4	1-0	1-0	1-1	2-0	2-4	2-4	4-2	

	IFA Premiership	Pd	Wn	Dw	Ls	GF	GA	Pts	
1.	Cliftonville FC (Belfast)	38	29	4	5	95	38	91	
2.	Crusaders FC (Belfast)	38	26	5	7	82	41	83	
3.	Linfield FC (Belfast)	38	17	11	10	69	48	62	
4.	Glentoran FC (Belfast)	38	15	12	11	63	44	57	
5.	Ballinamallard United FC (Ballinamallard)	38	15	8	15	49	43	53	
6.	Coleraine FC (Coleraine)	38	13	14	11	50	57	53	
7.	Portadown FC (Portadown)	38	15	10	13	55	55	55	
8.	Ballymena United FC (Ballymena)	38	11	13	14	54	68	46	
9.	Glenavon FC (Lurgan)	38	12	6	20	64	62	42	
10.	Dungannon Swifts FC (Dungannon)	38	9	13	16	42	58	40	
11.	Donegal Celtic FC (Belfast)	38	6	9	23	32	80	27	POR
12.	Lisburn Distillery FC (Lisburn)	38	4	7	27	29	90	19	R
		456	172	112	172	684	684	628	

After 33 games, clubs in the bottom half of the table at the split cannot finish in the top half, regardless of the number of points earned during the final 5 matches.

The 2-1 result of Donegal Celtic vs Lisburn Distillery played on 16th March 2013 was subsequently overturned after it was discovered that Donegal Celtic had fielded an ineligible player. The match was awarded to Lisburn Distillery with a 3-0 scoreline.

Promotion/Relegation Play-off

Warrenpoint Town FC (Warrenpoint)　　　　　1-0, 1-2　　　　　　　　Donegal Celtic FC (Belfast)
(Warrenpoint Town FC won on the away goals rule to secure promotion. Donegal Celtic FC were relegated)

Top goalscorers 2012-13

1) Liam BOYCE   (Cliftonville FC)   29
2) Andrew WATERWORTH (Glentoran FC)   20
3) Darren MURRAY   (Portadown FC)   18
4) Curtis ALLEN   (Coleraine FC)   17
   Joe GORMLEY   (Cliftonville FC)   17

IFA Championship 1 2012-2013	Ards	Bangor	Carrick Rangers	Coagh United	Dergview	Dundela	H & W Welders	Institute	Larne	Limavady United	Loughgall	Tobermore Utd	Warrenpoint Tn
Ards FC	■	1-0	1-0	2-0	2-0	5-2	2-1	1-1	2-1	4-0	3-2	2-0	2-0
Bangor FC	0-2	■	1-2	2-3	1-0	2-3	0-2	0-3	3-0	1-1	2-1	1-0	0-3
Carrick Rangers FC	1-1	1-2	■	2-0	6-0	3-0	1-0	2-2	1-1	2-0	0-0	5-0	2-1
Coagh United FC	1-5	3-1	2-3	■	0-1	0-3	1-1	1-2	3-0	3-3	3-1	2-3	1-4
Dergview FC	0-0	0-0	0-0	3-0	■	1-3	4-1	1-1	1-3	2-1	1-1	2-1	1-3
Dundela FC	2-2	5-1	5-3	0-5	4-0	■	2-3	2-1	1-1	4-4	1-2	4-2	1-0
Harland & Wolff Welders FC	2-3	4-1	1-2	5-1	3-1	2-1	■	0-2	0-0	2-3	0-2	2-0	1-1
Institute FC	2-2	0-1	5-0	2-3	2-0	0-0	2-0	■	2-0	1-0	2-0	3-2	1-2
Larne FC	1-2	0-0	0-6	0-0	1-1	3-5	1-2	0-4	■	2-0	0-0	1-0	1-1
Limavady United FC	0-5	3-1	3-1	1-1	0-2	3-4	0-1	1-2	0-1	■	5-2	2-0	0-2
Loughgall FC	0-4	1-1	2-1	3-1	0-4	1-4	4-2	1-3	2-0	1-1	■	0-1	1-4
Tobermore United FC	0-2	3-1	4-3	1-1	4-2	2-3	1-2	2-6	4-4	3-3	3-0	■	0-1
Warrenpoint Town FC	3-1	1-1	1-1	3-0	2-0	5-3	0-0	2-1	0-3	2-0	2-0	3-2	■

	IFA Championship 1	Pd	Wn	Dw	Ls	GF	GA	Pts	
1.	Ards FC (Bangor)	24	18	5	1	56	19	59	P
2.	Warrenpoint Town FC (Warrenpoint)	24	15	5	4	46	23	50	POP
3.	Institute FC (Londonderry)	24	14	5	5	50	23	47	
4.	Dundela FC (Belfast)	24	13	4	7	62	51	43	
5.	Carrick Rangers FC (Carrickfergus)	24	11	6	7	48	32	39	
6.	Harland & Wolff Welders FC (Belfast)	24	10	4	10	37	35	34	
7.	Dergview FC (Castlederg)	24	7	6	11	27	39	27	
8.	Larne FC (Larne)	24	5	9	10	24	40	24	
9.	Coagh United FC (Coagh)	24	6	5	13	35	51	23	
10.	Bangor FC (Bangor)	24	6	5	13	23	42	23	
11.	Loughgall FC (Loughgall)	24	6	5	13	27	48	23	
12.	Limavady United FC (Limavady)	24	5	6	13	34	49	21	
13.	Tobermore United FC (Tobermore)	24	6	3	15	38	55	21	R
		312	122	68	122	507	507	434	

IFA Championship 2 2012-2013	Annagh United	Armagh City	Ballyclare Com	Ballymoney Utd	Banbridge Town	Chimney Corner	Glebe Rangers	Killymoon Rang	Knockbreda	Lurgan Celtic	Moyola Park	Portstewart	P.S.N.I.	Queen's University	Sport & Leisure	Wakehurst
Annagh United FC	■	1–1	0–2	0–0	1–4	2–2	0–1	2–0	1–4	0–2	1–1	3–1	1–3	1–1	0–1	1–4
Armagh City FC	2–1	■	1–0	7–1	1–0	11–1	3–0	5–1	2–5	1–0	1–0	2–0	1–3	2–1	7–2	3–1
Ballyclare Comrades FC	3–1	2–0	■	0–2	2–1	4–1	1–1	2–0	1–0	2–1	1–2	2–0	2–1	2–1	6–0	2–0
Ballymoney United FC	1–1	1–5	1–4	■	2–3	5–1	1–0	4–1	1–1	0–2	1–1	4–0	1–1	0–5	4–1	0–4
Banbridge Town FC	1–2	0–2	3–2	3–1	■	5–0	0–2	4–1	0–4	2–2	2–2	6–2	3–2	0–2	3–3	0–1
Chimney Corner FC	1–2	0–4	2–6	3–2	1–2	■	1–2	2–1	0–3	0–7	2–1	1–2	1–6	0–4	0–6	0–4
Glebe Rangers FC	3–1	4–1	2–4	0–0	6–2	1–0	■	4–0	1–1	0–4	3–1	4–4	1–0	2–3	1–1	1–1
Killymoon Rangers FC	0–1	0–5	1–6	1–5	3–2	2–2	3–5	■	1–3	4–3	2–2	1–1	1–2	2–2	4–2	1–0
Knockbreda FC	6–1	1–0	1–2	6–1	4–0	5–0	3–1	2–1	■	8–0	3–0	8–0	2–1	6–2	4–1	4–2
Lurgan Celtic FC	2–2	4–1	2–1	3–1	3–0	3–0	2–1	3–1	0–3	■	1–0	5–2	2–1	1–0	5–0	2–5
Moyola Park FC	1–4	0–1	0–2	6–1	1–1	3–2	1–1	0–0	2–4	0–2	■	1–0	1–2	1–1	3–3	0–1
Portstewart FC	0–2	0–0	0–4	2–3	1–1	3–0	0–2	7–3	0–1	2–2	0–0	■	1–2	2–2	2–0	0–2
PSNI FC	0–2	1–3	1–5	2–3	1–2	2–0	1–3	4–0	1–3	3–1	0–1	3–1	■	0–1	4–0	7–2
Queen's University FC	1–0	1–2	2–2	3–1	0–3	5–0	0–3	0–0	1–3	0–1	5–0	4–1	1–3	■	7–0	3–1
Sport & Leisure Swifts FC	1–2	2–6	0–2	0–5	2–2	3–2	1–0	3–3	1–8	1–2	1–4	1–3	2–1	0–4	■	2–5
Wakehurst FC	4–3	1–1	1–3	1–1	2–2	2–1	1–3	2–0	1–0	2–4	3–0	1–0	1–2	4–3	2–1	■

	IFA Championship 2	Pd	Wn	Dw	Ls	GF	GA	Pts	
1.	Knockbreda FC (Belfast)	30	25	2	3	106	25	77	P
2.	Ballyclare Comrades FC (Ballyclare)	30	23	2	5	77	28	71	P
3.	Armagh City FC (Armagh)	30	21	3	6	81	34	66	
4.	Lurgan Celtic FC (Lurgan)	30	20	3	7	71	43	63	
5.	Glebe Rangers FC (Ballymoney)	30	15	7	8	58	41	52	
6.	Wakehurst FC (Castledawson)	30	16	4	10	61	50	52	
7.	Queen's University FC (Belfast)	30	13	6	11	65	43	45	
8.	P.S.N.I. FC (Belfast)	30	14	1	15	60	48	43	
9.	Banbridge Town FC (Banbridge)	30	11	7	12	57	58	40	
10.	Ballymoney United FC (Ballymoney)	30	10	7	13	53	67	37	
11.	Annagh United FC (Portadown)	30	9	7	14	39	53	34	
12.	Moyola Park FC (Castledawson)	30	6	10	14	35	51	28	
13.	Portstewart FC (Portstewart)	30	5	7	18	37	70	22	
14.	Sport & Leisure Swifts FC (Belfast)	30	5	5	20	41	101	20	
15.	Killymoon Rangers FC (Cookstown)	30	4	7	19	38	85	19	
16.	Chimney Corner FC (Antrim)	30	3	2	25	26	108	11	**
		480	200	80	200	905	905	680	

** As a result of Newry City FC dissolving, there was no relegation from Championship 2 this season

The Northern Ireland Football League took over the running of the league competition from the Irish Football Association from the 2013-2014 season onwards. No change was made to the structure of the league itself, but the divisions were renamed to the NIFL Premiership, NIFL Championship 1 and NIFL Championship 2 respectively.

IRISH CUP FINAL (Windsor Park, Belfast – 04/05/2013 – 9,825)
Cliftonville FC (Belfast)   1-3 (aet)   GLENTORAN FC (BELFAST)
Gormley 34'   *Waterworth 64', 101', Callacher 99'*

Cliftonville: Devlin, Seydak, Smyth, McGovern (O'Carroll 60), McMullan, Garrett (Cosgrove 82), Catney, Johnston, Caldwell, Gormley (Donnelly 70), Boyce.
Glentoran: Morris, Ward, Magee, Callacher, Hill (Nixon 109), McAlorum, M Clarke (O'Hanlon 70), R. Clarke, Howland, Carson, Waterworth.

Semi-finals

Portadown FC (Portadown)	0-1	Glentoran FC (Belfast)
Crusaders FC (Belfast)	0-2	Cliftonville FC (Belfast)

Quarter-finals

Cliftonville FC (Belfast)	2-0	Kilmore Recreation FC (Crossgar)
Coleraine FC (Coleraine)	0-3	Portadown FC (Portadown)
Crusaders FC (Belfast)	1-1, 1-1 (aet)	Lisburn Distillery FC (Lisburn)
	(Crusaders FC won 4-3 on penalties)	
Knockbreda FC (Belfast)	1-3	Glentoran FC (Belfast)

Round 6

Ballymena United FC (Ballymena)	2-3	Coleraine FC (Coleraine)
Bangor FC (Bangor)	2-5	Glentoran FC (Belfast)
Cliftonville FC (Belfast)	2-0	Donegal Celtic FC (Belfast)
Crusaders FC (Belfast)	4-1	Glenavon FC (Lurgan)
Institute FC (Londonderry)	0-2	Kilmore Recreation FC (Crossgar)
Lurgan Celtic FC (Lurgan)	0-3	Knockbreda FC (Belfast)
Portadown FC (Portadown)	1-0	Ards FC (Bangor)
Lisburn Distillery FC (Lisburn)	2-1	Dundela FC (Belfast)

Round 5

Ards FC (Bangor)	4-0	Immaculata FC (Belfast)
Ballyclare Comrades FC (Ballyclare)	2-3	Bangor FC (Bangor)
Ballymena United FC (Ballymena)	2-1	Warrenpoint Town FC (Warrenpoint)
Cliftonville FC (Belfast)	4-2	Ballinamallard United FC (Ballinamallard)
Coleraine FC (Coleraine)	7-0	Ballynahinch United FC (Ballynahinch)
Dundela FC (Belfast)	4-3	Queen's University FC (Belfast)
Glenavon FC (Lurgan)	5-1	Harland & Wolff Welders FC (Belfast)
Institute FC (Londonderry)	2-1	Rathfriland Rangers
Killymoon Rangers FC (Cookstown)	1-4	Glentoran FC (Belfast)
Knockbreda FC (Belfast)	5-1	Rosario Youth Club FC (Belfast)
Larne FC (Larne)	1-1, 1-4	Lurgan Celtic FC (Lurgan)
Linfield FC (Belfast)	2-2, 1-2	Crusaders FC (Belfast)
Lisburn Distillery FC (Lisburn)	5-1	Coagh United FC (Coagh)
Loughgall FC (Loughgall)	1-3	Donegal Celtic FC (Belfast)
Portadown FC (Portadown)	2-1	Dungannon Swifts FC (Dungannon)
Tobermore United FC (Tobermore)	2-2, 0-1	Kilmore Recreation FC (Crossgar)

2013-2014

NIFL Premiership 2013-2014	Ards	Ballinamallard U.	Ballymena Utd.	Cliftonville	Coleraine	Crusaders	Dungannon Sw.	Glenavon	Glentoran	Linfield	Portadown	Warrenpoint T.
Ards	■	4-1	2-0	0-4	3-1	1-4	2-3	1-2	0-0	1-3	3-1	1-2
	■	0-0	0-0	2-3	0-1		1-3		2-1		1-2	2-2
Ballinamallard United	1-0	■	1-0	0-2	1-1	1-0	1-1	0-2	1-4	1-2	2-1	3-0
	1-0	■		0-0		2-1	1-2	2-2	1-2	0-3		2-3
Ballymena United	4-2	2-0	■	0-1	2-2	1-0	2-1	3-6	3-4	1-4	2-1	0-1
	1-1	1-0	■		1-3	2-2		1-2	2-1		1-2	3-2
Cliftonville	4-2	1-0	2-1	■	1-3	0-2	2-2	2-1	4-1	3-0	1-2	1-1
		5-0		■	2-0	4-0		5-0	2-0	1-0	0-1	
Coleraine	2-1	1-2	2-3	3-4	■	2-2	0-2	3-2	1-3	2-3	2-2	3-2
	2-0	1-1	1-1		■	1-0	0-0			0-0	2-3	3-0
Crusaders	4-2	2-1	1-2	1-1	4-0	■	1-1	3-0	0-0	2-0	2-2	2-0
	4-1		1-0	2-3		■	5-1	2-2	2-1	2-3	3-1	
Dungannon Swifts	1-0	1-0	2-3	1-1	1-0	0-1	■	3-3	1-2	1-0	0-5	1-2
	2-0	1-1	2-3	1-2	0-2		■		0-1			0-4
Glenavon	4-1	2-3	0-0	1-0	2-2	2-2	1-3	■	1-2	1-3	3-2	3-1
	3-1		2-5	3-1	1-3	3-2		■	2-3	2-5	4-2	
Glentoran	5-0	0-0	0-0	1-1	1-1	0-3	2-1	0-0	■	1-2	0-2	3-0
		3-0	0-0	1-1	3-0		0-4		■	0-1	2-2	1-2
Linfield	5-2	3-0	4-1	2-4	1-0	0-0	2-0	3-2	0-0	■	3-2	5-1
	3-3	6-0		1-3		1-1	3-0	2-1	0-2	■	1-1	
Portadown	2-0	11-0	1-0	3-3	2-0	0-1	2-1	2-4	2-1	1-1	■	2-0
		1-0	1-0	0-2		1-1	4-2	3-0	1-2	1-2	■	3-0
Warrenpoint Town	2-0	2-2	0-2	2-4	2-1	1-1	2-3	1-2	0-1	0-2	2-2	■
	0-2	0-3	1-0	0-2	0-1	1-1	0-1	2-1			2-3	■

	NIFL Premiership	Pd	Wn	Dw	Ls	GF	GA	Pts	
1.	CLIFTONVILLE FC (BELFAST)	38	26	7	5	88	39	85	
2.	Linfield FC (Belfast)	38	24	7	7	81	46	79	
3.	Crusaders FC (Belfast)	38	18	12	8	67	42	66	
4.	Portadown FC (Portadown)	38	18	8	12	77	53	62	
5.	Glentoran FC (Belfast)	38	16	11	11	54	42	59	
6.	Glenavon FC (Lurgan)	38	15	6	17	75	79	51	
7.	Ballymena United FC (Ballymena)	38	13	8	17	48	59	47	
8.	Dungannon Swifts FC (Dungannon)	38	12	8	18	49	66	44	
9.	Coleraine FC (Coleraine)	38	10	12	16	51	61	42	
10.	Ballinamallard United FC (Ballinamallard)	38	10	9	19	35	70	39	
11.	Warrenpoint Town FC (Warrenpoint)	38	10	6	22	43	72	36	
12.	Ards FC (Bangor)	38	6	6	26	44	83	24	R
		456	178	100	178	712	712	634	

After 33 games, clubs in the bottom half of the table at the split cannot finish in the top half, regardless of the number of points earned during the final 5 matches.

No Promotion/Relegation play-off took take place this season because Bangor FC, runners-up of the NIFL Championship 1, did not possess the necessary licence to participate in top-flight football.

Top goalscorers 2013-14

1) Joe GORMLEY   (Cliftonville FC)   27
2) Darren MURRAY   (Portadown FC)   23
3) Andrew WATERWORTH   (Linfield FC)   22
4) Liam BOYCE   (Cliftonville FC)   21
5) Gary TWIGG   (Portadown FC)   19

NIFL Championship 2013-2014	Ballyclare Comrades	Bangor	Carrick Rangers	Coagh United	Dergview	Donegal Celtic	Dundela	Harland & Wolff Welders	Institute	Knockbreda	Larne	Limavady United	Lisburn Distillery	Loughgall
Ballyclare Comrades FC	■	0-1	0-1	1-2	2-0	1-1	5-3	2-2	5-1	2-5	4-0	3-2	0-3	2-0
Bangor FC	4-0	■	0-3	5-0	2-1	1-0	3-2	1-1	0-1	2-0	3-2	3-1	6-2	6-1
Carrick Rangers FC	4-2	2-2	■	1-0	3-1	3-4	0-1	3-2	1-2	3-0	1-2	1-0	3-1	1-2
Coagh United FC	0-2	1-6	1-6	■	2-3	3-1	0-2	2-2	1-1	2-3	1-1	2-1	4-4	2-3
Dergview FC	1-5	5-0	2-1	0-0	■	2-1	2-3	0-0	1-1	0-5	1-2	0-0	3-3	1-1
Donegal Celtic FC	1-6	1-4	0-0	6-1	0-1	■	5-3	0-3	0-5	1-0	1-1	2-1	1-1	4-2
Dundela FC	3-0	5-1	1-1	2-3	2-2	3-2	■	0-2	1-1	4-0	0-1	1-0	2-0	2-1
Harland & Wolff Welders FC	1-1	2-2	1-2	4-0	2-0	0-2	3-6	■	0-1	1-1	1-0	3-0	3-3	1-2
Institute FC	3-2	2-2	5-1	6-2	4-0	4-2	4-0	3-1	■	0-0	6-1	2-0	2-1	1-1
Knockbreda FC	2-0	3-0	3-1	5-1	1-2	4-1	5-4	0-1	2-2	■	1-0	4-0	2-2	3-1
Larne FC	0-1	0-4	1-2	3-3	2-1	1-1	0-2	0-3	4-3	1-5	■	5-1	1-0	2-0
Limavady United FC	3-3	1-2	0-5	1-0	2-1	0-4	1-3	0-5	1-2	0-0	■		1-0	1-2
Lisburn Distillery FC	1-0	1-3	1-1	1-3	2-0	2-0	3-6	0-1	2-2	3-1	1-2	2-0	■	2-1
Loughgall FC	6-4	2-2	0-2	4-2	1-1	1-3	3-3	2-3	5-5	1-0	1-0	4-1	1-2	■

	NIFL Championship	Pd	Wn	Dw	Ls	GF	GA	Pts	
1.	Institute FC (Londonderry)	26	15	9	2	72	35	54	P
2.	Bangor FC (Bangor)	26	16	5	5	65	39	53	
3.	Knockbreda FC (Belfast)	26	14	4	8	57	36	46	
4.	Dundela FC (Belfast)	26	14	4	8	65	47	46	
5.	Carrick Rangers FC (Carrickfergus)	26	14	4	8	52	34	46	
6.	Harland & Wolff Welders FC (Belfast)	26	11	8	7	46	34	41	
7.	Ballyclare Comrades FC (Ballyclare)	26	10	4	12	53	50	34	
8.	Loughgall FC (Loughgall)	26	9	6	11	48	56	33	
9.	Larne FC (Larne)	26	9	5	12	32	47	32	
10.	Lisburn Distillery FC (Lisburn)	26	8	7	11	43	49	31	
11.	Donegal Celtic FC (Belfast)	26	8	5	13	41	55	29	
12.	Dergview FC (Castlederg)	26	6	8	12	30	46	26	
13.	Coagh United FC (Coagh)	26	5	6	15	38	74	21	R
14.	Limavady United FC (Limavady)	26	4	3	19	19	59	15	R
		364	143	78	143	661	661	507	

NIFL Championship 2 2013-2014	Annagh United	Armagh City	Ballymoney United	Banbridge Town	Chimney Corner	Glebe Rangers	Killymoon Rangers	Lurgan Celtic	Moyola Park	Newington Youth Club	Portstewart	P.S.N.I.	Queen's University	Sport & Leisure Swifts	Tobermore United	Wakehurst
Annagh United FC		0-3	6-2	2-0	9-1	1-0	3-0	1-0	3-0	4-2	3-3	1-1	3-4	3-1	3-1	7-2
Armagh City FC	5-1		2-1	4-0	9-2	3-0	6-0	4-0	4-2	2-0	3-1	2-1	1-0	3-0	3-0	6-0
Ballymoney United FC	3-3	1-2		0-1	1-3	3-4	3-1	4-0	1-2	5-2	0-2	1-3	3-4	3-1	1-0	3-3
Banbridge Town FC	4-3	1-4	3-0		3-2	3-1	2-0	1-1	1-0	2-1	2-0	1-2	0-2	1-1	6-0	3-1
Chimney Corner FC	2-3	2-1	1-1	0-1		0-2	3-0	4-0	0-4	1-4	1-5	0-2	0-1	1-0	1-2	3-0
Glebe Rangers FC	0-3	0-2	1-2	2-1	3-2		1-0	1-3	3-5	1-1	1-2	1-8	1-2	4-0	2-4	4-0
Killymoon Rangers	1-2	0-4	1-0	0-7	4-2	3-3		3-3	1-6	0-4	0-1	2-2	0-2	2-4	2-5	5-4
Lurgan Celtic FC	1-1	0-1	0-4	1-4	0-1	3-2	5-1		3-0	2-2	0-5	2-0	0-1	3-3	0-2	2-1
Moyola Park FC	5-2	1-2	2-6	4-3	4-0	0-3	1-2	4-0		0-3	5-2	0-3	1-0	1-1	5-0	0-0
Newington Youth Club FC	1-1	1-0	2-2	2-0	2-1	2-0	2-0	2-2	1-0		0-1	1-1	3-0	4-0	2-1	4-1
Portstewart FC	1-1	4-1	0-1	1-0	2-2	1-2	3-0	0-1	0-0	0-3		0-5	0-1	4-1	3-1	2-3
P.S.N.I. FC	5-0	3-3	5-1	3-1	3-0	3-1	2-0	7-0	4-0	1-2	3-2		0-0	2-0	3-2	2-3
Queen's University FC	2-1	2-4	2-4	2-1	2-1	1-1	3-1	3-2	0-0	0-0	1-1	0-0		1-0	3-0	2-1
Sport & Leisure Swifts FC	3-1	2-2	0-2	3-2	2-1	1-3	2-4	3-4	1-3	3-3	0-1	0-3	0-1		3-3	1-1
Tobermore United FC	0-4	1-2	0-0	0-2	3-1	3-0	2-0	2-1	2-3	0-0	2-2	0-2	2-3	4-0		2-4
Wakehurst FC	0-0	0-2	3-3	2-4	2-0	2-1	3-0	0-2	2-3	1-0	3-3	2-5	1-2	0-1	2-3	

	NIFL Championship 2	**Pd**	**Wn**	**Dw**	**Ls**	**GF**	**GA**	**Pts**	
1.	Armagh City FC (Armagh)	30	25	2	3	90	26	77	P
2.	P.S.N.I. FC (Belfast)	30	20	6	4	84	28	66	P
3.	Queen's University FC (Belfast)	30	19	6	5	47	32	63	
4.	Newington Youth Club FC (Belfast)	30	15	9	6	56	32	54	
5.	Annagh United FC (Portadown)	30	15	7	8	75	53	52	
6.	Banbridge Town FC (Banbridge)	30	16	2	12	60	44	50	
7.	Moyola Park FC (Castledawson)	30	14	4	12	61	53	46	
8.	Portstewart FC (Portstewart)	30	12	7	11	52	46	43	
9.	Ballymoney United FC (Ballymoney)	30	11	6	13	61	59	39	
10.	Tobermore United FC (Tobermore)	30	10	4	16	47	63	34	
11.	Glebe Rangers FC (Ballymoney)	30	10	3	17	48	64	33	
12.	Lurgan Celtic FC (Lurgan)	30	9	6	15	41	67	33	
13.	Wakehurst FC (Castledawson)	30	7	6	17	47	75	27	
14.	Chimney Corner FC (Antrim)	30	7	2	21	38	75	23	
15.	Sport & Leisure Swifts FC (Belfast)	30	5	7	18	37	70	22	
16.	Killymoon Rangers FC (Cookstown)	30	5	3	22	33	90	18	R
		480	200	80	200	877	877	680	

Promoted to NIFL Championship 2: Dollingstown FC (Lurgan)

IRISH CUP FINAL   (Windsor Park, Belfast – 03/05/2014 – 7,282)

Ballymena United FC (Ballymena)   1-2   GLENAVON FC (LURGAN)
Jenkins 70'   *Neill 34', Patton 75'*

Ballymena: Shanahan, Ervin (Taggart 28), McBride, Taylor, Munster (Stewart 83), Kane, Thompson, Jenkins, Teggart, Cushley, Boyce (Davidson 65).

Glenavon: McGrath, Marshall, Lindsay, McKeown, Singleton, McGrory, Martyn, McCabe, Neill (Patton 67), Bates (Hamilton 90+1), Mulvenna (Murphy 79).

Semi-finals

Ballymena United FC (Ballymena)	3-0	Queen's University FC (Belfast)
Glenavon FC (Lurgan)	3-1 (aet)	Crusaders FC (Belfast)

Quarter-finals

Ballymena United FC (Ballymena)	4-1	Dungannon Swifts FC (Dungannon)
Crusaders FC (Belfast)	5-0	Ballyclare Comrades FC (Ballyclare)
Queen's University FC (Belfast)	3-2	Bangor FC (Bangor)
Glentoran FC (Belfast)	1-2	Glenavon FC (Lurgan)

Round 6

Armagh City FC (Armagh)	1-1, 1-2	Glentoran FC (Belfast)
Ballyclare Comrades FC (Ballyclare)	2-1	Carrick Rangers FC (Carrickfergus)
Coleraine FC (Coleraine)	2-3	Dungannon Swifts FC (Dungannon)
Crusaders FC (Belfast)	4-0	Ballymoney United FC (Ballymoney)
Linfield FC (Belfast)	1-2	Ballymena United FC (Ballymena)
Lisburn Distillery FC (Lisburn)	0-2	Queen's University FC (Belfast)
Warrenpoint Town FC (Warrenpoint)	0-0, 0-1	Bangor FC (Bangor)
Ballinamallard United FC (Ballinamallard)	0-3	Glenavon FC (Lurgan)

Round 5

Harland & Wolff Welders FC (Belfast)	2-2, 0-1	Ballymena United FC (Ballymena)
Queen's University FC (Belfast)	1-0	Limavady United FC (Limavady)
Lisburn Distillery FC (Lisburn)	0-0, 2-0	P.S.N.I. FC (Belfast)
Armagh City FC (Armagh)	2-2, 3-1	Ards FC (Bangor)
Ballinamallard United FC (Ballinamallard)	0-0, 1-0	Strabane Athletic FC (Strabane)
Ballyclare Comrades FC (Ballyclare)	3-0	Kilmore Recreation FC (Crossgar)
Ballymoney United FC (Ballymoney)	1-0	Banbridge Town FC (Banbridge)
Bangor FC (Bangor)	7-1	Glebe Rangers FC (Ballymoney)
Carrick Rangers FC (Carrickfergus)	3-2	Dundela FC (Belfast)
Cliftonville FC (Belfast)	2-2, 3-4	Coleraine FC (Coleraine)
Crusaders FC (Belfast)	2-1	Crumlin Star FC (Larne)
Glenavon FC (Lurgan)	7-0	Sport & Leisure Swifts FC (Belfast)
Linfield FC (Belfast)	5-0	Dergview FC (Castlederg)
Moyola Park FC (Castledawson)	1-5	Dungannon Swifts FC (Dungannon)
Portadown FC (Portadown)	1-3	Glentoran FC (Belfast)
Warrenpoint Town FC (Warrenpoint)	2-0	Chimney Corner FC (Antrim)

2014-2015

NIFL Premiership 2014-2015	Ballinamallard	Ballymena	Cliftonville	Coleraine	Crusaders	Dungannon	Glenavon	Glentoran	Institute	Linfield	Portadown	Warrenpoint
Ballinamallard United		3-0	0-4	1-0	1-1	2-0	1-0	2-2	2-3	1-3	0-2	3-1
		1-3	1-1	2-1		1-0	1-3		2-0	1-1	0-0	3-3
Ballymena United	3-0		2-2	0-2	0-2	2-2	1-4	2-2	2-1	2-3	3-2	2-0
	2-1		4-3	1-3	1-0	2-4	1-3	3-0			2-1	
Cliftonville	3-2	7-0		2-3	0-1	1-1	3-3	0-0	4-0	0-0	2-0	3-1
		1-0			0-1		2-3	1-1	5-1	2-2	4-0	2-2
Coleraine	1-1	1-2	2-0		2-6	1-2	2-1	1-0	NR	1-2	0-0	0-0
	1-2	0-1	0-0		1-5	1-2	1-1	1-1	3-1		0-1	2-1
Crusaders	3-1	2-2	0-1	3-0		1-0	1-4	1-0	3-2	2-2	2-3	3-0
	3-0		4-1			4-0	2-0	3-1	2-1	6-0	4-1	
Dungannon Swifts	1-1	0-3	1-3	0-1	2-2		2-1	2-3	2-2	0-1	2-3	0-2
	2-0	1-0	1-1	1-0	1-1			1-1	0-3		1-1	
Glenavon	1-0	2-1	1-3	2-3	2-2	0-2		1-2	1-1	1-2	2-4	3-2
		5-0		3-7	2-1			4-0	2-1	1-0	3-2	2-2
Glentoran	3-1	4-0	2-1	2-0	1-3	1-0	2-4		2-1	2-3	1-1	3-1
	4-0		1-0		1-2	2-0	1-2		4-1	1-2	0-0	
Institute	0-2	1-2	2-3	2-0	1-1	1-1	1-4	1-1		1-1	0-4	1-0
	1-1	1-2		0-2		1-2				0-1		1-1
Linfield	3-0	3-2	1-3	2-1	1-2	4-0	0-1	2-2	3-1		3-2	1-0
		2-1	2-2	1-1	3-1		0-2	2-1			1-2	3-0
Portadown	3-0	2-1	0-1	0-2	3-1	1-0	3-2	3-1	4-1	3-0		2-2
		5-5	0-2	1-0		1-1	3-3	1-1	2-1	1-1		
Warrenpoint Town	2-0	2-2	1-1	1-3	0-3	3-3	0-2	2-5	0-1	1-2	2-1	
	7-0	2-0		0-5		1-1		0-5	5-1		0-0	

Coleraine FC and Institute FC both fielded an ineligible player in the same match. The original 4-0 win for Coleraine was voided with a 3-0 loss being recorded for both clubs, resulting in the final league table containing two more losses than wins, and an overall goal difference of -6.

	NIFL Premiership	Pd	Wn	Dw	Ls	GF	GA	Pts	
1.	CRUSADERS FC (BELFAST)	38	25	7	6	93	43	82	
2.	Linfield FC (Belfast)	38	21	9	8	67	46	72	
3.	Glenavon FC (Lurgan)	38	20	6	12	82	65	66	
4.	Portadown FC (Portadown)	38	17	11	10	65	56	62	
5.	Cliftonville FC (Belfast)	38	16	13	9	71	47	61	
6.	Glentoran FC (Belfast)	38	16	10	12	67	51	58	
7.	Ballymena United FC (Ballymena)	38	15	6	17	62	75	51	
8.	Coleraine FC (Coleraine)	38	13	7	18	48	55	46	
9.	Ballinamallard United FC (Ballinamallard)	38	10	9	19	40	71	39	
10.	Dungannon Swifts FC (Dungannon)	38	8	13	17	38	56	37	
11.	Warrenpoint Town FC (Warrenpoint)	38	6	12	20	50	76	30	PO
12.	Institute FC (Londonderry)	38	4	9	25	36	84	21	R
		456	171	112	173	719	725	625	

After 33 games, clubs in the bottom half of the table at the split cannot finish in the top half, regardless of the number of points earned during the final 5 matches.

Promotion/relegation play-off

Bangor FC (Bangor)　　　　　　　　2-0, 0-2 (aet)　　　　Warrenpoint Town FC (Warrenpoint)
Aggregate 2-2. Warrenpoint Town FC won 3-1 on penalties to retain their NIFL Premiership status.

Top goalscorers 2014-15

1	Joe GORMLEY	(Cliftonville FC)	31
2	Paul HEATLEY	(Crusaders FC)	27
3	Jordan OWENS	(Crusaders FC)	26
4	Aaron BURNS	(Linfield FC)	17
	Daniel HUGHES	(Warrenpoint Town FC)	17

NIFL Championship 1 2014-2015	Ards	Armagh	Ballyclare	Bangor	Carrick Rangers	Dergview	Donegal Celtic	Dundela	Harland & Wolff	Knockbreda	Larne	Lisburn	Loughgall	PSNI
Ards		4-1	1-1	1-1	3-2	3-1	1-1	2-1	2-2	2-0	2-1	4-0	5-1	2-1
Armagh City	1-1		3-1	1-2	0-2	1-1	3-2	5-2	0-1	2-0	2-4	3-1	1-0	1-2
Ballyclare Comrades	1-1	4-0		1-2	0-2	2-2	2-2	3-1	3-0	0-1	0-2	1-2	1-2	1-0
Bangor	2-3	2-0	3-1		1-1	4-1	4-2	3-1	2-2	4-2	1-1	3-2	2-1	8-0
Carrick Rangers	1-0	3-1	2-0	2-2		3-1	2-0	1-0	4-0	2-1	2-1	3-2	2-0	2-1
Dergview	2-2	2-0	5-3	0-3	0-0		3-3	2-1	1-2	1-0	3-2	3-1	2-0	2-0
Donegal Celtic	1-2	2-3	4-1	0-1	0-1	1-1		1-1	2-6	2-0	2-1	0-1	2-2	0-0
Dundela	1-3	1-1	0-3	3-3	2-5	1-0	3-1		1-1	1-2	0-3	3-4	4-0	1-3
Harland & Wolff Welders	1-2	0-2	4-3	0-1	3-0	2-2	1-0	3-2		2-0	1-3	3-2	3-0	4-1
Knockbreda	3-1	2-0	2-1	2-4	0-5	3-2	1-1	3-1	1-2		2-2	0-2	0-1	4-1
Larne	1-2	4-1	4-1	1-2	1-2	2-0	1-0	3-0	0-5	2-0		1-2	0-3	1-1
Lisburn Distillery	1-3	1-2	2-6	0-3	1-1	1-1	0-0	3-0	0-6	2-0	0-4		1-1	5-1
Loughgall	2-2	1-1	1-2	2-7	1-1	2-1	0-3	4-2	3-3	0-2	2-4	3-1		0-1
PSNI	0-7	3-3	0-4	2-1	1-3	1-1	1-3	3-1	0-2	0-0	0-3	3-1	1-4	

	NIFL Championship 1	Pd	Wn	Dw	Ls	GF	GA	Pts	
1.	Carrick Rangers FC (Carrickfergus)	26	19	5	2	54	22	62	P
2.	Bangor FC (Bangor)	26	18	6	2	71	32	60	PO
3.	Ards FC (Newtownards)	26	16	8	2	61	30	56	
4.	Harland & Wolff Welders	26	15	5	6	59	37	50	
5.	Larne FC (Larne)	26	13	3	10	52	36	42	
6.	Dergview FC (Castlederg)	26	8	9	9	40	43	33	
7.	Armagh City FC (Armagh)	26	9	5	12	38	48	32	
8.	Knockbreda FC (Belfast)	26	9	3	14	31	43	30	
9.	Ballyclare Comrades FC (Ballyclare)	26	8	4	14	46	48	28	
10.	Lisburn Distillery FC (Lisburn)	26	8	4	14	38	58	28	
11.	Loughgall FC (Loughgall)	26	7	6	13	36	54	27	
12.	Donegal Celtic FC (Belfast)	26	5	9	12	35	42	24	
13.	PSNI FC (Belfast)	26	6	5	15	27	64	23	R
14.	Dundela FC (Belfast)	26	3	4	19	34	65	13	R
		364	144	76	144	622	622	508	

NIFL Championship 2 2014/2015	Annagh	Ballymoney	Banbridge	Coagh	Dollingstown	Glebe Rangers	Limavady	Lurgan	Moyola Park	Newington YC	Portstewart	Queen's University	Sport & Leisure	Tobermore	Wakehurst
Annagh United		5-1	0-0	3-2	4-3	5-3	0-6	1-1	1-2	3-2	3-1	1-2	3-4	2-1	2-3
Ballymoney United	3-5		3-3	3-0	2-6	1-1	2-3	0-5	0-6	0-2	1-2	1-2	0-1	2-1	1-2
Banbridge Town	0-4	1-1		4-3	0-4	3-1	0-1	0-0	3-4	0-3	0-2	0-0	3-2	4-1	3-2
Coagh United	0-3	1-1	1-3		0-2	2-1	0-1	2-4	1-1	3-3	0-1	1-4	0-2	2-2	1-0
Dollingstown	1-5	4-0	3-0	6-1		2-2	1-1	1-2	3-1	0-0	1-0	1-1	1-1	4-3	0-1
Glebe Rangers	1-2	2-2	4-0	3-1	1-1		4-1	1-0	3-3	0-1	1-4	0-4	0-3	1-3	8-0
Limavady United	2-2	3-0	3-0	4-0	3-1	2-0		3-4	3-2	2-0	1-2	2-2	3-0	2-0	1-1
Lurgan Celtic	4-0	2-0	2-3	9-0	2-0	4-2	2-0		1-0	0-1	3-0	2-1	5-0	2-2	1-0
Moyola Park	2-7	1-0	5-2	1-0	1-0	4-0	1-5	1-1		2-1	5-2	2-1	1-1	1-1	6-0
Newington YC	0-1	2-1	3-1	3-1	2-0	1-1	0-0	1-4	3-2		2-1	1-0	0-1	0-3	2-0
Portstewart	1-4	1-0	3-0	3-2	1-2	5-1	2-4	1-1	0-1	0-1		3-3	1-1	1-1	3-1
Queen's University	0-1	1-0	2-2	2-2	1-2	3-0	3-2	0-0	2-0	1-0	0-1		1-2	3-2	7-1
Sport & Leisure Swifts	0-0	7-0	4-2	1-2	1-1	3-1	2-0	0-2	1-0	1-3	1-2	1-0		4-1	2-0
Tobermore United	1-3	3-0	8-0	1-0	3-1	1-2	0-3	1-2	1-1	1-1	0-0	1-0	1-2		2-0
Wakehurst	0-3	4-1	1-1	1-1	0-2	3-1	1-6	0-3	1-2	0-2	0-0	3-2	1-2	2-3	

	NIFL Championship 2	**Pd**	**Wn**	**Dw**	**Ls**	**GF**	**GA**	**Pts**	
1.	Lurgan Celtic FC (Lurgan)	28	19	6	3	68	21	63	P
2.	Annagh United FC (Portadown)	28	18	4	6	73	46	58	P
3.	Limavady United FC (Limavady)	28	17	5	6	67	32	56	
4.	Sport & Leisure Swifts FC (Belfast)	28	16	5	7	50	34	53	
5.	Newington YC FC (Belfast)	28	15	5	8	40	29	50	
6.	Moyola Park FC (Castledawson)	28	14	6	8	58	44	48	
7.	Dollingstown FC (Dollingstown)	28	12	7	9	53	39	43	
8.	Portstewart FC (Portstewart)	28	12	6	10	43	40	42	
9.	Queen's University FC (Belfast)	28	11	7	10	48	34	40	
10.	Tobermore United FC (Tobermore)	28	9	7	12	48	45	34	
11.	Banbridge Town FC (Banbridge)	28	7	7	14	38	70	28	
12.	Glebe Rangers FC (Ballymoney)	28	6	6	16	45	64	24	
13.	Wakehurst FC (Castledawson)	28	6	4	18	28	68	22	
14.	Coagh United FC (Coagh)	28	3	6	19	29	72	15	
15.	Ballymoney United FC (Ballymoney)	28	2	5	21	26	76	11	R
		420	167	86	167	714	714	587	

IRISH CUP FINAL (The Oval, Belfast – 02/05/2015 – 8,072)

GLENTORAN FC (BELFAST)   1-0   Portadown FC (Portadown)

Scullion 54'

Glentoran: E. Morris, C. Birney, W. Garrett, N. Henderson (J. Addis 89'), B. Holland, D. Scullion (F. McCaffery 89'), S. McAlorum, M. Kane, S. Gordon, C. Allen, J. Stewart (K. Nelson 90+3').

Portadown: D. Miskelly, C. Casement, G. Breen, K. O'Hara, R. Redman, S. Mackle, R. Garrett, M. Gault, P. McMahon, M. McAllister (D. Murray 72'), G. Twigg.

Semi-finals

Crusaders FC (Belfast)	0-1	Glentoran FC (Belfast)
Ballymena United FC (Ballymena)	1-3	Portadown FC (Portadown)

Quarter-finals

Harland & Wolff Welders FC (Belfast)	2-3	Ballymena United FC (Ballymena)
Crusaders FC (Belfast)	4-1	Carrick Rangers FC (Carrickfergus)
Glentoran FC (Belfast)	3-0	Dungannon Swifts FC (Dungannon)
Portadown FC (Portadown)	3-2	Linfield FC (Belfast)

Round 6

Harland & Wolff Welders FC (Belfast)	2-0	Glenavon FC (Lurgan)
Portstewart FC (Portstewart)	0-2	Portadown FC (Portadown)
Ballyclare Comrades FC (Ballyclare)	0-0 (aet)	Dungannon Swifts FC (Dungannon)

Dungannon Swifts FC won 5-4 on penalties.

Bangor FC (Bangor)	0-2	Crusaders FC (Belfast)
Carrick Rangers FC (Carrickfergus)	3-1 (aet)	Institute FC (Londonderry)
Cliftonville FC (Belfast)	1-2	Ballymena United FC (Ballymena)
Glentoran FC (Belfast)	4-1	Armagh City FC (Armagh)
Linfield FC (Belfast)	5-0	Warrenpoint Town FC (Warrenpoint)

Round 5

Harland & Wolff Welders FC (Belfast)	2-0	Derriaghy Cricket Club FC (Derriaghy)
Portstewart FC (Portstewart)	3-2	Dundela FC (Belfast)
PSNI FC (Belfast)	1-2 (aet)	Portadown FC (Portadown)
Tobermore United FC (Tobermore)	0-2	Linfield FC (Belfast)
Annagh United FC (Portadown)	1-3	Ballyclare Comrades FC (Ballyclare)
Armagh City FC (Armagh)	3-0	Newtowne FC (Limavady)
Ballymena United FC (Ballymena)	4-0	Crumlin Star FC (Belfast)
Bangor FC (Bangor)	4-0	Brantwood FC (Belfast)
Cliftonville FC (Belfast)	6-0	Ards Rangers FC (Newtownards)
Coleraine FC (Coleraine)	1-3	Warrenpoint Town FC (Warrenpoint)
Crusaders FC (Belfast)	6-0	Newington YC FC (Belfast)
Dungannon Swifts FC (Dungannon)	4-2 (aet)	Ballinamallard United FC (Ballinamallard)
Glentoran FC (Belfast)	2-0	Ards FC (Newtownards)
Institute FC (Londonderry)	5-1	Loughgall FC (Loughgall)
Larne FC (Larne)	1-2	Carrick Rangers FC (Carrickfergus)
Moyola Park FC (Castledawson)	2-3	Glenavon FC (Lurgan)

2015/2016

NIFL Premiership 2015/2016	Ballinamallard	Ballymena	Carrick Rang.	Cliftonville	Coleraine	Crusaders	Dungannon	Glenavon	Glentoran	Linfield	Portadown	Warrenpoint
Ballinamallard United	■	0-1	1-3	0-2	1-2	1-1	0-0	0-1	2-4	0-1	1-2	3-0
	■	4-2	1-2			0-1	1-1		1-0		1-0	2-0
Ballymena United	1-1	■	1-1	6-1	0-2	2-4	1-0	1-7	0-1	1-3	1-1	4-2
	1-2	■	1-0	2-2	0-2		2-4			0-4	0-2	3-1
Carrick Rangers	1-1	2-2	■	1-2	1-2	0-4	2-2	2-2	1-1	0-3	0-1	1-2
	2-1	0-2	■		2-1	4-3	1-0	1-5	1-2		1-2	0-1
Cliftonville	3-1	4-2	1-0	■	4-0	0-1	1-0	1-1	1-0	3-3	3-0	2-1
	2-0		3-3	■		1-3	1-3		3-1	0-2	0-2	1-0	1-1
Coleraine	2-1	2-1	2-1	0-0	■	1-1	1-0	0-2	1-0	1-3	4-0	2-0
	1-0			3-0	■	0-2	0-1	0-1	1-1	2-3		
Crusaders	5-0	3-2	5-0	2-2	3-1	■	4-0	1-0	3-0	3-0	1-2	1-0
		0-0		1-0	1-0	■		2-0	1-1	4-2	2-0	
Dungannon Swifts	2-0	2-0	1-2	0-1	0-3	1-2	■	1-2	2-4	0-1	3-1	5-1
	4-2	2-4	1-3	2-2			■	0-1	3-1		2-1	0-1
Glenavon	5-1	3-1	2-0	0-1	3-0	1-2	3-1	■	0-0	3-2	1-0	1-1
	1-0	1-1		3-3	3-0	0-1		■	1-3	0-1	4-1	
Glentoran	0-2	1-3	2-0	2-0	1-1	2-2	1-1	2-0	■	1-2	1-0	2-1
		2-0		0-2	1-0	0-1		0-1	■	0-4	2-1	0-4
Linfield	1-1	4-0	1-1	1-2	1-0	0-1	5-1	4-3	1-1	■	3-0	5-1
	2-1		2-0	4-0	3-0	2-0	6-0	1-1	3-0	■		
Portadown	0-3	3-2	3-2	0-1	1-2	1-3	3-3	2-2	5-3	2-0	■	2-1
	0-0	3-4	0-0		0-1	0-1	1-2		2-1		■	1-3
Warrenpoint Town	0-3	1-2	1-1	2-2	0-4	1-3	0-2	0-3	0-1	0-3	2-0	■
	3-0	4-1	1-1		3-0	1-1	1-1	1-3		2-6	2-0	■

Warrenpoint Town FC vs Ballinamallard United FC was awarded 3-0 to Ballinamallard as Warrenpoint had fielded an ineligible player. Ballinamallard United had originally won the game with a 1-0 scoreline.

	NIFL Premiership	**Pd**	**Wn**	**Dw**	**Ls**	**GF**	**GA**	**Pts**	
1.	CRUSADERS FC (BELFAST)	38	28	7	3	79	28	91	
2.	Linfield FC (Belfast)	38	26	5	7	91	35	83	
3.	Glenavon FC (Lurgan)	38	20	9	9	72	40	69	
4.	Cliftonville FC (Belfast)	38	18	10	10	58	53	64	POQ
5.	Coleraine FC (Coleraine)	38	18	4	16	47	46	58	PO
6.	Glentoran FC (Belfast)	38	15	7	16	46	55	52	PO
7.	Dungannon Swifts FC (Dungannon)	38	12	7	19	51	66	43	
8.	Ballymena United FC (Ballymena)	38	11	7	20	57	81	40	
9.	Portadown FC (Portadown)	38	11	5	22	43	67	38	
10.	Carrick Rangers FC (Carrickfergus)	38	8	11	19	43	68	35	
11.	Ballinamallard United FC (Ballinamallard)	38	9	7	22	39	59	34	PO
12.	Warrenpoint Town FC (Warrenpoint)	38	9	7	22	45	73	34	R
		456	185	86	185	671	671	641	

UEFA Europa League play-offs

A two match play-off process to decide qualification for the UEFA Europa League was introduced from this season. The teams placed 3rd to 6th enter play-offs for a place in the initial stages of the Europa League place. Higher-placed qualifiers are given home advantage in the semi-finals of the play-offs with the two winners then meeting in the final. Glenavon FC, who finished in 3rd place, qualified outright for Europa League as winners of the Irish Cup. The play-offs would therefore have been played between team placed 4th and 7th placed. However, Dungannon Swifts FC, who finished in seventh place were ineligible for the Europa League play-offs as they did not apply for a UEFA licence. Therefore, only one semi-final match was played and 4th-placed Cliftonville FC were given a bye to the final.

Coleraine FC (Coleraine)	1-2	Glentoran FC (Belfast)
Cliftonville FC (Belfast)	3-2	Glentoran FC (Belfast)

NIFL Premiership Promotion/Relegation play-off

Institute FC (Londonderry)　　　　1-2, 3-3　　　Ballinamallard United FC (Ballinamallard)
Ballinamallard United FC won 5-4 on aggregate to retain their NIFL Premiership status.

Top Goalscorers 2015-16

1)	Paul HEATLEY	(Crusaders FC)	22
	Andrew WATERWORTH	(Linfield FC)	22
3)	Aaron BURNS	(Linfield FC)	19
4	Curtis ALLEN	(Glentoran FC)	18
	Jordan OWENS	(Crusaders FC)	18

NIFL Championship 1 2015/2016	Annagh	Ards	Armagh	Ballyclare	Bangor	Dergview	Donegal Celtic	Harland & Wolff	Institute	Knockbreda	Larne	Lisburn	Loughgall	Lurgan
Annagh United		1-3	2-1	1-1	1-3	3-3	2-3	0-5	0-2	1-2	0-5	1-2	3-2	2-3
Ards	4-0		1-0	2-1	2-1	0-2	2-1	3-3	0-2	2-0	2-2	5-2	3-0	1-1
Armagh City	1-1	4-3		4-0	3-4	3-1	2-2	1-2	3-1	2-1	0-1	3-0	4-0	6-0
Ballyclare Comrades	2-2	0-2	2-1		3-1	1-1	3-1	3-3	1-0	1-3	3-2	4-1	1-1	1-3
Bangor	1-3	2-4	2-0	0-1		2-0	5-0	1-2	1-0	2-2	2-1	3-0	2-2	0-3
Dergview	4-4	1-0	0-1	0-4	1-2		2-2	1-1	0-0	1-0	3-0	1-1	2-4	3-1
Donegal Celtic	0-1	2-3	1-3	0-4	1-3	2-6		1-2	1-4	1-2	1-6	1-4	0-1	1-2
Harland & Wolff Welders	3-0	3-4	1-1	3-0	1-0	3-0	6-2		3-0	1-0	2-1	1-0	2-0	0-2
Institute	0-1	1-2	2-0	1-1	0-0	0-0	3-1	2-0		4-0	1-1	3-0	2-0	3-0
Knockbreda	3-3	2-0	1-3	2-2	1-0	3-0	3-3	1-0	1-0		3-0	2-2	2-2	0-0
Larne	2-0	1-6	4-4	0-0	1-1	3-2	5-0	2-1	1-3	0-3		6-1	2-2	1-0
Lisburn Distillery	0-3	0-3	1-9	1-1	2-2	0-3	0-3	0-4	0-3	0-7			1-5	0-4
Loughgall	1-0	2-0	3-3	3-2	4-3	0-2	3-1	2-2	1-0	0-7	3-7	3-0		0-1
Lurgan Celtic	1-2	1-2	0-2	2-2	2-1	0-2	3-3	1-1	2-2	2-1	2-3	2-0	2-1	

	NIFL Championship 1	Pd	Wn	Dw	Ls	GF	GA	Pts	
1.	Ards FC (Newtownards)	26	17	3	6	59	35	54	P
2.	Harland & Wolff Welders	26	15	6	5	54	28	51	
3.	Armagh City FC (Armagh)	26	13	5	8	64	36	44	
4.	Knockbreda FC (Belfast)	26	12	7	7	48	32	43	
5.	Institute FC (Londonderry)	26	12	6	8	40	20	42	PO
6.	Larne FC (Larne)	26	12	6	8	64	45	42	
7.	Lurgan Celtic FC (Lurgan)	26	11	6	9	40	40	39	
8.	Ballyclare Comrades FC (Ballyclare)	26	9	10	7	44	40	37	
9.	Loughgall FC (Loughgall)	26	10	6	10	45	54	36	
10.	Bangor FC (Bangor)	26	10	5	11	44	40	35	R
11.	Dergview FC (Castlederg)	26	9	8	9	41	40	35	
12.	Annagh United FC (Portadown)	26	7	6	13	37	57	27	
13.	Donegal Celtic FC (Belfast)	26	2	4	20	34	80	10	R
14.	Lisburn Distillery FC (Lisburn)	26	2	4	20	18	85	10	R
		364	141	82	141	632	632	505	

Harland & Wolff Welders, Armagh City FC and Knockbreda FC did not apply for a Promotion Licence and were therefore ineligible to enter the promotion play-off. Institute FC therefore qualified for the promotion play-off against Ballinamallard United FC, the 11th-placed Premiership club.

Bangor FC were demoted to the third tier as their application a second tier Championship Licence was refused. PSNI FC were automatically promoted to replace Bangor FC in the second tier.

Limavady United FC (in Championship 2) were refused a second tier Championship Licence. As a result, Annagh United FC were reprieved from relegation.

At the end of the season, NIFL Championship 1 gained senior status and was renamed the NIFL Championship.

NIFL Championship 2 2015/2016	Banbridge Town	Coagh United	Dollingstown	Dundela	Glebe Rangers	Limavady United	Moyola Park	Newington YC	Portstewart	PSNI	Queen's University	Sport & Leisure	Tobermore United	Wakehurst
Banbridge Town	■	1-2	1-1	2-0	0-1	2-0	0-3	1-1	2-0	1-1	0-1	0-6	3-4	1-0
Coagh United	1-1	■	2-1	2-3	0-0	2-5	1-3	1-1	1-0	1-0	1-4	0-1	0-1	1-0
Dollingstown	1-5	3-1	■	4-0	2-2	0-1	1-0	3-3	3-0	1-2	1-2	2-2	0-0	4-2
Dundela	0-1	3-1	2-3	■	3-2	0-2	0-3	1-0	3-1	0-1	1-1	2-5	4-0	3-2
Glebe Rangers	1-0	3-2	3-4	3-1	■	0-4	1-3	1-1	1-3	1-2	1-0	0-4	2-1	2-1
Limavady United	2-2	4-1	3-1	2-0	1-1	■	1-0	4-0	3-1	4-2	1-1	2-2	2-0	5-1
Moyola Park	0-0	3-0	6-1	0-0	1-0	0-4	■	0-3	2-0	0-1	1-1	1-1	2-2	4-1
Newington YC	0-0	3-1	5-2	0-1	4-1	0-4	2-0	■	2-0	1-1	0-1	1-2	2-3	1-0
Portstewart	1-3	0-2	2-2	1-3	3-1	2-3	3-0	3-4	■	0-3	2-1	1-1	2-5	2-2
PSNI	3-3	3-0	3-1	3-2	1-0	3-0	7-0	3-0	5-0	■	4-0	4-2	2-0	2-0
Queen's University	1-1	3-2	0-2	0-0	0-3	0-2	3-2	1-0	4-5	4-0	■	1-2	0-2	3-1
Sport & Leisure Swifts	0-2	4-0	1-1	1-3	3-1	4-1	1-2	1-1	1-0	0-0	0-0	■	0-2	7-1
Tobermore United	3-1	2-1	2-0	5-0	0-1	1-1	0-1	2-1	1-0	1-1	1-0	0-4	■	0-1
Wakehurst	1-2	2-2	1-2	2-3	2-2	1-5	0-3	1-2	0-2	1-2	2-3	0-4	0-0	■

	NIFL Championship 2	Pd	Wn	Dw	Ls	GF	GA	Pts	
1.	Limavady United FC (Limavady)	26	18	5	3	66	27	59	P
2.	PSNI FC (Belfast)	26	18	5	3	59	23	59	P
3.	Sport & Leisure Swifts FC (Belfast)	26	13	8	5	59	28	47	
4.	Tobermore United FC (Tobermore)	26	13	5	8	38	31	44	
5.	Moyola Park FC (Castledawson)	26	12	5	9	40	34	41	
6.	Banbridge Town FC (Banbridge)	26	9	9	8	35	34	36	
7.	Queen's University FC (Belfast)	26	10	6	10	35	37	36	
8.	Dundela FC (Belfast)	26	11	3	12	38	47	36	
9.	Newington YC FC (Belfast)	26	9	7	10	38	38	34	
10.	Dollingstown FC (Dollingstown)	26	9	7	10	46	51	34	R
11.	Glebe Rangers FC (Ballymoney)	26	9	5	12	34	46	32	R
12.	Coagh United FC (Coagh)	26	6	4	16	28	54	22	R
13.	Portstewart FC (Portstewart)	26	6	3	17	34	58	21	R
14.	Wakehurst FC (Castledawson)	26	1	4	21	25	67	7	R
		364	144	76	144	575	575	508	

At the end of the season, the NIFL Championship 2 was renamed to the NIFL Premier Intermediate League after the NIFL Championship 1 gained senior status.

IRISH CUP FINAL (Windsor Park, Belfast – 07/05/2016 – 11,500)

GLENAVON FC (LURGAN)   2-0   Linfield FC (Belfast)
Braniff 45', Hall 48'   *(1-0)*

Glenavon: J. Tuffey, S. Kelly, R. Marshall, C. Dillon, C. Martyn (M. Sykes 68'), M. Patton, A. Kilmartin, A. Hall, J. Cooper (D. Kearns 90+1'), K. Braniff, E. Bradley (G. Hamilton 85').

Linfield: G. Deane, S. Ward, R. Gaynor, M. Haughey, M. Clarke (K. Millar 56'), J. Mulgrew, S. Lowry, J. Callacher (N. Quinn 77'), A. Waterworth, Aaron Burns, P. Smyth.

Semi-finals

Glenavon FC (Lurgan)	4-3	Crusaders FC (Belfast)
Linfield FC (Belfast)	3-0	Lurgan Celtic FC (Lurgan)

Quarter-finals

Crusaders FC (Belfast)	3-0	Carrick Rangers FC (Carrickfergus)
Cliftonville FC (Belfast)	0-3	Linfield FC (Belfast)
Glenavon FC (Lurgan)	2-1	Loughgall FC (Loughgall)
Portadown FC (Portadown)	2-3	Lurgan Celtic FC (Lurgan)

Round 6

Loughgall FC (Loughgall)	2-0	PSNI FC (Belfast)
Lurgan Celtic FC (Lurgan)	1-0	Knockbreda FC (Belfast)
Cliftonville FC (Belfast)	4-0	Sport & Leisure Swifts FC (Belfast)
Dungannon Swifts FC (Dungannon)	1-3	Crusaders FC (Belfast)
Glentoran FC (Belfast)	1-4	Glenavon FC (Lurgan)
Linfield FC (Belfast)	7-0	Armagh City FC (Armagh)
Portadown FC (Portadown)	3-1	Coleraine FC (Coleraine)
Carrick Rangers FC (Carrickfergus)	1-0	Crumlin Star FC (Belfast)

Round 5

Banbridge Town FC (Banbridge)	0-2	Carrick Rangers FC (Carrickfergus)
Crumlin Star FC (Belfast)	3-2	Oxford United Stars FC (Derry)
Harland & Wolff Welders FC (Belfast)	1-4	Glenavon FC (Lurgan)
Loughgall FC (Loughgall)	5-2	Larne FC (Larne)
Lurgan Celtic FC (Lurgan)	2-1	Bangor FC (Bangor)
Sport & Leisure Swifts FC (Belfast)	3-2 (aet)	Institute FC (Londonderry)
Tobermore United FC (Tobermore)	0-2	PSNI FC (Belfast)
Armagh City FC (Armagh)	2-2 (aet)	Portstewart FC (Portstewart)

Armagh City FC won 4-1 on penalties.

Cliftonville FC (Belfast)	2-0	Immaculata FC (Belfast)
Coleraine FC (Coleraine)	2-2 (aet)	Ballinamallard United FC (Ballinamallard)

Coleraine FC (Coleraine) won 4-2 on penalties.

Crusaders FC (Belfast)	3-0	Rathfriland Rangers FC (Rathfriland)
Dungannon Swifts FC (Dungannon)	4-3	Warrenpoint Town FC (Warrenpoint)
Linfield FC (Belfast)	2-1 (aet)	Ballymena United FC (Ballymena)
Portadown FC (Portadown)	6-1	Wakehurst FC (Castledawson)
Annagh United FC (Portadown)	1-5	Knockbreda FC (Belfast)
Glentoran FC (Belfast)	4-1	Ards FC (Newtownards)

2016/2017

NIFL Premiership 2016/2017	Ards	Ballinamallard	Ballymena	Carrick Rangers	Cliftonville	Coleraine	Crusaders	Dungannon	Glenavon	Glentoran	Linfield	Portadown
Ards		3-3	2-4	3-1	2-2	1-2	0-1	3-3	0-1	2-0	0-2	1-0
Ards		2-0	4-2	0-4			2-4	4-1	1-0	1-3		3-2
Ballinamallard United	2-1		0-1	1-3	1-2	0-3	0-1	2-0	1-1	2-1	1-2	1-2
Ballinamallard United	2-3		1-2	4-1	1-0	1-2		1-4		3-0	1-2	1-0
Ballymena United	3-4	4-0		2-0	3-2	2-0	2-1	1-4	3-3	4-1	1-4	2-0
Ballymena United				3-1	4-1	1-1	3-0	3-2	3-4	2-4	0-2	3-0
Carrick Rangers	1-1	3-3	1-4		0-3	2-0	1-4	0-3	0-0	1-2	0-2	1-1
Carrick Rangers	2-2	1-2						0-1	0-0	1-2	0-2	3-2
Cliftonville	2-0	1-0	2-0	1-0		1-0	0-4	1-2	3-0	2-0	2-1	1-0
Cliftonville	2-1		2-1	0-0		0-0	2-3		1-3	1-1	1-3	3-0
Coleraine	1-1	3-1	2-2	2-0	0-1		1-1	2-2	2-2	4-1	1-1	*3-0*
Coleraine	3-1		1-1	2-0	2-0		1-0	2-1	1-1	2-0	1-5	4-2
Crusaders	1-0	5-1	6-0	3-1	4-3	1-0		3-1	3-1	2-2	0-0	2-1
Crusaders		3-1	2-1	3-0	1-0	3-2			6-1		1-2	
Dungannon Swifts	1-2	3-2	2-2	3-1	1-1	4-0	0-1		1-1	0-1	0-4	6-0
Dungannon Swifts	3-3	2-2		4-0	2-2		1-2			2-1	1-4	2-0
Glenavon	1-0	0-1	5-0	4-0	3-2	1-0	3-3	0-1		1-1	2-2	1-0
Glenavon		3-0	3-0		2-2	1-2	0-1	2-0			1-2	
Glentoran	1-0	1-1	2-3	0-1	2-1	0-1	1-3	1-0	2-2		1-2	0-0
Glentoran	1-1	0-1		1-0			0-3	2-2	0-0		0-1	3-0
Linfield	4-0	4-0	2-1	3-0	1-2	1-1	0-0	1-1	4-0	1-1		4-1
Linfield	5-1		2-0		2-0	0-1	1-0		3-0			1-1
Portadown	*0-3*	2-1	0-2	4-0	0-3	0-1	0-1	2-0	*3-0*	0-1	0-5	
Portadown	0-3	1-0		2-1			1-1	0-1	1-2	0-5		

Coleraine FC vs Portadown FC was awarded 3-0 to Coleraine as Portadown forfeited the game because they were suspended from all football activity for non-payment of a fine.

Portadown FC vs Ards FC was subsequently awarded 3-0 to Ards after Portadown fielded a suspended player. The original result of the game was Portadown FC 3-1 Ards FC.

Portadown FC vs Glenavon FC was subsequently awarded 3-0 to Portadown after Glenavon fielded a suspended player. The original result of the game was a 2-2 draw.

	NIFL Premiership	Pd	Wn	Dw	Ls	GF	GA	Pts	
1.	LINFIELD FC (BELFAST)	38	27	8	3	87	24	89	
2.	Crusaders FC (Belfast)	38	27	6	5	83	36	87	
3.	Coleraine FC (Coleraine)	38	18	11	9	56	42	65	
4.	Ballymena United FC (Ballymena)	38	18	5	15	75	73	59	POQ
5.	Cliftonville FC (Belfast)	38	17	7	14	55	50	58	PO
6.	Glenavon FC (Lurgan)	38	13	13	12	55	55	52	PO
7.	Dungannon Swifts FC (Dungannon)	38	14	10	14	67	59	52	PO
8.	Ards FC (Newtownards)	38	13	8	17	61	70	47	
9.	Glentoran FC (Belfast)	38	12	10	16	45	53	46	
10.	Ballinamallard United FC (Ballinamallard)	38	10	5	23	45	72	35	
11.	Carrick Rangers FC (Carrickfergus)	38	5	7	26	31	79	22	PO
12.	Portadown FC (Portadown)	38	7	4	27	28	75	13	R-12
		456	181	94	181	688	688	625	(-12)

Portadown FC had 12 points deducted following a breach of the player registration regulations.

UEFA Europa League play-offs

As Linfield FC won an NIFL Premiership and Irish Cup double, 3rd placed Coleraine FC automatically entered the Europa League first qualifying round. The teams who finished in 4th to 7th place then played-off for a further qualifying round place.

Ballymena United FC (Ballymena)	5-2	Dungannon Swifts FC (Dungannon)
Cliftonville FC (Belfast)	3-5	Glenavon FC (Lurgan)

Ballymena United FC (Ballymena)	2-1	Glenavon FC (Lurgan)

Ballymena United FC entered the Europa League first qualifying round

NIFL Premiership play-offs

Ballyclare Comrades FC (Ballyclare)	1-0, 1-3	Institute FC (Londonderry)

Institute FC (Londonderry)	1-1, 1-4	Carrick Rangers FC (Carrickfergus)

Carrick Rangers won 5-2 on aggregate to retain their NIFL Premiership status.

Top goalscorers 2016-17

1)	Andrew MITCHELL	(Dungannon Swifts FC)	25
2)	Paul HEATLEY	(Crusaders FC)	21
3)	Andrew WATERWORTH	(Linfield FC)	20
	Jordan OWENS	(Crusaders FC)	20
5)	Cathair FRIEL	(Ballymena United FC)	17

NIFL Championship 2016/2017	Annagh	Armagh	Ballyclare	Dergview	Harland & Wolff	Institute	Knockbreda	Larne	Loughgall	Lurgan	PSNI	Warrenpoint
Annagh United		3-0	0-4	0-8	1-4	2-2	0-7	0-4	0-5	2-4	0-0	2-2
		4-4			1-2		1-2	3-1		1-1		
Armagh City	4-2		3-1	1-3	2-2	1-4	4-0	1-0	2-3	1-3	0-1	2-1
	0-0				0-3		1-2	1-1		3-0		
Ballyclare Comrades	3-1	2-0		5-1	0-2	2-2	1-3	3-2	5-2	2-1	3-2	2-2
				2-1		2-4			1-0		0-3	1-0
Dergview	9-0	4-0	0-2		0-3	1-1	2-1	2-0	6-2	3-4	0-0	2-3
			1-0			1-5		2-0			1-2	2-0
Harland & Wolff Welders	1-1	3-0	0-1	1-1		0-2	0-2	3-2	1-1	1-0	2-2	1-2
	2-0	2-1				0-1	1-1		4-1			
Institute	5-0	2-0	1-1	1-1	3-1		3-1	1-1	2-0	2-1	4-0	0-1
			2-2	2-1				1-0		1-1	0-1	
Knockbreda	1-2	1-1	0-5	1-2	0-2	1-1		1-1	0-2	4-2	3-1	1-2
	6-1	1-0		1-0				4-0		1-2		
Larne	4-1	2-1	2-3	3-2	2-1	6-0	3-1		1-4	2-0	2-2	0-1
	2-0	0-1			2-3		2-1		3-0			
Loughgall	7-0	3-1	2-1	0-4	3-0	1-2	2-3	1-1		0-2	3-0	2-2
		4-2	1-0		0-4					2-0		1-4
Lurgan Celtic	3-1	0-2	3-1	3-3	2-3	4-3	3-3	2-0	2-0		2-5	2-6
	0-2	0-2			2-3		3-1	2-0				
PSNI	3-1	1-1	4-4	1-1	3-1	1-0	0-1	1-1	4-2	3-0		1-0
		1-0	4-1		0-1			1-0				1-3
Warrenpoint Town	7-0	1-1	3-3	3-1	1-0	2-1	3-1	4-1	4-1	4-2	3-0	
		4-0	4-1		3-2			1-0		1-1		

	NIFL Championship	Pd	Wn	Dw	Ls	GF	GA	Pts	
1.	Warrenpoint Town FC (Warrenpoint)	32	22	6	4	78	35	72	P
2.	Institute FC (Londonderry)	32	16	9	7	64	39	57	PO
3.	Ballyclare Comrades FC (Ballyclare)	32	15	6	11	64	56	51	PO
4.	PSNI FC (Belfast)	32	13	10	9	49	44	49	
5.	Dergview FC (Castlederg)	32	12	6	14	67	55	42	
6.	Loughgall FC (Loughgall)	32	12	3	17	54	59	39	
7.	Harland & Wolff Welders FC (Belfast)	32	15	6	11	52	41	51	
8.	Knockbreda FC (Belfast)	32	14	4	14	56	52	46	
9.	Larne FC (Larne)	32	11	7	14	52	51	40	
10.	Lurgan Celtic FC (Lurgan)	32	12	3	17	56	71	39	
11.	Armagh City FC (Armagh)	32	9	7	16	41	55	34	POR
12.	Annagh United FC (Portadown)	32	4	7	21	32	107	19	R
		384	155	74	155	665	665	539	

Teams played each other twice (22 matches), before the league split into two groups (the top six and the bottom six) for the last ten matches.

NIFL Championship Promotion/Relegation play-off

Newry City AFC (Newry) 4-0, 3-1 Armagh City FC (Armagh)
Newry City won 7-1 on aggregate and were promoted to the NIFL Championship.
Armagh City FC were relegated to the NIFL Premier Intermediate League.

Promoted to NIFL Championship: Limavady United FC (Limavady), Newry AFC (Newry)

IRISH CUP FINAL (Windsor Park, Belfast – 06/05/2017 – 12,500)

Coleraine FC (Coleraine) 0-3 LINFIELD FC (BELFAST)
A. Waterworth 29', 33', 87'

Coleraine: C. Johns, D. Ogilby, G. McConaghie, A. Mullan, L. Kane, B. Lyons, C. Harkin, D. McCauley, J. McLaughlin (I. Parkhill 57'), E. Bradley, J. McGonigle (J. Allan 82').
Linfield: R. Carroll, M. Haughey, M. Stafford, N. Quinn, J. Mulgrew, S. Lowry, J. Callacher, R. Clarke, A. Waterworth, Aaron Burns (C. Stewart 82'), P. Smyth.

Semi-finals

Linfield FC (Belfast)	1-0	Dungannon Swifts FC (Dungannon)
Coleraine FC (Coleraine)	2-1	Glenavon FC (Lurgan)

Quarter-finals

Ballymena United FC (Ballymena)	0-4	Coleraine FC (Coleraine)
Crusaders FC (Belfast)	0-2	Linfield FC (Belfast)
Dungannon Swifts FC (Dungannon)	2-1 (aet)	Warrenpoint Town FC (Warrenpoint)
Portadown FC (Portadown)	0-5	Glenavon FC (Lurgan)

Round 6

Armagh City FC (Armagh)	0-2	Glenavon FC (Lurgan)
Coleraine FC (Coleraine)	1-0	Tobermore United FC (Tobermore)
Crusaders FC (Belfast)	2-0	PSNI FC (Belfast)
Dungannon Swifts FC (Dungannon)	4-1	Dollingstown FC (Dollingstown)
Harland & Wolff Welders FC (Belfast)	1-3	Ballymena United FC (Ballymena)
Institute FC (Londonderry)	0-2	Linfield FC (Belfast)
Loughgall FC (Loughgall)	1-2	Portadown FC (Portadown)
Warrenpoint Town FC (Warrenpoint)	5-0	Crewe United FC (Glenavy)

Round 5

Annagh United FC (Portadown)	0-2	Tobermore United FC (Tobermore)
Armagh City FC (Armagh)	2-1	Trojans FC (Derry)
Ballyclare Comrades FC (Ballyclare)	2-4	Institute FC (Londonderry)
Ballymena United FC (Ballymena)	1-1 (aet)	Cliftonville FC (Belfast)
Ballymena United FC (Ballymena) won 4-3 on penalties.		
Coleraine FC (Coleraine)	5-1	Carrick Rangers FC (Carrickfergus)
Crusaders FC (Belfast)	2-0	Ards FC (Newtownards)
Dungannon Swifts FC (Dungannon)	3-0	Dergview FC (Castlederg)
Glenavon FC (Lurgan)	4-1	Portstewart FC (Portstewart)
Glentoran FC (Belfast)	1-2 (aet)	Linfield FC (Belfast)
Harland & Wolff Welders FC (Belfast)	1-0	Lurgan Celtic FC (Lurgan)
Knockbreda FC (Belfast)	1-2	Crewe United FC (Glenavy)
Larne FC (Larne)	1-2	Portadown FC (Portadown)
Loughgall FC (Loughgall)	3-0	Fivemiletown United FC (Fivemiletown)
PSNI FC (Belfast)	2-1	Lisburn Distillery FC (Lisburn)
Richhill AFC (Richhill)	1-4	Dollingstown FC (Dollingstown)
Warrenpoint Town FC (Warrenpoint)	0-0 (aet)	Ballinamallard United FC (Ballinamallard)
Warrenpoint Town FC (Warrenpoint) won 5-4 on penalties.		

2017/2018

NIFL Premiership 2017/2018	Ards	Ballinamallard	Ballymena	Carrick Rangers	Cliftonville	Coleraine	Crusaders	Dungannon	Glenavon	Glentoran	Linfield	Warrenpoint
Ards		2-1	1-0	1-0	0-1	0-3	2-4	0-1	0-2	0-1	0-2	2-1
		1-1	1-0	0-4		1-3		3-4	1-6	1-4	0-3	4-2
Ballinamallard United	0-2		1-3	2-0	1-1	0-2	1-5	0-1	0-3	1-2	0-6	1-1
	0-4			2-1	6-4	2-5	0-3	2-2		2-2	2-2	2-0
Ballymena United	6-3	2-1		3-1	1-0	0-2	1-4	2-1	1-6	1-3	2-1	3-3
		2-0		3-0	0-3	0-2	1-2		3-1		2-2	1-3
Carrick Rangers	0-1	2-0	1-1		1-2	1-3	0-3	2-1	0-2	1-1	0-1	0-2
	0-1	2-2			0-1			1-0	1-2	1-2		1-2
Cliftonville	6-3	5-0	1-0	3-0		1-2	1-2	2-1	1-1	1-0	3-2	2-0
	3-0		1-2			0-0	3-1	3-0	1-3		1-2	
Coleraine	4-1	2-1	1-1	3-0	2-0		1-1	1-0	4-2	3-0	2-1	2-1
			1-0	3-2	2-1		3-3		1-1		2-2	1-0
Crusaders	0-0	2-0	2-1	7-1	2-0	1-2		1-1	2-3	1-0	2-1	5-0
	1-0		3-1	6-0	1-1	1-1		3-0	1-1	4-2	2-0	
Dungannon Swifts	0-0	2-0	2-1	4-0	0-4	1-3	0-4		0-3	0-2	0-4	2-1
	1-0	2-0	2-3	2-0		0-1			3-2	0-0		4-2
Glenavon	3-0	6-2	4-0	2-0	3-1	2-2	3-4	1-1		2-2	0-1	1-0
			0-0		1-1	0-0	1-6			2-2	2-3	3-3
Glentoran	0-2	2-1	1-1	1-1	0-2	0-0	0-3	2-0	1-3		2-1	2-0
	1-2	1-3	1-2	1-2	1-0	0-2		4-2				5-0
Linfield	2-0	4-0	1-0	2-0	2-0	2-1	2-5	1-0	2-3	1-0		3-3
		2-0	2-0	1-2	2-2	1-2	0-0	0-2	1-1			
Warrenpoint Town	1-0	2-1	1-3	2-2	1-3	0-2	2-3	1-2	2-3	2-3	1-4	
	3-3	1-0		2-3	1-3		1-4	3-0		1-0	1-3	

	NIFL Premiership	Pd	Wn	Dw	Ls	GF	GA	Pts	
1.	CRUSADERS FC (BELFAST)	38	28	7	3	106	38	91	
2.	Coleraine FC (Coleraine)	38	26	11	1	76	31	89	
3.	Glenavon FC (Lurgan)	38	19	12	7	85	52	69	
4.	Linfield FC (Belfast)	38	20	7	11	72	45	67	PO
5.	Cliftonville FC (Belfast)	38	20	5	13	68	45	65	POQ
6.	Ballymena United FC (Ballymena)	38	14	6	18	53	65	48	PO
7.	Glentoran FC (Belfast)	38	14	9	15	52	52	51	PO
8.	Dungannon Swifts FC (Dungannon)	38	13	6	19	42	62	45	
9.	Ards FC (Newtownards)	38	12	4	22	42	74	40	
10.	Warrenpoint Town FC (Warrenpoint)	38	8	6	24	52	86	30	
11.	Carrick Rangers FC (Carrickfergus)	38	6	5	27	31	78	23	POR
12.	Ballinamallard United FC (Ballinamallard)	38	5	8	25	38	89	23	R
		456	185	86	185	717	717	641	

UEFA Europa League play-offs

Coleraine FC, who finished in 2nd place, also won the Irish Cup. Therefore, their original runners-up berth in the Europa League first qualifying round was passed on to 3rd placed Glenavon FC. As a result, the four teams finishing 4th-7th took part in Europa League play-offs to decide which one team would qualify for the 2018-19 UEFA Europa League first qualifying round.

Linfield FC (Belfast)	3-4	Glentoran FC (Belfast)
Cliftonville FC (Belfast)	4-0	Ballymena United FC (Ballymena)
Cliftonville FC (Belfast)	3-2	Glentoran FC (Belfast)

Cliftonville FC entered the Europa League first qualifying round

NIFL Premiership play-offs

Harland and Wolff Welders did not apply for a Premiership licence so Newry City AFC advanced directly to the play-off.

Newry City AFC (Newry)   3-2, 3-1   Carrick Rangers FC (Carrickfergus)

Newry City won 6-3 on aggregate and were promoted to the NIFL Premiership.
Carrick Rangers FC were relegated into the NIFL Championship.

Top goalscorers 2017-18

1)	Joe GORMLEY	(Cliftonville FC)	24
2)	Gavin WHYTE	(Crusaders FC)	22
3)	Curtis ALLEN	(Glentoran FC)	20
4)	Paul HEATLEY	(Crusaders FC)	19
	Jay DONNELLY	(Cliftonville FC)	19

NIFL Championship 2017/2018	Ballyclare	Dergview	Harland & Wolff	Institute	Knockbreda	Larne	Limavady	Loughgall	Lurgan	Newry	Portadown	PSNI
Ballyclare Comrades	■	1-1	4-3	2-4	2-3	0-2	2-1	2-1	4-0	0-3	1-0	0-3
	■	0-2	2-4				2-1		0-3	1-0		
Dergview	1-1	■	1-1	1-2	2-2	2-2	0-1	1-5	3-2	2-2	3-1	0-1
		■			1-1	1-0	3-2		8-0			2-1
Harland & Wolff Welders	1-0	5-1	■	3-2	0-3	6-1	3-2	2-0	1-0	0-0	3-2	2-1
	2-1		■		1-2			1-0		0-3	1-3	
Institute	2-1	2-0	2-1	■	2-1	3-0	2-0	3-0	1-1	0-0	2-2	1-0
	1-0		1-2	■				3-0		0-1	2-1	
Knockbreda	1-2	0-0	1-2	0-1	■	1-3	2-1	0-3	4-2	0-1	1-2	3-0
		1-4			■	3-3	6-1		7-0			2-2
Larne	1-1	3-0	1-1	0-1	3-1	■	2-1	1-1	2-2	3-2	0-3	2-1
	3-0				8-0	■	2-1		2-0			1-1
Limavady United	3-5	1-0	3-1	2-2	3-1	1-1	■	3-1	2-3	1-3	1-1	2-1
		0-0			2-2	1-0	■		6-0			0-0
Loughgall	2-1	2-0	1-2	3-1	0-1	2-1	2-1	■	3-2	0-4	1-4	2-1
	3-5		3-1	1-3				■		1-1	1-2	
Lurgan Celtic	0-1	1-3	2-2	0-1	1-1	2-2	3-3	1-2	■	2-1	1-1	3-0
		1-4			1-1	0-5	0-3		■			2-4
Newry City	4-1	1-0	1-1	0-1	1-0	3-1	2-2	1-0	5-0	■	1-4	1-2
	2-1		0-3	3-1				1-0		■	0-0	
Portadown	1-2	7-0	0-0	1-2	0-1	2-2	2-1	3-0	6-0	1-4	■	3-0
	2-0		0-0	1-1				2-1		2-1	■	
PSNI	5-0	5-2	1-1	2-3	0-0	1-1	4-1	1-2	2-0	0-3	1-1	■
		3-2			1-0	2-2	3-0		11-1			■

	NIFL Championship	**Pd**	**Wn**	**Dw**	**Ls**	**GF**	**GA**	**Pts**	
1.	Institute FC (Londonderry)	32	21	5	6	55	36	68	P
2.	Newry City AFC (Newry)	32	17	8	7	58	31	59	POP
3.	Harland & Wolff Welders FC (Belfast)	32	16	8	8	54	42	56	
4.	Portadown FC (Portadown)	32	14	9	9	61	36	51	
5.	Ballyclare Comrades FC (Ballyclare)	32	15	3	14	56	52	48	
6.	Loughgall FC (Loughgall)	32	12	2	18	45	59	38	
7.	Larne FC (Larne)	32	12	11	9	59	47	47	
8.	PSNI FC (Belfast)	32	11	8	13	55	50	41	
9.	Limavady United FC (Limavady)	32	10	7	15	52	58	37	
10.	Knockbreda FC (Belfast)	32	9	9	14	50	54	36	
11.	Dergview FC (Castlederg)	32	9	9	14	49	59	36	PO
12.	Lurgan Celtic FC (Lurgan)	32	3	7	22	32	102	16	R
		384	149	86	149	626	626	533	

Promoted to NIFL Championship: Dundela FC (Belfast)

NIFL Championship Promotion/Relegation play-off

Queen's University FC (Belfast)   0-1, 1-3   Dergview FC (Castlederg)

Dergiew FC won 4-1 on aggregate to retain their place in the NIFL Championship.

IRISH CUP FINAL (Windsor Park, Belfast – 05/05/2018 – 12,012)

Cliftonville FC (Belfast)   1-3   COLERAINE FC (COLERAINE)

Donnelly 55'   *McCauley 50', Burns 78', Bradley 90+4'*

Cliftonville: Neeson, Ives (Grimes 85'), Breen (Harkin 85'), Harney, Curran (Garrett 73'), Bagnall, Gormley, J. Donnelly, Cosgrove, McDonald, Donnelly.

Coleraine: Johns, Mullan, Harkin, McCauley (Smith 86'), Bradley, McConaghie, Lyons, O'Donnell, Traynor, McGonigle (Burns 61'), Dooley (Parkhill 32').

Semi-finals

Cliftonville FC (Belfast)	4-1	Loughgall FC (Loughgall)
Coleraine FC (Coleraine)	3-1	Larne FC (Larne)

Quarter-finals

Ballymena United FC (Ballymena)	1-2	Larne FC (Larne)
Coleraine FC (Coleraine)	1-0	Glentoran FC (Belfast)
Glenavon FC (Lurgan)	1-2	Loughgall FC (Loughgall)
Linfield FC (Belfast)	0-1	Cliftonville FC (Belfast)

Round 6

Linfield FC (Belfast)	1-0	Newry City AFC (Newry)
Cliftonville FC (Belfast)	4-1	Crusaders FC (Belfast)
Loughgall FC (Loughgall)	2-1	Ards FC (Newtownards)
Ballyclare Comrades FC (Ballyclare)	0-4	Glentoran FC (Belfast)
Coleraine FC (Coleraine)	4-0	Institute FC (Londonderry)
Ballymena United FC (Ballymena)	2-2 (aet)	Ballinamallard United FC (Ballinamallard)

Ballymena United FC won 4-3 on penalties.

Larne FC (Larne)	6-1	Dundela FC (Belfast)
Glenavon FC (Lurgan)	3-0	Dungannon Swifts FC (Dungannon)

Round 5

Knockbreda FC (Belfast)	0-2	Institute FC (Londonderry)
Queen's University FC (Belfast)	0-1	Dundela FC (Belfast)
Lurgan Celtic FC (Lurgan)	1-2	Glentoran FC (Belfast)
Larne FC (Larne)	3-0	Dergview FC (Castlederg)
Carrick Rangers FC (Carrickfergus)	1-3 (aet)	Glenavon FC (Lurgan)
Coleraine FC (Coleraine)	7-0	Lisburn Distillery FC (Lisburn)
Crusaders FC (Belfast)	2-0	Maiden City FC (Derry)
Ballinamallard United FC (Ballinamallard)	4-2	Immaculata FC (Belfast)
Cliftonville FC (Belfast)	4-3 (aet)	Warrenpoint Town FC (Warrenpoint)
Loughgall FC (Loughgall)	4-1	PSNI FC (Belfast)
Ballymena United FC (Ballymena)	4-0	Moyola Park FC (Castledawson)
Newry City AFC (Newry)	2-0	Harland & Wolff Welders FC (Belfast)
Portadown FC (Portadown)	1-2 (aet)	Ballyclare Comrades FC (Ballyclare)
Ards FC (Newtownards)	4-1	Crumlin Star FC (Belfast)
Linfield FC (Belfast)	5-0	Glebe Rangers FC (Ballymoney)
Dungannon Swifts FC (Dungannon)	4-0	Limavady United FC (Limavady)

2018/2019

NIFL Premiership 2018/2019	Ards	Ballymena	Cliftonville	Coleraine	Crusaders	Dungannon	Glenavon	Glentoran	Institute	Linfield	Newry	Warrenpoint
Ards		1-2	1-3	0-0	0-1	2-2	0-2	0-2	0-1	2-1	4-0	1-1
			1-2	2-2	1-0		1-1	0-3	0-2	3-1		0-1
Ballymena United	2-0		2-1	3-3	3-0	1-1	2-1	2-1	6-1	2-1	3-0	1-2
	4-1		2-1	1-0	3-0	2-2	4-3	0-2		0-1	3-1	
Cliftonville	3-1	3-2		1-2	1-5	5-1	4-2	1-0	3-0	1-1	3-1	3-1
	4-1	1-1		4-2	2-0		1-1	2-1	1-0	0-2	1-0	
Coleraine	1-0	2-2	1-2		1-0	2-1	1-4	1-1	2-2	0-0	0-1	3-0
		0-4	4-1		4-2	1-2	1-1	2-0		1-1		
Crusaders	4-2	2-2	3-2	0-3		1-0	3-0	3-0	3-2	0-2	1-0	3-1
		3-2	2-0	4-2			1-1		0-1			
Dungannon Swifts	0-0	0-2	1-1	0-2	3-2		1-1	1-0	2-1	1-2	1-1	0-2
	0-3		3-1		1-0		1-2	2-1	0-5	2-1	4-3	
Glenavon	3-1	4-0	0-2	4-0	3-2	2-1		1-1	3-3	0-1	2-0	1-1
	2-0	0-2	4-0	1-1	2-1	1-0			3-3	2-0		1-3
Glentoran	4-0	0-1	1-2	2-2	2-2	2-1	1-2		2-1	0-1	4-1	3-1
	1-1			0-1	2-4	1-2			2-0		2-1	2-2
Institute	1-0	1-2	6-4	1-2	1-4	0-0	1-4	3-3		1-4	1-0	2-0
	0-1	1-2		1-0	1-3	2-0		0-2			2-1	2-1
Linfield	0-0	2-1	4-2	1-2	4-1	3-0	0-0	4-0	3-0		3-1	1-1
		1-0	5-1	3-2	0-0		0-4	4-2	2-0			4-0
Newry City	2-0	1-2	1-0	1-1	0-3	2-1	1-2	1-1	0-2	0-2		1-1
	3-0		1-4	0-1	0-1	0-1	0-2	1-2	0-1			0-2
Warrenpoint Town	1-0	1-6	2-1	2-1	1-2	1-1	2-4	1-1	0-1	0-5	2-2	
	1-1	2-4	0-2	0-1	1-3	5-3		0-5	4-0		2-4	

The result of Ballymena United FC vs Crusaders FC was awarded to Ballymena with 3-0 scoreline after they fielded an ineligible player. The game had originally finished Ballymena United FC 0-3 Crusaders FC.

	NIFL Premiership	**Pd**	**Wn**	**Dw**	**Ls**	**GF**	**GA**	**Pts**	
1.	LINFIELD FC (Belfast)	38	26	7	5	77	27	85	
2.	Ballymena United FC (Ballymena)	38	24	6	8	83	47	78	
3.	Glenavon FC (Lurgan)	38	20	10	8	74	46	70	PO
4.	Crusaders FC (Belfast)	38	20	5	13	68	55	65	
5.	Cliftonville FC (Belfast)	38	19	4	15	70	66	61	POQ
6.	Coleraine FC (Coleraine)	38	15	11	12	59	55	56	PO
7.	Glentoran FC (Belfast)	38	13	10	15	58	53	49	PO
8.	Institute FC (Londonderry)	38	13	5	20	50	72	44	
9.	Dungannon Swifts FC (Dungannon)	38	11	9	18	44	65	42	
10.	Warrenpoint Town FC (Warrenpoint)	38	10	9	19	51	79	39	
11.	Ards FC (Newtownards)	38	6	9	23	31	63	27	R
12.	Newry City AFC (Newry)	38	6	5	27	31	68	23	R
		456	183	90	183	696	696	639	

UEFA Europa League play-offs

Crusaders FC won the Irish Cup and therefore qualified for the Europa League directly. Therefore, the play-off took place between the teams in 3rd, 5th, 6th and 7th place.

Glenavon FC (Lurgan)	2-4	Glentoran FC (Belfast)
Cliftonville FC (Belfast)	5-3 (aet)	Coleraine FC (Coleraine)
Cliftonville FC (Belfast)	2-0 (aet)	Glentoran FC (Belfast)

Cliftonville FC entered the Europa League first qualifying round.

NIFL Premiership Promotion/Relegation play-offs

Carrick Rangers FC (Carrickfergus)	2-0	Portadown FC (Portadown)
Carrick Rangers FC (Carrickfergus)	1-0, 2-1	Ards FC (Newtownards)

Carrick Rangers won 3-1 on aggregate and were promoted to the NIFL Premiership.
Ards FC were relegated into the NIFL Championship.

Top goalscorers 2018-19

1) Joe GORMLEY (Cliftonville FC) 20
2) Michael McCRUDDEN (Institute FC) 19
3) Andrew WATERWORTH (Linfield FC) 17
4) Cathair FRIEL (Ballymena United FC) 16
5) Stephen MURRAY (Glenavon FC) 15

NIFL Championship 2018/2019	Ballinamallard	Ballyclare	Carrick	Dergview	Dundela	Harland & Wolff	Knockbreda	Larne	Limavady	Loughgall	Portadown	PSNI
Ballinamallard United		1-0	1-2	1-4	1-1	2-0	0-1	2-0	3-0	1-2	1-2	3-0
			1-2		2-0	3-0		0-5			1-0	
Ballyclare Comrades	2-0		1-4	2-2	3-3	0-2	2-1	0-4	1-1	2-1	2-1	2-2
				2-3			1-1		4-1	1-4		1-3
Carrick Rangers	1-3	2-0		1-0	0-5	1-4	3-0	2-0	3-1	1-1	2-0	4-2
	2-1				3-2	7-2		1-0			4-0	
Dergview	1-2	1-2	0-2		1-3	2-1	3-0	1-1	0-2	1-3	1-2	2-3
		2-0					3-0		0-1	1-0		2-1
Dundela	3-2	2-4	0-0	3-2		1-4	1-1	0-2	2-2	5-2	2-3	3-3
	4-0		1-2			4-1		0-5			2-0	
Harland & Wolff Welders	2-0	3-4	1-0	2-1	1-0		1-3	2-3	1-2	0-2	0-2	1-1
	2-1		1-2		2-2			0-2			0-6	
Knockbreda	1-2	3-2	0-2	5-3	0-4	1-2		1-1	0-1	3-2	2-2	2-2
		2-1		0-4					1-3	0-0		5-2
Larne	1-0	3-1	4-0	2-0	5-0	3-0	2-0		6-0	4-1	2-2	4-0
	3-0		4-0		3-0	2-1				3-0		
Limavady United	1-2	3-3	2-1	1-2	1-4	1-2	1-2	1-3		1-1	2-2	3-4
		0-1		1-4			3-0			1-3	1	1-1
Loughgall	2-2	4-2	1-1	6-0	1-2	0-2	4-0	2-3	2-1		1-1	3-2
		3-5	0-0			1-1		1-1				1-2
Portadown	5-0	3-1	0-2	2-1	0-4	3-2	4-3	0-3	2-2	2-1		2-0
	2-1		2-2		3-2	3-1		1-2				
PSNI	0-0	1-4	2-0	0-1	1-2	4-2	1-3	1-2	1-0	3-1	3-2	
		2-2		0-3		0-3		0-4	1-4			

	NIFL Championship	**Pd**	**Wn**	**Dw**	**Ls**	**GF**	**GA**	**Pts**	
1.	Larne FC (Larne)	32	26	3	3	87	19	81	P
2.	Carrick Rangers FC (Carrickfergus)	32	20	4	8	59	42	64	POP
3.	Portadown FC (Portadown)	32	15	6	11	59	55	51	
4.	Dundela FC (Belfast)	32	13	7	12	67	60	46	
5.	Ballinamallard United FC (Ballinamallard)	32	12	3	17	39	51	39	
6.	Harland & Wolff Welders FC (Belfast)	32	11	2	19	45	68	35	
7.	Loughgall FC (Loughgall)	32	11	9	12	60	52	42	
8.	Dergview FC (Castlederg)	32	13	3	16	51	51	42	
9.	Ballyclare Comrades FC (Ballyclare)	32	11	7	14	58	68	40	
10.	Knockbreda FC (Belfast)	32	10	7	15	45	63	37	
11.	PSNI FC (Belfast)	32	9	7	16	48	72	34	PO
12.	Limavady United FC (Limavady)	32	8	8	16	45	62	32	R
		384	159	66	159	663	663	543	

NIFL Championship play-off

Annagh United FC (Portadown)   1-4, 2-1   PSNI FC (Belfast)

PSNI FC won 5-3 on aggregate to retain their NIFL Championship status.

Promoted to NIFL Championship: Queen's University FC (Belfast)

IRISH CUP FINAL   (Windsor Park, Belfast – 04/05/2019 – 5,744)

Ballinamallard United FC (Ballinamallard)   0-3   **CRUSADERS FC (BELFAST)**
J. Owens 6', P. Lowry 47', R. Clarke 53'

Ballinamallard: J. Connolly, R. O'Reilly, R. Taheny, M. Smyth, R. Clarke, C. Kelly (S. Warrington 80'), A. Arkinson, N. Cashel, J. McCartney (R. Hume 68'), R. Campbell, D. McBrien (D. McManus 59').

Crusaders: H. Doherty, S. Ward, B. Burns, C. Coates, M. Ruddy, D. Cushley (R. Clarke 52'), D. Caddell, P. Lowry, J. Forsythe, P. Heatley, J. Owens (R. Patterson 87').

Semi-finals

Ballinamallard United FC (Ballinamallard)	0-0 (aet)	Warrenpoint Town FC (Warrenpoint)
	Ballinamallard United FC won 5-4 on penalties.	
Coleraine FC (Coleraine)	0-2	Crusaders FC (Belfast)

Quarter-finals

Larne FC (Larne)	3-5 (aet)	Coleraine FC (Coleraine)
Crusaders FC (Belfast)	3-0	Ballymena United FC (Ballymena)
Dungannon Swifts FC (Dungannon)	2-2 (aet)	Ballinamallard United FC (Ballinamallard)
	Ballinamallard United FC won 3-2 on penalties.	
Warrenpoint Town FC (Warrenpoint)	3-1	Larne Tech Old Boys FC (Larne)

Round 6

Ballinamallard United FC (Ballinamallard)	1-0	Carrick Rangers FC (Carrickfergus)
Ballymena United FC (Ballymena)	4-1	Portadown FC (Portadown)
Coleraine FC (Coleraine)	3-0	Dergview FC (Castlederg)
Glenavon FC (Lurgan)	0-1	Dungannon Swifts FC (Dungannon)
Larne FC (Larne)	3-1	Crumlin Star FC (Belfast)
Larne Tech Old Boys FC (Larne)	3-1	Strabane Athletic FC (Strabane)
Linfield FC (Belfast)	1-2	Crusaders FC (Belfast)
Warrenpoint Town FC (Warrenpoint)	2-0	Queen's University FC (Belfast)

Round 5

Ards FC (Newtownards)	0-1	Carrick Rangers FC (Carrickfergus)
Ballinamallard United FC (Ballinamallard)	5-1	PSNI FC (Belfast)
Cliftonville FC (Belfast)	0-1	Dungannon Swifts FC (Dungannon)
Coleraine FC (Coleraine)	2-0	Harland & Wolff Welders FC (Belfast)
Crusaders FC (Belfast)	4-1	Glentoran FC (Belfast)
Dergview FC (Castlederg)	3-2	Maiden City FC (Derry)
Dundela FC (Belfast)	1-3	Ballymena United FC (Ballymena)
Glenavon FC (Lurgan)	5-0	Rosemount Recreation FC (Greyabbey)
Institute FC (Londonderry)	0-2	Warrenpoint Town FC (Warrenpoint)
Knockbreda FC (Belfast)	1-2	Strabane Athletic FC (Strabane)
Larne FC (Larne)	2-1	Newry City AFC (Newry)
Limavady United FC (Limavady)	0-2	Larne Tech Old Boys FC (Larne)
Linfield FC (Belfast)	1-0	Ballyclare Comrades FC (Ballyclare)
Loughgall FC (Loughgall)	1-4	Crumlin Star FC (Belfast)
Portadown FC (Portadown)	5-1	Abbey Villa FC (Millisle)
Queen's University FC (Belfast)	6-0	Lisburn Distillery FC (Lisburn)

2019/2020

NIFL Premiership 2019/2020	Ballymena	Carrick Rangers	Cliftonville	Coleraine	Crusaders	Dungannon	Glenavon	Glentoran	Institute	Larne	Linfield	Warrenpoint
Ballymena United	■	1-2	2-1	1-1	1-1	3-2	2-1	1-2	1-1	0-3	1-2	4-0
	■	0-2		0-2		0-3			2-3	1-4		
Carrick Rangers	0-1	■	0-1	1-4	1-3	1-0	6-2	0-1	3-0	1-2	0-3	1-0
		■	1-0	0-2		1-2					0-2	1-2
Cliftonville	1-0	3-1	■	1-0	0-2	5-0	3-1	0-2	1-0	1-0	0-1	4-0
	1-1		■			1-1	1-0			1-2		
Coleraine	2-0	3-2	1-1	■	4-2	5-0	4-0	2-2	0-0	0-0	1-0	3-0
		1-0		■	0-1		2-1			1-1		
Crusaders	0-1	3-0	1-2	0-2	■	3-0	3-2	5-2	1-1	2-2	1-0	4-0
	2-0		0-0		■	5-0			2-1	3-0		
Dungannon Swifts	2-2	2-1	0-4	0-2	1-6	■	2-1	3-1	2-2	0-1	1-4	3-1
	1-0					■	0-2	2-0	0-2			4-4
Glenavon	3-1	1-0	1-2	0-4	2-2	5-0	■	1-1	3-1	1-3	1-0	2-0
				2-1			■	2-2	2-2			1-1
Glentoran	3-1	3-1	0-1	2-2	1-1	6-1	4-0	■	4-0	2-1	3-0	2-1
	2-0	0-0	0-2	0-1				■				2-1
Institute	1-1	0-2	0-3	2-0	0-6	2-3	1-4	1-1	■	1-4	0-3	0-1
		0-3		0-4				0-2	■	0-4		
Larne	2-4	0-0	1-1	2-2	0-0	0-0	6-0	2-3	1-1	■	3-1	6-0
		4-0	1-2			1-0	2-1			■		1-0
Linfield	2-1	2-0	1-0	2-4	1-1	0-0	7-0	1-0	3-1	1-0	■	7-0
					4-0	2-1	8-1		3-0		■	
Warrenpoint Town	2-1	0-3	1-5	3-1	0-1	4-3	1-3	0-4	1-3	0-2	0-2	■
				0-4	0-4				2-2		1-2	■

	NIFL Premiership	Pd	Wn	Dw	Ls	GF	GA	Pts	PPG	
1.	LINFIELD FC (Belfast)	31	22	3	6	71	24	69	2.23	
2.	Coleraine FC (Coleraine)	31	19	8	4	64	24	65	2.10	
3.	Crusaders FC (Belfast)	31	17	8	6	66	30	59	1.90	
4.	Cliftonville FC (Belfast)	31	18	5	8	48	22	59	1.90	
5.	Glentoran FC (Belfast)	31	17	7	7	60	33	58	1.87	
6.	Larne FC (Larne)	31	16	8	7	59	29	56	1.81	
7.	Glenavon FC (Lurgan)	31	10	5	16	46	71	35	1.13	
8.	Carrick Rangers FC (Carrickfergus)	31	10	2	19	34	47	32	1.03	
9.	Dungannon Swifts FC (Dungannon)	31	8	6	17	36	76	30	0.97	
10.	Ballymena United FC (Ballymena)	31	7	6	18	34	54	27	0.87	
11.	Warrenpoint Town FC (Warrenpoint)	31	5	3	23	26	85	18	0.58	
12.	Institute FC (Londonderry)	31	2	9	20	23	72	15	0.48	R
		372	151	70	151	567	567	523		

The season was curtailed after 31 fixtures due to the effects of the COVID-19 pandemic. Standings were decided by a points per game average.

Promotion/Relegation play-offs were cancelled and Warrenpoint Town FC were therefore reprieved from the risk of relegation.

The Europa League play-offs were also cancelled so Coleraine FC automatically entered the Europa League first qualifying round as runners up in the NIFL Premiership.

Top goalscorers 2019-20

1) Joe GORMLEY   (Cliftonville FC)   18
2) Robbie McDAID   (Glentoran FC)   15
3) Andrew WATERWORTH   (Linfield FC)   13
4) David McDAID   (Larne FC)   12
   Jamie McGONIGLE   (Crusaders FC)   12
   Hrvoje PLUM   (Glentoran FC)   12

NIFL Championship 2019/2020	Ards	Ballinamallard	Ballyclare	Dergview	Dundela	Harland & Wolff	Knockbreda	Loughgall	Newry	Portadown	PSNI	Queen's University
Ards		3-2	2-0	5-2	1-1	1-0	2-3	3-0	0-3	2-4	3-0	3-2
			2-2	3-1		1-2				1-1	0-1	
Ballinamallard United	1-1		5-0	2-1	4-0	4-2	0-1	2-3	0-1	4-2	5-0	2-0
	2-2			3-0	1-0			1-2			6-4	
Ballyclare Comrades	1-1	2-0		1-1	0-1	8-0	4-0	4-5	0-1	0-1	1-2	3-2
				2-0			0-1	1-1	1-1			2-0
Dergview	3-1	2-0	1-1		0-2	0-3	3-1	1-2	1-2	1-2	2-4	3-2
					1-0					3-1		2-0
Dundela	0-3	0-4	0-0	1-0		3-2	5-0	1-3	1-1	1-1	5-2	3-1
	1-5	4-2				1-0		1-1	0-0			
Harland & Wolff Welders	1-2	0-2	3-0	2-2	1-2		2-3	1-2	2-0	2-1	2-2	2-1
		1-2		1-1						2-4	3-1	
Knockbreda	0-1	1-4	1-3	1-1	0-2	2-2		3-0	1-4	0-5	1-1	1-3
	0-8					2-6					4-2	
Loughgall	0-3	1-2	1-4	2-1	0-0	4-1	0-3		1-0	0-0	6-0	0-1
				2-1		3-1	4-0			0-2		
Newry City	5-1	1-3	5-1	1-2	4-0	1-2	2-2	3-4		1-2	1-2	1-0
		1-0					0-0	3-1	0-3		3-0	
Portadown	2-1	0-1	5-0	2-0	2-0	2-0	3-0	2-1	0-0		5-0	3-1
		3-3	0-2			4-0						7-1
PSNI	0-4	0-4	2-6	3-1	0-1	1-4	3-2	1-4	1-6	0-1		5-3
					2-4					0-2		0-4
Queen's University	3-1	0-2	1-2	2-1	5-2	5-2	3-2	0-4	1-3	3-3	5-1	
	1-2			3-1			4-0	2-5	0-1			

Knockbreda FC vs Loughgall FC was awarded 3-0 to Knockbreda after Loughgall fielded an ineligible player.
Loughgall FC vs Ards FC was awarded 3-0 to Ards after Loughgall fielded an ineligible player.

	NIFL Championship	Pd	Wn	Dw	Ls	GF	GA	Pts	PPG	
1.	Portadown FC (Portadown)	31	20	6	5	72	30	66	2.13	P
2.	Ballinamallard United FC (Ballinamallard)	30	19	3	8	71	34	60	2.00	
3.	Loughgall FC (Loughgall)	31	18	4	9	64	45	58	1.87	
4.	Ards FC (Newtownards)	31	16	6	9	68	44	54	1.74	
5.	Newry City AFC (Newry)	30	15	6	9	55	32	51	1.70	
6.	Dundela FC (Belfast)	31	13	7	11	43	49	46	1.48	
7.	Ballyclare Comrades FC (Ballyclare)	30	11	7	12	53	49	40	1.33	
8.	Harland & Wolff Welders FC (Belfast)	31	10	5	16	52	63	35	1.13	
9.	Queen's University FC (Belfast)	31	11	1	19	59	69	34	1.10	
10.	Dergview FC (Castlederg)	30	8	5	17	38	54	29	0.97	
11.	Knockbreda FC (Belfast)	30	7	4	19	36	84	25	0.83	
12.	PSNI FC (Belfast)	30	7	2	21	40	98	23	0.77	R
		366	155	56	155	651	651	521		

Play was suspended on 13th March 2020 due to the effects of the COVID-19 pandemic and the season was officially curtailed during June 2020. Final standings were calculated on a points per game average.

The promotion and relegation play-offs were cancelled so Ballinamallard United FC remained in the NIFL Championship and Knockbreda FC were reprieved from the risk of relegation.

Promoted to NIFL Championship: Annagh United FC (Portadown)

IRISH CUP FINAL   (Windsor Park, Belfast – 31/07/2020 – 500)

Ballymena United FC (Ballymena)   1-2 (aet)   GLENTORAN FC (BELFAST)
Friel 48'   *O'Neill 22', McDaid 115'*

Ballymena United: R. Glendinning, J. Ervin, J. Addis (Aaron Burns 116'), S. McCullough, S. Whiteside, A. McGrory (T. Kane 37' (K. Balmer 116')), J. Winchester (J. Knowles 61'), L. Millar, J. Kelly, C. Friel (K. Kane 106'), A. Lecky.
Glentoran: E. Morris, K. Cowan, J. Crowe (C. O'Connor 67'), P. McClean, M. Kane, N. Nasseri, C. Gallagher, R. Donnelly (G. Peers 118'), E. van Overbeek (M. Smith 88'), R. McDaid, P. O'Neill (J. Frazer 83').

Semi-finals

Ballymena United FC (Ballymena)	1-1 (aet)	Coleraine FC (Coleraine)
	Ballymena United FC won 3-1 on penalties.	
Cliftonville FC (Belfast)	1-1 (aet)	Glentoran FC (Belfast)
	Glentoran FC won 7-6 on penalties.	

Quarter-finals

Ballinamallard United FC (Ballinamallard)	0-2	Ballymena United FC (Ballymena)
Dungannon Swifts FC (Dungannon)	1-2	Cliftonville FC (Belfast)
Glentoran FC (Belfast)	2-1	Crusaders FC (Belfast)
Larne FC (Larne)	2-3	Coleraine FC (Coleraine)

Round 6

Ballyclare Comrades FC (Ballyclare)	0-1	Larne FC (Larne)
Carrick Rangers FC (Carrickfergus)	1-5	Crusaders FC (Belfast)
Cliftonville FC (Belfast)	3-1	Rathfriland Rangers FC (Rathfriland)
Coleraine FC (Coleraine)	3-0	Banbridge Town FC (Banbridge)
Dungannon Swifts FC (Dungannon)	4-2	Newry City AFC (Newry)
Knockbreda FC (Belfast)	2-5	Ballinamallard United FC (Ballinamallard)
Queen's University FC (Belfast)	2-3	Glentoran FC (Belfast)
Warrenpoint Town FC (Warrenpoint)	1-2	Ballymena United FC (Ballymena)

Round 5

Ards FC (Newtownards)	1-3	Carrick Rangers FC (Carrickfergus)
Ballinamallard United FC (Ballinamallard)	1-0	Dollingstown FC (Dollingstown)
Ballyclare Comrades FC (Ballyclare)	2-1	Harland & Wolff Welders FC (Belfast)
Ballymena United FC (Ballymena)	2-0	Crumlin Star FC (Belfast)
Banbridge Town FC (Banbridge)	2-2 (aet)	East Belfast FC (Belfast)

Banbridge Town FC won 5-4 on penalties.

Cliftonville FC (Belfast)	6-0	Hanover FC (Portadown)
Crusaders FC (Belfast)	3-0	Dundela FC (Belfast)
Glenavon FC (Lurgan)	0-2	Coleraine FC (Coleraine)
Glentoran FC (Belfast)	2-2 (aet)	Portadown FC (Portadown)

Glentoran FC won 5-4 on penalties.

Institute FC (Londonderry)	2-3	Dungannon Swifts FC (Dungannon)
Knockbreda FC (Belfast)	3-2	Dergview FC (Castlederg)
Larne FC (Larne)	8-0	Belfast Celtic FC (Belfast)
Loughgall FC (Loughgall)	1-2	Rathfriland Rangers FC (Rathfriland)
Newry City AFC (Newry)	3-1	Bangor FC (Bangor)
Queen's University FC (Belfast)	2-1	Linfield FC (Belfast)
Warrenpoint Town FC (Warrenpoint)	3-1	PSNI FC (Belfast)

2020/2021

NIFL Premiership 2020/2021	Ballymena	Carrick Rangers	Cliftonville	Coleraine	Crusaders	Dungannon	Glenavon	Glentoran	Larne	Linfield	Portadown	Warrenpoint
Ballymena United		2-0	1-1	0-1	1-4	0-1	0-2	1-1	1-1	2-3	2-1	2-0
		2-0		1-2	0-1	5-1	3-1	2-2		2-1	4-2	3-0
Carrick Rangers	0-2		0-1	0-2	1-3	0-0	3-4	0-5	1-2	1-1	4-1	1-3
	0-4				1-1	1-1	3-6		1-3		5-3	1-1
Cliftonville	0-4	3-0		0-2	2-2	3-0	1-1	1-0	1-0	4-3	5-0	3-0
	2-1	5-0		2-1	1-1		2-1	0-2	1-2	0-2		3-0
Coleraine	0-1	3-0	2-2		2-1	2-0	0-0	2-1	0-2	0-2	1-1	2-1
		1-0	2-0		2-0			1-1	2-0	1-1	2-0	2-1
Crusaders	2-1	1-3	1-0	1-0		3-1	0-1	2-0	3-3	1-2	5-0	4-0
			2-2	0-1			6-1	1-0	1-3	1-2		0-2
Dungannon Swifts	1-5	0-2	2-1	2-0	2-1		1-2	0-1	0-2	0-2	0-3	0-2
	1-3	0-2	1-2	2-3	0-2		0-4			0-1	0-1
Glenavon	2-1	1-1	1-1	4-4	3-1	0-0		2-1	1-4	1-2	2-4	1-0
	3-2	1-1		1-1		1-1			2-2	3-2	4-1	4-0
Glentoran	0-2	6-0	1-0	2-2	1-0	5-1	1-1		0-0	3-1	2-1	0-0
		2-0	0-2	1-1	2-0	2-0	3-1		3-2	0-0	4-0	
Larne	2-0	3-0	1-0	1-2	2-1	3-0	2-1	1-1		3-1	2-2	1-1
	0-1		0-0	1-2	0-3	3-0		0-1		1-1		5-0
Linfield	2-1	5-1	2-0	0-0	2-1	4-0	2-0	3-3	2-1		3-0	6-0
		7-0	2-0	2-1	3-1	2-0		0-1	1-2			5-0
Portadown	0-0	2-0	1-1	0-3	2-2	1-0	4-1	1-2	1-2			0-2
	1-2	2-1	1-2		1-2	4-2	1-2		2-1	0-1		1-2
Warrenpoint Town	1-1	0-0	0-5	1-2	0-1	1-1	1-2	0-2	1-1	2-1	1-1	
	2-2	3-1			4-1	3-4	1-2			1-3	

	NIFL Premiership	Pd	Wn	Dw	Ls	GF	GA	Pts	
1.	LINFIELD FC (Belfast)	38	24	6	8	83	38	78	
2.	Coleraine FC (Coleraine)	38	21	10	7	57	35	73	
3.	Glentoran FC (Belfast)	38	20	11	7	65	32	71	
4.	Larne FC (Larne)	38	18	10	10	64	41	64	POQ
5.	Cliftonville FC (Belfast)	38	17	9	12	59	42	60	PO
6.	Crusaders FC (Belfast)	38	16	6	16	62	50	54	PO
7.	Glenavon FC (Lurgan)	38	17	11	10	72	65	62	PO
8.	Ballymena United FC (Ballymena)	38	18	7	13	67	44	61	
9.	Portadown FC (Portadown)	38	10	6	22	50	78	36	
10.	Warrenpoint Town FC (Warrenpoint)	38	9	9	20	38	74	36	
11.	Carrick Rangers FC (Carrickfergus)	38	5	8	25	35	92	23	
12.	Dungannon Swifts FC (Dungannon)	38	4	5	29	22	83	17	
		456	179	98	179	674	674	635	

UEFA Europa Conference League play-offs

A new competition, the UEFA Europa Conference League commenced during the 2021/2022 season. The NIFL was allocated 3 places for teams to enter the first qualifying round of this new competition. The 2nd placed team, Coleraine FC earned one of these places by right and another was to be given to the winners of the Irish Cup. However, as Linfield FC won the 2020/2021 Irish Cup and also qualified for the Champions League by winning the NIFL Premiership, 3rd placed team Glentoran FC qualified for the Europa Conference League first qualifying round directly, vacating one of the play-off places. As a result, the four clubs that finished in 4th to 7th place competed for the final berth in the 2021-2022 Europa Conference League first qualifying round.

Larne FC (Larne)	2-1	Glenavon FC (Lurgan)
Cliftonville FC (Belfast)	0-0 (aet)	Crusaders FC (Belfast)

Cliftonville FC won 5-4 on penalties.

Larne FC (Larne)	3-1	Cliftonville FC (Belfast)

Larne FC entered the Europa Conference League first qualifying round

Top goalscorers

1)	Shayne LAVERY	(Linfield FC)	23
2)	Shay McCARTAN	(Ballymena United FC)	18
3)	Jay DONNELLY	(Glentoran FC)	17
4)	Ryan CURRAN	(Cliftonville FC)	15
	Andrew WATERWORTH	(Linfield FC)	15

The NIFL Championship season was due to commence on 28th November 2020 as a 22 week season. However, the effects of the COVID-19 pandemic meant that this wasn't possible and the season was eventually declared null and void on 2nd February 2021. The NIFL Intermediate Premier League season was declared null and void at the same time.

As a result of the ongoing COVID-19 pandemic, the Irish Cup was played as a condensed format this season with just 32 clubs allowed to take part and all matches played during a 24 day period. Due to restrictions related to the pandemic, all matches were played behind closed doors with the exception of the Final itself where 1,000 spectators were permitted.

IRISH CUP FINAL   (Mourneview Park, Lurgan – 21/05/2021 – 1,000)

Larne FC (Larne)   1-2   LINFIELD FC (BELFAST)
Hughes 90+2'   *Lavery 5', Cooper 32'*

Larne: C. Mitchell, A. Watson, D. Jarvis, J. Robinson, J. Hughes, M. Donnelly (D. McDaid 46'), J. Herron, L. Lynch (M. Randall 53'), T. Cosgrove, F. Sule, R. Hale (J. McMurray 76').

Linfield: C. Johns, M. Haughey, M. Clarke, N. Quinn, J. Mulgrew, J. Callacher, K. Millar, C. Pepper, J. Cooper, C. Palmer, S. Lavery (C. Manzinga 74').

Semi-finals

Larne FC (Larne)	1-1	Crusaders FC (Belfast)
	Larne FC won 6-5 on penalties.	
Ballymena United FC (Ballymena)	0-3	Linfield FC (Belfast)

Quarter-finals

Ballymena United FC (Ballymena)	5-0	Dergview FC (Castlederg)
Glentoran FC (Belfast)	0-1	Crusaders FC (Belfast)
Larne FC (Larne)	2-1	Carrick Rangers FC (Carrickfergus)
Loughgall FC (Loughgall)	1-3	Linfield FC (Belfast)

Round 2

Ballymena United FC (Ballymena)	5-0	PSNI FC (Belfast)
Carrick Rangers FC (Carrickfergus)	2-2	Bangor FC (Bangor)
	Carrick Rangers FC won 3-1 on penalties.	
Dergview FC (Castlederg)	2-0	St James' Swifts FC (Belfast)
Glentoran FC (Belfast)	1-0	Cliftonville FC (Belfast)
Knockbreda FC (Belfast)	0-5	Crusaders FC (Belfast)
Larne FC (Larne)	8-1	Dollingstown FC (Dollingstown)
Linfield FC (Belfast)	5-2	Dungannon Swifts FC (Dungannon)
Loughgall FC (Loughgall)	1-0	Warrenpoint Town FC (Warrenpoint)

Round 1

The draw for the first round took place on 17th December 2020, with the 32 teams drawn randomly into 16 ties. However, six NIFL Championship teams (Ards FC, Dundela FC, Harland & Wolff Welders FC, Institute FC, Newry City AFC and Queen's University FC) subsequently withdrew from the competition and their opponents were given a bye into the Second Round.

Ards FC (Newtownards) (withdrew)	bye	Dollingstown FC (Dollingstown)
Glentoran FC (Belfast)	bye	Dundela FC (Belfast) (withdrew)
Harland & Wolff Welders FC (Belfast) (withdrew)	bye	St James' Swifts FC (Belfast)
Institute FC (Londonderry) (withdrew)	bye	PSNI FC (Belfast)
Larne FC (Larne)	bye	Newry City AFC (Newry) (withdrew)
Queen's University FC (Belfast) (withdrew)	bye	Bangor FC (Bangor)
Ballinamallard United FC (Ballinamallard)	2-2	Dergview FC (Castlederg)
	Dergview FC won 9-8 on penalties.	
Ballymena United FC (Ballymena)	4-1	Portadown FC (Portadown)
Carrick Rangers FC (Carrickfergus)	3-0	Belfast Celtic FC (Belfast)
Cliftonville FC (Belfast)	5-1	Portstewart FC (Portstewart)
Coleraine FC (Coleraine)	0-1	Crusaders FC (Belfast)
Glenavon FC (Lurgan)	1-2	Dungannon Swifts FC (Dungannon)
Knockbreda FC (Belfast)	2-1	Newington FC (Belfast)
Linfield FC (Belfast)	2-0	Annagh United FC (Portadown)
Loughgall FC (Loughgall)	1-1	Banbridge Town FC (Banbridge)
	Loughgall FC won 3-2 on penalties.	
Warrenpoint Town FC (Warrenpoint)	2-1	Ballyclare Comrades FC (Ballyclare)